PRACTICAL MODEL-BASED TESTING

PRACTICAL MODEL-BASED TESTING

TESTING

A TOOLS APPROACH

Mark Utting

Bruno Legeard

ELSEVIER

AMSTERDAM • BOSTON • HEIDELBERG • LONDON
NEW YORK • OXFORD • PARIS • SAN DIEGO
SAN FRANCISCO • SINGAPORE • SYDNEY • TOKYO

Morgan Kaufmann Publishers is an imprint of Elsevier

MORGAN KAUFMANN PUBLISHERS

Publisher	Denise E. M. Penrose
Publishing Services Manager	George Morrison
Assistant Editor	Mary E. James
Project Manager	Marilyn E. Rash
Cover Design	Yvo Design
Composition and Illustrations	VTeX
Copyeditor	Joan M. Flaherty
Proofreader	Carol Leyba
Indexer	Ted Laux
Interior printer	Sheridan Books
Cover printer	Phoenix Color Corp.

Morgan Kaufmann Publishers is an imprint of Elsevier.
500 Sansome Street, Suite 400, San Francisco, CA 94111

This book is printed on acid-free paper.

Library of Congress Cataloging-in-Publication Data
Utting, Mark.
    Practical model-based testing : a tools approach / Mark Utting,
Bruno Legeard.
        p. cm.
    Includes bibliographical references and index.
    ISBN-13: 978-0-12-372501-1 (alk. paper)
    ISBN-10: 0-12-372501-1 (alk. paper)
    1. Computer software—Testing. 2. Computer software—Testing—
    Automation. I. Legeard, Bruno. II. Title.
    QA76.76.T48U98 2006
    005.3028'7–dc22   2006034511

ISBN 13: 978-0-12-372501-1
ISBN 10: 0-12-372501-1

For information on all Morgan Kaufmann publications, visit our
Web site at *www.mkp.com* or *www.books.elsevier.com*

Printed in the United States of America
06 07 08 09 10   5 4 3 2 1

This book is dedicated to the memory of Julien Orsat,
an enthusiastic practitioner of model-based testing
and valued employee of LEIRIOS Technologies,
whose life was tragically cut short on the icy roads
of Franche-Comté on December 28, 2005.

CONTENTS

PREFACE

Software testing is vitally important in the software development process, as illustrated by the growing market for automated testing tools. Moreover, software testing generally consumes between 30 and 60 percent of the overall development effort.

Many companies are already using automated test execution tools. Model-based testing pushes the level of automation even further by automating the design, not just the execution, of the test cases. Model-based testing tools automatically generate test cases from a model of the software product. This gives a repeatable and rational basis for product testing, ensures coverage of all the behaviors of the product, and allows tests to be linked directly to requirements. Intensive research on model-based testing in the last 5 to 10 years has demonstrated the feasibility of this approach, has shown that it is cost-effective, and has developed a variety of test generation strategies and model coverage criteria. A range of commercial model-based testing tools are now available (see Appendix C for a brief list of commercial tools), as are many research tools and experimental prototypes.

This book gives a practical introduction to model-based testing, showing how to write models for testing purposes and how to use model-based testing tools to generate test suites. It focuses on the mainstream practice of functional black-box testing rather than the more specialist areas of testing real-time software or concurrent software. It covers different styles of model, especially transition-based models (e.g., finite state machines and UML state machines) and pre/post models (e.g., B machines and UML/OCL specifications). It uses examples and case studies from a variety of software domains, including embedded software and information systems. It shows how model-based testing can be used with existing test execution environments such as Mercury Test Director, JUnit, and proprietary test execution environments.

From reading this book, you will learn the following:

- The basic principles and terminology of model-based testing
- A step-by-step process for applying model-based testing

- How model-based testing differs from other testing processes
- How model-based testing fits into typical software life cycles
- The benefits and limitations of model-based testing, its cost effectiveness, and the preconditions for adopting it
- Guidelines for using different modeling techniques for model-based testing
- Useful test generation strategies and how they are used in model-based testing tools
- Some common test selection criteria, the differences among them, and how they can be used to control the test generation process
- How model-based testing connects with automated test execution platforms
- How to apply model-based testing techniques to real applications, as illustrated by case studies taken from different domains, including telecommunications, electronic banking, and embedded controllers

This book takes a practical and easy-to-understand approach to model-based testing, aimed more at software developers who wish to use the techniques and tools than at the developers of those techniques and tools. The only background assumed is basic knowledge of software development, programming languages, and the role of testing. Both authors have connections with LEIRIOS Technologies (see *http://www.leirios.com*), a company formed to commercialize model-based testing tools developed during the 1990s in university research projects. The book reflects their experiences in deploying model-based testing in dozens of industrial validation projects in domains such as smart cards, electronic transaction, automotive control software, and banking or administrative information systems.

Some examples in this book are inspired by these industrial experiences applications. Several chapters use the LEIRIOS Test Generator tools (LTG/B and LTG/UML) as examples of model-based testing tools, as well as a variety of other tools such as Microsoft Spec Explorer and Conformiq Qtronic, to illustrate complementary approaches. We focus on the general principles of using the tools rather than the detailed interaction with the tools because the details tend to change with each tool release.

Table P.1 gives an overview of the examples and case studies that we use throughout the book, the application domain of each example, the kind of model, and the model-based testing tool that we illustrate, along with the section of the book in which they appear.

The book is designed to be read sequentially, but it is possible to start with any chapter and refer to the concept chapters (2, 3, and 4) as desired. Chapters 1, 2, and 11 deal with the general *what*, *why*, and *when* questions (e.g., *What is model-based testing?*, *Why should we use it?*, and *When should we start model-based testing?*).

TABLE P.I   Examples and Case Studies in This Book

Section	Example	Application Domain	Model	Tool
1.3	Smartcard	Banking	UML	LTG/UML
3.3	Coffee machine	Embedded	UML	–
3.4	Coffee machine	Embedded	B, Z	–
5.1	Qui-Donc	Telephone	FSM	Chinese Postman
5.2	ZLive	Java unit tests	EFSM	ModelJUnit
6.2	Scheduler	Embedded	B	LTG/B
6.3	Triangle	Data processing	B	LTG/B
6.5	Chat System	Distributed system	Spec#	Spec Explorer
7.2	eTheater	Online shopping	UML	LTG/UML
7.3	Protocol	Telecommunications	UML	Qtronic
9	GSM 11.11	Telecommunications	B	LTG/B
10	ATM	Banking	UML	LTG/UML

They are intended for a general audience, including managers, developers, testers, and researchers. The remaining chapters are more technically oriented and aimed at test engineers because they deal with the *how* of model-based testing.

Here is a brief overview of the chapters.

- Chapter 1 gives an overview of model-based testing and uses a small example to illustrate the process of generating tests from a UML model.

- Chapter 2 compares model-based testing with other approaches to testing and describes the costs and benefits of using model-based testing, using a hypothetical example and real examples from industry.

- Chapter 3 takes a detailed look at the different models used for model-based testing and compares some of the different notations used to write models.

- Chapter 4 introduces the large variety of test selection criteria that can be used to control the generation of tests.

- The core of the book comprises Chapters 5, 6, and 7, which walk the reader through a series of examples showing how to use model-based testing. Each chapter takes examples from different domains, uses different modeling notations, and applies different model-based testing tools. These three chapters allow us to draw comparisons among the various approaches, give guidelines for writing good models, describe the various algorithms for model-based testing, and demonstrate some typical model-based testing tools.

- Chapter 8 deals with issues of executing the generated tests. The generated tests are often more abstract than the system under test, so they must be mapped into executable test scripts.

- Chapters 9 and 10 describe two larger case studies, going through the whole testing process from designing the model to executing the generated tests.
- The final chapter presents several practical issues and techniques for adopting model-based testing. It gives a taxonomy of approaches to model-based testing, introduces organizational issues concerning people and training, reviews how model-based testing can fit with two major software development processes (agile methods and the UML Unified Process), and discusses current and future trends in model-based testing.

This book will be a valuable resource for anyone seeking to improve functional testing skills and use up-to-date testing methods and tools. A companion website (*http://www.cs.waikato.ac.nz/~marku/mbt*) makes available machine-readable versions of some of the examples and case studies in the book. It also provides links to free or demonstration versions of some of the model-based testing tools discussed in the book, and maintains a current list of commercial model-based testing tools.

ACKNOWLEDGMENTS

It is a pleasure for us to thank the many colleagues from whom we received valuable help and contributions for this book. We are grateful to the reviewers of the initial drafts of this text for their helpful comments and suggestions: Arnaud Gotlieb, INRIA Research Institute; Wolfgang Grieskamp, Microsoft Research; Alan Hartman, IBM Haifa Research Laboratory; Robert Hierons, Brunel University; Fabrice Bouquet, Jacques Julliand, and Stephane Debricon, the University of Franche-Comté; Thierry Machicoane, Parkeon; and Paul Strooper, The University of Queensland.

Special thanks to Alexander Pretschner of ETH Zürich for many influential interactions and exciting discussions regarding the scope and methods of model-based testing.

Colleagues from LEIRIOS—Olivier Albiez, Fabrice Ambert, Eddy Bernard, Amandine Charbonnier, Severine Colin, Eddie Jaffuel, Christophe Grandpierre, Michel Guez, Franck Lebeau, Fabien Nicolet, Frederic Oehl, Fabien Peureux, Laurent Py, Eric Torreborre and Nicolas Vacelet—brought useful comments and some material for examples and case studies. Thanks to Antti Huima of Conformiq for providing material about the Qtronic example; to Tuong Nguyen for his comments about the Qui-Donc FSM model; and to Jean-Daniel Nicolet, CTI Geneva, for his feedback about integrating model-based testing with the Unified Process.

Finally, we owe a great debt to our families for their encouragement throughout the years and their patience during the writing of this book. Mark would like to thank his wife, Lynda, for her wonderful support and love, and his children Larissa, Jeremy, Julian, and Kaylee for washing more dishes, allowing Dad to use the computer sometimes, and reminding him that there are more important things to life than writing books. Bruno would like to thank his wife, Oumhanie, and children Anissa, Loïc, Fabien, and Maëva for their support, love, and understanding.

ABOUT THE AUTHORS

Mark Utting is a senior lecturer in the Department of Computer Science at The University of Waikato, New Zealand. Before this position, he was an analyst/programmer in the Australian software industry for several years, and a postdoctoral researcher working on theorem proving and real-time refinement.

Dr Utting has been a consultant to the BZ Testing Tools project on model-based testing since 2000, and a consultant to LEIRIOS Technologies since its creation. For the past four years, he has been leading the Community Z Tools (CZT) project, which has developed analysis and animation tools for the Z specification language. He is the author of more than 40 refereed publications in the areas of formal methods for object-oriented software, real-time software, and model-based testing. He is a member of the IFIP WG2.3 Working Group on Programming Methodology.

Bruno Legeard is chief technology officer at LEIRIOS Technologies and professor of software engineering at the University of Franche-Comté (France). Dr. Legeard is the author of more than 50 journal papers and refereed conference publications in the domain of software validation, model-based testing, and test automation. He started working on model-based testing in the mid-1990s and is one of the designers of the LTG model-based testing tool. He has extensive experience in applying model-based testing to information systems, e-transaction applications, and embedded software.

PRACTICAL MODEL-BASED TESTING

## CHAPTER 1

THE
CHALLENGE

The lakes and rivers of New Zealand are a fisherman's paradise. But one threat to the quality of streams and fishing in New Zealand is the koi carp, which was introduced accidentally in the 1960s as part of a goldfish consignment and is now classified as a noxious species. Koi carp resemble huge goldfish, but they destroy native plants and fish habitats, eat indiscriminately like vacuum cleaners, and grow to about 75 cm long. They are found mostly in the Auckland/Waikato region, and the goal is to prevent them from spreading further.

Imagine that you are a regional manager of the Fish and Game Council and you been given the job of eliminating carp from a stream, so that rainbow trout and other fish can thrive there. How would you do it? Would you take any or all of the following actions?

- Employ hundreds of amateur fishermen to fish with rods and hooks and offer a bounty payment for each koi carp caught.
- Place nets at strategic places, with regular inspections to kill all koi carp and release all other fish.

Note: The photo here is of the Waikato River in Hamilton, New Zealand.

FIGURE 1.1   New Zealand's first electrofishing boat looks like something from a science fiction movie. But Waikato University's *Te Waka Hiko Hi Ika* is the first successful electrofishing boat. It has spectacular electronic prongs in front that dangle under the water and generate a 5 kilowatt pulsating electronic fishing field. Fish are temporarily stunned by the field and float to the surface. Pest fish, such as koi carp, can be scooped out with a net, while other fish are left unharmed. Some advantages of electrofishing over conventional fish-capturing techniques, such as netting, are that it captures fish of all sizes and from all locations, including bottom-dwelling ones. *Source*: Centre for Biodiversity and Ecology Research, University of Waikato, Hamilton, NZ. Used with permission.

- Use an advanced technology solution, such as an electrofishing boat (see Figure 1.1) that attracts all fish and allows pest fish like koi carp to be killed while other fish can be returned to the water unharmed [HOL05, H+05].

Now imagine that you are the validation manager of a software development company that is finalizing the development of a new smart card payment system for car parking. To thoroughly test your system, which of the following actions would you take?

- Employ a dozen full-time testers to manually design tests, record the tests on paper, and then manually perform the tests each time the system changes.

- Manually design a set of tests and then use automated test execution tools to rerun them after every change and report tests that fail.

- Use state-of-the-art tools that can automatically generate tests from a model of your requirements, can regenerate updated test suites each time the requirements change, and can report exactly which requirements have been tested and which have not.

In both cases, the third solution takes advantage of new technology to get faster results with lower costs than traditional methods, and it ensures a more systematic, less ad hoc, coverage (of the fish in the stream, or the failures in the program).

This book will show you how to test your software systems using the third approach. That is, it will explain how a new breed of test generation tools, called *model-based testing* tools, can improve your testing practices while reducing the cost of that testing.

1.1 WHAT DO WE MEAN BY TESTING?

Testing is an activity performed for evaluating product quality, and for improving it, by identifying defects and problems.

This definition of testing, from the IEEE *Software Engineering Body of Knowledge* (SWEBOK 2004),[1] describes the top-level goals of testing. It goes on to give more detail:

*Software testing consists of the *dynamic* verification of the behavior of a program on a *finite* set of test cases, suitably *selected* from the usually infinite executions domain, against the *expected* behavior.*

We've emphasized in italics the words that capture the key features of software testing; these are their definitions as they relate to this book.

Dynamic: This means that we execute the program with specific input values to find failures in its behavior. In contrast, *static* techniques (e.g., inspections, walkthroughs, and static analysis tools) do not require execution of the program. One of the big advantages of (dynamic) testing

---

[1] The SWEBOK can be downloaded from *http://www.swebok.org* or purchased from the IEEE.

is that we are executing the actual program either in its real environment or in an environment with simulated interfaces as close as possible to the real environment. So we are not only testing that the design and code are correct, but we are also testing the compiler, the libraries, the operating system and network support, and so on.

Finite: Exhaustive testing is not possible or practical for most real programs. They usually have a large number of allowable inputs to each operation, plus even more invalid or unexpected inputs, and the possible sequences of operations is usually infinite as well. So we must choose a smallish number of tests so that we can run the tests in the available time. For example, if we want to perform nightly regression testing, our tests should take less than 12 hours!

Selected: Since we have a huge or infinite set of possible tests but can afford to run only a small fraction of them, the *key challenge* of testing is how to select the tests that are most likely to expose failures in the system. This is where the expertise of a skilled tester is important—he or she must use knowledge about the system to guess which sets of inputs are likely to produce the same behavior (this is called the *uniformity assumption*) and which are likely to produce different behavior. There are many informal strategies, such as equivalence class and boundary value testing,[2] that can help in deciding which tests are likely to be more effective. Some of these strategies are the basis of the test selection algorithms in the model-based testing tools that we use in later chapters.

Expected: After each test execution, we must decide whether the observed behavior of the system was a failure or not. This is called the *oracle* problem. The oracle problem is often solved via manual inspection of the test output; but for efficient and repeatable testing, it must be automated. Model-based testing automates the generation of oracles, as well as the choice of test inputs.

Before describing the various kinds of testing, we briefly review some basic terms according to standard IEEE software engineering terminology.

A *failure* is an undesired behavior. Failures are typically observed during the execution of the system being tested.

A *fault* is the *cause* of the failure. It is an error in the software, usually caused by human error in the specification, design, or coding process. It is the execution of the faults in the software that causes failures. Once we have

---

[2] See Lee Copeland's book [Cop04] for a comprehensive overview of the most popular informal test design techniques.

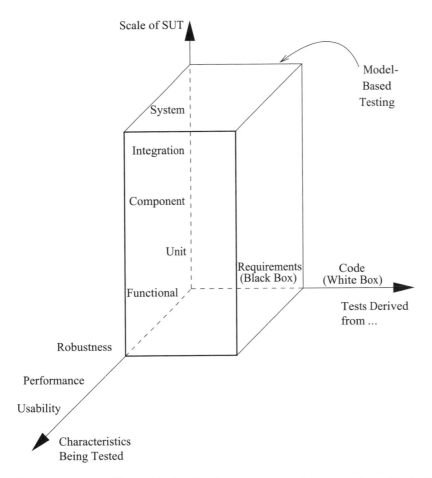

FIGURE 1.2   Different kinds of testing. *Source*: From Tretmans [Tre04]. Used with permission.

observed a failure, we can investigate to find the fault that caused it and correct that fault.

So *testing* is the activity of executing a system in order to detect failures. It is different from, and complementary to, other quality improvement techniques such as static verification, inspections, and reviews. It is also distinct from the debugging and error-correction process that happens after testing has detected a failure.

In fact, there are many kinds of testing. Figure 1.2 shows one way to classify various kinds of testing along three dimensions (adapted from [Tre04]). One axis shows the *scale* of the system under test (SUT), ranging from small units up to the whole system. *Unit testing* involves testing a single unit at a time, such as a single procedure or a single class. *Component testing* tests each component/subsystem separately, and *integration testing* aims at testing to ensure that several components work together correctly. *System testing* involves testing the system as a whole. Model-based testing can be applied to any of these levels.

Another axis shows the different *characteristics* that we may want to test. The most common kind of testing is *functional testing* (also known as *behavioral testing*), where we aim to find errors in the functionality of the system—for example, testing that the correct outputs are produced for given inputs. *Robustness testing* aims at finding errors in the system under invalid conditions, such as unexpected inputs, unavailability of dependent applications, and hardware or network failures. *Performance testing* tests the throughput of the system under heavy load. *Usability testing* focuses on finding user interface problems, which may make the software difficult to use or may cause users to misinterpret the output.

The main use of model-based testing is to generate functional tests, but it can also be used for some kinds of robustness testing such as testing the system with invalid inputs. It is not yet widely used for performance testing, but this is an area under development.

The third axis shows the kind of information we use to design the tests. *Black-box testing* means that we treat the SUT as a "black box," so we do not use information about its internal structure. Instead, the tests are designed from the system requirements, which describe the expected behavior of that black box. On the other hand, *white-box testing* uses the implementation code as the basis for designing tests. For example, we might design a set of tests to ensure *statement coverage* of a procedure, meaning that each statement will be executed by at least one of the tests.

Much has been written about the pros and cons of black-box and white-box testing. However, the most common practice is to use black-box testing techniques to design functional and robustness tests. Some testers then use white-box coverage metrics to check which parts of the implementation have not been tested well so that extra tests can be designed for those cases. Model-based testing is a form of black-box testing because tests are generated from a model, which is derived from the requirements documentation. The next section describes model-based testing in more detail.

1.2 WHAT IS MODEL-BASED TESTING?

Model-based testing has become a bit of a buzzword in recent years, and we have noticed that people are using the term for a wide variety of test generation techniques. The following are the four main approaches known as model-based testing.

1. Generation of test input data from a domain model
2. Generation of test cases from an environment model
3. Generation of test cases with oracles from a behavior model
4. Generation of test scripts from abstract tests

We will briefly describe these approaches and then explain why this book focuses mostly on the third meaning of model-based testing and covers the other meanings more briefly.

When model-based testing is used to mean the generation of test input data, the *model* is the information about the domains of the input values and the test generation involves clever selection and combination of a subset of those values to produce test input data. For example, if we are testing a procedure that has three inputs, $A : \{red, green, yellow\}$, $B : 1..4$, and $C : \{car, truck, bike\}$, then we might use a *pairwise* algorithm[3] to generate a minimal set of tests that exercise all possible pairs of input values. For this example, a good pairwise algorithm would generate just 12 tests[4] rather than the $3 \times 4 \times 3 = 36$ tests that we would need if we tried all possible combinations. The automatic generation of test inputs is obviously of great practical importance, but it does not solve the complete test design problem because it does not help us to know whether a test has passed or failed.

The second meaning of model-based testing uses a different kind of model, which describes the expected *environment* of the SUT. For example, it might be a statistical model of the expected usage of the SUT [Pro03] (operation frequencies, data value distributions, etc.). From these environment models it is possible to generate sequences of calls to the SUT. However, like the previous approach, the generated sequences do not specify the expected *outputs* of the SUT. It is not possible to predict the output values because the environment model does not model the behavior of the SUT. So it is difficult to determine accurately whether a test has passed or failed—a crash/no-crash verdict may be all that is possible.

---

[3] See Chapter 4 for further discussion of pairwise testing, and the Pairwise website, *http://www.pairwise.org*, for tools, articles, and case studies on pairwise testing.

[4] For example, the 12 triples (*red*, 1, *car*), (*red*, 2, *truck*), (*red*, 3, *bike*), (*red*, 4, *car*), (*green*, 1, *truck*), (*green*, 2, *car*), (*green*, 3, *truck*), (*green*, 4, *bike*), (*yellow*, 1, *bike*), (*yellow*, 2, *bike*), (*yellow*, 3, *car*), (*yellow*, 4, *truck*) cover all pairs of input values. That is, all 12 combinations of color and number appear; so do all 12 combinations of number and vehicle and all 9 combinations of color and vehicle.

The third meaning of model-based testing is the generation of executable test cases that include *oracle* information, such as the expected output values of the SUT, or some automated check on the actual output values to see if they are correct. This is obviously a more challenging task than just generating test input data or test sequences that call the SUT but do not check the results. To generate tests with oracles, the test generator must know enough about the expected behavior of the SUT to be able to predict or check the SUT output values. In other words, with this definition of model-based testing, the model must describe the expected *behavior* of the SUT, such as the relationship between its inputs and outputs. But the advantage of this approach is that it is the only one of the four that addresses the whole test design problem from choosing input values and generating sequences of operation calls to generating executable test cases that include verdict information.

The fourth meaning of model-based testing is quite different: it assumes that we are given a very abstract description of a test case, such as a UML sequence diagram or a sequence of high-level procedure calls, and it focuses on transforming that abstract test case into a low-level test script that is executable. With this approach, the model is the information about the structure and API (application programming interface) of the SUT and the details of how to transform a high-level call into executable test scripts. We discuss this process in more detail in Chapter 8.

The main focus of this book (Chapters 3 to 7 and 9 and 10) is the third meaning of model-based testing: the generation of executable test cases that include oracle information, based on models of the SUT behavior. This generation process includes the generation of input values and the sequencing of calls into test sequences, but it also includes the generation of oracles that check the SUT outputs. This kind of model-based testing is more sophisticated and complex than the other meanings, but it has greater potential paybacks. It can automate the complete test design process, given a suitable model, and produces complete test sequences that can be transformed into executable test scripts.

With this view of model-based testing, we define model-based testing as *the automation of the design of black-box tests*. The difference from the usual black-box testing is that rather than manually writing tests based on the requirements documentation, we instead create a *model* of the expected SUT behavior, which captures some of the requirements. Then the model-based testing tools are used to automatically generate tests from that model.

Key Point   Model-based testing is the automation of the design of black-box tests.

That leads us to two questions: What is a model? What notation should we use to write models? Here are two illuminating definitions of the word *model*, from the *American Heritage Dictionary* [Ame00]:

- A small object, usually built to scale, that represents in detail another, often larger object.
- A schematic description of a system, theory, or phenomenon that accounts for its known or inferred properties and may be used for further study of its characteristics.

These definitions show the two most important characteristics of models that we want for model-based testing: the models must be small in relation to the size of the system that we are testing so that they are not too costly to produce, but they must be detailed enough to accurately describe the characteristics that we want to test. A UML class diagram or an informal use case diagram by itself is not precise or detailed enough for model-based testing; some description of the dynamic behavior of the system is needed. Yes, these two goals (small, detailed) can be in conflict at times. This is why it is an important engineering task to decide which characteristics of the system should be modeled to satisfy the test objectives, how much detail is useful, and which modeling notation can express those characteristics most naturally. Chapter 3 gives an introduction to various kinds of modeling notations and discusses guidelines for writing effective models for testing purposes.

Once we have a model of the system we want to test, we can then use one of the model-based testing tools to automatically generate a test suite from the model. There are quite a few commercial and academic model-based testing tools available now, based on a variety of methods and notations. Many of the tools allow the test engineer to guide the test generation process to control the number of tests produced or to focus the testing effort on certain areas of the model.

The output of the test case generator will be a set of *abstract test cases*, each of which is a sequence of operations with the associated input values and the expected output values (the *oracle*). That is, the generated test cases will be expressed in terms of the abstract operations and values used by the model.

The next step is to *transform* (concretize) these abstract test cases into executable test scripts. This may be done by the model-based testing tool, using some templates and translation tables supplied by the test engineer. The resulting executable tests may be produced directly in some programming language, such as JUnit tests in Java, or in a dynamic language such as Tcl or Python, or in a dedicated test scripting language. These executable test scripts can then be executed to try to detect failures in the SUT. The execution of the tests may be controlled and monitored by a *test execution tool*—different varieties of these tools are available for various types of SUT. The process of transforming the abstract test cases into executable tests and executing them is covered in Chapter 8.

In the next chapter, we will discuss the benefits and limitations of model-based testing and its impact on the software life cycle. But before that, let us look at a realistic example of model-based testing to get a clearer picture of what it involves.

1.3 A SMART CARD EXAMPLE

To give a good overview of what model-based testing can do, we will show how we can use it to test a simplified smart card system. Figure 1.3 shows a UML class diagram for this system. We will not describe the system in detail or show the entire model, but we note that it is sophisticated enough to allow each smart card to be used for a variety of applications, such as banks and retailers, and it even supports loyalty programs.

The Smartcard class in Figure 1.3 is annotated with ≪SUT≫ to indicate that it is the SUT. A Smartcard instance can contain several Applications and one of those Applications may be the selectedApplication. Each Application can be either an EPurse application, which stores real money, or a Loyalty application, which keeps track of reward points and prizes such as free trips. Finally, each Application has one or more Profiles associated with it that define the PINs (personal identification numbers) needed to use that Application and indicate whether those PINs have been entered correctly.

This class diagram by itself is not enough. It tells us the classes that make up the system, their data fields, and the signatures of the methods, but it says nothing about the behavior of those methods. To get a UML model that is suitable for model-based testing, we need to add details about the *behavior* of the methods shown in the class diagram.

UML offers many ways and notations for specifying behavior. The two that we will illustrate in this example are *OCL postconditions* and *state machine diagrams*. We will explain these notations more fully in Chapter 3, so here we have just a brief introduction.

OCL (Object Constraint Language) is a textual notation, somewhat similar to the expression part of a programming language, that can be used to define constraints within class diagrams or specify preconditions or postconditions for operations. For example, here is an OCL postcondition to specify

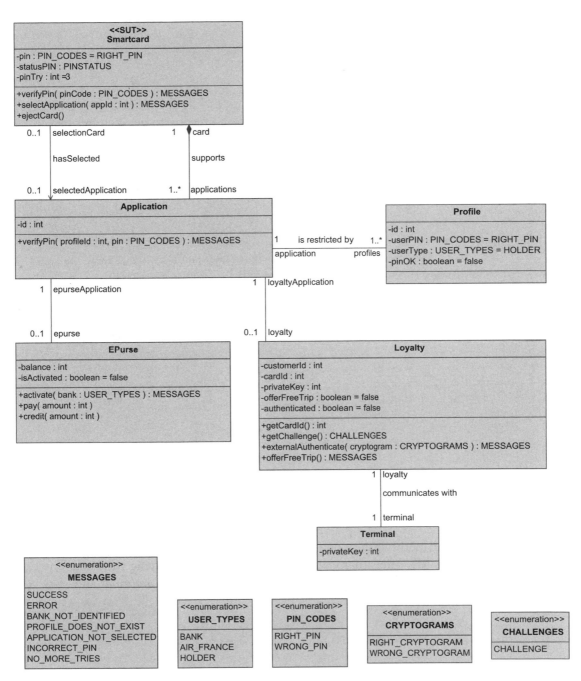

FIGURE 1.3   UML class diagram for the smart card system.

the behavior of the *credit* operation of the EPurse class. Note that the expression self.balance@pre gives the value of the balance field before the method executes, so this postcondition says that the balance is increased by amount if this EPurse is activated, but is left unchanged otherwise.

```
post: if (self.isActivated) then
         self.balance = self.balance@pre + amount
      else
         self.balance = self.balance@pre
      endif
```

Here is a more complex example, for the *activate* operation of the EPurse class. It illustrates some of the OCL operators for collections, which allow us to write expressive but concise conditions. The expression self.epurseApplication.profiles navigates through the class diagram, starting from the current EPurse object and returning its collection of Profile objects. Then the .userType->excludes(bank) part checks that none of those Profile objects are BANK profiles. The second if generates the same set of Profile objects and then checks that there is a BANK profile among them and that a valid PIN has been entered for that BANK profile.

```
post: if (self.epurseApplication.profiles.userType
            ->excludes(USER_TYPES::BANK)) then
         result = MESSAGES::ERROR
      else
         if (self.epurseApplication.profiles->
               exists(p:Profile | p.userType
               = USER_TYPES::BANK and p.pinOK)) then
            result = MESSAGES::SUCCESS and self.isActivated
         else
            result = MESSAGES::BANK_NOT_IDENTIFIED
         endif
      endif
```

Some class behaviors are better specified with *state machine diagrams*. UML state machine diagrams represent the various states that an object may be in and the transitions between those states. Figure 1.4 shows a state machine for the Smartcard class. Note that some transitions have labels in the form *Event*[*Guard*]/*Action*, which means that the transition is triggered by *Event* but is taken only if *Guard* evaluates to true. When the transition is taken, then *Action* (which is written in OCL in this example) can specify how the instance variables of the class are modified. The *Guard* and *Action* parts are optional, so the ejectCard() event is always enabled and has an

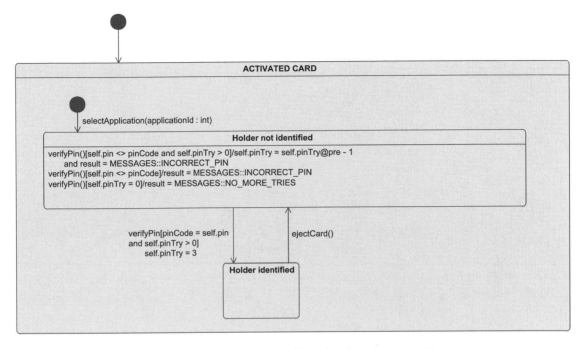

FIGURE 1.4   UML state machine for the Smartcard class.

empty action that does not change any variables. The transitions within the "Holder not identified" state are *self-transitions* that can change state variables and produce outputs, but do not move to a different state.

In addition to these details about the behavior of objects, it is useful to give a concrete scenario for testing purposes. Figure 1.5 shows a UML object diagram that specifies a single smart card that can interact with a bank and an airline.

After specifying all these elements, we can finally use a model-based testing tool to automatically generate some tests. We can choose various criteria to determine how many tests we want. For example, we might choose *all-transitions* coverage for a state machine to get a basic set of tests or *all-transition-pairs* coverage to get a larger set of tests that tests interactions between adjacent pairs of transitions. For the methods specified with OCL postconditions, we could choose basic *branch* coverage to make sure that all branches of if-then-else constructs are tested or something like *Modified Condition/Decision Coverage* (MC/DC) to give a larger set of tests that tests each condition more thoroughly and independently. Most tools offer a variety of coverage criteria or allow you to specify manually exactly which class or method or sequence of events you want to test.

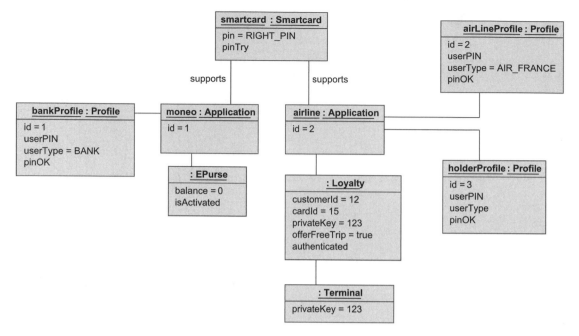

FIGURE 1.5   UML object diagram that defines an initial state.

For example, if we use the LTG/UML tool from LEIRIOS[5] Technologies, with its default settings of branch coverage and transition coverage, we get 29 abstract tests. Each abstract test is a short sequence of operation calls with appropriate input values, plus the expected output value of the method if it has an output. In addition, some oracle information is included (shown in italics in the following sample test), saying how the internal state of each object should have changed after each method call.

Here is one of the abstract tests that is generated, showing a successful withdrawal of one cent from the moneo application within the card. We write the actual test invocations in bold, where $Obj.M(...) = R$ means that method M of object Obj should be called and its expected return value is R.

```
test001 =
    moneo.verifyPin(pin=RIGHT_PIN, profileId=1)=SUCCESS;
    bankProfile={id=1, userPIN=RIGHT_PIN, pinOK=true,
                        userType=BANK}
```

[5]LEIRIOS Technologies is a software company that produces model-based testing tools and other model-based testing services. LTG/UML is the LEIROS Test Generator tool for UML.

```
moneo.epurse.activate(bank=BANK)=SUCCESS;
```
moneo.epurse={isActivated=true, balance=0}
```
moneo.epurse.credit(amount=1);
```
moneo.epurse={isActivated=true, balance=1}
```
moneo.epurse.pay(amount=1);
```
moneo.epurse={isActivated=true, balance=0}

Why does this test do *credit*(1) before the *pay*(1) call? Because in this model, the precondition of *pay* is that *balance* $>=$ amount, so the model-based test generation determined that it was necessary to increase the initial balance (which was 0) before the *pay* method could be tested. Similarly, it generated the necessary setup code to verify that the PIN was correct and to activate the bank's EPurse.

We say that this is an *abstract* test because it is written using the concepts, classes, and values of the model rather than the real SUT. The actual concrete API of the SUT may be quite different from the abstract model. So we need to define how each abstract method maps to the concrete operations of the system, how the abstract data values should be transformed into concrete data, and whether we can use query methods to observe some of the internal states of the objects. Most model-based testing tools provide some way to define these mappings, either by writing an *adaptation layer* that gives the SUT an interface similar to the model or by writing some templates in the target language for your tests so that the model-based testing tool can translate all the abstract tests into executable code.

For example, the preceding abstract test could be translated into a scripting language, such as Tcl, or into C++ or Java. Listing 1.1 shows how it might look if we translated it into Java code that uses the JUnit testing framework[6] (we assume that the RIGHT_PIN constant is mapped to 3042 and that we have query methods for accessing the pinOK and id fields of the Profile class and the balance field of the EPurse class, but not for accessing other data fields).

This example illustrates some of the tradeoffs of model-based testing. The tests do not come for free; there is the cost of writing the model or

---

[6]JUnit is a widely used Java library for unit testing of Java applications. See *http://www.junit.org* for details and downloads.

LISTING 1.1 The JUnit test script generated from test001.

```
public class  extends junit.framework.TestCase
{
    private Smartcard smartcard;
    private Application moneo;
    private Application airline;

    public setUp()
    {
        /* Code to set up the initial network of objects */
        ... reinitializes smartcard, moneo, airline, etc.
    }

    public void test001()
    {
        MESSAGES result = moneo.verifyPin(3042,1);
        assertEqual(result, MESSAGES.SUCCESS);
        assertTrue(moneo.getProfile().pinOk());
        assertTrue(moneo.getProfile().getId() == 1);

        result = moneo.getEPurse().activate(USER_TYPES.BANK);
        assertEqual(result, MESSAGES.SUCCESS);
        assertEqual(moneo.getEPurse.getBalance() == 0);

        moneo.epurse.credit(1);
        assertEqual(moneo.getEPurse.getBalance() == 1);

        moneo.epurse.pay(1);
        assertEqual(moneo.getEPurse.getBalance() == 0);
    }

    // ...the other 28 tests...
}
```

at least of making an existing model precise enough so that it can be used for model-based testing. In this example, it is likely that the class diagram already existed but that the OCL postconditions for eight methods, the state machine diagram, and the object diagram were developed specifically for the model-based testing. So the cost of using model-based testing is mostly the time to write these 2 or 3 pages of model details. The benefit is that we can then automatically obtain a comprehensive set of 29 executable tests that cover all the different behaviors of each method and class.

The cost of writing these 10 to 15 pages of tests manually would have been greater than the additions we made to the model, and the coverage of the manually written test set would probably be less systematic. Furthermore, with model-based testing we can easily generate a larger test suite from the same model or regenerate our test suite each time we change the system requirements and therefore the model.

Other advantages of the model-based approach are discussed in the next chapter. We will also see there how model-based testing changes the software life cycle and the software development process.

1.4 SUMMARY

Model-based testing is the automation of black-box test design. A model-based testing tool uses various test generation algorithms and strategies to generate tests from a behavioral model of the SUT.

The model must be concise and precise: concise so that it does not take too long to write and so that it is easy to validate with respect to the requirements but precise enough to describe the behavior that is to be tested.

Test cases (including test data and oracles) can be automatically generated from the model using a model-based testing tool. The test engineer can also control the tool to focus the testing effort and manage the number of tests that are generated.

The tests produced from the model are abstract tests, so they must be transformed into executable tests. This also requires some input from the test engineer, but most model-based testing tools provide assistance with this process.

1.5 FURTHER READING

To understand model-based testing, it helps to have a good knowledge of general testing practices and techniques, so we will start by recommending a few good testing books.

Myers's book, *The Art of Software Testing* [Mye79], is a classic in the testing area—some sections are now a little out of date, but the first few chapters are well worth reading, and it has good descriptions of some widely used test design strategies, such as cause-effect and boundary testing.[7] Beizer's book [Bei90] covers a range of manual test design techniques from models, including path testing, data-flow testing, logic-based testing, graph-based testing, and state-machine-based testing. Whittaker's book, *How to Break Software* [Whi03], contains a series of testing techniques, called "attacks," that target common software errors. The list is based on an empirical analysis of a large number of bugs found in commercial software. Copeland's book [Cop04] gives an overview of classic and recent test design techniques. He does not explicitly introduce model-based testing, but many of the test design techniques that he discusses are used by model-based testing tools to automate test case generation.

Binder's 1200-page book on testing object-oriented systems [Bin99] is the biggest and best guide to designing and automating tests for object-oriented applications. He explains that, in one sense, all testing must be model-based, whether the model is just in the tester's mind or is a sketch on paper or is a formal model that can be analyzed by tools (which is the focus of our book). He covers a wide variety of techniques for designing tests from state machine models, combinational logic and the Unified Modeling Language (UML), plus a large library of patterns for writing tests. The scope of his book is much broader than ours because we focus more on *tool-supported* model-based testing and on the kinds of models and test generation techniques that we have found to work best with automated tools.

For more information about model-based testing, we suggest that you go online to the website associated with this book (*http://www.cs.waikato.ac. nz/~markut.mbt*). There you will find up-to-date links to other model-based testing resources and lists of model-based testing tools and examples.

If you want to know more about the theory behind model-based testing, the book *Model-Based Testing of Reactive Systems* (BJK⁺05) is a valuable collection of survey papers on testing of finite state machines, testing of labeled transition systems, model-based test case generation, tools and case studies, and so forth.

---

[7]A second edition (2004) updates some chapters and covers new kinds of testing such as extreme testing and Internet testing.

## CHAPTER 2

"Life is too short for manual testing."

Harry Robinson, test architect for Microsoft's Engineering Excellence Group and a driving force behind Microsoft's model-based testing initiative, 1999–2004.

THE PAIN AND THE GAIN

This chapter describes the impact of model-based testing on the testing life cycle and the benefits and challenges associated with adopting model-based testing.

We start with an overview of some traditional testing processes and show how these differ from the model-based testing process. Then we discuss maturity levels, look at several case studies that demonstrate the pain and the gain of putting model-based testing into practice, and finish by discussing the benefits and limitations of model-based testing.

2.1 CLASSIC TESTING PROCESSES

When doing functional testing, there are three key issues:

Designing the test cases: The test cases have to be designed starting from the system requirements and taking into consideration the high-level

Note: The quote is from "Bumper Stickers for Testers," Stickyminds.com, December 2004. Available at *www.stickyminds.com/se/S8299.asp*.

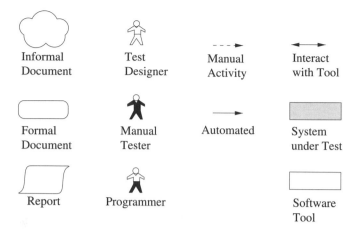

FIGURE 2.1   Key to the notation used in process diagrams.

test objectives and policies. Each test case is defined by a test context, a scenario, and some pass/fail criteria.

Executing the tests and analyzing the results: The test cases have to be executed on the system under test (SUT). The test results are then analyzed to determine the cause of each test execution failure.

Verifying how the tests cover the requirements: To manage the quality of the testing process (and therefore the quality of the product), one must measure the coverage of the requirements by the test suite. This is usually done by a *traceability matrix* between test cases and requirements.

This section describes several classic testing processes that are widely used in industry. We start by describing a simple manual testing process, and then we progress through several testing processes that use automated test execution. We finish with a table that shows how each of these testing processes addresses the three stated testing issues, and what issues remain unsolved.

Figure 2.1 shows the notations that we use in the process diagrams in this chapter. *Informal Document* means a document in natural language, such as English, while *Formal Documents* are written in some precise notation (such as models and test scripts) that can be parsed or executed by tools.

2.1.1 A Manual Testing Process

The left side of Figure 2.2 shows a completely manual testing process. This was the earliest style of testing, but it is still widely used.

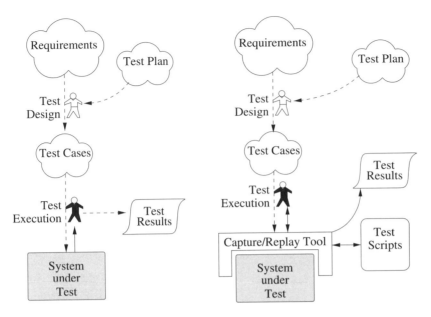

FIGURE 2.2   A manual testing process (*left*) and a capture/replay testing process (*right*).

The test plan gives a high-level overview of the testing objectives, such as which aspects of the SUT should be tested, what kinds of test strategies should be used, how often testing should be performed, and how much testing will be done.

The test design is done manually, based on the informal requirements documents. The output of the design stage is a human-readable document that describes the desired test cases. The description of test cases can be quite concise and high-level; many of the low-level details about interacting with the system under test can be left to the common sense of the test execution person, who is called a *manual tester*. However, the manual designing of the tests is time-consuming and does not ensure systematic coverage of the SUT functionality.

The test execution is also done manually. For each test case, the manual tester follows the steps of that test case, interacts directly with the SUT, compares the SUT output with the expected output, and records the test verdict.

In embedded applications, where it is often not possible to interact directly with the SUT (it may be just a black box with some wires coming out), a *test execution environment* may be used to allow the tester to enter inputs and observe outputs. However, the execution of each test case is still performed manually.

Note that the required skills of the test designer and manual tester are rather different. The test designer needs to have expert knowledge about the SUT, plus some skill with test design strategies. The manual tester has a much more menial task, which requires some knowledge of how to interact with the SUT but mostly involves simply following the steps of the test case and recording results.

This manual test execution process is repeated each time a new release of the SUT needs to be tested. This quickly becomes a very boring and time-consuming task. Since there is no automation of the test execution, the cost of testing each SUT release is constant and large. In fact, the cost of repeating the manual test execution is so high that, to keep testing costs within budget, it is often necessary to cut corners by reducing the number of tests that are executed after each evolution of the code. This can result in software being delivered with incomplete testing, which introduces a significant risk regarding product maturity, stability, and robustness.

The next few testing processes propose various ways of automating the test execution, to reduce this cost and permit more comprehensive testing.

2.1.2 A Capture/Replay Testing Process

Capture/replay testing attempts to reduce the cost of test re-execution by *capturing* the interactions with the SUT during one test execution session and then *replaying* those interactions during later test execution sessions. In this process, test cases are still manually designed.

The right side of Figure 2.2 shows how this is different from manual test execution. The interaction with the SUT is managed by a testing tool that we call the *capture/replay* tool. This records all the inputs sent to the system under test and the outputs that result (e.g., procedure return results, screen snapshots, data files, etc.). Then when a new release of the SUT must be tested, the capture/replay tool can attempt to rerun all the recorded tests and report which ones fail. To rerun each recorded test, the tool sends the recorded inputs to the SUT and then compares the new outputs with the recorded outputs from the original test execution.

The main problem with capture/replay testing is that it is very fragile. For example, a change to the layout of a window in the SUT (such as changing from a combo box to a radio button) or a small change to the interface of one procedure in an API can cause a large number of the recorded tests to fail. These have to be tested manually again and recorded for future sessions. This inability to adapt to small changes in the SUT creates a huge maintenance problem with the recorded tests and often leads to the capture/replay method being abandoned after several SUT releases.

This problem comes from a *lack of abstraction* in the recorded tests. That is, it is the low-level details of the actual SUT input and output values that are recorded rather than a higher-level, more abstract, view. The verification of the correctness of the outputs is also usually too low-level and based on comparing screen snapshots or strings rather than checking just the relevant higher-level features of the output.

The key issue of automating the test execution is only partially solved by the capture/replay approach. This is due to the extreme sensitivity of this approach to any changes in the SUT. Notice also that this approach is usually used only to automate the testing of the graphical user interface (GUI) of the SUT, which is only one part of the desired functional test suite.

2.1.3 A Script-Based Testing Process

The left side of Figure 2.3 shows a testing process that uses *test scripts* to automate the execution of tests.

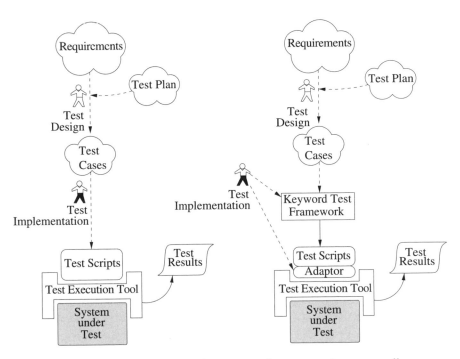

FIGURE 2.3   Testing processes with automated test execution: manually developed test scripts (*left*) and data-driven or keyword-driven testing (*right*).

A test script is an executable script that runs one or more test cases. This usually involves initializing the SUT, putting the SUT in the required context, creating the test input values, passing those inputs to the SUT, recording the SUT response, comparing that response with the expected outputs, and assigning a pass/fail verdict to each test. The test scripts may be written in some standard programming or scripting language or in a special testing language such as TTCN-3 (Testing and Test Control Notation) [WDT$^+$05]. So writing test scripts is now a programming task, which requires different skills from test design or test execution.

Test scripts must *control* and *observe* the SUT using some API. This is a strong design constraint on the application—it must offer the required *points of control and observation* for testing purposes. These are important testability criteria, which are standard quality criteria in most software engineering processes. These points of control and observation are then invoked in the test scripts both to stimulate the SUT and to observe if the actual states or responses are the expected ones.

The script-based testing approach solves the test execution problem by automating it. Each time that we want to rerun the tests for regression testing, this can be done for free by just running the test scripts again.

However, this increases the test maintenance problem because the test scripts must evolve not only when some requirements change, but also whenever some implementation details change (e.g., when some parameters change in the API used to stimulate the SUT). Since the total size of test scripts can be nearly as big as the application under test and the details of one interface to the SUT are usually spread out over many tests, maintenance of the test scripts becomes very costly.

Abstraction is the key to reducing the maintenance costs of test scripts, but the level of abstraction depends on the individual skill of the test script designer.

2.1.4 A Keyword-Driven Automated Testing Process

Data-driven testing, table-driven testing, action-word testing, and keyword-driven testing [MP02] have the common goal of overcoming the maintenance problems of low-level test scripts by raising the abstraction level of the test cases.

The idea is to express each test case as abstractly as possible while making it precise enough to be executed or interpreted by a test execution tool.

Data-driven testing uses a fixed set of test scripts, which are parameterized by different data values from each test case. This makes the test scripts more generic and allows them to be reused in many test cases, which reduces the test script maintenance problem.

Keyword-driven testing, or *action-word testing*, takes this a step further by using *action keywords* in the test cases, in addition to data. Each action keyword corresponds to a fragment of a test script (the "Adaptor" code on the right in Figure 2.3), which allows the test execution tool to translate a sequence of keywords and data values into executable tests. Note that the implementation of these keywords still requires programming skills, but the design of test cases is now at a more abstract and concise level (keywords and data values), so it can be done by test designers who are not programmers.

One example of a keyword-based testing framework is the FitNesse tool,[1] based on FIT (Framework for Integrated Testing) [MC05]. With this tool, the test cases are defined within web pages (using a wiki interface), the Adaptor code is written as a set of "Fixture" classes, and the Keyword Test Framework merges these two to produce executable tests, which are immediately executed.

One strong point of keyword-driven testing comes from the high abstraction level of the test cases, which are easy for non-programmers to read and write but are still executable. The high level of abstraction also reduces maintenance problems because the test cases can often be adapted to a new version of the SUT or its environment simply by changing the scripts associated with a few keywords. However, the test data and oracles are still designed manually, and the verification of test coverage with respect to requirements has to be done and maintained manually. In the next section we will see how model-based testing addresses these problems.

2.1.5 Solved and Remaining Problems

In Table 2.1 we summarize the testing problems that are solved by each of the mentioned approaches, as well as the problems that remain unsolved. As we go down the table, the testing processes become more sophisticated and provide better solutions for minimizing the cost of executing and reexecuting tests. However, all these processes still rely on manual design of the test cases and manual tracking of the relationship between the requirements and the tests. In addition, because they all rely on manual design of the tests, none of them guarantees very systematic and repeatable coverage of the SUT behavior.

The model-based testing process aims to solve the following three remaining problems that the other testing processes do not fully address:

---

[1] See *http://fitnesse.org*.

TABLE 2.1   Comparison of Testing Approaches

Testing Process	Solved Problems	Remaining Problems
Manual Testing	Functional testing	Imprecise coverage of SUT functionality
		No capabilities for regression testing
		Very costly process (every test execution is done manually)
		No effective measurement of test coverage
Capture/ Replay	Makes it possible to automatically reexecute captured test cases	Imprecise coverage of SUT functionality
		Weak capabilities for regression testing (very sensitive to GUI changes)
		Costly process (each change implies recapturing test cases manually)
Script-Based Testing	Makes it possible to automatically execute and reexecute test scripts	Imprecise coverage of SUT functionality
		Complex scripts are difficult to write and maintain
		Requirements traceability is developed manually (costly process)
Keyword-Driven Testing	Easier development of high-level test scripts	Imprecise coverage of SUT functionality
		Requirements traceability is developed manually (costly process)

- Automation of the *design* of functional test cases (including generation of the expected results) to reduce the design cost and to produce test suites with systematic coverage of the model
- Reduction of the maintenance costs of the test suite
- Automatic generation of the traceability matrix from requirements to test cases

The next section presents the model-based testing process and describes each step of the process in more detail.

2.2 THE MODEL-BASED TESTING PROCESS

Model-based testing automates the detailed design of the test cases and the generation of the traceability matrix. More precisely, instead of manually writing hundreds of test cases (sequences of operations), the test designer writes an abstract model of the system under test, and then the model-based testing tool generates a set of test cases from that model. The overall test design time is reduced, and an added advantage is that one can generate a variety of test suites from the same model simply by using different test selection criteria.

The model-based testing process can be divided into the following five main steps, as shown in Figure 2.4.

1. *Model* the SUT and/or its environment.
2. *Generate* abstract tests from the model.
3. *Concretize* the abstract tests to make them executable.

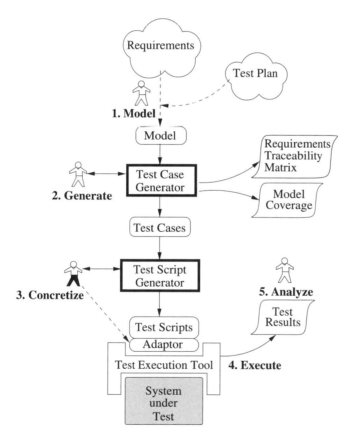

FIGURE 2.4   The model-based testing process (testing tools are in the boxes with very bold lines).

4. *Execute* the tests on the SUT and assign verdicts.

5. *Analyze* the test results.

Of course, steps 4 and 5 are a normal part of any testing process, even manual testing. Step 3 is similar to the "adaptor" phase of keyword-based testing, where the meaning of each keyword is defined. The first two steps distinguish model-based testing from other kinds of testing. In *online* model-based testing tools, steps 2 through 4 are usually merged into one step, whereas in *offline* model-based testing, they are usually separate. But it is still useful to explain the steps separately to ensure a clear understanding of the model-based testing process.

We will now give a more detailed description of each step of the process and mention some of the practical issues about using model-based testing in large projects.

The first step of model-based testing is to write an *abstract model* of the system that we want to test. We call it an *abstract* model because it should be much smaller and simpler than the SUT itself. It should focus on just the key aspects that we want to test and should omit many of the details of the SUT. Later chapters give detailed guidelines for how to perform this modeling step using various modeling notations. While writing the model, we may also annotate it with requirements identifiers to clearly document the relationship between the informal requirements and the formal model.

After writing the model, it is advisable to use tools to check that the model is consistent and has the desired behavior. Most modeling notations provide some automated verification tools (such as typecheckers and static analysis tools), as well as some interactive tools (such as animators) that allow us to explore the behavior of the model and check that it is what we expect. The use of an animator is highly recommended for novice modelers, but experienced modelers may prefer to save time by omitting animation—any errors that remain in the model will be noticed during later steps, and the animator can be used then to pinpoint the problem in the model.

The second step of model-based testing is to generate abstract tests from the model. We must choose some *test selection criteria*, to say which tests we want to generate from the model, because there are usually an infinite number of possible tests. For example, we might interact with the test generation tool to focus on a particular part of the model or to choose a particular model coverage criterion, such as *all-transitions*, or we might write some *test case specifications* in some simple pattern language to specify the kinds of test we want generated.

The main output of this step is a set of abstract tests, which are sequences of operations from the model. Since the model uses a simplified view of the SUT, these abstract tests lack some of the detail needed by the SUT and are not directly executable.

Most model-based testing tools also produce a *requirements traceability matrix* or various other *coverage reports* as additional outputs of this step. The requirements traceability matrix traces the link between functional requirements and generated test cases. This is generally a many-to-many relation: a requirement can be covered by several test cases, and a single test case may exercise several requirements. The coverage reports give us some indications of how well the generated test set exercises all the behaviors of the model. Note that these reports are talking about coverage of the *model*, not coverage of the SUT—we have not even executed the tests on the SUT yet! For example, a coverage report may give us some coverage statistics for the operations or transitions of the model, tell us what percentage of boolean decisions in the model have been tested with true and false values, or give the coverage results for many other kinds of coverage measure (see Chapter 4).

We can use such coverage reports simply for statistical feedback about the quality of the generated test set, or we can use them to identify parts of the model that may not be well tested and investigate why this has happened. For example, if a particular path through the model has no tests generated for it, we could try changing some of the test generation parameters and repeat the test generation step. This is where it can be useful to use an animation tool to investigate the behavior of the path in the model and decide whether the lack of tests is due to an error in the model, a normal feature of the model, or inadequate test generation. In the latter case, if we want to improve the coverage of our test set, we could add an abstract test for this path by hand or give the test generation tool some explicit hints about how to find the desired test.

The third step of model-based testing is to transform the abstract tests into executable concrete tests. This may be done by a *transformation* tool, which uses various templates and mappings to translate each abstract test case into an executable test script. Or it may be done by writing some *adaptor* code that wraps around the SUT and implements each abstract operation in terms of the lower-level SUT facilities. Either way, the goal of this step is to bridge the gap between the abstract tests and the concrete SUT by adding in the low-level SUT details that were not mentioned in the abstract model.

One advantage of this two-layer approach (abstract tests and concrete test scripts) is that the abstract tests can be quite independent of the language used to write tests and of the test environment. By changing just the adaptor code or the translation templates, we can reuse the same set of tests in different test execution environments.

The fourth step is to execute the concrete tests on the system under test. With online model-based testing, the tests will be executed as they are produced, so the model-based testing tool will manage the test execution process and record the results. With offline model-based testing, we have just generated a set of concrete test scripts in some existing language, so we can continue to use our existing test execution tools and practices. For example, we might use Mercury TestDirector[2] to manage the tests, execute them regularly, and record the results.

The fifth step is to analyze the results of the test executions and take corrective action. For each test that reports a failure, we must determine the fault that caused that failure. Again, this is similar to the traditional test analysis process. As usual, when a test fails, we may find that it is due to a fault in the SUT or we may find that it is due to a fault in the test case itself. Since we are using model-based testing, a fault in the test case must be due to a fault in the adaptor code or in the model (and perhaps also the requirements documents).[3] So this is another place where we get feedback about the correctness of the model.

In our experience, the first execution of the test set usually sees a high percentage of the tests fail—typically because of some minor errors in the adaptor code. Once these are fixed, the remaining failures are more interesting and require deeper analysis to find the fault. Perhaps roughly half of these failures will result from faults in the SUT and the other half from faults in the model and the requirements. However, this ratio can vary widely, depending upon the experience of the testers, the kind of project, the rate of change in the requirements and the model, and the rate of change in the SUT.

To finish this section, let us step back and take a more philosophical view of model-based testing.

It is always the case that test design is based on some kind of model of expected behavior, but with manual test design, this model is usually just an informal mental model. By making the model explicit, in a notation that can be used by model-based testing tools, we are able to generate tests automatically (which decreases the cost of testing), generate an arbitrary number of tests, as well as obtain more systematic coverage of the model. These changes can increase both the quality and quantity of our test suite.

---

[2]A trademark of Mercury Interactive Corporation; see *http://www.mercury.com.*

[3]We should also mention the possibility of an error in the model-based testing tools themselves. Of course, this is unlikely, since they are surely well tested!

2.3 MODELS: BUILD OR BORROW?

By now, you have seen that a good model is the most essential thing to have before we can start generating tests using model-based testing. So let's consider where this model comes from. For example, does the testing team have to build their own model for testing purposes, or can they borrow (reuse) the models that the development team has already developed?

In fact, there is a whole spectrum of possibilities, ranging from reusing the existing development model without change, all the way to developing a test-specific model from scratch. That is, the level of reuse of the development model for testing purposes can range all the way from 100 percent down to 0 percent. Let us briefly consider each of these extremes and then discuss the middle path.

At first glance, it seems very attractive to just reuse the development model, without change, as the input for the model-based testing process. This would give us 100 percent reuse and would obviously save time. However, this level of reuse is rarely possible, and when it is possible, it is often a very bad idea.

It is usually not possible for two reasons. First, development models frequently have too much detail and much of their detail concerns the low-level implementation issues of the SUT—these are not needed for test generation and only complicate the process. Second, development models do not usually describe the SUT *dynamic behavior* in enough detail for test generation—they often concentrate on describing the structural aspects of the SUT and the interfaces between subsystems, but they omit most of the details of the processing that happens within each subsystem or method, the contents of files or messages, and so on. So it is rare for a development model to be abstract enough, yet precise enough, for test generation.

Probably the only people who write development models that describe the full dynamic behavior of the SUT are those who intend to generate code automatically from the model rather than develop the code by hand. This is becoming more common in the area of embedded software, where the model might be, for example, a detailed statechart model with pseudocode that defines how a set of control functions interact to control a system, and automatic code generation tools are used to generate the implementation of that system. In this case, using the same model for test generation would be a very bad idea because it would mean that the tests and the implementation of the SUT are both being derived from the same source. So any errors in that model will generate incorrect implementation code, but the tests will contain the *same* errors, so no test failures will be found. The problem is that the tests and the implementation are not sufficiently *independent*.

The essence of testing is to execute the SUT to find *differences* between its behavior and the behavior expected by the tests. To find as many failures as possible, we want the design of the SUT and the design of the tests to be as independent as possible. So deriving them both from the same model is useless, unless our goal is just to test the correctness of the test generation and code generation tools themselves. By the way, the same *lack-of-independence* problem would arise if we used a sophisticated UML tool to reverse-engineer our SUT implementation code back into a UML model and then tried to generate tests from that.

The other extreme, where we develop a test model from scratch (0 percent reuse), is actually quite common and useful. This maximizes independence and allows us to customize the model for our current test purposes. In some situations, it is necessary to develop a test model from scratch because there is no development model, or the development model is designed for human consumption only and is so informal that tools cannot make use of it. In other situations, you might want to have independent testing, with a high level of independence between the tests and the SUT implementation, so you decide that the test engineers will develop their models directly from the system requirements rather than being influenced by any development models.

However, a middle path can be useful as well. For example, it is common to reuse a high-level class diagram and some use cases from the development model and then add the behavioral details that are necessary for model-based testing.

In this book, we show how to build testing models directly from the informal requirements documents. We recommend that you also follow this approach because it maximizes the independence between your test model and your SUT implementation. However, it is also fine to start with an existing high-level development model, such as a UML class diagram, throw away the parts of it that are unnecessary for the current test purpose, then look at the requirements documents, and add all the details that are necessary to make your model *test ready*, that is, sufficiently precise for test generation. We will talk more about how precise the model needs to be in Section 2.4.2 and Chapter 3. Whichever approach you take, the emphasis should be on relating your model to the informal requirements as closely as possible so that your tests accurately reflect the user's needs.

2.4 YOUR MATURITY LEVEL

The CMM (Capability Maturity Model) for Software, and its newer form, CMMI[4] (Capability Maturity Model Integration) for Software Engineering, are well-established methods for measuring and improving the maturity of a software development group. They identify five maturity levels:

Level 1, initial: Ad hoc and chaotic processes.

Level 2, managed: Requirements are managed, and processes are planned and measured.

Level 3, defined: Processes are standardized across the organization and tailored by each project.

Level 4, quantitatively managed: Processes are measured and controlled using statistics.

Level 5, optimizing: Processes are continually improved.

A collection of concrete goals and practices is associated with each level. Numerous studies have demonstrated that higher maturity levels result in lower cost, more predictable schedules, and better quality software.[5]

If your software development processes are somewhere between the initial (ad hoc) and managed levels, like the majority of software developers, is it wise to start using model-based testing? To explore this a little, let's investigate two maturity models that are more closely related to model-based testing.

In the following two subsections, we discuss *testing maturity levels* and *modeling maturity levels*. This will give us a good background for discussing the benefits, costs, and limitations of model-based testing in Sections 2.7 and 2.8.

2.4.1 Your Testing Maturity Level

Over the last 10 years, there have been many proposals for process improvement models for testing [Wea01], such as the Testing Maturity Model (TMM) from Illinois Institute of Technology [BSC96a, BSC96b] and the

---

[4]CMM and CMMI are registered trademarks of Carnegie Mellon University. See *http://www.sei. cmu.edu* for more information.

[5]See *http://www.sei.cmu.edu/cmmi/results.html* for a summary of CMMI performance results and links to more detail.

Test Process Improvement (TPI) model [KP99] from Sogeti.[6] These focus primarily on the wider management and organizational issues of testing, whereas in this section we focus mostly on the technical issues of test design and implementation. However, as we will see, a reasonably mature test process is an important prerequisite for adopting model-based testing. The various process improvement models are useful in measuring and improving the maturity of your existing process and evaluating whether it is mature enough to introduce model-based testing.

For example, TPI defines maturity levels 0 to 13. The basic "Use of tools" for supporting testing is expected by level 3; the "Managed test automation" level, which includes systematic use of test execution tools, is associated with level 7; and "Optimal test automation," where periodic evaluations are carried out to determine where test automation could give further gains, is associated with level 10.

Model-based testing tools are sophisticated testing tools since they automate the test *design* stage, and this usually implies that the test execution phase is already automated. So the adoption of model-based testing would correspond to at least level 7 of TPI. A company whose testing maturity level is significantly lower than this will face an increased risk when adopting model-based testing because they must leap multiple levels of test maturity in a single bound.

2.4.2 Your Modeling Maturity Level

It is also useful to consider the modeling maturity level of a company that is adopting model-based testing.

The UML/OCL and MDA (model-driven architecture) community has identified six levels of modeling maturity for UML development models and MDA [WK03]:

Level 0, No Specification: The software specifications are only in the heads of the developers.

Level 1, Textual: The software specifications are written down in informal natural-language documents.

Level 2, Text with Diagrams: The textual specifications are augmented with some high-level diagrams.

Level 3, Models with Text: A set of models (diagrams or text with well-defined meanings) form the backbone of the specification. Natural lan-

---

[6]See *http://www.sogeti.nl/tpi*.

guage is used to motivate and explain the models and to fill in many details within the models. The transition from models to code is still manual, and it can be difficult to keep models up to date after changes to the code.

Level 4, Precise Models: This is the level where MDA becomes possible, with code being generated from the model and then modified to fulfill special requirements. The model has a precise meaning, which does not rely on natural language even though natural language is still used to explain the background of the model.

Level 5, Models Only: At this level, the model is used like a high-level programming language, the model-to-code generation is automatic and used just like a compiler, and the generated code is used directly without changes. In 2003, the authors commented that this level has not yet been reached anywhere in the world, but it is a good ultimate goal.

Model-based testing corresponds to a modeling maturity level of 3—that is, somewhere between levels 3 and 4. The test models need to be precise enough to specify some of the SUT behavior, which implies level 3 maturity or a little higher. But since the test model is just for testing purposes, rather than for development, it is usually much simpler and does not specify all the SUT details that would be necessary for code generation. This is one of the differences that makes model-based testing much more feasible than full MDA.

In our experience, many companies that adopt model-based testing successfully have a modeling maturity level of only 1 or 2, but they have little difficulty in developing precise testing models, even though their development models remain much less precise. Furthermore, as we will see in the next section, the added precision of the test model can have surprising feedback to the requirements and the development process.

2.5 HYPOTHETICAL CASE: TOTAL TESTING HOURS

In this section, we simulate the experiences of a hypothetical company that wishes to test a series of versions of a small application (around 15K noncomment lines of code). For each of the testing processes described earlier in this chapter, we estimate the total time that they will devote to testing over the life cycle of this application. The goal is to compare the cost (in hours) of the various processes.

Warning This is a rather academic simulation exercise. If you are a practical person who likes to see just the bottom-line results, we suggest that you skip the next subsection, which describes the details of the simulation, and go straight to the graph and the conclusions in Section 2.5.2 on page 38.

2.5.1 Assumptions

Here are the assumptions that we make for our simulation. These are very open to debate, so if you disagree with some of our assumptions or want to put your own figures into the simulation, please download our simulation spreadsheet from the website associated with this book and experiment.

1. For the first version, we want about 300 tests (which is 20 tests per thousand lines of code).
2. Each subsequent version will have some new functionality, so we will add another 10 percent of tests.
3. The time to design tests manually (T_d) is around 10 minutes per test.
4. The time to execute tests manually (T_e), including analyzing and recording the results, is around 6 minutes per test.
5. The time to write an automated test script (T_s) is around 10 minutes per test (this is in addition to the design time T_d of the test).
6. With each version, there are minor and major changes to the APIs and the interfaces of the application, and these cause about 50 percent of the existing capture/replay tests and automated test scripts to fail (usually for trivial reasons). For the capture/replay process, this just means that those tests must be captured (reexecuted) manually again. For the scripting process, this means that those test scripts must be modified slightly to account for the changes.
7. The time to fix a broken test script (T_f) is around 3 minutes per test.
8. The human time required to start and monitor the execution of an automated test suite (T_a) is around 2 hours.
9. The time required to write the test adaptor (i.e., to define the keyword scripts for each test keyword, or the adaptor module for model-based testing) is around 15 hours.
10. The time required to model the application for model-based testing is around 30 hours.
11. The time required to tune test-selection criteria for model-based testing is around 5 hours.

Based on these assumptions, we can calculate the total number of tests (N) for each version as:

$$N_1 = 300 \text{ tests}$$

$$N_{i+1} = N_i + N_i \times 10\%$$

To manually design the 300 tests for version 1 takes $300 \times 10 = 3000$ minutes, which is 50 hours. This applies to all the test processes except model-based testing because model-based testing is the only process where the test design is automated.

The cost of manual test execution for the first version is $300 \times T_e = 1800$ minutes, which is 30 hours. For the subsequent versions, we design 10 percent of additional tests, and then we manually execute the original and new tests, so the cost in person-hours (M) is:

$$M_1 = 300 \times T_e/60 = 30 \text{ hours}$$

$$M_{i+1} = N_i \times 10\% \times T_d/60 + N_{i+1} \times T_e/60 \text{ hours}$$

The cost of capture/replay testing (R) for the first version is the same as the cost of manual testing because all the tests must be executed manually so that they can be captured. For subsequent versions, the cost is lower since the captured tests can simply be replayed. However, we assume that 50 percent of these fail to replay and must be executed manually again; plus our new 10 percent of tests must be designed and executed, so the cost is:

$$R_{i+1} = N_i \times 10\% \times (T_d + T_e)/60 + N_i \times 50\% \times T_e/60$$

For the test scripting process (S), as well as the test design time, we have the cost of writing the automated test scripts, which is $300 \times T_s = 3000$ minutes (50 hours). Once these are written (and debugged!), we can just run them, which takes $T_a = 2$ person-hours to manage. For subsequent versions, we assume that changes in the application mean that 50 percent of the original test scripts need minor fixes ($N_i \times 50\% \times T_f$ minutes), plus we must design and code the new tests. So the cost of each version is:

$$S_1 = 300 \times (T_d + T_s)/60 + T_a = 300 \times 20/60 + 2 = 102 \text{ hours}$$

$$S_{i+1} = N_i \times 50\% \times T_f/60 + N_i \times 10\% \times (T_d + T_s)/60 + T_a$$

For the action-word or keyword-based testing process (KW), we must design the high-level tests (50 hours), plus we have the additional overhead of mapping each action/keyword into an executable script. We allow

15 hours for this (about a third of the test design time). For subsequent versions, we design 10 percent of new tests ($N_i \times 10\% \times T_d$ minutes). We assume that the overhead of defining any new actions/keywords and fixing any existing action/keyword definitions is about half of the original effort ($50\% \times 15$ hours), and after this is done, all the existing high-level test scripts rerun without change. So the cost of each version is:

$$KW_1 = 300 \times T_d/60 + 15 + T_a = 50 + 15 + 2 = 72 \text{ hours}$$
$$KW_{i+1} = N_i \times 10\% \times T_d/60 + 50\% \times 15 + T_a$$

For model-based testing (*MBT*), instead of the manual design of the 300 tests, we must write the test model of the application (30 hours) and then use a model-based testing tool to choose our test selection criteria and generate some tests (15 hours). We also have the overhead of mapping the abstract operations of the model to the concrete operations of the application—this is the same task as defining the actions/keywords in action-word or keyword-based testing, so it takes about the same time (15 hours). For subsequent versions, we must update the model and our test selection criteria to cover the new functionality ($[30 + 15] \times 10\%$ hours), and we may have to add to or update the adaptor code as well, just as in the action-word or keyword-based testing process ($50\% \times 15$ hours). So the costs are:

$$MBT_1 = 30 + 15 + 15 + T_a = 62 \text{ hours}$$
$$MBT_{i+1} = (30 + 15) \times 10\% + 50\% \times 15 + T_a = 14 \text{ hours}$$

2.5.2 Conclusions

Table 2.2 shows the hours required for each version of each testing process, as well as the total number of tests for each version. Figure 2.5 shows the same figures plotted as the *cumulative* total hours devoted to testing all 10 versions of the application.

You can see that manual testing (and capture/replay testing) have the lowest initial design costs, but their ongoing execution costs make them expensive as the number of releases increases. Automated test scripts are more expensive to design initially but can become cheaper than manual testing or capture/replay testing after several releases. The keyword-based testing and model-based testing are the most economical as the number of releases increases because the tests are designed at a higher level of abstraction (keywords and models, respectively), so they are easier to design, automate, and maintain.

TABLE 2.2   Person-Hours Spent on Testing for Each Version

Activity	Tests (No.)	Manual	Replay	Script	Keywd	MBT
Initial Manual Test Design		50	50	50	50	0
Initial Modeling						30
Initial Test Generation						15
Initial Adaptor Coding				50	15	15
Initial Test Execution		30	30	2	2	2
Total for Version 1	300	80	80	102	67	62
Total for Version 2	330	38	23	20	15	14
Total for Version 3	363	42	25	21	15	14
Total for Version 4	399	46	28	23	16	14
Total for Version 5	439	51	31	25	16	14
Total for Version 6	483	56	34	28	17	14
Total for Version 7	531	61	37	30	18	14
Total for Version 8	585	67	41	33	18	14
Total for Version 9	643	74	45	36	19	14
Total for Version 10	707	81	49	40	20	14
Total Hours		596	392	358	220	188

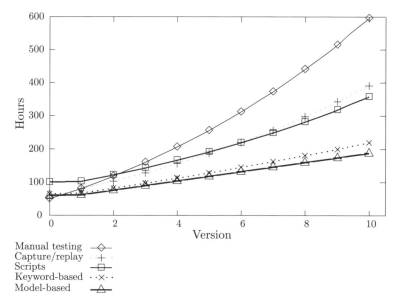

FIGURE 2.5   Total testing hours for each testing process. Release 0 shows the initial design cost of the tests, excluding the cost of the initial test execution.

Our hypothetical study has concentrated on the time costs of testing, showing that model-based testing can have a small cost-benefit (7–15%) over keyword-based testing and a significant cost-benefit over the other testing processes. But before finishing this section, it is worth mentioning a couple of other advantages of model-based testing over all the other testing processes.

One is that with model-based testing it is very easy to generate more tests; with the push of another button or a few minutes choosing some more test selection criteria, we can quickly generate 600 or 6000 executable test scripts (with oracles!) from one model. As well as the quantity of tests, the *quality* of the test suite is also very important, and several studies have shown that the use of a model tends to increase fault detection effectiveness [DJK+99, FHP02, PPW+05].

The other major benefit comes from the modeling stage—it is usual to find numerous "issues" (faults) in the requirements and design documents as a side-effect of modeling. The detection of such faults at an early stage can be a major benefit of model-based testing. We will discuss these benefits and others in more detail in Section 2.7.

2.6 MODEL-BASED TESTING EXPERIENCE REPORTS

The previous section discussed a hypothetical company. Now let's look at the experience of some real companies that have used model-based testing on their applications.

2.6.1 Model-Based Testing at IBM

IBM reported significant cost reductions as well as good fault-finding capability in two industrial case studies where they used a model-based test generator named GOTCHA-TCBeans [FHP02]. This generates tests from finite state machine (FSM) models. In both case studies, the FSM models were derived from informal English specifications of the requirements. Another tool, TCtranslator, was used to translate the generated abstract tests into C and Java test scripts, respectively. In both case studies, they augmented the generated test suites with a few well-chosen manual tests to cover requirements that were outside the scope of the model.

The first case study was to test an implementation of the POSIX (Portable Operating System Interface) `fcntl` byte range locking feature. The implementation of this subsystem had been thoroughly tested by a manually developed test suite (12 person-months, 18 defects found).

The model-based testing took 10 person-months (including the time required to learn GOTCHA) and found an additional 2 defects. Postmortem analysis showed it would also have detected 15 of the 18 defects found earlier. So the fault-detection power was roughly similar, but the cost of model-based testing was 17 percent lower [FHP02]. They commented that, "In future use of the techniques, one could reasonably expect additional resource savings."

The second case study was to test part of a Java garbage collector that analyzes the control flow of Java programs—particularly complex when the program includes exception handling. The SUT component in this case study contained 6914 lines of C code distributed over 2681 basic blocks.

Initially, they used the standard JCK 1.3 (Java Compatibility Kit) and SpecJVM programs as test cases. This found 16 defects (3 design defects and 13 implementation defects), with statement coverage of the SUT being 78 percent.

Then they used model-based testing with two FSM models, one derived from the operational semantics of Java and the other based on the syntax of catch, try, and finally statements. When they ran the tests generated via model-based testing, 4 new defects were found (2 design and 2 implementation defects) and the statement coverage rose to 83 percent. The time spent on modeling and testing was 3 to 4 person-months, which is roughly half the time spent on testing similar systems.

They also made some interesting observations about the skills required of testers when using model-based testing.

> The skills required for the use of our techniques are not usually found in existing testing organizations. Testers with some programming knowledge can acquire these skills quickly. In the first case study, the testers received an intensive four-day course on the tools and methodology; in the second study, the testers studied the manuals and had a two-day course. [FHP02, 107]

2.6.2 Model-Based Testing at Microsoft

There have been at least three generations of model-based testing tools developed and used within Microsoft over the past few years [Sto05, VCST05].

The first generation tool, called Test Model Toolkit (TMT), was developed by the Internet Explorer (IE) team, won the testing best practice award inside Microsoft in 2001, and by 2004 was in use by at least 20 teams within Microsoft. It uses simple finite state machine models, which are written as transition tables [tables of (*StartState*, *Action*, *EndState*) triples]. It supports six test generation algorithms, including random exploration, some shortest path algorithms, and several algorithms that take the shortest path to a specified state and then generate tests that start from that state. The generated test cases are output as XML files, along with a template driver program for executing the tests.

Their experience with TMT was that it reduced the time to develop automated tests, made it easy to generate more tests, increased the code coverage, and uncovered many specification and implementation bugs. For example, the BizTalk team had spent 8 weeks writing a test suite manually, but in 1 week with TMT they generated a larger test suite that increased code coverage by 50 percent.

The second and third generations of MBT tools (ASML/T[7] and Spec Explorer [CGN+05]) were developed by the Foundations of Software Engineering (FSE) group within Microsoft Research. These two tools use more powerful executable specification languages that are interoperable with the .NET framework. The ASML is based on the theory of abstract state machines, while the Spec Explorer modeling language is called Spec# and is an extension of C#.

The FSE group worked with several teams within Microsoft to run pilot testing projects using ASML/T. For example, the Indigo[8] team used it to model parts of the industry-defined standards for web services and found it to be extremely effective in exposing requirements and design issues [Sto05]. Keith Stobie's comments on the adoption of ASML modeling and the lack of recognition for testers who detect bugs too early are thought-provoking:

> Few testers successfully pick up ASML all on their own (but there are some stellar examples). Indigo testers were provided with a two-day training course each year to get them started. Many, but not all, students quickly embraced the concept and attempted usage. However, the cost of developing a model is high, and most industry practices do not adequately measure prevented bugs or improved quality. Consequently, testers struggle to get credit for preventing bugs by asking clarifying questions and removing specification bugs long before executable code or test cases are ever developed. [Sto05, 8]

The Indigo team used ASML/T for test generation and found bugs in early versions of several web services implementations. However, practical issues such as lack of documentation, unfamiliar concepts, a steep learning curve, and the research prototype nature of ASML/T meant that adoption was limited. These issues led to the development of the third generation tool, Spec Explorer [Res06b], which we explore further in Section 6.5.

---

[7]ASML/T is a tool that generates tests from models written in ASML/T (Abstract State Machine Language).

[8]Indigo, now called the Windows Communication Foundation, is part of Microsoft's Web services platform and is the communications infrastructure of Windows Vista.

Spec Explorer is used daily by several Microsoft product teams. For example, in one project that tested an interaction protocol between components of the Windows operating system,[9] Spec Explorer discovered 10 times more errors than traditional manual testing, while the time to develop the Spec# model was about the same as the time taken to develop the manual test cases. The model-based testing also increased the coverage of the implementation code from 60 to 70 percent. Even more significant was that the modeling process exposed twice as many design issues as implementation bugs. Discovering these design errors enabled them to be fixed early and prevented them from going into the code.

See the Microsoft FSE website[10] for more recent papers and news about Spec Explorer.

2.6.3 Model-Based Testing in the Smart Card Industry

This section reports on several experiences of using one of the LEIRIOS Test Generator tools in the smart card industry. This started in 2000, with various case studies and trials of applying model-based testing to smart card software (see, for example [BL03, BLPT04, BLLP04, BJL+05]), and now the major card manufacturers, such as Axalto, Gemplus,[11] and Giesecke & Devrient, are regularly deploying model-based testing in their validation processes.

Smart card software validation is an exemplar of the main characteristics that make it easy to integrate model-based testing into the existing test process and obtain a high level of return on investment. These characteristics are as follows.

Strong validation needs: Smart card software is on-chip software that is embedded in mobile devices like mobile phones, bank cards, passports, and health cards. In the case of software bugs, it is not possible to patch the application without asking the owner to return the smart card. Therefore, product quality is a major issue and the level of testing is very high in this industry (typically, 50 percent of the development effort is devoted to testing). Another reason for the high level of testing is that most smart card software specifications are standards (like the GSM 11.11 standard in Chapter 9), and extensive testing is needed to ensure conformance to these standards and interoperability among various smart card manufacturers. In this context of strong validation needs,

---

[9] The WP1 and WP2 case studies reported in [VCST05].

[10] *http://research.microsoft.com/fse*.

[11] Axalto and Gemplus merged in 2006 and became Gemalto.

model-based testing practices help to reduce testing effort while increasing test quality.

High level of test execution automation: Smart card software can be tested in a simulated environment or tested on-card by using various hardware and software test harnesses. To perform these two kinds of testing, card manufacturers use powerful test execution environments that support test scripting languages for expressing tests, provide domain-specific facilities such as cryptographic functions, and completely automate test execution and verdict assignment. Some of these test execution environments are developed in-house and others are available from independent tool providers (e.g., KaNest® tool by KaSYS). So the test automation problem is already solved in the smart card industry, but a huge effort is required for test design. Model-based testing is a good solution for this because it can automate the design of tests and connect to the existing test execution tools.

Good level of development maturity: The general software development maturity level in the smart card industry is high. One major player, Gemplus, has reached level 3 of CMMI. This implies strong expertise in traceability issues, from requirements to code and test development. Model-based testing helps to industrialize this kind of process. However, this industry usually has a low level of maturity in modeling. The specifications (standards) are usually some informal text plus diagrams, and the practice of modeling for development purposes is only starting to be adopted. Fortunately, this has not been a barrier to the deployment of model-based testing. The smart card validation engineers are software engineers, typically with four-year college degrees, and they have no difficulty in developing abstract models. Moreover, they greatly appreciate the opportunity to develop test models and define test selection criteria instead of doing the tedious work of manually developing test scripts. Model-based testing makes the validation work more interesting for testers.

In the rest of this section, we describe two applications of model-based testing in the smart card area:

- an identity card (PIV II) validation at Gemplus, and
- the IAS (Identification, Authentication, and electronic Signature) application at Axalto.

Both these validation projects used B machines [Abr96] as models and the model-based testing tool LTG for Smartcard from LEIRIOS Technologies. This is a similar approach to what we do in Chapter 9, where we test another smart card application—an implementation of GSM 11-11 standard for mobile phones.

PIV II PROJECT AT GEMPLUS

The US National Institute of Standards and Technology (NIST) has established the Personal Identity Verification (PIV) program to validate the identity of federal employees and contractors.[12] The PIV II smart card application is used for physical access control systems such as entry into buildings or rooms. The smart card stores data about the holder, such as name, identity photo, and fingerprints. Some pieces of data are protected by a personal identification number (PIN) to ensure that they are accessed only with the holder's agreement. Secure communication with a terminal card reader involves dedicated protocols, symmetric and asymmetric keys, and certificates stored in the card.

The goal of this testing project was the functional black-box testing of the application. A model was developed using the B notation, and then the test cases were automatically generated by LTG and transformed into executable test scripts.

The B model contained 15 operations, of which 5 were related to a single smart card command (*General Authenticate*), which has multiple uses in the PIV II application. LTG computed 487 *test targets* (this terminology is explained in detail in Section 6.2.3) in one test campaign. Of these targets, 353 targets were used to generate 897 test cases, 46 targets failed to produce tests, and the remaining 88 targets were proved to be unreachable. The generated test cases were functional tests based strictly on the PIV II standard, without Gemplus's proprietary extensions, and used the card's contact interface rather than its contactless interface.

The generated test scripts were executed using a proprietary test execution environment that provided a C language interface. Scripts were compiled to build one .exe file per script. Dedicated libraries were linked with these executable test scripts so that they could communicate with the tested application and perform common tasks such as cryptographic computations. Script generation was quite simple: there was one template file that defined the script structure and one template fragment that defined how to call the C procedures provided by the adaptation layer.

---

[12] See *http://csrc.nist.gov/npivp* for more information on the PIV application.

TABLE 2.3   Person-Days Required for PIV Test Generation

Task	Workload (Days)	Percentage
Modeling of the functional and syntactic behavior	16	59
Design of the adaptation layer	4	15
Test generation	7	26
Total for test generation	27	100

The workload statistics for tasks related to test generation (*days* means *person-days*) are shown in Table 2.3. Manual test design and scripting took 42 person-days, whereas the model-based testing approach took 27 person-days. The difference was 15 person-days, which is a workload reduction of 35 percent using model-based testing.

IAS PROJECT AT AXALTO

The *Identification, Authentication, and electronic Signature* (IAS) specification defines a common base for interoperability among different smart cards being issued by the French government (National ID card, Health Vitale card, Agent card, Daily Life card). The smart cards have a contactless interface that supports the biometrics authentication of the holder and a contact interface that supports electronic signature services.

IAS is a large smart card application with more than 30 smart card commands including functionality such as authentication and cryptographic protocol, data management, and electronic signature.

The purpose of this validation project was the functional and robustness testing of an IAS smart card manufactured by Axalto. This project was performed as a partnership between Axalto and LEIRIOS in 2004 and 2005. The model was developed with the B notation, the test cases were generated using LTG for Smartcard, and the automated test execution environment, which was used for both on-card testing and simulator testing, was a proprietary tool developed by Axalto for its own needs.

Within the project, two models were developed. One was a syntactic model aimed at format testing, which is a kind of robustness testing that checks the expected behavior of the smart card when commands are called with incorrect argument formats. The other model, the main one, was aimed at normal functional testing, including nominal and error cases. This functional model formalized the expected behavior of each command of the IAS standard. The motivation to develop two models comes from the difference in abstraction levels between format testing and functional testing. Using separate models made each of those models easier to develop and maintain than a single model that mixed both aspects would have been.

The IAS models contained 15,000 lines of textual B modeling code: 5,000 for the syntactic model and 10,000 for the functional one. Ninety person-days were required to develop, validate, and verify the two models.

Test generation used model coverage criteria, such as coverage of all effects of each operation, coverage of all conditions in the decisions of the model, and boundary testing of the input parameter domains. The test generation process was split into 12 test campaigns, for a total of 5100 test cases. The traceability matrix from IAS functional requirements to test cases was also generated, thanks to the tagging of the model with requirements identifiers. A few IAS functions were not modeled because the modeling effort was judged to be quite high relative to the desired number of tests, so modeling was not cost-effective. Instead, 200 test cases were developed manually to test these functions and complement the generated test cases.

Test scripts were automatically generated using the LTG test script generator. The adaptation layer cost about 40 person-days to develop.

An iterative testing process led to the correction of about 100 errors, equally distributed among the model, the adaptation layer, and the implementation. The use of model-based testing was considered successful particularly because of the high level of requirements coverage that was obtained and because of easier maintenance of a large test suite, thanks to the high abstraction level of the model and the automated generation of tests from that model.

Following this testing project, the same approach has been chosen for functional certification purposes within a national certification program that has been launched by the French DGME (Direction Générale de la Modernisation de l'Etat). This procedure includes generating certification test suites using an IAS model that is aimed at interoperability testing. The test suites that are generated from this model are then inspected and validated by a technical committee of the DGME.

2.6.4 Model-Based Testing in the Automotive Industry

Pretschner and colleagues [PPW+05] report on a comparison study that applied model-based testing to the network controller of an "infotainment network" in vehicles. The goal of the study was to systematically compare automatically generated test suites with hand-crafted ones and to try to precisely measure the fault-detection benefits of model-based testing. It did not try to compare the cost of the various approaches.

They started from existing requirements documents (informal message sequence charts, MSCs) and built an executable behavior model of the network controller. During this modeling phase, they found 30 requirements problems (3 inconsistencies, 7 omissions, and 20 ambiguities), which were fixed before continuing. The corrected requirements were then used (1) by developers of a third-party software simulation of the controller (this was used as the system under test), (2) by test engineers who, without the model, had to test this system, and (3) by different engineers who both manually and automatically derived tests based on the model. As test selection criteria, they explored random generation as well as generation based on *functional test case specifications*—33 specifications derived from 7 scenarios.

In total, 26 faults were found: 2 were errors in the model (from mistaken requirements), 13 were programming errors in the SUT, and the remaining 11 were errors both in the SUT and the requirements. Of the 24 errors in the SUT, 15 were considered severe by the domain experts, and 9 were considered not severe.

This case study yielded the following conclusions:

- The model-based test suites detected roughly the same number of programming errors as the hand-crafted test suites.

- The model-based test suites detected significantly more requirements-related errors than the hand-crafted test suites.

- The randomly generated model-based tests detected roughly as many errors as manually designed tests but with a higher proportion of requirements-related errors.

- There was a positive correlation between the level of condition/decision coverage of the model and the number of errors detected. However, increasing the condition/decision coverage level of the model does not always guarantee a larger number of detected errors.

- A sixfold increase in the size of the automatically generated test suite led to an 11 percent increase in the errors detected.

2.7 BENEFITS OF MODEL-BASED TESTING

In this section, we discuss the various benefits that model-based testing can have. We group these into six areas: SUT fault detection, reduced testing cost and time, improved test quality, requirements defect detection, traceability, and requirements evolution.

2.7.1 SUT Fault Detection

The main goal of testing is to find errors in the SUT. The experience reports in the previous section illustrate that model-based testing is indeed good at finding SUT errors. In the IBM and BMW case studies, model-based testing found roughly the same number of SUT errors as manually designed test suites, while in one of the Microsoft applications, it found 10 times more. In the smart card industry, the model-based testing practice is deployed daily. When this has been compared to manual testing (see Section 2.6.3), the number of faults detected by the model-based testing process has always been greater than or equal to the number of faults detected with the manual process.

Of course, model-based testing is not magic. Its fault-detection power still depends on the skill and experience of the people who write the model and choose the test selection criteria, so it is not possible to say that model-based testing always detects more faults than manually designed tests, or vice versa. The experience of the tester with the SUT drives the test generation, using the test selection criteria supported by the model-based testing tool.

Comparative studies show that model-based testing is as good as or better at fault detection than manually designed tests [DJK+99, FHP02, BLLP04, PPW+05]. In all the case studies reported in [HPER05], model-based testing was successful in detecting SUT faults, even though some of those SUTs had already been in the field for some time.

2.7.2 Reduced Testing Cost and Time

Model-based testing can lead to less time and effort spent on testing if the time needed to write and maintain the model plus the time spent on directing the test generation is less than the cost of manually designing and maintaining a test suite.

Our hypothetical study in Section 2.5 illustrates the possible cost savings, and an increasing number of published case studies show that the cost of model-based testing is typically less than manual test design [DJK+99, FHP02, BBN04, BLLP04, HPER05, JJ05]. However, one case study at Intrasoft International, where a graphical web-based application was tested using model-based testing tools developed by the AGEDIS project[13] and also using Intrasoft's usual test process based on Mercury WinRunner,[14] found that the skills needed to use the AGEDIS tools required a considerable ramp-up time, so the total testing time using WinRunner (around 30 days) was less

---

[13]AGEDIS was a three-year European project to develop and evaluate model-based testing tools. It ran from 2001 to 2003 and had seven industrial and academic partners. See *http://www.agedis.de* for details, especially the Final Report, which is available in the Downloads page.

[14]Mercury WinRunner is a capture/replay tool for testing Microsoft Windows graphical applications that does some abstraction and allows test scripts to be recorded and programmed. See *http://www.mercury.com/us/products* for details.

than the total time to use the AGEDIS tools (around 47 days). In this case, the other benefits of model-based testing that they reported (more tests and easier requirements evolution) had to be balanced against the increased time [CSH03, Har04].

Clarke [Cla98] reports that the costs of using model-based testing to test features of digital switching systems were 90 percent less than the cost of manual test design (0.192 person-months rather than 2.04 person-months for testing call management features, and 0.6 person-months rather than 5.4 person-months for testing the number portability feature).[15]

In the smart card area, several studies (see Section 2.6.3) show a reduction of test development costs of more than 25 percent compared with a manual test design process.

As well as costing less to design, model-based tests may also save time during the failure-analysis stage that follows test execution. First, because the tests are generated, they follow a consistent style, and they report failures in a consistent way. Second, some model-based testing tools are capable of generating or finding the *shortest* test sequence that causes the failure—this makes the failures easier to analyze. Third, when a particular test fails, we can inspect not only the code of that test but also the corresponding abstract test (which gives a concise overview of the test sequence) and the path that it took through the model. We can even use an animation tool to explore the behavior of that path through the model. If the model-based testing tool supports requirements traceability, then we also know which informal requirements are being tested by this test. All this extra information can make it easier to understand the test and the reasons for its failure and to find and correct the fault more quickly.

2.7.3 Improved Test Quality

When test design is done manually, the quality of the tests is very dependent on the ingenuity of the engineers, the design process is not reproducible, the rationale for each test case is usually not recorded, and the resulting test cases are not easy to relate to the original system requirements.

Model-based testing can ameliorate many of these problems. The use of an automated test case generator based on algorithms and heuristics to choose the test cases from the model makes the design process systematic and repeatable. It becomes possible to measure the "quality" of the test suite

---

[15] We have multiplied Clarke's "technical head count years" by 12 to convert them into person-months.

by considering its coverage of the model.[16] Also, model-based testing can be used to generate many more tests than is possible with manual test design. By changing the model-based test selection criteria slightly or telling the tools to generate more tests, we can easily obtain very large test suites. Since the test input data and the test oracles are both generated from the model, the cost of generating more executable test scripts is just the computing time required to generate them. For SUTs where it is feasible to execute large numbers of tests, this can help to find more errors [PPW[+]05].

2.7.4 Requirements Defect Detection

A sometimes unexpected benefit of model-based testing is that writing the model exposes issues in the informal requirements. These requirements are typically recorded in a large, natural-language document that may contain omissions, contradictions, and unclear requirements. But the first step of model-based testing is to clarify this intended behavior of the SUT by building an abstract model of the SUT. The model has a precise semantics so that it can be analyzed by a machine. As one writes this model, the increased precision raises lots of questions about the requirements, such as "What should happen when this input is out of range?" and "Can both these conditions be true at the same time?" So the modeling phase typically exposes numerous requirements issues. In fact, this should not be surprising since writing the model is a bit like developing a small abstract prototype of the SUT, and it has long been known that prototyping is a good technique for finding requirements errors [BGS84].

Furthermore, when the generated tests are run, some of the test failures turn out to be caused by errors in the model. Our experience is that approximately half the failures may come from modeling or requirements errors. The Microsoft example in Section 2.6.2 reported that the modeling process exposed twice as many design issues as implementation bugs.

Finding requirements issues is a major benefit of model-based testing because requirements problems are the major source of system problems. Every requirements fault that is found is one less fault that enters into the design and implementation phases, and faults are much cheaper to fix at the requirements phase than in later phases.

This may be the area where model-based testing will have the largest impact on software development practices. It encourages early modeling, and

---

[16]We put "quality" in quotations here because the quality of a test suite is usually a rather subjective notion and does not necessarily correlate directly with coverage criteria or with the number of tests.

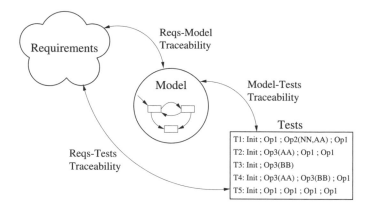

FIGURE 2.6   Traceability among requirements, model, and tests.

this early modeling finds requirements and design errors because the model is precise enough to be analyzed by computer. This can be done before the first line of implementation code has even been written. So one long-term effect of model-based testing might be to change the role of testers from catching errors at the bottom of the cliff (after the SUT has been built) to erecting fences at the top of the cliffs (during the requirements and design phases).

2.7.5 Traceability

Traceability is the ability to relate each test case to the model, to the test selection criteria, and even to the informal system requirements.

Traceability helps to explain the test case as well as give a rationale for why it was generated. Traceability can also be used to optimize test execution when the model evolves, because it enables us to execute just the subset of the tests that are affected by the model changes. And as discussed in Chapter 4, requirements traceability can also be used as a test selection criterion.

To illustrate traceability issues and benefits, we focus on traceability between informal requirements (*Reqs*) and test cases. As shown in Figure 2.6, this can be broken down into three aspects, *Reqs-Model* traceability, *Model-Tests* traceability, and *Reqs-Tests* traceability, which is the combination of the previous two.

It is not too difficult to provide Model-Tests traceability between the model and the generated test cases. The test generation algorithms must record which parts of the model contribute to each test case and output that information in a usable form. Abstractly, it is a relation between elements of the model and test cases. For example, when we use UML state machines as a modeling notation, the test generation algorithms would record which transitions of the model are used in each test case. This relationship can then be used to perform the following tasks.

- Show the transitions of the model that are not covered by any test.
- Find all test cases that exercise a given model transition.
- Visualize a given test case as a sequence of transitions in the model.

Generating a Reqs-Model traceability matrix, which shows the relationships between the informal system requirements and the model, is more challenging because the requirements are in natural-language, so they are not easily understood by a computer. The solution is to record the relationships between the model and the requirements when we design the model. For example, we can assign a unique identifier to each informal requirement, and then annotate the model elements (e.g., transitions or statements or predicates) with these identifiers. This gives us traceability between the requirements and the model, which can be used to answer queries such as the following:

- Which requirements are not yet modeled?
- How does a particular requirement influence the model?
- What is the rationale for a given transition or predicate in the model? That is, which requirements are related to it?

Finally, the composition of these two relationships gives us Reqs-Tests traceability, which is traceability between informal requirements and the generated test cases. This can be visualized as a traceability matrix between the requirements and the test cases. Since it circumvents the model, it is useful not only for the test engineers but also for nontechnical people who are not familiar with the modeling notation. It allows us to perform the following tasks:

- Identify the requirements that are not yet tested.
- Show all the tests that relate to a given requirement.
- Show the requirements that relate to a given test. (This provides an informal rationale for that test.)

Other uses of requirements traceability are as a measure of test suite quality (*What percentage of requirements are tested?*), as a test selection criterion during test generation (*Generate at least one test for each requirement.*), or as a test suite reduction mechanism (*Retain only the first* N *tests for each combination of requirements.*).

2.7.6 Requirements Evolution

If you use manual testing or manual test design and the requirements of your system change, a large amount of effort is often required to update the test suite to reflect the new requirements.

With model-based testing, it suffices to update the model and then regenerate the tests. Since the model is usually much smaller than the test suite, it usually takes less time to update the model than it would to update all the tests. This results in faster response to changing requirements. This was illustrated in our hypothetical study (Section 2.5).

Also, when the requirements or the model evolve, it is useful for tools to provide *incremental traceability*. The idea of incrementality can be applied to any of the three kinds of traceability relationships, but we use Reqs-Tests traceability as an example. *Incremental Reqs-Tests traceability* means that the model-based testing tool can analyze the differences between the original requirements and the new (modified) requirements, and then it can report which tests generated from the original requirements are no longer relevant, which tests are unaffected by the requirements changes, which tests relate to the modified requirements, and which tests relate to the newly added requirements. That is, after a change to the model, it can generate the new test suite and partition all the tests into four groups: *deleted, unchanged, changed,* and *added.*[17] When testing execution time is limited, it can be useful to rerun just the latter two groups of tests.

2.8 LIMITATIONS OF MODEL-BASED TESTING

A fundamental limitation of model-based testing is that it cannot guarantee to find *all* the differences between the model and the implementation, not even if we generate an infinite stream of tests and run them on 1000 machines for thousands of hours. This is a limitation of all kinds of testing.

---

[17] Note that the same effect could in principle be obtained by comparing the new test suite against the old test suite. But in practice, a small change to the model may cause large changes to the generated test suite, and the generation process often involves some randomness, so it is difficult to decide when two generated tests are equivalent and when they are different. To know accurately whether a given test has been affected by recent requirements changes, it is best to trace that test back to certain parts of the model and the test selection criteria, and see whether they were affected by the requirements changes—that is, determine whether the *reason* for generating that test has changed.

A more practical limitation on adopting model-based testing is that it requires somewhat different skills from manual test design. The model designers must be able to abstract and design models, in addition to being expert in the application area. This may require some training costs and an initial learning curve when starting to use model-based testing.

Another limitation is that model-based testing is usually used only for functional testing. We have little experience with model-based testing for other kinds of testing, although it is sometimes used to generate stress tests for testing the performance of web-based applications under heavy load. Furthermore, some kinds of testing are not easily automated, such as testing the installation process of a software package. These are better tested manually.

As discussed in Section 2.4.1, model-based testing is a more sophisticated approach to testing than the earlier generations of testing tools, so it requires a reasonable level of test maturity. For example, it would probably be unwise to start using model-based testing without some experience with automated test execution.

To finish this section, we should mention some of the "pain" factors that can occur *after* one has started to use model-based testing and overcome the initial learning curve:

Outdated requirements: As a software project evolves, it sometimes happens that the informal requirements become out of date. If some model-based testers start working from those outdated requirements, they will build the wrong model and find lots of "errors" in the SUT!

Inappropriate use of model-based testing: As noted in several of the experience reports in Section 2.6, some parts of the SUT may be difficult to model, and it may be quicker to test them with a few manually designed tests. The risk here is that it takes some experience to know which aspects of the SUT should be modeled and which should be tested manually.

Time to analyze failed tests: When one of the generated tests fails, we must decide whether the failure is caused by the SUT, the adaptor code, or an error in the model. This is similar to the traditional task of deciding whether a test failure is due to a fault in the SUT or to a fault in the test script. But the test sequences generated by model-based testing may be more complex and less intuitive than a manually designed test sequence, which may make it more difficult and time-consuming to find the cause of failed test. The techniques discussed in Section 2.7.2 can ameliorate this problem, but it is still a risk.

Useless metrics: When tests are designed manually, most managers use the number of test cases designed as a measure of how the testing is progressing. But with model-based testing it is easy to generate huge numbers of tests, so the number-of-tests metric is not useful. It becomes necessary to move toward other measurements of test progress, such as SUT code coverage, requirements coverage, and model coverage metrics [Rob03].

2.9 SUMMARY

Model-based testing builds on previous generations of testing tools. Like the action-word and keyword-based approaches to testing, model-based testing relies on abstraction, and like the automated test script approach, it produces executable test scripts.

It is typically not practical to directly reuse your development models for model-based testing. Some customization of those models, or construction of test-specific models, is usually necessary. But including the work of developing the model, model-based testing is cost-effective because it automates the generation of test scripts and makes it easier to handle requirements evolution by modifying the model and regenerating the tests, rather than maintaining the test suite itself. This can dramatically reduce the cost of test maintenance.

Before adopting model-based testing, it is desirable to have a reasonably mature testing process and some experience with automated test execution.

Model-based testing has been used successfully on numerous industrial applications, and most studies have shown it to be an effective way of detecting SUT faults as well as a cost-effective technique.

One limitation of model-based testing is that it requires different skills of your testers: modeling skills for the test designers and programming skills for the test adaptor implementors. This may imply some training costs and an initial learning curve.

2.10 FURTHER READING

The Encyclopedia of Software Engineering (second edition) has a 12-page introduction to model-based testing [EFW02] that suggests a process similar to the one we have described.

Two very practical books about automated test execution are *Software Test Automation*, by Fewster and Graham [FG99], and *Just Enough Test Automation*, by Mosley and Posey [MP02].

The four generations of test automation tools are described in two papers by Blackburn and colleagues [BBN03, BBN04]. These papers also contain good examples of the benefits of model-based testing and the organizational, personnel, and development changes that result from using model-based testing.

The book *Practical Software Testing: A Process-Oriented Approach*, by Burnstein [Bur03], describes the Testing Maturity Model (TMM), which can be used to measure and improve your current test maturity level. Similarly, the TPI book [KP99] gives more detail on the Test Process Improvement approach. Weatherill [Wea01] compares six test maturity models and concludes that TMM and TPI were the best.

Sections 2.6 and 2.7 gave several references to papers that describe industrial case studies that used model-based testing.

CHAPTER 3

A MODEL OF
YOUR SYSTEM

This chapter shows how to write models of the system that you want to test. In Section 3.1 we give some guidelines for writing a concise and abstract model of the behavior of a system under test (SUT). We also discuss several styles of notation for models and give some recommendations about how to choose an appropriate notation for modeling your system. Throughout the chapter we illustrate these notations using several variants of a drink vending machine or coffee vending machine, introduced in Section 3.2.

The goal is to write models that are useful for test generation, so we focus on the most useful notations and abstraction techniques for model-based testing. Section 3.3 introduces transition-based models and Section 3.4 gives guidelines and examples of developing pre/post models. We use finite state machines (FSMs) and UML state machines as examples of transition-based notations and the B abstract machine notation as our main example of pre/post notations, with brief examples of five other pre/post notations.

A key goal of this chapter is to show you the relationship between these styles of modeling notations (transition-based and pre/post) and their

Note: Photo courtesy of VE Global Solutions, LLC (8200 Brookpak Road, Cleveland, OH 44111; *www.veglobal.com*).

strengths and weaknesses, so that you can decide which style of notation is best for your application.

3.1   HOW TO MODEL YOUR SYSTEM

The first and most important step in modeling a system for testing is deciding on a good level of *abstraction*, that is, deciding which aspects of the SUT to include in your model and which aspects to omit. Since the model is just for test generation purposes, it does not have to specify all the behavior of the system. Several smaller partial models are often more useful than one huge and complex model. For example, it may be useful to write a model for each subsystem or component and to test them independently, before writing a top-level model for the whole system. So your decisions about which operations to include in the model should be driven by your top-level test objectives.

Once you have decided which aspects of the SUT you wish to model, the next step in modeling a system is to think about the data that it manages, the operations that it performs, and the subsystems that it communicates with. A good notation for this is a UML class diagram, perhaps enhanced with a few textual UML use cases for the most important operations.

If you already have a UML class diagram that describes the design of the SUT, you may be able to use that as a starting point for the testing model. However, a class diagram for testing purposes should be much simpler than the full class diagram that is used for design purposes. The following are some typical simplifications:

- Focus primarily on the SUT
- Show only those classes (or subsystems) associated with the SUT and whose values will be needed in the test data
- Include only those operations that you wish to test
- Include only the data fields that are useful for modeling the behavior of the operations that will be tested
- Replace a complex data field, or a class, by a simple enumeration. This allows you to limit the test data to several carefully chosen example values (one for each value of the enumeration).

For each operation that you decide to model, you should also apply the abstraction principle to its input and output parameters. If the value of an input parameter changes the behavior of an operation, and you want to test those different behaviors, then put that input parameter into your model. Otherwise, it is generally better to leave the input parameter out of the model to keep it simple—an appropriate input value can be chosen after test generation when the abstract tests are being translated into executable tests. The difficulty of test generation is usually highly dependent on the number and range of the input parameters (in addition to the state variables), so reducing this helps to control the test generation effort. Output parameters should be modeled only if their value is useful as an oracle for the test.

> **Key Point**   Design your model to meet your test objectives.
> When in doubt, leave it out!

Note that the operations in your model do not have to be exactly the same as the operations of the SUT. If your system has a complex operation *Op*, you may want to split its behavior into several cases and define one model operation *Op_i* for each case. On the other hand, you may want to define one model operation that corresponds to a sequence of operations in the actual system, perhaps to summarize a complex initialization sequence into a single model operation, or to reach a particular state that you want to test thoroughly.

> **Key Point**   You can have a many-to-many relationship among the
> operations of your model and the operations of the SUT.

The next step is to decide which notation to use for your model. This decision is often influenced by the model-based testing tools you have available and the notations they support. But in addition to this factor, it is important to consider which style of notation is most suitable for your system. In the next section, we give an overview of the different modeling notations that are available and some guidelines for choosing an appropriate notation.

After you have chosen a notation and written a model of your system in that notation, the next step is to ensure that your model is accurate. You will want to *validate* your model (check that it does indeed specify the behavior that you want to test) and *verify* it (check that it is correctly typed and consistent). This is where good tool support can help. Most tool suites offer an *animation tool* for simulating the behavior of your model, which helps you to validate your model. They also provide tools for checking the syntax and types in your model and may offer more sophisticated tools for checking deeper properties of your model, such as an automatic prover that tries to prove that each operation of a B machine preserves the invariant or a model checker that searches for states where no operations are enabled (*deadlocked* states).

The final step is to use your model to generate tests. This is the subject of the next few chapters. Note that your model will continue to be validated throughout the test generation process. After you generate tests from your model and execute those tests on your system, each test that fails will point either to an error in the implementation of your system or to a mistake or inadequacy in your model. The value of model-based testing comes from the automated cross-checking between these two independent works of art: the model and the system implementation.

3.1.1 Notations for Modeling

Dozens, perhaps even hundreds, of different modeling notations have been used for modeling the functional behavior of systems. We group them into the following paradigms, adapted from van Lamsweerde [vL00].

Pre/post (or state-based) notations: These model a system as a collection of variables, which represent a snapshot of the internal state of the system, plus some operations that modify those variables. This is similar to an object in Java or C++. Rather than the operations being defined with programming language code, each operation is usually defined by a *precondition* and a *postcondition*. Examples of these notations include B [Abr96], the UML Object Constraint Language (OCL) [WK03], the Java Modeling Language (JML) [L+06], Spec# [Res06a], VDM [Jon90, FLM+05] and Z [ISO02, Bow06]. *Note:* The traditional name for these notations is "model-based." However, this is rather confusing in our context, where all kinds of notations are being used to define models of the SUT. So, in this book, we call them *pre/post* notations.

Transition-based notations: These focus on describing the *transitions* between different states of the system. Typically, they are graphical node-and-arc notations, such as FSMs, where the nodes of the FSM represent the major states of the system and the arcs represent the actions or operations of the system. Textual or tabular notations are also used to specify the transitions. In practice, transition-based notations are often made more expressive by adding data variables, hierarchies of machines, and parallelism between machines. Examples of transition-based notations include FSMs, statecharts (e.g., UML State Machines, STATEMATE statecharts, and Simulink Stateflow charts), labeled transition systems, and I/O (input/output) automata.

History-based notations: These notations model a system by describing the allowable traces of its behavior over time. Various notions of time can be used (discrete or continuous, linear or branching, points or intervals, etc.), leading to many kinds of temporal logics.

We also include message-sequence charts (MSC) and related formalisms in this group. These are graphical and textual notations for specifying sequences of interactions among components. They are often used for modeling telecommunication protocols, particularly in combination with the System Description Language (SDL).[1] MSCs were adopted into UML, where they are called *sequence diagrams*, which are one kind of interaction diagram. MSCs are good for visually showing interactions among components, but not so good at specifying the detailed behavior of each component. So, although they are sometimes used as a basis for model-based testing, our preference is to use them to describe the generated tests. That is, they are better used for visualizing the tests that result from model-based testing than for defining the model that is the input to model-based testing.

Functional notations: These describe a system as a collection of mathematical functions. The functions may be first-order only, as in the case of algebraic specifications, or higher-order, as in notations like HOL (an environment for interactive theorem proving). For example, the property *push*; *pop* = *skip* specifies that the *pop* operation undoes the effect of a *push* operation. Algebraic specifications tend to be more abstract and more difficult to write than other notations, so they are not widely used for model-based testing (but see [Mar95] for one test generation tool based on algebraic models).

Operational notations: These describe a system as a collection of executable processes, executing in parallel. They are particularly suited to describing distributed systems and communications protocols. Examples include process algebras such as CSP and CCS on the one hand and Petri net notations on the other hand.

Statistical notations: These describe a system by a probabilistic model of the events and input values. They tend to be used to model environments rather than SUTs. For example, Markov chains are often used to model expected usage profiles, so the generated tests exercise that usage profile.

Statistical notations are good for specifying distributions of events and test inputs for the SUT but are generally weak at predicting the expected

---

[1] See the SDL Forum Society, *http://www.sdl-forum.org*, for more details of SDL and MSC.

outputs of the SUT; therefore, with only a statistical model it is not usually possible to generate automated oracles as part of the tests. However, it is possible to combine a statistical model with one that models the SUT behavior. This allows the statistical model to drive the choice of test sequences and inputs, while the other model predicts the expected outputs of the SUT.

Data-flow notations: These notations concentrate on the flow of data through the SUT, rather than its control flow. Some examples of this style are Lustre [MA00] and the block diagram notations that are used in Matlab Simulink[2] for the modeling of continuous systems.

3.1.2 Choosing a Notation

For model-based testing, the transition-based notations and the pre/post notations are the most used for developing behavioral models of the SUT.

Which notation will be the best for modeling your SUT? In addition to practical factors, such as the availability of model-based testing tools for each notation and the degree of familiarity that you have with some notations, the answer will depend on the characteristics of your SUT.

The basic guideline is to look at whether your system is more data-oriented or control-oriented. A data-oriented system typically has several state variables, with rich types such as sets, relations, maps, and sequences of values. The operations of a data-oriented system operate on that data to access and manipulate it. Data-oriented systems are most easily specified using pre/post notations, like B, which offer powerful libraries of data structures.

In a control-oriented system, the set of available operations varies according to which state the system is in. For example, in the drink vending machine that we will study later in this chapter, some operations are enabled only when the machine is out of service, and others are enabled only when the machine is in service. Control-oriented systems are most easily specified using transition-based notations, such as UML state machines, because the set of transitions can be different for each state machine node.

> **Key Point**   Pre/post notations are best for data-oriented systems.
> Transition-based notations are best for control-oriented systems.

Of course, your system may not be so easy to classify. It may show signs of being both data-oriented and control-oriented. These classifications are

---

[2]See the MathWorks website, *http://www.mathworks.com*, for information on the Simulink product family.

not opposites, but rather two independent dimensions, so you must make a judgment call about which dimension is dominant in your system.

We close by noting that it is always possible to specify control-oriented aspects of a system in a pre/post notation, and it is usually possible to specify data-oriented systems in a transition-based notation.

If several "states" of your system have different behavior and could easily be modeled by nodes in a transition-system, you can still model this using a pre/post notation. You simply introduce one or more state variables to tell you which of those "nodes" your system is currently in (like *state* : {*InService*, *OutOfService*}), and then you add appropriate preconditions (like *state* = *InService*) or if-then-else conditions into the operations to enable the desired operations. Operations that correspond to a transition from one state to another must also update the state variables to reflect this change (like *state* := *InService*).

On the other hand, a transition-based notation may have good enough support for complex data structures that it can be used for data-oriented systems. With UML state machines, OCL offers *Set*, *OrderedSet*, *Bag*, and *Sequence* data types, and associations among classes can be used to model many-to-many relations, many-to-one functions, one-to-one functions, and so on. OCL has fewer built-in operators than the B toolkit, but has a good set of quantifiers that can be used to express sophisticated queries.

So choosing the "wrong" notation may make it a little more difficult to model your system. The goal is to choose the notation that suits your system best and one for which you have good tool support.

Whatever notation you choose, the important thing for model-based testing is that the notation be formal. *Formal* means that the notation has a precise and unambiguous meaning, so that the behavior of your model can be understood and manipulated by various tools. This precise meaning makes it possible to simulate the execution of the model and to use the model as an *oracle* by predicting the expected output of the SUT or checking the actual output of the SUT against the model.

Moreover, the precise semantics of modeling notations allow tools to perform deep consistency checks on your model, such as proving that every operation preserves the desired properties of your data structures (the *invariant*) or that all states are reachable.

> **Key Point**   Model-based testing requires an accurate model, written in a formal modeling notation that has precise semantics.

For example, a UML class diagram by itself does not give enough detail for test generation. One must add behavioral detail in some way, perhaps by writing OCL preconditions and postconditions for the methods of the class or perhaps by writing a state machine diagram with detailed transitions.

3.2   A CASE STUDY

We use several variants of a simple drink vending machine as a common case study thoughout this chapter. This section gives the informal requirements of a drink vending machine (DVM) that distributes prepackaged drinks, such as those in cans.

3.2.1   DVM Requirements

A typical usage of the DVM is that the consumer inserts coins into the machine and then selects the desired drink via several buttons. If enough money has been entered and the selected drink is available, then the DVM ejects the drink into the bottom drawer of the machine, so that the consumer can retrieve it. Use Case 3.1 shows a simple use case for a successful interaction with the machine. If the amount of money inserted was more than the price of the drink, then the machine will return the correct change to the consumer. When any of these conditions are not met (for example, the correct change is not available), the transaction is aborted with an appropriate message and all the inserted coins are returned to the consumer. The consumer can also press a Return button at any time to retrieve all the money that has been inserted but not yet spent.

The DVM must also support several service operations, such as restocking it with drinks and emptying its money box. Finally, the DVM may go into *out of service* mode when something goes seriously wrong, for example, when its money box becomes too full or it detects some internal malfunction. This out of order mode can be reset only by the service personnel.

3.2.2   DVM High-Level Design

The goal of our testing is to test the controller of the DVM. However, before we can model the behavior of the controller, we need to decide on the high-level architecture within the DVM so that we know how the controller interacts with the other components of the DVM.

Figure 3.1 gives a class diagram for the drink vending machine, showing the controller unit and some of the components that it communicates with. Each DrinkShelf object corresponds to one row of drinks, which must all be of the same type. The release() method drops the front drink in that row down into a bin where the consumer can retrieve the drink. The avail

USE CASE 3.1   Use case for the drink vending machine.

Use Case: Buy a drink
Scope: Drink vending machine
Primary Actor: Consumer
Goal: The customer wants to obtain a drink in exchange for money.
Precondition: The drink machine is not "Out of service."

Main Success Scenario

1. Consumer inserts one or more coins into the machine.
2. Consumer chooses a drink from a fixed menu.
3. Vending machine checks that enough money has been inserted, then dispenses the requested drink and returns any excess money and to the consumer.
4. Consumer takes the drink from the machine.

Extensions

1a. When a MAXMONEY value is reached, further coins are rejected.
2a. If the chosen drink is not available, a "Not available" message is displayed.
3a. If not enough money has been inserted, an "Insufficient funds" message is displayed.
4a. Until the consumer takes the drink, the machine cannot dispense further drinks.

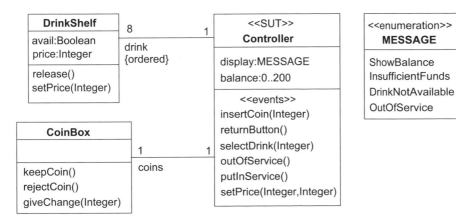

FIGURE 3.1   UML class diagram for the drink vending machine.

flag becomes false whenever the row of drinks is empty. The CoinBox corresponds to the physical coin box in the machine, which detects and classifies inserted coins and is able to output a given value of change by combining several coins. To keep our case study simple, we assume that the CoinBox can always generate any desired value of change up to $2.00 (in a real DVM, this would be another condition the controller must check before selling a drink). The Controller class is responsible for most of the logic within the machine. Its main output is the display state variable, which models the message that is displayed on the LCD screen of the drink machine (the message ShowBalance means that the current balance of the CoinBox is displayed on the screen). The Controller class reacts to events such as button presses, as well as events such as insertCoin(50) from the CoinBox.

To explain this design a little more, we go through Use Case 3.1 and describe how the various components of the DVM interact to fulfill the use case. The goal is to buy a 60-cent drink, with two 50-cent coins.

- Consumer inserts the first 50-cent coin.

- CoinBox detects the coin and sends the event insertCoin(50) to the controller. It holds the coin in its classification area until it receives a response from the controller.

- Controller decides to accept the coin, so increments balance by 50 and calls the keepCoin() method of the CoinBox. The display is set to ShowBalance, which means that it displays 50 cents.

- The CoinBox moves the coin into its internal storage area.

- Consumer inserts the second 50-cent coin and the same sequence of events occurs, resulting in balance being set to 100.

- Consumer presses the third drink button, which sends the selectDrink(3) event to the controller.

- Controller checks that drink[3].avail is true, then calls the drink[3].release() method to release one of those drinks, calls the giveChange(40) method of the CoinBox and resets balance to zero.

These informal descriptions in English give us a rough idea of what the DVM controller does, but they do not specify all the input conditions, alternatives, and exception cases that we want to test. So this description alone is not precise enough to be the basis of our test generation. The rest of this chapter explores various formal models of the Controller component of several versions of the DVM. These models will be precise enough to be used for test generation.

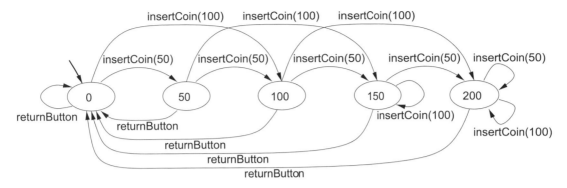

FIGURE 3.2   Finite state machine of drink vending machine money operations.

3.3 TRANSITION-BASED MODELS

This section shows you how to write transition-based models, starting with simple finite state machines and then progressing to more complex transition-based notations such as the UML 2.0 state machine diagrams.

3.3.1 Finite State Machines

A *finite state machine* (FSM) is usually drawn visually as a graph, with the nodes of the graph representing the states of the system and the directed arcs representing the *transitions* of the system from one state to another. The important restriction on FSMs is that the number of states must be finite,[3] and so must the number of transitions.

FSMs are very useful for modeling small reactive systems but rapidly become too large to be manageable when you try to apply them naively to something like the drink vending machine. For example, Figure 3.2 shows an FSM that handles just the insertCoin and returnButton operations, with the entry coins restricted to only 50-cent and $1.00 coins. As you can see, if we extended this FSM to handle all the coins (5, 10, 20, 50 cents, and $1 coins), the FSM diagram would become rather large (41 nodes and more than 200 transitions)!

The problem here is that we were silly to represent each different value of the balance variable by a different node of the FSM because many values of balance produce similar behavior. For example, all the nodes, except the rightmost one, behave the same for insertCoin(50). There are much

---

[3]In practice, it is wise to keep the number of states quite small. It becomes difficult to design or understand an FSM with more than a few dozen states.

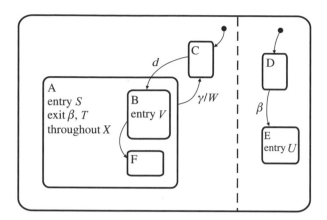

FIGURE 3.3   An example statechart. *Source*: From Harel [Har87], Figure 37. Used with permission.

more concise ways of expressing this than an FSM! Next we will see how *extended finite state machines* (EFSMs), such as UML state machines, allow us to use data variables like balance to represent some aspects of the state while continuing to use the nodes of an FSM to represent other aspects of the state.

3.3.2 Overview and History of Statecharts

Statecharts are a visual notation for describing the behavior of reactive systems, introduced by Harel [Har87]. He describes them as FSMs[4] extended with hierarchy, concurrency, and communication. Or in other words,

$$\text{Statecharts} = \text{FSMs} + \text{depth} + \text{orthogonality}$$
$$+ \text{ broadcast communication}$$

He shows that these extensions allow small diagrams to express complex behavior in a modular way.

Figure 3.3 shows a statechart, from Harel's original paper [Har87], that illustrates the main features of statecharts. The top-level chart contains two subcharts: the left one has states A and C and the right one has states D and E. These two charts are separated by a dotted line, which means that they are *orthogonal*, so they act in parallel and a snapshot of the state of the whole machine will be a pair of states like (C, D), (C, E), or (A, D). However, state A is actually a *superstate* that is decomposed into the substates B

---

[4]He uses the term *state diagrams* for FSMs.

and F, so whenever the left machine is in state A, it is actually in either state B or state F. Superstates and substates are intended to give a hierarchical mechanism for controlling complexity, and tools should allow the internal states (B and F) to be hidden so that only A is displayed or to open up A and see its internal behavior. These substates can be nested to any depth.

In addition to helping to control the visual complexity of the diagram, superstates and substates reduce the number of transitions because a transition that leaves a superstate like A is a shorthand for a whole set of transitions that leave each of its substates. So the γ transition from A to C is actually equivalent to two transitions, one from B to C and the other from F to C. This is a powerful abstraction mechanism because a single transition out of a superstate can replace many transitions out of a whole hierarchy of substates.

The label on a transition can include a *trigger*, a *condition* (or *guard*), and an *action*, using the following syntax:[5]

$$\textit{Trigger}[\textit{Guard}]/\textit{Action}$$

All these parts are optional. The *Trigger* is the name of an event, such as the arrival of some external signal, a timeout, or a signal generated by some other transition in the statechart. If it is omitted, then the transition may be taken whenever the *Guard* is true. The *Guard* part is a boolean condition that must be true for the transition to be taken. It defaults to true if it is omitted. The *Action* describes the effect of the transition, such as how the state variables are updated and what events are generated. Generated events may trigger other transitions. This is the *broadcast communication* aspect of statecharts: a transition in one part of the statechart may generate an event that triggers some transitions in other parts of the statechart. This allows very complex models to be written. Harel says that "Defining the formal semantics of these action-enriched statecharts is quite a delicate matter" [Har87, 257].

The remaining features illustrated by Figure 3.3 are the *entry*, *exit*, and *throughout* actions within state A as well as several other states. An *entry action* within a state is executed every time a transition enters that state, and an *exit action* is executed every time a transition leaves the state. These actions, like the actions attached to the transitions, are considered instantaneous occurrences that ideally take zero time. In contrast, the *throughout X* construct (which would be written as *do/X* in a UML state machine) in state A specifies an ongoing activity X that is carried on continuously while the system is within state A.

---

[5]Harel originally used the syntax "Trigger(Guard)/Action" but switched to "Trigger[Guard]/Action" in later papers and books. We use the later syntax, which is also used in UML state machines.

To finish the Figure 3.3 illustration, let us consider how the statechart reacts when the sequence of events α, then β, arrives from some external source. Initially the statechart is in state (C, D), so when α arrives, the transition $C \xrightarrow{\alpha} B$ fires and the current state becomes (B, D). The entry into state B (and thus state A) causes the actions S and V to be executed (simultaneously). While in state (B, D), the X activity is ongoing. When the γ event arrives, the transition $B \xrightarrow{\gamma/W} C$ is taken, which causes the exit actions of A to be executed (β and T), and this β triggers the transition $D \xrightarrow{\beta} E$, which in turn causes the entry action of E to be executed (U) and leaves the statechart in the state (C, E).

During the late 1980s and the 1990s, this statecharts notation was adopted by several companies and communities. The STATEMATE tool was developed at I-Logix[6] by Harel and others. It is a commercial tool that supports modeling with statecharts, animation, model checking, and code generation. Another variant of statecharts is the *stateflow* notation, which is part of the MATLAB system from The MathWorks[7] and is often used for modeling embedded real-time systems. Yet another variant of statecharts was adopted into UML, as described in the next section.

3.3.3 UML State Machines

UML state machines are a modified form of Harel's statecharts, with some of the more complex features removed and a different set of complex features added. However, in this book we use just a subset of the UML state machine notation and do not try to cover all its features.

The role of a UML state machine is to help define the state-related behavior of an existing class. The class is usually defined by a UML class diagram, so it already has data fields, methods, and associations with other classes. The transitions of the state machine can read and update these data fields. The trigger events of the transitions must be one of the following:

- A *call* of one of the methods of the class
- A *signal* received from somewhere else in the state machine
- A *change* in the value of an attribute (for example, *when*(*attribute > value*))
- A *timeout*

---

[6] See *http://www.ilogix.com.*

[7] See *http://www.mathworks.com.*

The first step in designing our UML state machine for the DVM controller is to decide what states it should have. Note that in our Controller class in Figure 3.1, we used an integer data field called balance to record how much money has been inserted so far. So we no longer need to have a large number of different states for each possible value of balance. In other words, the use of data variables solves the problem of having too many states in the state machine.

If we took this to the extreme, we could use data fields for *all* our state variables and have just a single node in our state machine, with all transitions starting and ending with that node. However, this would be silly because it does not take advantage of the power of state machines. The best approach is to create separate nodes for states that have *significantly different behavior*. For example, if we look at the use cases and think about the transitions that we need for a drink vending machine, we quickly realize that quite a few of the operations behave differently when the machine is out of service. This is a good indication that our machine should have at least two states: one for normal operation and one for OutOfService operation. We could also split the normal operation state into one state where balance=0 and another state where balance>0, but it turns out that there is no advantage in doing this, since there are no significant differences in behavior.

Figure 3.4 shows a statechart specification of the behavior of the Controller class with two states, InService and OutOfService.

> **Key Point**   The main step in designing a transition-based model is choosing the states (the nodes). A good choice of states will result in the system exhibiting different behavior for each state.

We now explain some of the features of UML state machines using Figure 3.4 as an example. As in Harel's statecharts, the two inner states correspond to different states of the Controller object. The transitions between those states define a change of state within the Controller, and the guards and actions of the transition can access and modify the attributes and associations of the Controller class. In Figure 3.4 we also have several *internal transitions* defined inside each of the states, such as the insertCoin and selectDrink transitions. These internal transitions are the same as a self-transition that loops from that state back to the same state, except that the internal transitions do not trigger *entry* or *exit* actions (our two states do not have entry or exit actions anyway).

Several different notations may be used in the action part of the transitions. For example, in Section 7.3 we will see a Java-like notation being used

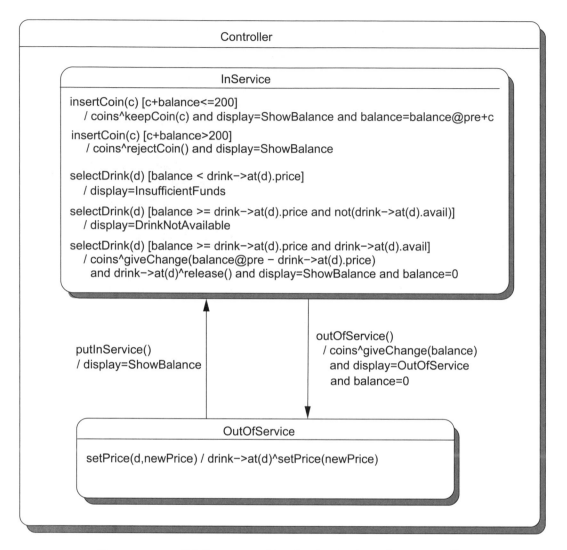

FIGURE 3.4 UML state machine for the drink machine controller.

within state machine transitions. The notation that we use in Figure 3.4 is the UML *Object Constraint Language* (OCL), which we describe more fully in the next subsection. The OCL predicates in the guards of Figure 3.4 are like conditions in many object-oriented programming languages, except that we write `drink->at(N)` to access the *N*th element in the `drink` sequence. The OCL postconditions (the action parts of the transitions, after the "/") contain two new OCL constructs:

- `balance@pre` (in the third `selectDrink` transition) gives the initial value of the `balance` field *before* the transition is taken. If we wrote just `balance`, it would be the value of the `balance` field *after* the transition is taken, which would be zero.
- `drink->at(d)^release()` sends the `release()` message to the `drink->at(d)` object, which tells it to release one drink.

UML state machines have many features that are not illustrated by our simple DVM state machine. Like statecharts, they allow nested states and parallel state machines. They also provide entry/*Action*, exit/*Action*, and do/*Action* facilities, history states, and several other kinds of connectors for making transitions more concise. These features make UML state machines a very expressive notation for specifying reactive control systems.

3.3.4 The UML Object Constraint Language

In several examples in this book, we use the UML Object Constraint Language to clarify the meaning of UML diagrams. For example, it can be used to constrain class diagrams, to specify the preconditions and postconditions of methods, to specify the guards of transitions within a UML state machine, and even to specify the action part of transitions within a UML state machine. This section gives a brief overview of OCL.

The UML OCL is a declarative language designed for object-oriented programmers. It avoids use of unfamiliar mathematical symbols, its syntax is quite straightforward, and it is fairly easy for someone who is familiar with object-oriented programming languages to learn to read and write simple OCL constraints. However, it also supports a large range of powerful operators on collections, some of which are unfamiliar to programmers, so it can take a while to master the whole language.

Some strengths of OCL are its four kinds of collections, the high-level operators on those collections, and its good facilities for navigating associations between classes. The latter feature is particularly useful when navigating associations with multiplicity greater than one. For example, in Figure 1.3, one Smartcard object could be connected to several Application objects, and each Application object could have one or more Profile objects associated with it. If we have a card, and we want to find all the Profile objects associated with it that have a `userType` field equal to `HOLDER`, we could simply write the OCL expression:

```
card.applications.profiles->select(userType=USER_TYPES::HOLDER)
```

By comparison, in Java we could not do this with just a single expression. We would first have to write the following helper method, which uses nested loops to handle the two one-to-many associations. Then we could get the same effect as the OCL expression by calling getHolderProfiles(card).

```
Set<Profile> getHolderProfiles(Smartcard card)
{
  Set<Profile> result = new HashSet<Profile>();
  for (Application app : card.applications())
  {
    for (Profile prof : app.profiles())
    {
      if (prof.userType == USER_TYPES.HOLDER)
      {
        result.add(prof);
      }
    }
  }
  return result;
}
```

Every OCL predicate or expression has a *context*—usually a class or a method within a particular class. Here are some of the main OCL constructs:

OCL Construct	Purpose
context *class* **inv:** *predicate*	Class invariant
context *class* **def:** *name* : *type* = *expr*	Define an attribute
context *class::attribute* **init:** *expr*	Define an initial value
context *class::method* **pre:** *predicate*	Precondition
context *class::method* **post:** *predicate*	Postcondition
context *class::method* **body:** *expr*	Define a query method

In addition to the usual arithmetic and logical operators, there are just three basic concepts in the OCL language:

- Access an attribute, *object.attribute*, where *attribute* is an attribute in the class of *object* or is an association leading out of that class. For example, in the context of the Controller class of Figure 3.1, `self.coins` (or just `coins`) gives the unique CoinBox object associated with the Controller, while `drink` will give a collection of DrinkShelf objects and `drink.price` will give a collection of all the prices of those drinks.

- Call a function, *object.function*(*args*...), where *function* must be a pure query function (usually, the meaning of *function* is specified via an OCL **body:** constraint).

- Select objects or get information from a collection, (*collection->op*(...)), where *op* is one of the OCL collection operators, such as *isEmpty*(), *size*(), *sum*(), *includes*(*collection*), *union*(*collection*), and *select*(*predicate*).

Note the distinction between the dot and arrow operators. The dot operator accesses one of the *user-defined* attributes or query functions in the class diagram, whereas the arrow operator calls one of the *OCL* collection operators. To take an extreme example of this, if we defined a query method called `size()` in our `DrinkShelf` class that tells us the number of drinks remaining on the shelf, then `drink.size()` would apply our query method to every drink object and return the collection (Bag) of those integers, whereas `drink->size()` would call the OCL *size* operator, so it would return 8 because we have eight DrinkShelves. It can even be useful to use the dot and arrow operators in the same expression, such as `drink.size()->sum()`, which would calculate the total number of drinks remaining in the machine.

OCL supports four kinds of collection: Set, OrderedSet, Bag, and Sequence, as well as Collection, which is the abstract supertype of these four collection types. Appendix B contains a summary of some common OCL operators.

The transitions in Figure 3.4 illustrate a few of the features of OCL but do not use any of the collection operators except for `at(N)` to access the Nth element of a Sequence collection. Note that sequences are indexed from 1 up to N in OCL, rather than starting from 0 as in C and Java. In Section 7.2 we will use the OCL Set operators to keep track of the customers of a web-based system for buying movie tickets.

There are no side-effect or assignment statements in OCL, so changes in the values of variables are specified as equations like `balance = balance@pre + c`, which says that the new (postoperation) value of `balance` equals the original (preoperation) value of `balance` plus c. OCL is not very precise about how to specify which variables have *not* changed value (the *frame problem*), but in Section 7.2.3 we will discuss one way of interpreting Object

Constraint Language postconditions that allows us to decide which variables can change and which cannot.

3.4 PRE/POST MODELS IN B

The B *abstract machine notation* is a formal modeling notation for specifying software systems. We choose it as a good example of pre/post notations because

- it has a clear and precise semantics;
- there are several good commercial and freely available tools for checking B models and reasoning about them;
- it uses a codelike notation for postconditions that is more familiar to engineers than raw predicate calculus; and
- it provides a high-level library of data structures (sets, relations, functions, sequences, etc.) that helps to make models simple and abstract.

In fact, the data structure toolkit of B is basically the same as the toolkit of the Z specification language and is quite similar to the libraries used within JML, Spec#, and OCL, so most of the advice that we give about writing models in B will transfer to those notations as well.

The B abstract machine notation is the basis of the complete B method, which we will now describe briefly. It is interesting to compare the complete B method with our use of the B notation for model-based testing.

3.4.1 The Complete B Method

The complete B method allows one to develop *provably correct* software. The development starts from an abstract model of the system. By *abstract model* we mean a model that gives a high-level functional view of the system and defines its interfaces and expected behaviors, as well as any invariant properties that the modeled operations should respect.

In the complete B method, one then writes a series of increasingly detailed designs, each of which refines the previous design. The B support tools automatically generate mathematical proof obligations to ensure that each new design is indeed a correct refinement. Once a sufficiently detailed design has been reached, the B tools can automatically generate executable code from that design. If one discharges all the proof obligations (which can require a huge amount of time and expertise), then the generated implementation is guaranteed to be correct. That is, it will have the same behavior properties as the original abstract model. This complete B method has been used successfully to develop some significant safety-critical software, such as the train control software for the driverless trains on Line 14 of the Paris Metro.

In contrast, our use of the B abstract machine notation for model-based testing is much more lightweight and does not require proof expertise. Like the complete B method, the B abstract machine notation is used to define an abstract model of the system, but this model is usually a small partial model, written just for testing purposes, rather than a complete model of the desired system. So, unlike with the complete B method, we do not use refinement and proof to generate a correct implementation; rather, we assume that the implementation has been coded manually, in some programming language, and is likely to contain errors. We use model-based testing tools to automatically generate a systematic set of tests from the model. When these tests are executed on the implementation, they expose differences between the behavior of the implementation and the behavior of the model. Each such difference should then be investigated to either correct the error in the implementation or perhaps to find a mistake in the model (which often indicates a lack of clarity in the original informal requirements of the system).

> **Key Point**   The complete B method uses automatic and interactive proof to *guarantee* that the code implements the model correctly. Model-based testing also checks the model against the code, but only via testing, so it does not guarantee to find all errors.

3.4.2 A Simple Drink Vending Machine

We will start by writing an extremely simple B abstract machine that describes just the money-related services offered by a DVM. Each of these services is described as an operation that modifies the internal state of the DVM.

To illustrate this, Listing 3.1 is a very abstract, partial model of the drink vending machine that models only the insertion and return of money, ignoring drinks completely. The functionality of this simple B model is similar to the simple FSM in Figure 3.2, except that here we handle all the possible coins.

The balance variable in Listing 3.1 models the total number of cents that the customer has entered, and the limit variable is the maximum balance that the machine accepts before returning coins. We will discuss the

LISTING 3.1   A simple DVM model, which models money only.

```
MACHINE
    DVM1
VARIABLES
    balance, limit
INVARIANT
    limit : INT & balance : INT &
    0 <= balance & balance <= limit
INITIALISATION
    balance := 0  || limit := 200
OPERATIONS
    reject <-- insertCoin(coin) =
        PRE coin : { 5, 10, 20, 50, 100 }
        THEN
        IF coin + balance <= limit
        THEN
            balance := balance + coin ||
            reject := 0
        ELSE
            reject := coin
        END
    END;
    money <-- returnButton =
        money := balance || balance := 0
END
```

meaning of B machines shortly, but you should be able to read this one reasonably well by analogy with a module or class definition in your favorite programming language.

Note that *out*<--name(*in*)=... defines an operation (procedure) with input variables *in* and output variables *out*. The parallel operator, ||, allows us to perform multiple assignments without worrying about which order they must go in. (To implement a parallel assignment on a sequential machine, it is necessary in general to evaluate all the right side expressions before updating any of the left side variables.) For example, the following three commands are all equivalent:

```
money := balance  ||  balance := 0
balance := 0  ||  money := balance
money,balance := balance,0
```

Note that this is quite different from using sequential composition,

```
balance:=0;   money:=balance,
```

which would have the effect of setting both `balance` and `money` to 0.

This DVM1 model is written in the ASCII syntax of B, which is what we shall use most of the time throughout this book because it is exactly what most tools take as input. There is also a typeset form, where `0 <= balance` appears as $0 \leq balance$ and `balance : INT` appears as $balance \in \mathbb{Z}$, and so on. There are tools for converting from the ASCII syntax to the typeset one.

One possible execution (animation) of the DVM model in Listing 3.1 is as follows. We could use a B tool[8] to execute this sequence to check that our model works as expected.

```
init;              /* sets balance to 0 */
insertCoin(50);    /* balance is now 50 cents */
insertCoin(10);    /* balance is now 60 cents */
r:=returnButton;   /* balance is now 0.  r=60 */
```

This simple model of the drink vending machine is a very *abstract* model. That is, it *abstracts* away from many (most!) of the concrete details of the real machine, including:

- how many drinks of each type are in stock (data abstraction);
- the service operations for restocking drinks and resetting the machine (operation abstraction);
- the `requestDrink` operation—the main one that the consumer is interested in! (operation abstraction); and
- details of exactly which coins are returned—it models the collection of coins by a single integer, which means that the model does not distinguish between returning two 10-cent coins versus one 20-cent coin (output abstraction).

Key Point   A model can give a *partial* view of the SUT.

Even though this model is very abstract, we could use it for test generation. It would generate a few test sequences, depending on which model-

---

[8]For example, the ProB tool supports several kinds of model animation and consistency checking. See *http://www.stups.uni-duesseldorf.de/ProB*.

based testing tool we used. For example, we might get the following two tests (we write insertCoin(100)= 0 to mean *call the insert operation with input 100 and check that it returns 0*):

```
Test1:  init;
        returnButton = 0
        insertCoin(5) = 50
        returnButton = 5

Test2:  init;
        insertCoin(100) = 0
        insertCoin(100) = 0
        insertCoin(5) = 5
```

These two tests check that the initial balance is zero, that money is rejected when more than $2.00 is entered, and that the reject button returns the money entered. These two simple tests would be enough to achieve statement coverage of the B model, which is a weak check on the adequacy of our test set. (In fact, for this model, statement coverage could be achieved with a single test sequence—you might like to try to find such a sequence.)

However, we would be rather ashamed to claim that this tiny set of tests is sufficient testing for a real DVM! To obtain a richer set of tests, we need a richer model that includes the requestDrink operation, some details of what drinks are in stock, and so on. We do this in Section 3.4.5, but first we discuss the structure and meaning of B machines and the toolkit of data structures provided by B.

3.4.3 Overview of B Machines

A B machine is conceptually not very different from a Java object (a single instance of a class) or a module in Modula-2 or Ada. That is, it defines some private state plus several public operations that manipulate and access that state. As you have seen, the B abstract machine notation is a textual notation. The structure of the machine is a series of clauses; the common B clauses are summarized in Listing 3.2. The full B notation also allows parameterized machines and several kinds of import, but these are beyond the scope of this book. We now briefly describe the purpose of each clause.

The MACHINE clause contains the name of the machine. This is similar to the name of a class in Java.

The SETS clause is for defining data types that the machine will use. We give the name of each data type and if it is a finite enumerated type, we can

LISTING 3.2   Structure of a B machine.

```
MACHINE
        name
SETS
        basic_types
CONSTANTS
        constant_names
PROPERTIES
        properties_of_constants
VARIABLES
        variable_names
INVARIANT
        properties_of_variables
INITIALISATION
        initial_state
DEFINITIONS
        macros
OPERATIONS
        operations
END
```

list all its members. For example, it would be good style to define a data type for the set of allowable coins in our vending machine.

```
SETS
    COINS = { 5, 10, 20, 50, 100 }
```

The CONSTANTS clause contains the names of any constants used in the machine, and the PROPERTIES clause specifies the values of those constants. For example, if we decide that the limit value of our DVM1 machine will never change, we could define it as a named constant.

```
CONSTANTS
    limit
PROPERTIES
    limit = 200
```

Since this constant has a unique value, an alternative would be to define it in the DEFINITIONS clause.

```
DEFINITIONS
    limit == 200
```

Such definitions are like C macros—they are unfolded as the B machine is read. It is also possible to write parameterized definitions, which allows you to extend the B notation in a simple way.

The VARIABLES clause specifies all the data variables of the machine, and the INVARIANT clause specifies the allowable range of each variable, plus any constraints *between* the variables. To be more precise, for each variable v in the VARIABLES clause, the INVARIANT must contain a conjunct of the form $v \in S$ or $v \subseteq S$. But it typically also specifies relationships between variables, like the `balance <= limit` constraint in the DVM1 machine. Such relationships capture important knowledge about the SUT, and a good tight invariant can be a big help in generating more accurate tests.

The INITIALISATION clause is a set of parallel assignments, giving a value to each state variable.

The OPERATIONS clause defines all the operations of the machine. Some of these will be *query* operations, which return a value but do not change the state variables. Other operations will be *update* operations, which do change the state variables. The behavior of each operation is specified by a *precondition*, which says what input values are allowed, and a *substitution*, which is a set of parallel assignments. These assignments must update all the output variables of the operation and may also update some of the state variables. To enhance expressiveness, there are several conditional constructs, like IF-THEN-ELSE and CASE statements, which allow us to specify conditional updates. However, no looping or sequential composition is allowed, and a given variable cannot be updated twice in parallel. (The syntax of substitutions is given in Appendix A.) These restrictions mean that every execution of an operation updates each variable at most once. This makes the operations easy to reason about and easier to use as the basis for test generation.

To summarize, the data part of a B abstract machine (its constants and variables) is an abstraction of the important internal state of the SUT, while the operations of the B abstract machine specify the dynamic behavior of the SUT. Although the internal state of the B machine is hidden, its design is actually one of the most important aspects of the machine. Just as a database schema tells you a lot about a database system and its capabilities, the state of a B machine tells you a lot about the system being modeled and what it is capable of. Furthermore, a good choice of state variables will make the operations easy to specify, but a bad choice can make them much more complex.

> **Key Point**   The main step in designing a pre/post model is choosing its state variables and their types.

Our simple DVM1 example uses only integers, but typically, B abstract machines use high-level data structures such as sets, relations, and functions. These give a high degree of expressiveness and make it easy to define an abstract model of the SUT internal state. Before we write a more sophisticated DVM model, we will investigate the data structures available in B.

3.4.4 The B Toolkit

The B notation includes a rich toolkit of data structures for use within machines, including sets, relations, functions, sequences, bags (or multisets), and trees. These data structures make it possible to represent complex information and the data structures of the application at an abstract level. Efficiency is irrelevant here, because the model is not the implementation of the system. Instead, the goal of using these high-level data structures is to write a clear, simple, and abstract behavior model.

This section gives a brief introduction to the B notation for logic, sets, relations, and functions. We use these data structures to specify a richer DVM model and in other examples throughout the book. See Appendix A for a summary of the syntax and operators of B.

LOGIC

B has the usual boolean operators that most programming languages have, such as *conjunction*, *disjunction*, and *negation*, plus equality and inequality on all types of data, and the usual integer arithmetic operators. It also provides logical *implication* and *equivalence* operators. The main logical operators are summarized in Table 3.1.

TABLE 3.1   Logical Operators in B

ASCII	Typeset	Name	True when ...
P & Q	$P \wedge Q$	conjunction	P and Q are both true
P or Q	$P \vee Q$	disjunction	at least one of P, Q is true
not(P)	$\neg P$	negation	P is false
P => Q	$P \Rightarrow Q$	implication	$(\neg P) \vee Q$
P <=> Q	$P \Longleftrightarrow Q$	equivalence	$(P \wedge Q) \vee (\neg P \wedge \neg Q)$
E = F	$E = F$	equality	E and F have the same value
E /= F	$E \neq F$	inequality	E and F have different values

When we have a large data structure, or one that varies in size, and we want to say something about all the elements, we can use the *universal quantifier*. This is written `!x.(x:S => P)`, or $\forall x.(x \in S \Rightarrow P)$ when typeset, and is true when the predicate P is true for *every* $x \in S$.

Similarly, if we want to search a data structure, or say that it is possible to find a solution to some problem, we can use the *existential quantifier*. This is written `#x.(x:S & P)`, or $\exists x.(x \in S \wedge P)$ when typeset, and is true when there is at least one member $x \in S$ that makes the predicate P true.

For example, $\forall x.(x \in 1 .. 9 \Rightarrow x \times x < 50)$ is false because $x \times x < 50$ is not true for every number from 1 to 9 (it is false when $x = 8$ and when $x = 9$). On the other hand, $\exists x.(x \in 1 .. 9 \wedge x \times x < 50)$ is true because $x \times x < 50$ is true when, for example, $x = 3$.

SETS

Sets are collections of elements of the same type, without repetition. They are not ordered. They are written using braces, { and }. For example, the set of prime numbers less than 10 can be written {2, 3, 5, 7} or {2, 5, 7, 3} or even {2, 2, 3, 5, 7, 7}. These are all equivalent to {2, 3, 5, 7}.

We call the number of elements in a set its *cardinality*, written `card(S)`. Elements of a set can be numbers, enumerated values (for example, the set of primary colors {red, yellow, blue}), or even sets. Set operators include the familiar operators such as union (written \/ in the ASCII form of B, or ∪ when typeset), intersection (/\ or ∩), and subtraction (-). Here are some examples of set operators:

$$5 .. 7 = \{5, 6, 7\}$$

$$\{2, 3, 5, 7\} \cup (5 .. 7) = \{2, 3, 5, 6, 7\}$$

$$\{2, 3, 5, 7\} \cap (5 .. 7) = \{5, 7\}$$

$$\{2, 3, 5, 7\} - (5 .. 7) = \{2, 3\}$$

In addition to equality and inequality, there are several boolean operators on sets to allow us to check their members.

The *membership* operator is written `E:S`, or $E \in S$ when typeset, and is true when the value of E is one of the elements of S. The *non-membership* operator, written `E /: S`, or $E \notin S$ when typeset, is the logical negation of membership, so it is true when the value of E is *not* one of the members of S.

The *subset* operator is written `S <: T`, or $S \subseteq T$ when typeset, and is true when *every* member of S is also a member of T. That is,

$$S \subseteq T \iff \forall x.(x \in S \Rightarrow x \in T)$$

To say that S is not a subset of T, we write S /<: T, or $S \nsubseteq T$ when typeset.

The final piece of set notation that we will mention is in fact the most powerful. The *set comprehension*, $\{x|P\}$, returns the set of all values of x that satisfy P. However, P must contain a conjunct that gives us an upper bound for the resulting set, such as $x \in S$. So set comprehension gives us a way of finding the subset of S that satisfies some desired property.

For example, if our vending machine had a set of available coins, $Coins = \{5, 10, 20, 50, 100\}$, with unlimited numbers of each coin, we could use set comprehension to define the possible amounts of change the machine could give, using one, two or three coins.

$$withOneCoin = Coins$$

$$withTwoCoins = \{value|value \in \mathbb{N} \wedge$$

$$\exists c1, c2.(c1 \in Coins \wedge c2 \in Coins \wedge value = c1 + c2)\}$$

$$withThreeCoins = \{value|value \in \mathbb{N} \wedge$$

$$\exists c1, c2, c3.(\{c1, c2, c3\} \subseteq Coins \wedge value = c1 + c2 + c3)\}$$

It would be interesting to generalize this solution to N coins and to take into account that we may have limited numbers of some coins. However, we have not yet seen enough of the B toolkit to do this here because the most elegant way of doing it is to use a function or a bag (multiset) to record the number of available coins of each denomination and the B summation operator SIGMA to calculate the total value (see Appendix A).

RELATIONS

Often we need to define various kinds of relationships between two collections. For this, we use *relations*, which are sets of pairs.

A *pair* (or more precisely, an *ordered pair*) is written c |-> d, or $c \mapsto d$ in typeset format. This pair associates the elements c and d. Note that c and d may have different types. For example, the pair $3 \mapsto red$ links the integer 3 with the color red. The first element of a pair is called its *antecedent*, and the second element is called its *image*. So in the pair $3 \mapsto red$, 3 is the antecedent and red is the image of the pair.

A set of pairs between two sets is a *relation*. The set of possible relations from a set A to a set B is written A <-> B, or $A \leftrightarrow B$ when typeset.

To illustrate relations, let us consider the relationship "plays" between a set of people and a set of musical instruments.

Let P be the set of people, $\{Kay, Peter, Paul, Angela\}$. Let I be the set of musical instruments, $\{guitar, piano, drums, flute\}$. The relation *plays*, defined by

$$plays = \{Kay \mapsto piano,\ Peter \mapsto flute,\ Peter \mapsto drums,\ Angela \mapsto flute\}$$

belongs to the set of relations between P and I. That is, $plays \in P \leftrightarrow I$.

Figure 3.5 shows a graphical representation of the *plays* relation. Since relations are just sets of pairs, we can use all the set operators to manipulate relations. For example, if Peter learns the guitar, we could define a new relation to reflect this:

$$plays2 = plays \cup \{Peter \mapsto guitar\}$$

However, the B toolkit also has many operators specifically for relations. We will now review the most useful of these, using the *plays* relation as an example.

The *domain* of a relation R, written dom(R), is the set of all the antecedents of R. For example,

$$\mathrm{dom}(plays) = \{Kay, Peter, Angela\}$$

The *range* of a relation R, written ran(R), is the set of all the image elements of R. For example,

$$\mathrm{ran}(plays) = \{piano, drums, flute\}$$

The *domain restriction* operator, written S <| R, or $S \lhd R$ when typeset, selects from the relation R those pairs whose antecedent belongs to the set S. For example, what instruments do the men play?

$$\{Peter, Paul\} \lhd plays = \{Peter \mapsto flute, Peter \mapsto drums\}$$

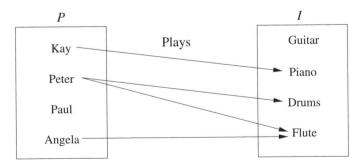

FIGURE 3.5   Graphical representation of the *plays* relation.

A variant of domain restriction, called *domain antirestriction* or *domain subtraction*, is useful when you want to select the pairs whose antecedents are *not* in S. This is written S <<| T, or $S \triangleleft\!\!\!- R$ when typeset. In fact, $S \triangleleft\!\!\!- R = (\mathrm{dom}(R) - S) \triangleleft R$. For example, even if we did not know the ladies' names, we could still find out what instruments they play:

$$\{Peter, Paul\} \triangleleft\!\!\!- plays = \{Kay \mapsto piano, Angela \mapsto flute\}$$

The *range restriction* operator, written R |> S, or $R \triangleright S$ when typeset, is used to select from the relation R those pairs whose image belongs to the set S. And of course, there is also a *range antirestriction* (or *range subtraction*) operator, R |>> S or $R \triangleright\!\!\!- S$. For example:

$$plays \triangleright \{flute\} = \{Peter \mapsto flute, Angela \mapsto flute\}$$
$$plays \triangleright\!\!\!- \{flute\} = \{Kay \mapsto piano, Peter \mapsto drums\}$$

The *relational override* operator, R <+ U, or $R \triangleleft\!\!+ U$ when typeset, is useful for creating an updated version of a relation. The pairs in U *override* any pairs in R that have the same antecedent. That is,

$$R \triangleleft\!\!+ U = (\mathrm{dom}(U) \triangleleft\!\!\!- R) \cup U$$

To illustrate these operators, let us experiment with this $plays : P \leftrightarrow I$ relation. We can use the preceding operators to answer questions like the following:

- Who plays the flute?
  $\mathrm{dom}(plays \triangleright \{flute\})$
- Is it true that at least one person plays the drums?
  $plays \triangleright \{drums\} \neq \{\}$
- Who are the people who don't play an instrument?
  $P - \mathrm{dom}(plays)$
- What are the instruments that nobody plays?
  $I - \mathrm{ran}(plays)$
- What are the instruments played by Kay or Peter?
  $\mathrm{ran}(\{Kay, Peter\} \triangleleft plays)$
- Define a new relation to show that Peter has learned to play the guitar and refuses to play anything else (so he no longer plays the flute and drums).
  $plays2 = plays \triangleleft\!\!+ \{Peter \mapsto guitar\}$
  $= \{Kay \mapsto piano, Peter \mapsto guitar, Angela \mapsto flute\}$

Note that relations are like binary relations in a relational database: the *dom* and *ran* operators select one of the columns of the relation (a *projection* in database terms), while operators such as ◁, ▷, ◀, ▶ select a subset of the records in the relation (a *selection* in database terms).

Just as one can define relations with more than two columns in a relational database, it is possible in B to define relations between more than two sets, using tuples like (*Peter*, *piano*, 5). However, these are less common than binary relations, so we do not describe them further here.

FUNCTIONS

Functions are just a special case of relations. They are the many-to-one and "one-to-one" relations—that is, the relations in which each element of the domain is mapped to at most one image element.

Functions are very common in B machines because they provide a powerful way to express a relationship between two sets. They can be used to model arrays, maps, permutations, and many other functional relationships. Since many kinds of relationship are possible, B gives us seven flavors of function to choose from. But in this book we use only the two most common kinds of function, which are partial functions and total functions. The difference is that a *total function* maps every element of its input type to some value, whereas a *partial function* may leave some elements undefined.

Since functions are relations, they are sets of pairs, so we can use all the set and relation operators to define and manipulate functions. For example, the *dom* operator tells us all the input values of the function, and the relational override <+ operator allows us to update the function.

Here is an example of a function that squares its inputs. We can define it using set comprehension,

$$square = \{in, out \mid in \in \mathbb{Z} \land out \in num \land out = in \times in\}$$

or we could write it as a *lambda function* (named after the Greek letter λ):

$$square = \lambda in.(in \in \mathbb{Z} \mid in \times in)$$

This defines a function whose input is called *in* and whose output is the expression *in* × *in*. This is equivalent to the preceding set comprehension, but the lambda function is more concise and makes it clear that we are defining a function rather than an arbitrary relation or set. So we generally use the lambda notation when defining function values in this book.

The most useful operation on a function is *function application*, written $f(arg)$. This takes the antecedent element *arg* and returns the unique image element that *f* maps it to. That is, $f(arg) = v$ means that $(arg \mapsto v) \in f$. It is important to note that *arg* must be in the domain of f for $f(arg)$ to be well defined. If $arg \notin \text{dom}(f)$, then the expression $f(arg)$ has an undetermined value—all we know about it is that it is some member of the image type.

3.4.5 A Richer DVM Model

Now we can use the sets and functions of the B toolkit to make our model of the drink vending machine much more sophisticated. In fact, we will model a hot coffee machine that is capable of making several recipes, such as expresso, cappuccino, and hot chocolate. Each of these has different amounts of hot water, coffee beans, whitener, and chocolate. It also allows customers to choose the sweetness of their drink by adjusting the sugar content on a 0..4 scale (the default is 2).

We model just the controller. In fact, this controller must communicate with the coinbox, a hot water boiler, several ingredient dispensers (similar to the DrinkShelf objects in our earlier DVM design except that these ingredient dispensers measure out a given number of grams of ingredients), the mixer, and the cup dispenser. We model the interactions between the controller and these other components using the inputs and outputs of the methods in our B model.

To simplify the example, the model developed here ignores the timing of the output signals and just outputs the amount of each ingredient that should be dispensed. Other simplifications include:

- not modeling the boiler control functionality (which ensures that the water is within a desired temperature range);
- modeling the water as a finite resource rather than as a continuous stream; and
- not modeling various safety signals to indicate hardware failure.

These features could easily be added to the model to allow us to generate more sophisticated test suites, but here we focus on the recipe and ingredient aspects to illustrate how it is possible to model the more data-intensive aspects of the DVM by using functions in the B model.

We start by designing the signatures of the B operations.

```
reject <-- insertCoin(coin);
reject <-- returnButton();
reject, makeDrink <-- selectDrink(drink);
moreSweet();
lessSweet();
```

```
setPrice(drink, newPrice);
refillIngredient(ingredientNumber, grams);
reject <-- outOfService();
putInService();
```

The `reject` output is the amount of money (in cents) that the coinbox should return to the consumer. Note that the `outOfService` operation must have a `reject` output, in case the service technician has to put the machine out of order after a consumer has started to use it. We model the current sweetness value, the current balance, and the contents of the LCD display using state variables within the Controller model, so they do not need to be treated as outputs of the operations.

Listing 3.3 shows all the set, constants, and state variables of the coffee machine, and Listing 3.4 shows how the state variables are initialized. A real controller would support a wider range of drinks and ingredients than this model, but three drinks and five ingredients is enough for testing purposes. Our controller is actually quite sophisticated because its `avail` function maintains an estimate of how much of each ingredient is available. Some machines use this information to send a telephone request for refilling when the level falls below a given point or to allow remote querying of the current ingredient levels. The `MAXQUANTITY` constant gives an arbitrary maximum for all the ingredient containers.

The `display` and `balance` variables model the contents of the LCD screen on the front of the coffee machine. Various messages can be displayed, but when the `DisplayBalance` message is output, the current value of `balance` is displayed. The *sweet* variable allows the customer to choose how much sugar he or she wants. The current level of this variable is displayed on the screen by a sequence of five lights. Note that these kinds of convention about the relationship of the model variables to the real world are just described informally at this stage, but they are made explicit later when we define how to transform the generated abstract tests into executable test scripts.

The `recipes` variable has the most complex type in this model. It is a function from `COMPOSITION` to `QUANTITY`, but since `COMPOSITION` is all pairs of drinks and ingredients, this means that `recipes` is like a two-dimensional array. That is, for every ingredient of every drink, `recipes` tells us how much of that ingredient is required in the drink. In `recipes`, the `Sugar` content is always zero, because it is overridden later by the customer-chosen sweetness level (`sweet`).

Listing 3.5 shows the operations for inserting coins, returning coins, and adjusting the sweetness level (see page 95). Note that the `insertCoin` operation rejects the entered coin (but retains the previously entered coins) if it

LISTING 3.3   B model of a coffee machine: sets, constants, and variables.

```
MACHINE
    COFFEE
SETS
    DRINK = {Expresso,Cappuccino,HotChoc};
    INGREDIENT = {Coffee,Sugar,Milk,Chocolate,Water};
    MESSAGE = {ShowBalance, InsufficientFunds,
                DrinkNotAvailable, OutOfService}
CONSTANTS
    MAXMONEY, MAXPRICE, MAXQUANTITY, COMPOSITION, none
PROPERTIES
    MAXMONEY = 200 & /*? max money before it rejects coins ?*/
    MAXPRICE = 100 & /*? max price of drinks ?*/
    MAXQUANTITY = 1000 &
    COMPOSITION : DRINK <-> INGREDIENT &
    COMPOSITION = DRINK * INGREDIENT &
    none : INGREDIENT --> NAT &
    none = %i.(i:INGREDIENT | 0)
DEFINITIONS
    MONEY   == 0..MAXMONEY;
    PRICES  == 0..MAXPRICE;
    QUANTITY == 0 .. MAXQUANTITY;
    SWEETNESS == 0..4;
    DEFAULTSWEET == 2;
    COIN == {5,10,20,50,100}
VARIABLES
    avail, price, balance, display, sweet, recipes
INVARIANT
    avail   : INGREDIENT --> QUANTITY  &
    price   : DRINK --> MONEY      &
    balance : MONEY               &
    display : MESSAGE & /*? The message on the screen ?*/
    sweet   : 0..4 &    /*? Displayed as a row of 5 lights ?*/
    recipes : COMPOSITION --> QUANTITY
```

causes the total value to be too high. This models the finite capacity of the coin-handling subsystem.

Listing 3.6 shows the most interesting operation, which dispenses the drink (see page 96). It starts by selecting the appropriate recipe for the

LISTING 3.4   B model of a coffee machine: initialisation.

```
INITIALISATION
    /*? All ingredients are initially empty ?*/
    avail := %i.(i:INGREDIENT | 0) ||

    /*? All prices default to $0.40 ?*/
    price := %d.(d:DRINK | 40) ||

    sweet := DEFAULTSWEET ||

    /*? The display starts off showing 0 balance. ?*/
    display := ShowBalance ||
    balance := 0 ||
    recipes := none  <+ {(Expresso  |-> Coffee) |-> 10,
                         (Expresso  |-> Water) |-> 50,
                         (Cappuccino |-> Coffee) |-> 5,
                         (Cappuccino |-> Chocolate) |-> 2,
                         (Cappuccino |-> Milk) |-> 30,
                         (Cappuccino |-> Water) |-> 210,
                         (HotChoc |-> Chocolate) |-> 10,
                         (HotChoc |-> Milk) |-> 10,
                         (HotChoc |-> Water) |-> 230}
```

requested drink and constructing a modified version of that recipe whose sugar level corresponds to the customer's desired sweetness level. Then it checks that enough money has been entered. If it has not, then the InsufficientFunds message is displayed and no drink is produced (in the model, this is indicated by makeDrink having zero levels for all ingredients). Then it checks that there are sufficient amounts of all the ingredients. If there are, the drink is dispensed (makeDrink says how much of each ingredient should be used), excess money is returned (the reject output), and the availability levels of the ingredients are reduced. Note that the high-level B operators, such as relational override and universal quantification, enable a concise description of this operation.

Listing 3.7 shows the remaining operations, which are for use by the service personnel (see page 97). In fact, the outOfService operation can be invoked manually by a service technician, but it is also invoked automatically when the machine detects a serious malfunction such as the coinbox being too full to handle more coins.

The operations of this machine have used simple B commands such as assignment, if-then-else, precondition, and local variables (the LET recipe BE

LISTING 3.5   B model of a coffee machine: coin and sweetness operations.

```
OPERATIONS
reject <-- insertCoin(coin) =
    PRE
        coin : COIN & display /= OutOfService
    THEN
        display := ShowBalance  ||
        IF balance + coin <= MAXMONEY
        THEN
            balance := balance + coin  ||
            reject  := 0
        ELSE
            reject  := coin
        END
    END;

reject <-- returnButton =
    /*? Release all current money and set display to 0 ?*/
    BEGIN
        balance := 0                ||
        reject := balance           ||
        IF display /= OutOfService THEN
            display := ShowBalance
        END
    END;

moreSweet =
    IF sweet < max(SWEETNESS) THEN
        sweet := sweet + 1
    END;

lessSweet =
    IF sweet > min(SWEETNESS) THEN
        sweet := sweet - 1
    END;
```

command in selectDrink). B also provides several more sophisticated commands, which can be nondeterministic. One of the most useful commands is the ANY v WHERE P THEN C END command, which creates new local variables v and nondeterministically chooses their values so that the predicate P is satisfied. Typically the command C then assigns those v variables to output or state variables.

LISTING 3.6   B model of a coffee machine: the selectDrink operation.

```
reject, makeDrink <-- selectDrink(drink) =
    PRE
        drink : DRINK & display /= OutOfService
    THEN
        LET recipe BE
            recipe = (({drink} <| COMPOSITION) <| recipes)
                    <+ {(drink |-> Sugar) |-> sweet}
        IN
            IF balance < price(drink) THEN
                display := InsufficientFunds ||
                reject  := 0 ||
                makeDrink := none
            ELSIF /*? we have enough ingredients ?*/
              !i.(i:INGREDIENT=>avail(i)>=recipe(drink|->i)) THEN
                makeDrink := recipe             ||
                display := ShowBalance           ||
                balance := 0                     ||
                reject := balance - price(drink) ||
                avail := %i.(i:INGREDIENT | avail(i) - recipe(i))
            ELSE
                display := DrinkNotAvailable ||
                reject  := 0 ||
                makeDrink := none
            END /* IF */
        END /* LET */
    END; /* PRE */
```

For example, if the coinbox of our vending machine has to be told exactly how to make up a given change value using the coins available, we could write a loose specification that nondeterministically chooses any available collection of coins that adds up to the desired reject value (SIGMA calculates the sum of a collection):

```
ANY coins WHERE coins : COIN --> NAT
    & reject = SIGMA(c).(c:dom(coins) | c * coins(c))
    & !c.(c:COIN => (coins(c) <= availCoins(c)))
THEN
    coinbox := coins
END
```

LISTING 3.7   B model of a coffee machine: service personnel operations.

```
reject <-- outOfService =
    BEGIN
        balance := 0            ||
        reject   := balance     ||
        display := OutOfService
    END;

setPrice(drink, newPrice) =
    PRE
        display = OutOfService &
        drink : DRINK &
        newPrice : PRICES &
        newPrice mod 5 = 0
    THEN
        price(drink) := newPrice
    END;

refillIngredient(ingred,amount) =
    PRE
        display = OutOfService &
        ingred : INGREDIENT &
        amount : QUANTITY
    THEN
        avail(ingred) := amount
    END;

putInService =
    display := ShowBalance
END /* MACHINE */
```

When reject $= 20$, and availCoins $= \{5 \mapsto 3, 10 \mapsto 3, 20 \mapsto 2, \ldots\}$, this might choose any of the following solutions:

$$\text{coins} = \{5 \mapsto 0, 10 \mapsto 0, 20 \mapsto 1, 50 \mapsto 0, 100 \mapsto 0\}$$

$$\text{coins} = \{5 \mapsto 0, 10 \mapsto 2, 20 \mapsto 0, 50 \mapsto 0, 100 \mapsto 0\}$$

$$\text{coins} = \{5 \mapsto 2, 10 \mapsto 1, 20 \mapsto 0, 50 \mapsto 0, 100 \mapsto 0\}$$

This illustrates how the ANY command is a useful and abstract way of specifying the properties of the results that we want without giving an exact algorithm for computing the results. The nondeterminism gives the implementor some freedom in how to choose values that satisfy *P*.

> **Key Point**   Pre/post notations allow you to develop behavior models that are good for generating functional test cases. The precondition of an operation specifies when and how the environment can call that operation. The postcondition describes how the operation changes the state of the model, which is an abstraction of how it changes the internal state of the SUT.

3.4.6   Other Pre/Post Notations

We will now briefly discuss how models like this DVM model could be written in other pre/post notations, such as the ISO Standard Z specification language, the Java Modeling Language (JML), Spec# (an extension of C#), SeC (an extension of C), and the UML Object Constraint Language. We include this comparison so that readers who are not familiar with some of the notations can get a quick glimpse of how the various notations differ on this common example. This may help with deciding which pre/post notation to use for model-based testing.

Listing 3.8 shows a Z version of the `insertCoin` operation (see Listing 3.5). We assume that a separate Z state schema called DVM would define the types and invariants of the six state variables (`avail`, `price`, `balance`, `display`, `sweet`, and `recipes`), just as the B machine does in Listing 3.3.

There are several interesting differences between this and the B model.

1. In Z, input and output variables are distinguished by naming conventions. The ? suffix indicates an input variable; the ! suffix indicates an output variable.
2. In Z there is no clear distinction between the precondition predicates and the postcondition predicates. Since the distinction is important for model-based testing, it is necessary to identify the precondition part of the operation before starting test generation. This usually requires some human input because automatic calculation of the precondition does not always produce the simplest form of the precondition.
3. The ΔDVMState line says that this operation can change the state variables. The default in Z is that *every* state variable can change value, so it is necessary to add an equality like $avail' = avail$ for each variable that does not change. This makes some operations a little

LISTING 3.8   Z version of the DVM `insertCoin` operation.

`insertCoin`

```
ΔDVMState
coin? : COIN
reject! : COIN
```
```
coin ∈ {5,10,20,50,100}
display ≠ OutOfService
avail' = avail
price' = price
sweet' = sweet
display' = ShowBalance
(balance + coin ⩽ MAXMONEY ⇒
      balance' = balance + amount ∧
      reject' = 0)
(balance + coin > MAXMONEY ⇒
      balance' = balance ∧
      reject' = coin)
```

more verbose in Z than in B, where variables do not change unless they are assigned to.

4. The B IF-THEN-ELSE construct must be expanded into two separate implications in the Z version, one for the THEN branch and one for the ELSE branch. This also makes some operations slightly more verbose in Z than in B.

Listing 3.9 shows a JML specification of the `insertCoin` operation. Note that the specifications are written within the Java comments for backward compatibility with standard Java tools. The precondition and postcondition predicates within those comments are written using Java syntax, with a few extensions, such as the JML implication operator (==>), the `spec_public` modifier,[9] and the \old(...) notation. The primary goal of JML is to provide sophisticated specification facilities using expressions that are as familiar to Java programmers as possible.

The precondition is given by the `requires` clauses. To keep the example simple, we have relaxed the precondition to allow any coin value between 5 and 100, but it would be possible to check that it is an exact coin value

---

[9]The spec_public modifier allows the private `balance` and `display` variables to be readable within other specifications (but not within code).

LISTING 3.9   JML specification of the insertCoin operation.

```
class DVM
{
    // An 'enumeration' for the MESSAGE values.
    public static final int ShowBalance = 1;
    public static final int InsufficientFunds = 2;
    public static final int DrinkNotAvailable = 3;
    public static final int OutOfService = 4;

    public static final int MAXMONEY = 200;

    private /*@spec_public@*/ int balance;
    private /*@spec_public@*/ int display;

    //@requires 5 <= coin && coin <= 100;
    //@requires display != OutOfService;
    //@assignable balance, display;
    //@ensures display == ShowBalance;
    /*@ensures \old(balance)+coin <= MAXMONEY
              ==> balance==\old(balance)+coin
                  && \result == 0;
      @ensures \old(balance)+coin > MAXMONEY
              ==> balance==\old(balance)
                  && \result == coin;
      @*/
    public int insertCoin(int coin)
    { ... }

    // other operations ...
}
```

by initializing a JMLEqualsSet called COIN and then checking that coin is a member of the COIN set by writing COIN.has(coin). Like the other specification languages, JML provides a rich set of specification-oriented data structures including sets, maps, and relations.

The JML postcondition is given in the ensures clauses. It is rather similar to the postcondition in the Z schema, with the if-then-else written as two implications. One difference is that in JML, undecorated variables refer to the *final* state of the operation, and the old(...) decoration is used to refer to the *initial* values of variables. The other main difference is that fewer equality predicates are needed than in Z because the assignable clause lists all the variables that may be updated by the operation, so all other variables implicitly remain unchanged.

Listing 3.10 shows the same model in Spec#, with the returnBalance operation as well. This is like the B model in that the precondition is given as predicates, but the body of the operation is written as code. The code parts of Spec# are just normal C#, but with several restrictions and extensions to make it more suitable for modeling purposes. We discuss the Spec# modeling language, and the Spec Explorer test generation tool that uses it, further in Section 6.5. If we use the Spec Explorer tool to explore the full state space of

LISTING 3.10   Spec# model of the insertCoin and returnBalance operations.

```
enum MESSAGE {ShowBalance, InsufficientFunds,
              DrinkNotAvailable, OutOfService};
MESSAGE display = MESSAGE.ShowBalance;
int balance = 0;

[Action]
int insertCoin(int coin)
requires 5 <= coin && coin <= 100;
requires display != MESSAGE.OutOfService;
{
  display = MESSAGE.ShowBalance;
  if (balance + coin <= 200)
  {
    balance = balance + coin;
    return 0;
  }
  else
  {
    return coin;
  }
}

[Action]
int returnBalance()
{
  int temp = balance;
  balance = 0;
  return temp;
}
```

the model in Listing 3.10, with the coin input being restricted to 50 or 100, then we get exactly the same FSM for the DVM machine that we designed manually in Figure 3.2. If we allow all the coins (5, 10, 20, 50, and 100), then we get a rather larger FSM with 41 states and 246 transitions.

Listing 3.11 shows the insertCoin operation specified in SeC (*Specification extension of the C programming language*). SeC is the modeling notation for the CTesK model-based testing tool from UniTesk.[10] This SeC version

LISTING 3.11   The insertCoin operation in SeC.

```
specification int insertCoin(int coin)
  reads    coin
  updates balance display
{
  pre
  {
    return 5 <= coin && coin <= 100
        && display != MESSAGE_OutOfService;
  }
  coverage C
  {
    if (coin + balance > 200)
      return { OVER, "Too much money" };
    else
      return { UNDER, "Less than the 2 dollar limit" };
  }
  post
    {
      if (coin + balance > 200)
        return balance == @balance
            && display == MESSAGE_ShowBalance
            && insertCoin == coin; /* the return value */
      else
        return balance == @balance + coin
            && display == MESSAGE_ShowBalance
            && insertCoin == 0; /* the return value */
    }
}
```

---

[10] See *http://www.unitesk.com* for details of SeC and the CTesk tool, plus other tools that use extensions of other programming languages.

of the insertCoin operation has the same style of precondition and post-condition as the JML and Z examples, where the postcondition checks the relationship between the updated variables and their original values. Like JML (but unlike Z), it also has a precise *frame* specification, which says not only which variables the SUT insertCoin operation can update, but also which variables it can read. But the most interesting feature of the SeC version is the **coverage** clause, which is between the **pre** and **post** clauses. The coverage clause allows the modeler to partition the expected behavior into interesting cases, so that the test generation process can try to test all the different cases. SeC allows several independent coverage clauses, which gives the test generator considerable freedom in choosing how to test the various combinations of partitions.

OCL can also be used as a pre/post notation. Earlier in this chapter (see Figure 3.4), we saw how the insertCoin operation could be specified as two separate transitions with the help of some OCL guards and postconditions. By combining those transitions and writing them as an OCL precondition and postcondition for the insertCoin method, we can specify the complete behavior of that method.

```
context  Controller::insertCoin(c:Integer)
  pre:     5 <= c and c <= 100 and display <> OutOfService
  post:    (c+balance<=200 and coins^keepCoin(c)
      and display=ShowBalance and balance=balance@pre+c)
  or
      (c+balance>200 and coins^rejectCoin()
        and display=ShowBalance)
```

This concludes our brief comparison of some pre/post notations.

3.5 SUMMARY

In this chapter we have seen how to write transition-based models, using UML statecharts as an example notation, and how to write pre/post models, using B as an example notation.

A general guideline is that the transition-based style is preferable for control-oriented systems, and the pre/post style is preferable for data-oriented systems.

In each notation, we saw several models of the drink vending machine, with varying amounts of detail. This illustrates that it is possible and useful to write *partial models* of a system and use those as a basis for test generation.

> **Key Point**　The quality and number of tests that you get from model-based testing depend upon the quality and precision of your model.

A very abstract model will generate a few high-level tests covering just a few aspects of the system. A more detailed, precise model will generate more tests, covering more of the system. The design of the model is the first and most important weapon of the test engineer against the dragon of exhaustive testing. We will see other weapons for fighting complexity in later chapters (like test selection criteria in the next chapter), but a good modeling strategy is a prerequisite.

3.6　FURTHER READING

The best overview of UML notations is undoubtedly the slim *UML Distilled* by Martin Fowler [Fow04]. For an overview of statecharts in general, the original paper by Harel [Har87] is a good read. For a more detailed introduction to UML state machines, an inspiring book that describes both how to write UML state machines and ways to implement them in C/C++ is *Practical Statecharts in C/C++: Quantum Programming for Embedded Systems*, by Miro Samek [Sam02]. The associated website is *http://www.quantum-leaps.com/writings/book.htm*.

Of course, the OMG's UML website (*http://www.uml.org*) is the first stop for downloadable versions of the UML 2.0 specification, tutorials, and lists of UML tools.

For a comprehensive introduction to the B notation and method, we recommend *The B-Method, An Introduction* by Schneider [Sch01]. For even more detail, the bible of the B method is Abrial's book, *The B-Book: Assigning Programs to Meanings* [Abr96]. The use of B for the development and proof of the train control software of Line 14 of the Paris Metro is described in a paper presented at the B98 conference [BDM98].

Here is a brief list of key references for the other pre/post notations that we looked at in Section 3.4.6.

Z:　Spivey [Spi92] gives a nice informal introduction to classic Z, which is gradually being superseded by ISO Standard Z [ISO02]. For up-to-date information on Z and Z tools, check the Z website.[11] There has been

---

[11] The Z website is *http://vl.zuser.org*.

quite a bit of research on test generation from Z [CS94, Hie97, Meu97, CMM⁺00, HSS01, Bur02, LPU02, HHS03] but not many available test generation tools.

JML: Good overviews of JML and its tool support can be obtained from [BCC⁺05] and the JML website.[12] One of the tools is JMLUnit, which uses the JML pre/post method specifications to help automate unit testing of the SUT methods. It does this by generating lots of input values for the method, selecting only the combinations of inputs that satisfy the precondition, running the SUT method on those inputs, and then checking that the resulting outputs or exceptions satisfy the postcondition. This can be a good way to produce lots of unit tests, but it does not yet address the problem of generating test sequences that call a series of SUT methods.

Spec#: We discuss Spec# [BLS04] and its associated model-based testing tool, Spec Explorer [CGN⁺05], in more detail in Section 6.5.

SeC: The UniTesk approach is described in several papers [KPB⁺02, KPKB03] and much more documentation of the SeC language and the CTesK tool is available from the UniTesk website.[13]

OCL: The best introduction to OCL is Warmer and Kleppe's book [WK03]. We will use OCL for test generation in Section 7.2 and Chapter 10.

---

[12]The JML website is *http://www.jmlspecs.org*.

[13]The UniTesk website is *http://www.unitesk.com*.

## CHAPTER 4

SELECTING
YOUR TESTS

This chapter gives an overview of the kinds of *test selection criteria* that you can give to a model-based testing tool to control the choice of tests. Your expert knowledge of the system under test (SUT) is the key factor in generating a good suite of tests and achieving the test objectives of your validation project. Test selection criteria are the means of communicating your choice of tests to a model-based testing tool. A good tool will support several kinds of criterion, to give as much control over the generated tests as possible.

It is important to realize that all of the test selection criteria that we discuss in this chapter are related to *models* and *requirements*. Many of them are coverage criteria that measure how well the generated test suite covers the model. None of them rely on the source code of the SUT or on coverage measurements made on the SUT. This means that it is possible to use any of the test selection criteria in this chapter whenever you want. For example, you can choose some test selection criteria and start generating tests in January, even though the development team will start coding in February and is not expected to finish until June.

> **Key Point**   Test selection criteria help you to *design* your black-box test suites. They do not depend on the SUT code.

Of course, by the time the developers finish coding (probably in August!), you will have generated a comprehensive set of black-box tests and will be able to thoroughly test the new SUT code. As you execute the test suites, we recommend that you record the *code coverage statistics* of the SUT code, such as statement coverage or branch coverage, because these statistics give an independent measurement of how well the SUT has been tested and how comprehensive your test suites are.

> **Key Point**   Model coverage criteria and SUT code coverage criteria are complementary, so use both.

In fact, many of test selection criteria for models have actually been stolen (adopted) from the well-researched field of code coverage (white-box coverage criteria). So we will see terms like *statement coverage* and *MC/DC* that may be familiar to you from the world of white-box testing, but in this chapter they refer to how well the statements or branches of the *model* have been covered, rather than to the coverage of the SUT code.

In white-box testing, we use coverage criteria for two main purposes:

Measuring the adequacy of a test suite: After a new recruit has designed a test suite for a module, the test manager might ask to see the statement coverage of the test run as an indicator of the quality of the test suite. If the statement coverage is only 40 percent (meaning that 60 percent of the SUT statements were never executed by the test suite), then the manager is likely to say that the test suite is not adequate and more tests must be designed.

Deciding when to stop testing: After the above incident, the manager might introduce the guideline that testing must continue until the statement coverage (or branch coverage, or some other coverage metric) reaches 80 percent. This is an example of using that coverage criteria as a *stopping condition*.

We can apply these two ideas to models as well. We might use a certain algorithm (for example, random generation) to generate a test suite and then apply one or more model coverage criteria to the test suite to measure the adequacy of the test suite. Or we can choose a criterion and use it as a stopping condition by saying that the test generator should continue generating tests until the test suite achieves 90 percent "transition-pair" coverage (or one of the other criteria in this chapter).

But we can also use a coverage criterion in a *prescriptive* fashion, as a command to the model-based test tool. For example, "Try to achieve all-transitions coverage." This means that it will try to generate a test suite that traverses all of the transitions of our FSM or UML state machine model. Our choice of coverage criteria determines the algorithms that the tool uses to generate tests, how large a test suite it generates, how long it takes to generate them, and which parts of the model are tested. This is why we call them *test selection criteria*—because we are using the coverage criteria in a prescriptive way to control the design of our test suites.

We should not lift our expectations too high, however. The model-based testing tool may not be able to achieve 100 percent coverage of the criterion that we request. For example, we might use *all-states coverage* to drive test generation on a UML state machine, but if some states of that machine are unreachable, the test generator will obviously not be able to generate tests for those states. Another possibility is that the automated test generator may not be powerful enough to find a path to a particular state, even though that state is a reachable state (this can happen when the state machine contains data variables and complex guards and actions). In both cases, the test generation tool can provide metrics on how well the generated test suite satisfies the requested coverage criterion and which parts of the model were not covered, so that we can investigate why. This issue of "getting less than we asked for" applies to most of the criteria in this chapter.

Here is an overview of the families of test selection criteria covered in this chapter:

Structural model coverage criteria (4.1): These deal with coverage of the control-flow through the model, based on ideas from control-flow through programs. Some of the structural coverage criteria that we describe are specific to certain styles of model.

Data coverage criteria (4.2): These deal with coverage of the input data space of an operation or transition in the model.

Fault-model criteria (4.3): These criteria generate test suites that are good at detecting certain kinds of fault in the model. Assuming that the SUT has similar kinds of faults, then the test suite is likely to detect those faults.

Requirements-based criteria (4.4): These aim to generate a test suite that ensures that all the informal requirements are tested. Traceability of requirements to the model can make it possible to automate this process.

Explicit test case specifications (4.5): These allow a validation engineer to explicitly say that a certain test, or set of tests, should be generated from the model. Various test specification languages have been defined for model-based testing, and these can be an expressive way of controlling test generation.

Statistical test generation methods (4.6): Random generation is an easy way to generate tests that explore a wide range of system behaviors.

This large set of possible test selection criteria gives the validation engineers control over the test generation process. Currently, there are no tools that implement all of these methods, but each model-based testing tool offers a subset of these test selection criteria, depending on their approach to test generation.

In Section 4.7, we look at three business cases that illustrate how different test selection criteria can be *combined* to meet the validation goals of some realistic projects.

4.1   STRUCTURAL MODEL COVERAGE

One major issue in model-based testing is to be able to measure and maximize coverage of the model. The intention is not to guarantee test coverage of the SUT—its structure may be quite different from that of the model. Rather, the formal model represents the high-level test objectives: it expresses the aspects of the system behavior that the engineer wants to test. So, covering all parts of those behaviors is important.

Some families of structural model coverage criteria originate from code-based coverage criteria, which consider the control-flow and the data-flow of a program. Other families of structural model coverage criteria are derived from the key concepts of the modeling paradigms used for model-based testing. For example, transition-based notations have given rise to a family of coverage criteria that includes *all-states*, *all-transitions*, and *all-transition-pairs*. Pre/post notations directly lead to predicate coverage of decisions in the model.

The rest of this section introduces the following families of structural model coverage criteria:

- Control-flow-oriented coverage criteria (4.1.1)
- Data-flow-oriented coverage criteria (4.1.2)
- Transition-based coverage criteria (4.1.3)
- UML-based coverage criteria (4.1.4)

For each family, we define the main criteria and discuss their usability for model-based testing.

4.1.1 Control-Flow-Oriented Coverage Criteria

Control-flow coverage criteria for models are derived from the classical coverage criteria for code, which are based on the statements, decisions (or branches), loops, and paths in source code.

In modeling notations such as UML/OCL postconditions or B abstract machines, the same concepts of statements, decisions, and paths arise. However, there are no loops.[1] For example, consider the following OCL operation, which specifies the behavior of the verify_pin operation of the Smartcard class introduced in Section 1.3:

```
context  SmartCard::verifyPin(p:PIN_CODES):MESSAGES
 post:
    if pinTry = 0 then
        result = MESSAGES::NO_MORE_TRIES
    else
        if (p=pin or statusPin=PINSTATUS::DISABLE) then
            result = MESSAGES::SUCCESS
        else
            result = MESSAGES::ERROR
        endif
    endif
```

In this OCL expression, we can see decisions such as pinTry=0, statements such as result=MESSAGES::SUCCESS, and control-flow paths that arise from the structure of the nested if-then-else expressions.

Many of the traditional code-based coverage criteria are focused on ensuring good coverage of loop constructs. With no loops or jumps in pre/post notations, criteria such as *linear code sequence and jump (LCSAJ)* [ZHM97],

---

[1] Because loops are considered a lower-level implementation technique, they are not allowed in those high-level modeling notations.

for example, are not relevant. The following are most relevant coverage criteria.

Statement coverage (SC): The test suite must execute every reachable statement.

Decision coverage (DC): The test suite must ensure that each reachable *decision* is made true by some tests and false by other tests. *Decisions* are the branch criteria that modify the flow of control in selection and iteration statements, and so on. For a test suite to satisfy decision coverage, we also require it to satisfy statement coverage (for example, this ensures that straight-line methods with no decisions are executed). (Decision coverage is also called **branch coverage**.)

Path coverage (PC): The test suite must execute every satisfiable path through the control-flow graph.

As noted in the testing literature [Mye79], for code-based coverage, some of these coverage criteria are stronger than others. We say that one coverage criterion C_1 *subsumes* another criterion C_2 (we write this as $C_1 \longrightarrow C_2$) if every test suite that satisfies C_1 also satisfies C_2. In other words, C_1 is a stronger coverage criterion than C_2. Of these three code-based coverage criteria, path coverage is the strongest and statement coverage is the weakest:

$$PC \longrightarrow DC \longrightarrow SC$$

We can apply these code-based coverage criteria to preconditions and postconditions, if we view their if-then-else expressions and disjunctions as defining alternative control paths. The resulting control-flow graphs are much simpler than code-based control-flow graphs, because they do not contain loops or sequencing.[2] In fact, we have shown elsewhere [LPU04] that for the restricted control-flow graphs that are derived from B operations (with if-then-else statements, but no if-then statements), statement coverage and decision coverage are equal.

$$DC = SC$$

Path coverage is generally impossible to achieve in code-based testing because the presence of loops usually gives an infinite number of paths. However, in the pre/post-oriented modeling notations there is a finite set

---

[2]There is no sequencing because a postcondition defines a single state change. This is simpler than a sequence of statements in an imperative language like C, which defines a series of state changes.

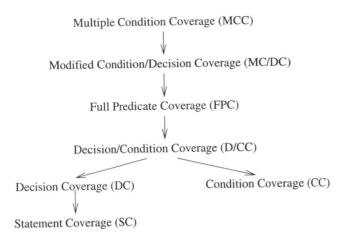

FIGURE 4.1   The hierarchy of control-flow coverage criteria for multiple conditions. $A \rightarrow B$ means that criterion A is stronger than (subsumes) criterion B.

of paths for each operation that corresponds exactly to the set of satisfiable combinations of decisions in the control-flow graph. This means that if all combinations of decision outcomes are tested, path coverage is obtained.

The testing of a decision depends on the structure of that decision in terms of conditions. Note the terminology: a *decision* contains one or more primitive *conditions*, combined by *and*, *or*, and *not* operators. For example, in the second decision of the verify_pin operation,

```
p = pin or statusPin = PINSTATUS::DISABLE
```

you might want to have just one test for that decision or two tests that exercise each condition (one for condition p=pin and one for statusPin = PINSTATUS::DISABLE) or three tests that cover the three mutually exclusive cases:

```
p = pin  and statusPin <> PINSTATUS::DISABLE
p <> pin and statusPin = PINSTATUS::DISABLE
p = pin  and statusPin = PINSTATUS::DISABLE
```

Figure 4.1 shows the *subsumes* relationships among the most common structural coverage criteria for complex decisions. These can all be used in model-based testing to control test generation.

Condition coverage (CC): A test set achieves CC when each condition in the program is tested with a true result and also with a false result. For a decision containing N conditions, two tests can be sufficient to achieve CC (one test with all conditions true, one with them all false), but dependencies between the conditions typically require several more tests.

Decision/condition coverage (D/CC): A test set achieves D/CC when it achieves both decision coverage (DC) and CC.

Full predicate coverage (FPC): A test set achieves FPC when each condition in the program is forced to true and to false in a scenario where that condition is *directly correlated* with the outcome of the decision. A condition c is directly correlated with its decision d when either $d \Leftrightarrow c$ holds or $d \Leftrightarrow not(c)$ holds [OXL99]. For a decision containing N conditions, a maximum of $2N$ tests are required to achieve FPC.

Modified condition/decision coverage (MC/DC): This strengthens the *directly correlated* requirement of FPC by requiring the condition c to *independently affect* the outcome of the decision d. A condition is shown to independently affect a decision's outcome by varying just that condition while holding fixed all other possible conditions [RTC92]. For a decision containing N conditions, a maximum of $2N$ tests are required to achieve MC/DC (the same upper bound as FPC), so the number of tests is proportional to the complexity of the decision (the number of conditions within it).

Multiple condition coverage (MCC): A test set achieves MCC if it exercises all possible combinations of condition outcomes in each decision. This requires up to 2^N tests for a decision with N conditions so is practical only for simple decisions (for example, those that contain fewer than 5 conditions).

Notice that these decision-oriented coverage criteria are usable any place you have decisions in a model. This is naturally the case for OCL postconditions and the preconditions or postconditions of a pre/post model, and also for the guards on transitions of UML state machines. Therefore, this family of coverage criteria is often combined with other criteria such as transition-based coverage criteria and data-oriented coverage criteria.

4.1.2 Data-Flow-Oriented Coverage Criteria

Control-flow graphs can be annotated with extra information regarding the *definition* and *use* of data variables. These are data-flow graphs, and the corresponding testing techniques are called data-flow testing. Data-flow criteria attempt to cover all definition-use paths, all definitions, or all uses, among others.

FIGURE 4.2   The hierarchy of data-flow criteria. $A \to B$ means that criterion A is stronger than (subsumes) criterion B.

Informally, a definition of a variable is a write to the variable, and a use of a variable is a read from it. More precisely, a *definition* of a variable is a statement that sets the value of the variable, and a *use* of that definition is an expression or predicate that uses the value set by the definition. For a given variable v, we say that (d_v, u_v) is a a *def-use pair* if d_v is a definition of v, u_v is a use of v, and there is a path from d to u that is free of other definitions of v (this ensures that the value of v set by d_v is not overwritten before it is used by u_v). We say that a def-use pair (d_v, u_v) is *feasible* if there exist some test inputs that cause d_v and then u_v to be executed; otherwise, it is *infeasible*.

All-defs: The *all-definitions* criterion requires a test suite to test at least one def-use pair (d_v, u_v) for every definition d_v, that is, at least one path from each definition to one of its feasible uses.

All-uses: The *all-uses* criterion requires a test suite to test all def-use pairs (d_v, u_v). This means testing all feasible uses of all definitions.

All-def-use-paths: The *all-def-use-paths* criterion requires a test suite to test all def-use pairs (d_v, u_v) and to test all paths from d_v to u_v. This is the strongest data-flow criterion and usually requires unrealistically many test cases.

We define these criteria to be trivially true for a definition that is not reachable or that has no feasible uses (for example, its value is overwritten before it is used). The hierarchy of data-flow criteria is shown in Figure 4.2.

4.1.3 Transition-Based Coverage Criteria

Many structural coverage criteria have been developed for transition-based modeling notations such as finite state machines (FSM), extended finite

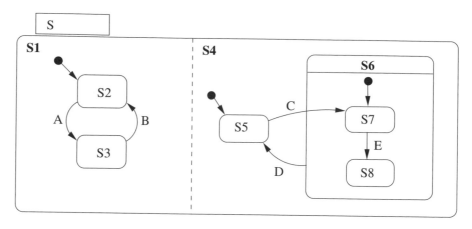

FIGURE 4.3   An example of a statechart.

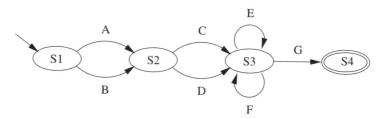

FIGURE 4.4   An example of a finite state machine.

state machines (EFSM), labeled transition systems (LTS) [Kel76], and state-charts [Har87] (for example, UML state machines).

In this section, we introduce the most common transition-based cover-age criteria used in model-based testing. First, we review the terminology for transition-based models and define the idea of *configuration*.

Transition-based models are made up of *states* and *transitions*. In some notations, like statecharts, the states may be nested so that one *superstate* contains several *substates*. For example, state S6 in Figure 4.3 has substates S7 and S8. A *transition* is a directed arc from one state to another. It is called a *self-transition* if its source state and destination state are the same state (e.g., transition F in Figure 4.4). Depending on which notation is used, a transition will be labeled with various kinds of information, such as inputs, outputs, events, guards, and/or actions.

Some notations, such as LTS and statecharts, allow these transition-based models to be put together in *parallel* (e.g., S1 and S4 in Figure 4.3). If we take a snapshot of such a parallel system during its execution, we will typi-cally find that it has two or more active states, one for each parallel part of the system. Each of these snapshots is called a *configuration*. More precisely, Harel and Naamad define a configuration to be the largest set of states that a system can be in simultaneously [HN96]. For example, if the statechart S in Figure 4.3 was in substate S2 of state S1 and substate S5 within state S4, then its configuration would be the set of states {S, S1, S2, S4, S5}. If the C transition was taken from this configuration while S2 stayed unchanged, the new configuration would be {S, S1, S2, S4, S6, S7}. Note that the super-state S has six possible configurations in total because it contains two parallel substates (S1 and S4), where S1 has two configurations and S4 has three configurations, and $2 \times 3 = 6$. The concept of configuration is a refinement of the concept of state that allows us to express the current state of a parallel statechart.

Note that when the following coverage criteria are applied to systems with state variables and guards on the transitions (e.g., EFSMs, LTSs, and statecharts), then it is usual to restrict the definitions to the *reachable* paths through the system, or the reachable configurations, so that impossible paths are ignored and do not distort our coverage measurements.

All-states coverage: Every state of the model is visited at least once.

For example, the single test A;C;G would be sufficient to give all-states coverage of the FSM in Figure 4.4. Similarly, the single test A;C;E gives all-states coverage of the statechart in Figure 4.3, because it starts in states S2 and S5, then the A transition visits S3, and the C and E transitions visit S7 and S8. This covers all the atomic states, which means that the superstates are covered too.

All-configurations coverage: Every configuration of a statechart is visited at least once. For systems that contain no parallelism, this coverage criterion is the same as all-states coverage.

For the statechart in Figure 4.3, it is necessary to visit all six of its configurations. This could be achieved by two tests C;E and A;C;E, or by a single test C;E;A;D;C.

All-transitions coverage: Every transition of the model must be traversed at least once.

For the example FSM in Figure 4.4, all-transitions coverage can be achieved with two tests, such as A;C;E;F;G and B;D (or B;D;G if one wants all tests to finish at the final state).

For the statechart in Figure 4.3, all-transitions coverage is more interesting because the transition D shown in the statechart is actually an abbreviation for two separate transitions: one from S7 to S5 and the other from S8 to S5. There seems to be no general agreement whether the term *all-transitions* should mean that just the explicit transition has been tested or that all the transitions that it expands to must be tested.

For example, the ACUTE-J tool [NML06] takes the explicit-only interpretation and would generate just one test for transition D, whereas Binder [Bin99, 221] says that "such a test suite could not be considered adequate." In Section 7.2 we compare these two interpretations on the UML state machine for an eTheater system.

In general, we recommend taking the stricter meaning of "all-transitions" for statecharts, so that transitions like transition D must be expanded into all their implicit transitions and all these implicit transitions must be tested. This means that compound states are tested more thoroughly, but a larger test suite is needed to achieve all-transitions coverage. Note that the same ambiguity applies to most of the following transition-based coverage criteria for statecharts, so when using one of these criteria with a given tool, it is wise to check which interpretation it uses.

All-transition-pairs coverage: Every pair of adjacent transitions in the FSM or statechart model must be traversed at least once.

For example, to obtain all-transition-pairs coverage at state S2 of Figure 4.4, it is necessary to test four pairs of transitions: A;C, A;D, B;C, and B;D. State S3 has two incoming transitions and three outgoing transitions, so it is necessary to test all $2 \times 3 = 6$ pairs of transitions.

All-loop-free-paths coverage: Every loop-free path must be traversed at least once. A path is *loop-free* if it does not contain repetitions of any configuration.

For the FSM example in Figure 4.4, this requires just the four paths: A;C;G, A;D;G, B;C;G, and B;D;G. Note that this does not test the E (or F) transition at all because any test that contains E will contain a loop. This shows that all loop-free paths coverage does not always cover all transitions. Similarly, if we added an extra state in the middle of the E transition, this state would not be tested by an all loop-free paths test suite, so all loop-free paths does not always cover all states either.

All-one-loop-paths coverage: Every path containing at most two repetitions of one (and only one) configuration must be traversed at least once. In other words, this requires all the loop-free paths through the model to be visited, plus all the paths that loop once.

For the FSM example in Figure 4.4, an all-one-loop-paths test suite would include the four paths of the all-loop-free-paths coverage criterion (A;C;G, A;D;G, B;C;G, and B;D;G), plus the combination of each of these with a single loop around either the E or the F transition, giving $3 \times 4 = 12$ tests in total.

All-round-trips coverage: This coverage criterion, which is recommended by Binder [Bin99], is similar to the all-one-loop-paths criterion because it requires a test for each loop in the model, and that test only has to do one iteration around the loop. But it is weaker than all-one-loop-paths because it does not require *all* the paths that precede or follow a loop to be tested—it is sufficient to achieve transition coverage on nonlooping parts of the model. This makes this criterion much more practical because it can be satisfied with a linear number of tests, whereas the various all-...-paths criteria may require an exponential number of tests if the model contains many alternative branches. Binder also gives detailed algorithms for constructing all round-trip paths from a given statechart. A case study by Antoniol and colleagues [ABPL02] applied this strategy to UML state machines and found that it detected 87 percent of faults, whereas random test suites of similar size detected only 69 percent.

For the FSM example in Figure 4.4, the all-round-trips test suite generated by Binder's algorithm (using breadth-first traversal) is A;C;E, A;C;F, A;C;G, A;D, and B. This covers each loop once and also covers all transitions in this example, but the test suite is much smaller than an all-one-loop-paths test suite.

All-paths coverage: Every path must be traversed at least once. The all-paths criterion corresponds to exhaustive testing of the control structure of the FSM or statechart model. In practice, this is usually not practical because such models typically contain an infinite number of paths, due to loops.

For the FSM example in Figure 4.4, the all-paths coverage criterion requires the same four paths as the all-loop-free-paths coverage criterion (A;C;G, A;D;G, B;C;G, and B;D;G), but each of those paths can be extended with *any number* of E and F transitions. This requires an infinite test suite that contains tests like A;C;G, A;C;E;G, A;C;E;E;G, A;C;E;E;E;G, and so on.

The hierarchy of transition-based criteria is shown in Figure 4.5. Note that the all-loop-free-paths, all-one-loop-paths, and all-round-trips coverage criteria can be rather inadequate by themselves, because they do not guarantee that all states, let alone all transitions, are covered. To take an extreme example, consider a statechart model in which the first thing we have to do is loop around a self-transition a few times until a counter reaches a particular value, which then enables a transition that leads to the rest of the

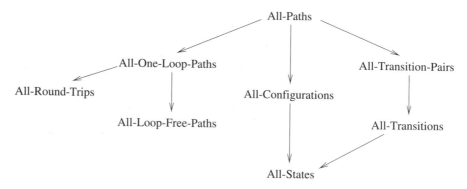

FIGURE 4.5   The hierarchy of transition-based criteria. $A \to B$ means that criterion A is stronger than (subsumes) criterion B.

statechart. For this example, the all-loop-free-paths criterion can be satisfied with an empty test suite, the all-round-trips criterion can be satisfied with just a single test (one loop around the self-transition), and Binder's algorithm for generating an all-round-trips test suite would generate tests that contained unsatisfiable guards, and so could not be executed. This shows that these coverage criteria should be combined with other criteria, such as all-states or all-transitions, to ensure that the whole statechart has been covered. As we discuss in Chapter 5, we recommend that all test suites generated from transition-based models satisfy all-transitions coverage as a minimum measure of quality.

4.1.4 UML-Based Coverage Criteria

The UML notation puts together more than a dozen kinds of diagrams used to describe either the structure or the behavior of an application. The criteria that have already been introduced in this chapter (control-flow, data-flow, and transition-based) are directly usable as test selection criteria for a UML model. For example, decision coverage criteria (DC, C/DC, MC/DC, etc.) can be used to drive test generation from OCL decisions, and transition-based coverage criteria can be used on UML state machines.

In this section, we introduce several coverage criteria that are not discussed in the previous sections. We consider coverage criteria based on two kinds of UML diagram:

- Class and object diagrams
- Sequence diagrams

We discuss these two kinds of diagram because they are often used for model-based testing, in conjunction with state machines and activity diagrams. Control-flow and transition-based coverage criteria are useful for state machines and activity diagrams, but class, object, and sequence diagrams require dedicated criteria.

CLASS DIAGRAM COVERAGE CRITERIA

Class diagram coverage criteria have been proposed for testing the UML model itself [AFGC03], but they can also be used for model-based testing of an SUT from the UML model.

Association-end multiplicity (AEM) coverage: An *association-end multiplicity* specifies how many instances of a class at the opposite end of the association link can be associated with a single instance of a class at the association end. This criterion requires that each representative multiplicity pair has to be created in the test suite. For example, if a class A has an association to another class B, with multiplicity $1..1$ at the A end and $0..4$ at the B end, AEM coverage with a default partitioning strategy would partition the B multiplicity into the three equivalance classes $\{0\}$, $1..3$ and $\{4\}$ and then choose one multiplicity from each of these equivalence classes, such as 0, 1, and 4. The same is done for the A multiplicity (one instance of A is the only possibility in this example), and then all pairs of the A and B multiplicities are tested: $(1, 0)$, $(1, 1)$, $(1, 4)$.

Generalization (GN) coverage: This criterion requires that for every specialization defined in a generalization relationship, an instance of that specialization be created by the test suite. For example, this requires testing every subclass of a given superclass.

Class attribute (CA) coverage: This criterion requires coverage of a set of attribute value combinations for each class in the class diagram. This is actually a metalevel coverage criterion because one must use other data coverage criteria to choose test values for each attribute and then test all combinations of those values that satisfy the class invariant.

The class diagram attribute coverage criteria are directly connected to the data coverage criteria that are presented in Section 4.2.

SEQUENCE DIAGRAM COVERAGE CRITERIA

A sequence diagram describes some object interactions arranged into a time sequence. A sequence diagram is often used to represent a set of possible scenarios.

All-paths sequence diagram coverage: This criterion requires that all *start-to-end message paths* of the sequence diagram be covered in the test suite.

A *start-to-end message path* in a sequence diagram is a sequence of messages that starts from an externally generated event and ends with the response message. Testing all start-to-end message sequences corresponds to covering all the scenarios in the sequence diagram. This is often realistic because a sequence diagram typically records just the interactions that correspond to a single use case.

4.2   DATA COVERAGE CRITERIA

Data coverage criteria are useful for choosing a few good data values to use as test inputs when there is a huge number of possible input values.

Let's consider the subpart of a UML state machine given in Figure 4.6. This state machine describes the behavior of a front wiper controller embedded in a car. In automatic mode, the transition that changes the front wiper engine from low speed to high speed depends on the speed of the car and the intensity of the rain. Testing all the possible data values is not realistic; in this case, even if you consider car_speed and rain_level to be integers, the total number of combinations will be $250 \times 5 = 1250$ test cases, just to test that one transition. You need to make a choice on the basis of *data coverage criteria*.

For a single variable whose values can range over a domain D, you could choose two extreme data coverage criteria:

One-value: This criterion simply requires the test suite to test at least one value from the domain D. Testing one value is so simplistic that it might seem useless, but in combination with other test selection criteria it can be useful because it helps to minimize the number of tests.

All-values: This criterion requires the test suite to test every value in the domain D. This is unlikely to be practical if D is large (e.g., $0..999999$), but when D is small, such as an enumerated type, it can be useful to test all possibilities.

Of course, we most often want to use a test selection criterion that lies somewhere between these two extremes, so that we get more than one test, but not too many. We often have many input variables rather than just one, and this quickly leads to a combinatorial explosion if we just naively test all

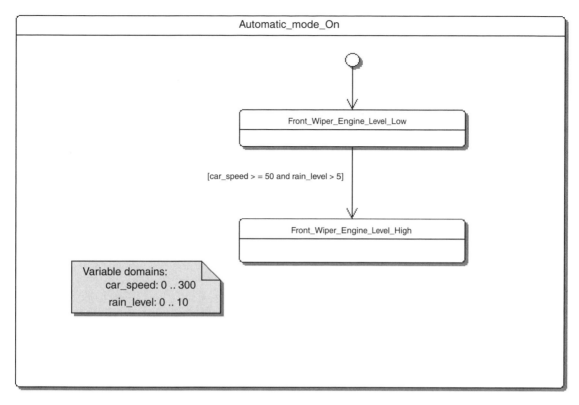

FIGURE 4.6   Extract of a state machine specifying an automobile's front-wiper controller.

the combinations of values. So in the remainder of this section, we explore three families of data coverage criteria that can be applied either to a single variable to produce a reasonable number of tests or to a collection of variables with the aim of combining their possible values in more intelligent ways. The three widely used families of data coverage criteria that we study are *boundary values*, *statistical data coverage*, and *pairwise testing*.

The following subsections explore these families of data coverage criteria in more detail and give examples of how they can be used to control test generation.

4.2.1 Boundary Value Testing

The intuitive idea of *boundary value testing* is to choose test input values at the boundaries of the input domains. The rationale for boundary testing is straightforward: lots of faults in the SUT are located at the frontier between two functional behaviors.

This approach clearly works for ordered domains such as numbers (integers, reals), but we can also apply it to structured domains if we define a suitable[3] ordering over those domains (e.g., ordering strings lexicographically or ordering sets of elements by the size of those sets).

When you consider a single variable, such as car_speed in Figure 4.6, boundaries correspond to the minimum and maximum of the variable domain—that is, 50 and 300 for the low to high transition. We can also combine the various boundaries (min and max) of several variables to compute our test data. For this example, this will give us four tests:

$$[\,\texttt{car\_speed} = 50,\ \texttt{rain\_level} = 6\,]$$

$$[\,\texttt{car\_speed} = 50,\ \texttt{rain\_level} = 10\,]$$

$$[\,\texttt{car\_speed} = 300,\ \texttt{rain\_level} = 6\,]$$

$$[\,\texttt{car\_speed} = 300,\ \texttt{rain\_level} = 10\,]$$

More generally, when we consider several variables, with some predicates that constrain the values of those variables, the boundaries correspond to the *frontier* of the shape that satisfies those predicates. For example, consider the region that satisfies the following conditions, where x and y are integers:

$$\left(x^2 + y^2 \leq 25\right) \ \& \ (0 \leq y) \ \& \ (x + y \leq 5).$$

Such a predicate could be a guard of a transition in a state-transition model or the decision of an IF...THEN...ELSE predicate within a pre/post model. Figure 4.7 shows the 22 boundary points of this region.[4]

All boundaries corresponds to all the points located at the frontier of some given region. The number of boundaries can be very high, so often we are more interested in a subset of all boundaries. This is the role of boundary-value-oriented coverage criteria—to give us a way to select which boundaries we are interested in. Here we introduce some boundary-oriented coverage criteria that can be useful for model-based testing:

All-boundaries coverage: For each predicate to which it is applied, the *all-boundaries* criterion requires a test case for every boundary point that

---

[3]We can use any total ordering. Recall that a *total ordering* is any ordering relation $\leq$ that returns true or false for any two elements. That is, the order of two elements is never undefined or unknown.

[4]Technically, we define an integer *boundary point* to be any point (x, y) *inside* the region, such that $(x \pm 1, y)$ or $(x, y \pm 1)$ is a point *outside* the region. This definition can easily be generalized to N dimensions [KLPU04]. It is also possible to define boundaries over continuous domains.

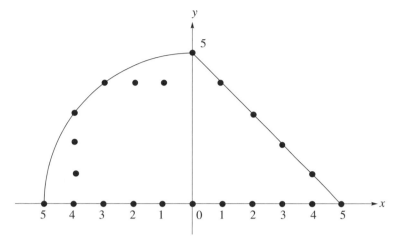

FIGURE 4.7   Example of the integer boundary points of a shape.

satisfies the predicate. This is often not practical because a given predicate may have too many boundary points, particularly if it involves many variables.

Multidimensional-boundaries coverage: A test suite satisfies the *multidimensional-boundaries* criterion on a given predicate if every variable is assigned its minimum value (that is, the minimum value for that variable that satisfies the predicate) in at least one test of the test suite and similarly for its maximum value. This coverage criterion requires at most two tests per variable, so the number of tests is linear in the number of variables. Intuitively, this criterion ensures that the bounding box of the shape has been tested.

For the example in Figure 4.7, multidimensional-boundaries coverage would require us to test the two points $(5, 0)$ and $(-5, 0)$ for the x-dimension maximum and minimum, and $(0, 5)$ and any of the points with $y = 0$ for the y-dimension maximum and minimum. So three or four tests would suffice, rather than the 22 tests required to satisfy all-boundaries coverage.

All-edges coverage: It is often possible to view the input region as an N-dimensional shape, with a predicate defining each edge of the shape. For the example region in Figure 4.7, we have a two-dimensional shape, with three edge predicates ($x^2 + y^2 \leq 25$, $0 \leq y$ and $x + y \leq 5$). The goal of all-edges coverage is that all of these edges should be tested. The most basic form of all-edges coverage is that at least one point on each edge must be tested. For our example, this is easily satisfied with the two points $(5, 0)$ and $(0, 5)$.

Note that several stronger kinds of edge coverage have been defined in the literature [WC80, Bei90, Bei95, Bin99]. For example, the *domain strategy* of White and Cohen [WC80] is designed for continuous domains (real-valued variables) and for *linear* edge predicates ($x + y \leq 5$ is linear, but $x^2 + y^2 \leq 25$ is not). It requires tests for two points *on* each edge (usually near the ends of that edge), plus one point that lies a small distance ϵ just *off* the edge, outside the domain being tested. For an input domain with N variables and E edges, they show that a maximum of $N \times (E + 3)$ tests is required. Similar domain testing techniques are discussed in more detail by Beizer [Bei90, Bei95] and Binder [Bin99, Section 10.2.4]. We do not focus further on these domain-testing strategies in this book because most of our examples use discrete inputs rather than continuous inputs.

One-boundary coverage: For each predicate to which it is applied, this criterion requires a test case for at least one boundary point of the predicate. This criterion requires only one test.

Figure 4.8 shows the hierarchy of boundary-oriented coverage criteria.

We can further refine each of these criteria by limiting them to just the minimum boundaries or the maximum boundaries. For example, we could refine the multidimensional-boundaries criterion to *multidimensional-max-boundaries*, which means that we are interested only in the *maximum* value of each variable, rather than the maximum and minimum.

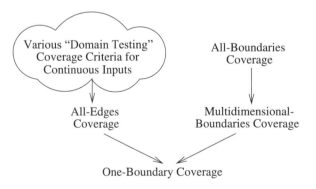

FIGURE 4.8   The hierarchy of boundary-oriented criteria. $A \rightarrow B$ means that criterion A is stronger than criterion B.

It is also possible to refine the all-boundaries criterion to *all-max-boundaries*, which means that we are interested only in those boundary points that maximize some global ordering function over all the variables. We can choose this global ordering function to reflect the properties of our application domain. For example, we might choose simply to sum all the variables, which means that for the example in Figure 4.7 we would want to maximize (or minimize) the value of $x + y$. With this choice of ordering function, there are six maximal boundaries $((0, 5), (1, 4), (2, 3), (3, 2), (4, 1), (5, 0))$, but only one minimal boundary $((-5, 0))$.

The same idea can be applied to the one-boundary criterion—to get more precise tests, we could refine it to one-max-boundary (or one-min-boundary), to specify which boundary we are interested in.

4.2.2 Statistical Data Coverage

In the area of choosing test input values, Duran and Ntafos [DN84] observed in 1984 that random testing is as good at finding faults as partition testing, unless some data partitions are known in advance to have a higher probability of errors. This led to a flurry of controversy and research about the merits of random testing versus partition-based testing [CY96, Nta01]. Some of the conclusions were that choosing random test inputs is a surprisingly good strategy for detecting errors and that random testing can be more cost-effective than partition strategies because random selection is usually a little easier to implement.

The following coverage criterion checks that a test suite uses a given statistical distribution for a given data variable v (e.g., uniform distribution; normal (gaussian) distribution, or poisson distribution):

Random-value coverage (with distribution D): This criterion requires the
   values of a given data variable v in the test suite to follow the statistical
   distribution D.

When we use a uniform distribution, we often omit the phrase "with distribution D" and just say "random-value coverage."

We illustrate this random-value coverage with some simple examples. Consider the guard on the transition in Figure 4.6.

```
car_speed >= 50 and rain_level > 5
and car_speed : 0 .. 300 and rain_level : 0..10
```

Using boundary testing we obtained four tests: all combinations of the boundary values of car_speed (50 and 300) and the boundary values of rain_level (6 and 10). But what if we want 100 tests of this transition? (It may be necessary to traverse this transition 100 times in order to get the desired level of coverage of the rest of the state machine.) Rather than reuse our four boundary values every time, it might be preferable to choose some additional test values for car_speed and rain_level. In situations like this, random choice is a good way to generate the desired number of values. For example, we might use a uniform distribution to choose values for the rain_level variable and a normal distribution (with mean 65 and standard deviation 20) to choose car_speed values.

Random-value coverage can also be useful for *unordered* domains, such as an enumerated domain of possible car colors:

```
car_colors : {Red, White, Gray, Black, Blue, Silver, ..., Other}
```

It is not useful to choose test data using boundary analysis here because all colors are equally ranked. However, we can use random-value coverage to choose a given number of values from this domain. For example, we might decide that all car color values are not equally likely, so we use an operational distribution profile[5] such as silver, 24.1%; black, 16.7%; blue, 12.7%; white, 11.8%; gray, 10.5%; red, 10.3%.

The nice thing about random generation of test values is that we can generate any number of values that we want. So given a variable $v : T$, we can choose an appropriate probability distribution for the values in the domain T and then do either of the following.

1. Generate a smaller number of test values than the size of T because we want to generate a small test suite.
2. Generate a larger number of test values than the size of T, perhaps because we want to do online testing all night, so we need an infinite sequence of tests.

4.2.3 Pairwise Testing

Pairwise testing is based on the assumption that most defects are created as a result of no more than two test parameters (test values) being in a certain combination. Let's look at a typical example: we are testing a system with three major parameters: OS, Web browser, and network.

---

[5]These are the actual top six car colors for 2005 in the United States. See *http://www.bankrate.com/brm/news/auto/20050119a1.asp*.

- OS domain: {Windows XP, Windows Vista, Linux}
- Web browser domain: {Firefox, IE7, Opera}
- Network domain: {IP, WiFi, VPN}

Under exhaustive testing, this would require $3 \times 3 \times 3 = 27$ tests. Using pairwise testing, we must follow the rule that each pair of parameters must be tested all ways—the pairs being OS & Web Browser, or OS & Network, and Web browser & Network.

Following the rule that all pairs of values must be tested, the pairwise test generation algorithms try to minimize the number of tests. On our example, the pairwise approach gives 9 test cases instead of 27. (You might want to calculate them yourself.)

The difference between pairwise testing and exhaustive testing becomes more pronounced as the number of variables and the sizes of the domains increase. For example, if we have 10 variables, each with 5 possible values, then testing all combinations would require $5^{10} = 9,765,625$ tests; pairwise testing can be satisfied with just 44 tests!

This pairwise approach (also called *all-pairs*) can be generalized to N-wise coverage—for example, all-triples or all-quadruples. This gives a family of combinatorial criteria:

Pairwise coverage: This criterion requires a test case for each possible combination of values of all pairs of parameters.

N-wise coverage: This criterion requires a test case for every possible combination of values of all combinations of N parameters. The number of tests grows rapidly as N increases, so all-triples can be practical with small domains, but all-quadruples and higher are usually not practical.

All-combinations coverage: This criterion requires a test case for each possible combination of values of all the parameters. This is usually not practical because it leads to a combinatorial explosion, which requires an exponential number of tests. This criterion is equivalent to applying the all-values criterion to all parameters.

Notice that in the case of two parameters, these three criteria give the same results (with $N = 2$ for the second criterion).

4.3   FAULT-BASED CRITERIA

The goal of software testing is obviously to detect faults in the SUT. *Fault-based testing* is defined as software testing techniques that use test data designed to demonstrate the absence of a set of *pre-specified faults*—typically, frequently occurring faults. This concept is generally based on specific fault models that are used to specify test data.

Since the mid-1970s, there have been several proposals of fault-based approaches for code-based testing [Mor90, DO91], mostly based on syntactic errors (e.g., errors in the use of relational or arithmetic operators, incorrect variable references, etc.). A popular instantiation of this concept is *mutation testing*, where program mutants are created by applying *mutation operators* that encode particular fault models. A program *mutant* results from a syntactic transformation of the program under test by applying a single mutation operator. For example, you can consider a mutation operator that changes arithmetic operators so that $+$ is transformed into $-$. By applying a few dozen mutation operators to a small program, it is easy to generate several hundred mutants of that program. If we execute a given test suite on all of these mutants, we can measure the percentage of mutants that are *killed* by the test suite (that is, at least one test exposes a fault in the mutant). This percentage gives us a measure of the *fault-finding power* of the test suite.

Another use of mutation operators is to guide the *design* of tests. For each mutant of the original program, we can design a test that distinguishes that mutant from the original program. The resulting test suite is therefore able to detect all faults that correspond to the set of mutation operators, which is all faults suggested by the fault model.

In model-based testing, techniques that use *mutations of the behavior models* to guide the test generation process have also been proposed [Sto93, ABM98, Par04]. Mutation operators appropriate for the modeling notation are defined and applied to the model to produce several mutants. A test input or test sequence that distinguishes each mutant from the original model is generated to be used as a test case. This approach also uses syntactic modifications of the model itself to represent some potential errors in the functional behavior of the system.

Fault-based criteria are not restricted to syntactic errors on the model. For example, the work presented by Marisa Sánchez [SAF04] extends the scope of traditional fault-based approaches to semantic errors. This approach characterizes possible behaviors using *fault tree analysis* to determine how an undesirable state (failure state) can occur in the system. Then fault tree analysis results are integrated with the model to act as test selection criteria over a transition-based model. This makes it possible to automatically derive fault-based test cases from the behavior model.

4.4 REQUIREMENTS-BASED CRITERIA

As stated by many authors (see, for example, Ian Sommerville's *Software Engineering* [Som00]), *requirements* is a general word with a wide variety of meanings.

In this book, we consider that a requirement is a *testable statement of some functionality that the product must have*. This is a restrictive definition, and such requirements correspond to detailed functional system requirements.[6] Requirements management is often supported by a dedicated tool, such as DOORS,[7] CALIBER-RM,[8] and SteelTrace[9] that makes it possible to work collaboratively to understand, define, communicate, and manage software requirements throughout the product life cycle.

Ensuring that each requirement will be tested is a key issue in the validation process. The implication is that if the software passes the test, the requirement's functionality is successfully included in the system. Therefore, requirements can be used both to measure a level of coverage for the generated test cases and to drive the test generation itself. Both of these issues relate to a single coverage criterion:

All-requirements coverage: This criterion requires that all requirements are covered in the test suite (also called simply **requirements coverage**).

In the model-based testing process, there are two main ways to achieve requirements coverage:

1. Record the requirements inside the behavior model (as annotations on various parts of the model) so that the test generation process can ensure that all requirements have been tested.
2. Formalize each requirement and then use that formal expression as a test selection criterion to drive the automated generation of one or more tests from the behavior model.

---

[6]There are other categories of requirements, such as user interface requirements, nonfunctional requirements, domain requirements, etc., but we do not need those in this book.

[7]See *http://www.telelogic.com*.

[8]See *http://www.borland.com*.

[9]See *http://www.steeltrace.com*.

The first method is based on the traceability capabilities of the model-based testing tool. In Chapter 6 we describe one technique for annotating the model with requirement identifiers. The requirement identifier is a unique identifier that makes it possible to trace that requirement through the overall test generation process. Requirement identifiers can be automatically extracted from the requirements management tool. For example, requirement identifiers can be attached to transitions of a UML state machine or to predicates within the postconditions of a pre/post model. Once this has been done, the *requirements* ↔ *model* relationship can be used as a coverage criterion to ensure that all the requirements that appear in the model have been tested.

The second method is directly linked to the notion of *explicit test case specifications* presented in the next section. The idea is to transform each high-level requirement into a test case specification that can be used by the automated test generator to produce covering test suites from the behavior model.

4.5   EXPLICIT TEST CASE SPECIFICATIONS

Explicit test case specifications can obviously be used to control test generation. In addition to the model, the validation engineer writes some test case specifications in some formal notation, and these are used to determine which tests will be generated. For example, they may be used to restrict the paths through the model that will be tested, to focus the testing on heavily used cases, or to ensure that particular paths will be tested.

The notation to express test objectives may be the same as the notation used for the model (e.g., STG [CJRZ02] uses extended labeled transition systems for both purposes), or it may be a different notation (e.g., in UML, a behavior model based on class diagrams and state machines, and explicit test case specifications formalized with message sequence chart diagrams). Notations commonly used for test objectives include FSMs, regular expressions, sequence diagrams, temporal logic formulae, constraints, and Markov chains (for expressing intended usage patterns).

The main advantage of explicit test case specifications is that they give extremely precise control over the generated tests. The drawback is that such specifications can be very labor intensive, much more so than choosing some structural model coverage criteria.

As discussed in Section 4.7 about combining test selection criteria, one useful strategy is to start generating tests using simple structural model coverage and data coverage criteria and then use explicit test case specifications to enhance the coverage of areas of the SUT that need more testing.

4.6 STATISTICAL TEST GENERATION METHODS

Section 4.2.2 discusses the use of statistical distributions to choose a given number of data values for input variables. This section discusses using statistical distributions to generate whole test cases—sequences of operation calls.

In model-based testing, statistical test generation is often used to generate test sequences from environment models because it is the environment that determines the usage patterns of the SUT. A typical approach is to use a Markov chain to specify the expected usage profile of the SUT. (A *Markov chain* [WT94] is essentially an FSM with probabilities attached to the transitions.) Test cases can be generated via a random walkthrough of the Markov chain, where the random choice of the next transition is made using the probability distribution of the outgoing transitions. This means that the test cases with greatest probability are likely to be generated first.

In this approach, the usage model is a representation of the system use, not its behavior. The usage model does not provide the expected response of the system; that is, no oracles are generated. With just a usage model, the oracle information has to be provided independently, either manually for each test case or by giving some general oracle criterion such as "no exceptions allowed," or "all output values must be in the range 10..100."

Another approach is to use this kind of statistical usage model (e.g., Markov chains) in *addition* to a behavioral model of the SUT. The statistical model acts as the test selection criterion and chooses the paths through the behavioral model, while the behavioral model is used to generate the oracle information for those paths. This generates a test suite that can perform accurate oracle checking but also follows the expected usage profile of the SUT.

4.7 COMBINING TEST SELECTION CRITERIA

The previous sections of this chapter introduce a large variety of coverage criterion that can be used to configure an automated test generation tool to generate test cases from various kinds of model.

These criteria have different scopes and purposes, but many of them are intended to be used in conjunction with other test selection criteria. That is, to obtain good quality test suites, you should combine different coverage criteria [ABPL02].

In the rest of this section, we review some typical combination schemes of test selection criteria. We take three application examples as business cases of combining test selection criteria to obtain the test suites required by the project validation objectives.

> **Key Point**   Combine test selection criteria to precisely tune the test generation configuration.

Business Case 1: Test a Large Tax Information System

Model-based testing is used to generate tests for various functionalities of the system, such as taxation-file life-cycle and tax computation. The input model is developed using UML with a class diagram; the behavior is modeled with state machines and some OCL specifications. The requirements from the informal specifications have been linked to the model.

The following combination of test selection criteria could be applied to generate a good quality test suite:

1. A basic all-transitions coverage of the state machines, augmented with all-transition-pairs coverage for some important parts (substates) of the state machines.
2. The guards of the transitions in the model, as well as the decisions in the OCL code, are all treated with condition/decision coverage (C/DC).
3. The data inputs for the taxation computation are treated with multidimensional-boundaries coverage, including both maximum and minimum values (this is a critical aspect of the system, and we want to test a larger number of combinations for such critical inputs).
4. The requirements identifiers are used to automatically check if all the requirements have been tested and to complete test generation to obtain full requirements coverage.

Business Case 2: Test a Vehicle Lighting Controller System

Model-based testing is used to generate tests for a car lighting controller system. This is an electronic embedded system that controls all the lighting features (low beam, high beam, fog lamp, automatic mode, etc.). The input model is expressed as a STATEMATE statechart (see Section 3.3.2).

The following combination of test selection criteria could be applied to generate a good quality test suite:

1. All-one-loop-path coverage is applied on the whole statechart.
2. The guards of the transitions in the model are treated with the condition/decision coverage, with some parts (that the validation engineer considers as critical) using modified condition/decision (MC/DC) coverage to give more intensive testing of those complex decisions.
3. The numeric data are generated using a random choice of data, with small intervals.

The car lighting controller is a safety-critical system, and therefore the test selection criteria are chosen to have a large exploration of the functional combinations defined by the model. But notice that this is still not testing all combinations—that would be completely impractical. Even for a safety-critical system, test case generation remains a trade-off that requires engineering expertise and risk analysis.

Business Case 3: Test a Pay Parking Card-Reader System

Model-based testing is used to test a security subsystem of the e-purse software within a pay parking card-reader system, a new generation of card reader that will be used within a wide variety of on-street, off-street, and mass transit ticketing products. These card readers comply with the EMV 2000 (Europay, MasterCard, Visa) standard. A high level of validation testing is necessary for this subsystem because faults could allow money to be redirected (stolen), and the cost of updating the software in all on-street terminals is prohibitive.

The model is written in UML 2.0, with a class diagram to show the relationships among three classes, and a state machine to describe the behavior of the main class. The state machine has around 50 states and 80 transitions, with the guards and actions of the transitions written as OCL predicates.

The following combination of test selection criteria are applied to generate a good quality test suite:

1. All-transition coverage is used for the state machine, with modified condition/decision coverage for the guards.
2. Multidimensional-boundaries coverage is used for the numeric data.
3. Twenty-five user scenarios (represented by UML message sequence chart diagrams) are added as explicit test case specifications.

The result of test generation with these test selection criteria gives an intensive test suite of 3500 test cases, which are executed completely automatically each night as a regression test suite.

4.8 SUMMARY

This chapter introduces the major test selection criteria that are commonly used in model-based testing. This is a large list, with different views of the model, including coverage of structural model elements (transitions, postconditions, etc.), data, and requirements. We also discuss test generation strategies based on statistical approaches and on explicit test selection criteria.

The key point is the complementarity of these test selection criteria. They are tools that allow the model-based tester to control the test generation, and any good model-based testing tool should support several families of test selection criteria. This is actually the case in commercial tools such as Reactis System, LEIRIOS Test Generator, and Qtronic from Conformiq.

These test selection criteria, and the ability to combine them in many ways, make it possible for the model-based tester to express his or her validation expertise with the SUT, to control the test generation process, and to produce the test suites that are required by the project test objectives.

4.9 FURTHER READING

A large amount of research on test coverage and adequacy criteria has been done since the 1970s. Goodenough and Gerhard [GG77] point out that test criteria are a key concept in software testing, both to estimate the adequacy of test data and to decide when to stop the testing process. A good general overview of various kinds of test coverage and adequacy criteria can be found in [ZHM97]. Sergiy Vilkomir maintains a website dedicated to the MC/DC criterion (see *http://www.dsl.uow.edu.au/~sergiy/MCDC.html*).

Lee and Sokolsky [HHL+03] have developed an approach to interpret data-flow criteria on transition-based models with temporal logic expressions to generate test cases using model-checking techniques.

Andrews and colleagues [AFGC03] propose ad hoc test adequacy criteria based on building blocks for UML class and interaction diagrams, for use in testing the UML model itself. McQuillan and Power [MP05] give an overview of a large list of UML-based coverage criteria from the testing literature.

The 1995 book by Beizer [Bei95] is still the best source for learning about domain and boundary testing techniques. Several boundary coverage criteria are discussed and formalized in [KLPU04].

See *http://www.pairwise.org* for papers and case studies on pairwise testing techniques and links to tools for generating test data that satisfy the pairwise coverage criterion.

A good introduction to random testing has been given by Hamlet [Ham02] in *Encyclopedia of Software Engineering*.

Prominent examples for the use of statistical criteria for test input generation include the work of Walton and Poore [WP00] as well as that of Musa [Mus04]. An example of one tool based on statistical usage models is the *Java Usage Model Builder Library* (JUMBL) [Pro03]. This is a model-based statistical testing tool [WPT95] developed at the University of Tennessee. JUMBL supports usage models based on Markov chain notation and provides model analysis facilities as well as test case generation.

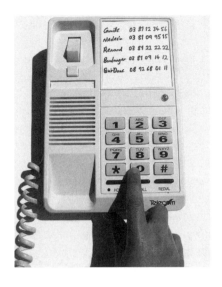

## CHAPTER 5

TESTING FROM FINITE STATE MACHINES

This chapter describes the simplest kind of model-based testing, which is based on finite state machines (FSMs). Each node of an FSM corresponds to a particular state of the SUT and each arc corresponds to an SUT action, so to generate test sequences we can just traverse the FSM.

We start with simple FSM models that are suitable for testing passive systems, such as unit testing of an object or class, and for testing deterministic reactive systems, where events occur in a known order. We use a simple FSM model to test the Qui-Donc service of France Telecom. Then we extend that to *extended finite state machines* (EFSM), which increase the expressiveness of FSMs by adding variables, state updating commands, and transition guards. We use a parameterized EFSM model to do unit testing of a hierarchy of Java classes.

Chapter 7 extends the ideas discussed in this chapter by using Unified Modeling Language (UML) state machines, which support nested machines and parallel machines.

5.1 TESTING QUI-DONC WITH A SIMPLE FSM

Qui-Donc (literal translation, "Who then?") is a service provided by France Telecom that does the opposite of the white pages—it allows you to enter a telephone number and find out the name and address associated with the number. It can be very useful in conjunction with caller ID! It is a vocal service, which you use by dialing the telephone number 08 92 68 01 11 and then listening to the vocal messages and pressing buttons on the keypad of your phone. Of course, the Qui-Donc service is actually all in French, but we've translated it into English for those readers who *ne parlent pas le français*.

Let's assume that we have been contracted to do some independent testing of the Qui-Donc system, to check that its behavior matches its requirements. The next section shows the informal requirements that we have been given. In Section 5.1.2 we develop a simple FSM model of the expected behavior of the Qui-Donc system, and in Section 5.1.3 we generate tests from that FSM. Since the outputs of the Qui-Donc system are all spoken phrases and we want to use a real telephone as our input device, we decided not to try to automate the execution of the tests. Instead, we will aim to choose test generation techniques that produce a smallish set of tests so that manual execution of the tests is practical.

5.1.1 Informal Requirements

After the caller dials 08 92 68 01 11, the Qui-Donc system responds by giving the WELCOME message, "Welcome to Qui-Donc. Please press the star key." This message is repeated up to three times, separated by a timeout of 6 seconds. If no star key is detected during this whole process, then the NOTALLOW message is given: "Your telephone does not allow access to the Qui-Donc service," and the call is disconnected.

If a star key is detected during the above process, then the ENTER message is given: "Please enter the 10-digit telephone number of the subscriber you are looking for, followed by the pound key." This message is repeated up to three times, but with a longer timeout of 20 seconds; if no numbers and hash, or pound (#), key are entered, then the call is terminated with the BYE message: "Thank you for using the Qui-Donc service."

If some digits followed by a pound key were detected, and the number was one of the emergency numbers, 15, 17, or 18 (for ambulance, police, and fire brigade, respectively), then an explanation of that emergency number is given, followed by the message: "If you want to do another search, press star." If the entered number did not contain 10 digits and was not one of the emergency numbers, then the ERROR message is given: "Invalid number entered. Please enter another number, followed by the pound key." However, if the entered number was 10 digits, then it is looked up in the white pages database. If the number is not in the database, then the SORRY message is given: "Sorry. The number NN NN NN NN NN does not appear in the white pages," and the caller goes back to the ENTER process.

If the entered number is in the database, the NAME message is given: "The number NN NN NN NN NN corresponds to SURNAME, INITIALS," then the Qui-Donc system enters the *information* menu.

The information menu gives the INFO message, "Press 1 to spell the name, press 2 to hear the address, or press star for a new search." If 1 is entered, then the name is spelled out and it returns to the information menu. If 2 is entered, then the address is given and it returns to the information menu. If star is entered, then it goes to the number-entry process, starting with the ENTER message. If no keys are pressed, then the INFO message is repeated after a timeout of 6 seconds; and after this message has been given three times without response, the call is terminated with the BYE message.

In addition to these processes, note that the caller can hang up at any moment.

5.1.2 Modeling Qui-Donc with an FSM

The first step in writing any model is always to decide what to *ignore*. That is, we need to take a very *abstract* view of the system to keep our FSM small enough. After all, there are 10^{10} possible 10-digit phone numbers—we cannot test all of those, and we certainly do not want to create an FSM that big! The kinds of fault that we want to find in the Qui-Donc system are logical faults, such as an incorrect message being given or the wrong menu being presented. We are not intending to test the contents of its database, which is all the numbers, names, and addresses in the white pages.

So, for testing purposes we decide that we will test just the four keys on the phone that Qui-Donc treats as special inputs (1, 2, * and #), plus four representative telephone numbers for when Qui-Donc asks for a telephone number:

18 This is the emergency number for the fire brigade. We make a *uniformity hypothesis* that if one of the emergency numbers behaves correctly, then all of them will, so testing one of them will be enough.[1]

---

[1] If Qui-Donc were a safety-critical application, we would not make this kind of assumption about the emergency numbers; rather we would want to test the set of emergency numbers exhaustively.

num1 (03 81 11 11 11). When we ring this number, it seems to be disconnected, so we assume that this number is not in the white pages database.

num2 (03 81 22 22 22). We found this number in the white pages by choosing *K. J. Renard* at random. His address is *45 rue de Vesoul, Besançon*, and we assume that this information is in the white pages database.

bad (12 34 56 78 9). The bad number is a number with just fewer than 10 digits. Here, we make another uniformity hypothesis, assuming that this number is a representative sample for all possible numbers that contain fewer than 10 digits or more than 10 digits. Thinking about boundary testing, it would be good to have an 11-digit input as well, but we leave this as an exercise for the reader.

So the *input alphabet* of our model (the set of all the different inputs that we will send to the Qui-Donc system) is:

`{dial,num1,num2,bad,18,1,2,*,#,wait}`

Let's just explain how these will relate to the real-world test inputs. The `dial` input means to pick up the phone (after resetting it by hanging up, if necessary), dial the Qui-Donc service (08 92 68 01 11), and wait for a response. The single digits, 1 and 2, and the * and # inputs mean that the person executing the tests should just press that key and wait for the Qui-Donc system to respond. The 18 means press 1, then 8, then the # key, taking a total of less than 6 seconds to do this. The `num1` input means press all 10 digits of that number (0, 3, 8, 1, 1, 1, 1, 1, 1, 1) followed by the # key and do all this in just less than 20 seconds.

Similarly for num2 (but to be different, we will enter num2 as quickly as we can), and for the bad input, which has only 9 digits (1, 2, 3, 4, 5, 6, 7, 8, 9, #). The `wait` input means wait, without pressing any keys, until the Qui-Donc system does something—it should time out after 20 seconds for the ENTER states and after 6 seconds for the other states. (For simplicity, we have not bothered to distinguish between these two timeouts in our model, but this could easily be done by annotating some of the output messages with the length of the pause that is expected before the output message is produced—for example, by having several different ENTER outputs, like $ENTER_0$, $ENTER_6$, and $ENTER_{20}$, so that the person executing the test knows exactly how long to wait before expecting the ENTER message.)

So, given a sequence of abstract input values like this,

```
dial, wait, *, Num1, 2, wait, wait, wait
```
our manual tester will know exactly what to press, and when. For this particular sequence of input stimuli, the resulting sequence of messages from the Qui-Donc system should be:

```
WELCOME, WELCOME, ENTER, NAME+INFO, ADDR, INFO,
INFO, BYE (it hangs up).
```

Rather than write each test case with its input sequence and expected output sequence separated like this, we usually write it as a sequence of input/output pairs:

```
dial/WELCOME, wait/WELCOME, */ENTER, num1/NAME+INFO,
2/ADDR, wait/INFO, wait/INFO, wait/BYE  (it hangs up).
```

Each transition of our finite state machine will be labeled with a single input/output pair like this. This means that our FSM is a *Mealy machine* [LY96], which is the most common kind of FSM used to specify software and hardware systems. In a Mealy machine, each transition is labeled with an input i and an output o. When used for testing purposes, each transition defines one step in a test case—the input i is the stimulus that is sent to the SUT, and the output o is the expected response of the SUT. We sometimes write a transition from state s to state s' as $s \xrightarrow{i/o} s'$.

When designing your FSM model, you may find that some transitions seem to need to be labeled with multiple outputs, or zero outputs, because your SUT does not always produce exactly one response for each input. For example, the Qui-Donc requirements show that the num1 input can result in our hearing two messages, the NAME message immediately followed by the INFO prompt message. In this case, we must package up those two outputs and model them as one single output message. You may also come across situations where your SUT does not produce any output for a given input/– this can be modeled as a transition labeled with something like "*input/*−," where the output symbol "−" just means "expect no response from the SUT."

The important thing about Mealy machine models is that every transition must be labeled with exactly one input. It is not acceptable to have transitions with no inputs because it would mean that the SUT could produce outputs spontaneously rather than being under the control of the test case. Later in the book (e.g., Sections 6.5 and 7.3), we discuss more powerful modeling notations that can be used for those kinds of *nondeterministic reactive systems*.

> **Key Point**   A Mealy machine model has a finite set of states, plus many transitions that go from one state to another. Each transition must be labeled with exactly one input and one output (which may be "–"). The machine must have one *initial* state and may optionally have one or more *final* states.

Each test generated from a Mealy machine FSM model is a sequence of transitions, which starts from the initial state and ends in one of the final states. If there are no final states, then the test case is allowed to end in any state. If your SUT requires a complete sequence of events (e.g., login, do some transactions, then logout), then adding a final state (after the logout transition) allows you to force all the generated test sequences to be complete.

Figure 5.1 shows the finite state machine that we can design from these requirements and assumptions. It is written graphically as a state transition diagram, and its output messages are listed in Table 5.1. Note that several of them are the concatenation of an informational message followed by the ENTER or INFO prompt, so the prompt strings are repeated in several messages. In this model, we have one final state, which is the same as our initial state. This means that we want all of the generated tests to end up in the Start state, ready to commence a new call.

Does this finite state machine seem to you to be quite complex for such a simple system? We agree. This is because the three levels of timeout create a lot of duplication and make the diagram rather cluttered. We will see later in this chapter that the use of *extended finite state machines* (EFSMs) can eliminate this kind of duplication and dramatically simplify the FSM by adding a variable to count the number of timeouts.

However, things may get worse before they get better because the FSM in Figure 5.1 is not even *complete* yet. That is, it has some states that do not have a transition for *every possible input*. Our input alphabet contains 10 symbols, so every state of our FSM should have 10 transitions leaving it, except the Start state, where we decide that dial is the only meaningful input because we are not yet connected to the Qui-Donc system. For example, the Star1 state does not specify what should happen if a number is pressed rather than *, and the Info1 state does not specify what happens if a phone number is entered. It is so tedious to specify all these transitions that it is usual to follow the convention that unexpected inputs are simply *ignored*, leaving the state unchanged. This effectively completes the FSM by adding implicit loop transitions from each state back to itself for each unspecified input. If we showed all those extra transitions on the diagram, it would be too cluttered to read.

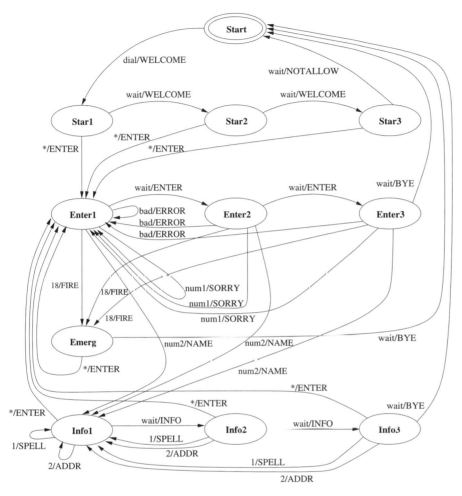

FIGURE 5.1   Qui-Donc FSM model.

Table 5.2 shows the same FSM written as a state table, with one column for each input symbol. This is a good representation for seeing missing transitions. The entries in italics show the transitions that we would need to add to make the FSM complete. The `dial` column models the effect of hanging up in the middle of a transaction and redialing the Qui-Donc system (it would be possible to divide this into separate `hangup` and `dial` inputs, but we have merged them for simplicity). The remaining italic entries show the effect of the *ignore unexpected inputs* convention—every missing transition is assumed to leave the state unchanged. If we add all these italicized transitions, the FSM is complete (except for the `Start` state) because each state has a transition for every input.

TABLE 5.1   The Output Alphabet of the Qui-Donc Model

Output Symbol	Concrete Message
WELCOME	"Welcome to Qui-Donc. Please press the star key."
NOTALLOW	"Your telephone does not allow access to the Qui-Donc service."
ENTER	"Please enter the 10-digit telephone number of the subscriber you are looking for, followed by the pound key."
ERROR	"Invalid number entered. Please enter another number, followed by the pound key."
FIRE	"18 is the emergency number for the fire brigade. If you want to do another search, press star."
SORRY	"Sorry. The number 03 81 11 11 11 does not appear in the white pages. Please enter the 10-digit telephone number of the subscriber you are looking for, followed by the pound key."
NAME	"The number 03 81 22 22 22 corresponds to Renard, K. J. Press 1 to spell the name, press 2 to hear the address, or press star for a new search."
INFO	"Press 1 to spell the name, press 2 to hear the address, or press star for a new search."
SPELL	"Renard is spelled R, E, N, A, R, D. Press 1 to spell the name, press 2 to hear the address, or press star for a new search."
ADDR	"The address of Renard, K. J. is 45 rue de Vesoul, Besançon. Press 1 to spell the name, press 2 to hear the address, or press star for a new search."
BYE	"Thank you for using the Qui-Donc service."

Another common way to represent an FSM is as a set of transitions, written as (CurrentState, Input, Output, NextState) quadruples.

```
(Start, dial,  WELCOME,  Star1 )
(Star1, wait,  WELCOME,  Star2 )
(Star1, *,     ENTER,    Enter1)
(Star2, wait,  WELCOME,  Star3 )
(Star2, *,     ENTER,    Enter1)
. . .
```

Whichever representation we use, after we have finished designing our model we should spend a little time validating it. The list on page 148 shows some of the properties that we could check.

TABLE 5.2 Qui-Donc FSM Model as a State Table

Input	dial	num1	num2	bad	18	1	2	*	#	wait
Start	WELCOME Star1									
Star1	WELCOME Star1	– Star1	– Star1	– Star1	– Star1	– Star1	– Star1	ENTER Enter1	– Star1	WELCOME Star2
Star2	WELCOME Star1	– Star2	– Star2	– Star2	– Star2	– Star2	– Star2	ENTER Enter1	– Star2	WELCOME Star3
Star3	WELCOME Star1	– Star3	– Star3	– Star3	– Star3	– Star3	– Star3	ENTER Enter1	– Star3	NOTALLOW Start
Enter1	WELCOME Star1	SORRY Enter1	NAME Info1	ERROR Enter1	FIRE Emerg	– Enter1	– Enter1	– Enter1	– Enter1	ENTER Enter2
Enter2	WELCOME Star1	SORRY Enter1	NAME Info1	ERROR Enter1	FIRE Emerg	– Enter2	– Enter2	– Enter2	– Enter2	ENTER Enter3
Enter3	WELCOME Star1	SORRY Enter1	NAME Info1	ERROR Enter1	FIRE Emerg	– Enter3	– Enter3	– Enter3	– Enter3	BYE Start
Emerg	WELCOME Star1	– Emerg	– Emerg	– Emerg	– Emerg	– Emerg	– Emerg	ENTER Enter1	– Emerg	BYE Start
Info1	WELCOME Star1	– Info1	– Info1	– Info1	– Info1	SPELL Info1	ADDR Info1	ENTER Enter1	– Info1	INFO Info2
Info2	WELCOME Star1	– Info2	– Info2	– Info2	– Info2	SPELL Info1	ADDR Info1	ENTER Enter1	– Info2	INFO Info3
Info3	WELCOME Star1	– Info3	– Info3	– Info3	– Info3	SPELL Info1	ADDR Info1	ENTER Enter1	– Info3	BYE Start

Deterministic: An FSM is *deterministic* if for every state, every transition out of that state is labeled with a different input. This is a crucial property for many FSM algorithms because otherwise, it is ambiguous which transition we should take out of that state.

Initially connected: An FSM is *initially connected* if every state is reachable from the initial state. If your FSM is not initially connected, then you have almost certainly made an error because it means that part of your FSM is unusable and cannot be tested. It is usually easy to see if an FSM is initially connected by a quick visual inspection of the FSM diagram.

Complete: An FSM is *complete* if for each state, the outgoing transitions cover all inputs. As mentioned, it is easy to make an FSM complete by adding all the self-transitions $s \xrightarrow{i/-} s$ for every state s that does not have an outgoing transition with an input i.

Minimal: An FSM is *minimal* if it has no redundant states. That is, it does not have two distinct states that generate the same set of input/output sequences. A nonminimal FSM is not a major problem; it just means that you could have designed a simpler FSM that was equivalent. There are efficient algorithms for transforming a nonminimal FSM into a minimal equivalent FSM [Hop71].

Strongly connected: An FSM is *strongly connected* if every state is reachable from every other state. This means that there are no states or loops that you can get stuck in—there is always a path out to the rest of the FSM. This is a strong restriction and not always desirable. However, if the SUT has a *reset* method that sets it back to the initial state (like hanging up the phone in the Qui-Donc example), then the FSM is automatically strongly connected whenever it is initially connected.

Our Qui-Donc FSM in Figure 5.1 is deterministic, initially connected, strongly connected, and minimal. This is good. Now that we have a model of the expected behavior of the Qui-Donc system, we consider how to generate tests from this model.

5.1.3 Generating Tests

We now show a series of simple techniques for generating tests from our Qui-Donc model, starting with some that generate small and rather inadequate test suites and progressing to techniques that generate such large and comprehensive test suites that they are rarely practical. We focus initially on generating tests from just the *explicit* Qui-Donc model that contains only the transitions shown in Figure 5.1, rather than from the *complete* model that also includes all the implicit transitions (italicized) shown in Table 5.2.

STATE, INPUT, AND OUTPUT COVERAGE

State coverage is a simple and popular coverage criterion. It measures the percentage of FSM states that are visited during the test execution. For example, here is a minimal length test suite (1 test, with just 12 transitions) that gives us 100 percent state coverage:

```
dial/WELCOME, wait/WELCOME, wait/WELCOME,
*/ENTER, wait/ENTER, wait/ENTER, 18/FIRE, */ENTER,
num2/NAME, wait/INFO, wait/INFO, wait/BYE.
```

As you can see, this is a very weak test suite. It does not test any bad numbers or unknown numbers and does not even ask for the spelling or address information.

Input coverage is another simple coverage metric. It measures how many distinct input symbols have been sent to the SUT. For example, here is a test sequence that gives us 90 percent coverage of our 10 possible inputs.

```
dial/WELCOME, */ENTER, bad/ERROR, num1/SORRY, num2/NAME,
1/SPELL, 2/ADDR, */ENTER, 18/FIRE, wait/BYE.
```

This is an even shorter test than the previous one, and it does not test the timeout behavior at all, so it is a very weak test suite.

Why didn't we get 100 percent input coverage? Because, surprisingly, the remaining input # does not appear on any transitions of our explicit FSM model (Figure 5.1). Failing to reach 100 percent coverage of a simple coverage metric like input coverage can be a useful warning sign that we have forgotten something in our model. However, in this case, our reason for including # in the set of inputs was just so that we could perform some robustness testing using the complete FSM model. So it is acceptable that we cannot reach 100 percent coverage in the explicit model. It is easy to reach 100 percent input coverage in the complete model—just add the transition #/— after the dial/WELCOME transition.

It is possible to define *output coverage* in a similar way to input coverage, so that it measures how many distinct output responses have been received from the SUT. For example, the short test that covers 9/10 of the inputs also covers 9/11 of the possible outputs. We have seen little discussion of output coverage in the testing literature, but it is similar to the *cause-effect* heuristic [Mye79], which says to try to test the inputs that cause the SUT to produce different responses/effects/outputs.

All these coverage metrics are too easily satisfied, so even 100 percent state coverage, input coverage, or output coverage gives us no confidence that we have generated a reasonably comprehensive test suite. In fact, the goal of this section is to persuade you to never be satisfied with just these weak metrics! Let us now investigate a stronger coverage, which covers every transition.

TRANSITION COVERAGE

Transition coverage measures how many of the transitions of the FSM have been tested. So 100 percent transition coverage means that every transition has been tested at least once. There are many ways to generate a test suite that has 100 percent transition coverage. For example, a random path through the FSM will eventually cover all the transitions.[2] However, the best way to generate the smallest possible test suite that has 100 percent transition coverage is to do a *transition tour* of the FSM. A transition tour is a minimum-length circular path through the FSM that visits every transition at least once.

The best way to generate a transition tour of an FSM is to use the *Chinese postman algorithm*, which was invented by the Chinese mathematican Guan Mei Gu [Gua62]. It finds the shortest path through a graph that visits every edge.[3] Thimbleby [Thi03] gives an excellent description of the algorithm and its applications and includes a full Java implementation.[4]

When we apply that algorithm to our Qui-Donc FSM, we get the tour shown in Listing 5.1, which dials up the Qui-Donc service just four times and contains a total of 61 steps. This is a very nice test suite, which exercises all the states, all the inputs, all the outputs, and all the transitions of our model, yet would take only about 15 minutes to execute (assuming that each transition takes an average of 15 seconds and to tap one or two keys and then listen to the response).

Transition coverage is stronger than state coverage because if we have tested all the transitions, we must also have visited every state at each end of those transitions (we assume that the FSM is *initially connected*). So if you use a transition-tour test generation algorithm, you not only have 100 percent transition coverage, but you also get 100 percent state coverage. State coverage is analogous to statement coverage in programming languages, and

---

[2]We assume here that the FSM is initially connected so that all states are reachable from the initial state. If the FSM graph is not also strongly connected, then the random path generator should occasionally perform a *reset* operation to return to the initial state and ensure that all transitions are reachable.

[3]Compare this with the well-known traveling salesman problem, which visits every node of the graph, but not necessarily every edge. A traveling salesman algorithm gives 100 percent state coverage of an FSM, but not necessarily 100 percent transition coverage.

[4]His Java implementation can be downloaded from *http://www.uclic.ucl.ac.uk/harold/cpp*.

LISTING 5.1   Transition tour of the Qui-Donc partial FSM (4 tests with a total of 61 transitions).

```
1. dial/WELCOME, */ENTER, wait/ENTER, num1/SORRY, wait/ENTER,
   bad/ERROR, wait/ENTER, 18/FIRE, */ENTER, num2/NAME,
   wait/INFO, */ENTER, wait/ENTER, num2/NAME, wait/INFO, 2/ADDR,
   wait/INFO, 1/SPELL, wait/INFO, wait/INFO, */ENTER, wait/ENTER,
   wait/ENTER, num1/SORRY, wait/ENTER, wait/ENTER, bad/ERROR,
   wait/ENTER, wait/ENTER, 18/FIRE, */ENTER, wait/ENTER,
   wait/ENTER, num2/NAME, wait/INFO, wait/INFO, 2/ADDR,
   wait/INFO, wait/INFO, 1/SPELL, 2/ADDR, 1/SPELL, wait/INFO,
   wait/INFO, wait/BYE
2. dial/WELCOME, wait/WELCOME, */ENTER, num1/SORRY, bad/ERROR,
   wait/ENTER, wait/ENTER, wait/BYE
3. dial/WELCOME, wait/WELCOME, wait/WELCOME, */ENTER, num2/NAME,
   */ENTER, 18/FIRE, wait/BYE
4. dial/WELCOME, wait/WELCOME, wait/WELCOME, wait/NOTALLOW,
```

---

transition coverage is analogous to branch coverage. In the case where every input appears somewhere in your explicit FSM model, then a transition tour also gives 100 percent input coverage. It works similarly for output coverage.

If we had included all the dial transitions in our FSM model to model the fact that from any state we can hang up the phone and then redial the Qui-Donc number to start a new session (these transitions are shown in the leftmost column of Table 5.2), then the transition tour would contain 14 tests, with a total of 89 transitions. This test suite extends the previous test suite by also testing that the Qui-Donc system resets itself correctly when a caller hangs up unexpectedly.

More interesting is Listing 5.2, which shows the test suite generated by a transition tour of the (almost) *complete* version of our FSM model, which includes all the default transitions shown in italics in Table 5.2, except for the italicized dial transitions. This test suite tries all the illegal and unexpected input values in each state, so it tries to test that the Qui-Donc system does indeed ignore all inputs that are not mentioned in its requirements.

However, if we execute this test suite, we find a few surprises (see the transitions in boxes in Listing 5.2):

- The 16th transition in test 1 has an input of # (from state Enter2), and we find that this is not ignored by Qui-Donc; because it is interpreted as a telephone number with zero digits, it produces the ERROR output. In fact, this is the correct behavior, so we realize that we have an error in

LISTING 5.2   Transition tour of the Qui-Donc complete FSM (4 tests with a total of 126 transitions).

1. `dial/WELCOME, #/-, 2/-, 1/-, 18/-, bad/-, num2/-, num1/-, dial/-, */ENTER, wait/ENTER, num1/SORRY, wait/ENTER, bad/ERROR, wait/ENTER, `‎`#/-`‎`, */-, 2/-, 1/-, dial/-, 18/FIRE, */ENTER, num2/NAME, wait/INFO, */ENTER, wait/ENTER, num2/NAME, wait/INFO, 2/ADDR, wait/INFO, 1/SPELL, wait/INFO, wait/INFO, */ENTER, wait/ENTER, wait/ENTER, num1/SORRY, wait/ENTER, wait/ENTER, bad/ERROR, wait/ENTER, wait/ENTER, #/-, */-, 2/-, 1/-, dial/-, 18/FIRE, */ENTER, wait/ENTER, wait/ENTER, num2/NAME, wait/INFO, wait/INFO, 2/ADDR, wait/INFO, wait/INFO, 1/SPELL, #/-, `‎`18/-`‎`, `‎`bad/-`‎`, num2/-, num1/-, dial/-, 2/ADDR, 1/SPELL, wait/INFO, #/-, 18/-, bad/-, num2/-, num1/-, dial/-, wait/INFO, #/-, 18/-, bad/-, num2/-, num1/-, dial/-, wait/BYE`

2. `dial/WELCOME, wait/WELCOME, #/-, 2/-, 1/-, 18/-, bad/-, num2/-, num1/-, dial/-, */ENTER, #/-, */-, 2/-, 1/-, dial/-, num1/SORRY, bad/ERROR, wait/ENTER, wait/ENTER, wait/BYE`

3. `dial/WELCOME, wait/WELCOME, wait/WELCOME, #/-, 2/-, 1/-, 18/-, bad/-, num2/-, num1/-, dial/-, */ENTER, num2/NAME, */ENTER, 18/FIRE, #/-, 2/-, 1/-, 18/-, bad/-, num2/-, num1/-, dial/-, wait/BYE`

4. `dial/WELCOME, wait/WELCOME, wait/WELCOME, wait/NOTALLOW`

our model—the three Enter_i states should each have a transition #/ERROR that goes back to the Enter1 state.

- The input 18, when in state Info_i, is not ignored because it contains a 1, which triggers the 1/SPELL transition. This is a consequence of our concrete test values—one input happens to be a prefix of another.

- The input bad, when in state Info_i, also triggers the 1/SPELL transition because the bad number is 81123456, which contains a 1. Similarly for the num1 and num2 inputs in these states.

We mention these "surprises" to illustrate that it is often very dangerous and error-prone to make a general assumption about the behavior of all omitted transitions in an FSM model, such as assuming that all unspecified inputs are ignored. Binder discusses this in more detail [Bin99, 223–228] and recommends that an explicit response matrix, similar to Table 5.2, be used to record the precise response to every input event.

In conclusion, a transition tour of the explicit FSM generates a useful test suite that gives 100 percent transition and state coverage (and usually input and output coverage too). A transition tour of the complete FSM generates a larger test suite that also does robustness testing by trying every possible input in each state. This is useful for detecting *sneak paths* (extra transitions) in the SUT.

We recommend that you treat transition coverage as your basic coverage metric when doing model-based testing from FSMs; you should expect to achieve 100 percent transition coverage of your explicit FSM model and preferably 100 percent transition coverage of the complete FSM model.

Of course, even 100 percent transition coverage is no guarantee that you have found all the errors in the SUT! It is quite possible that a particular sequence of three transitions would have exposed an SUT fault, but that particular sequence did not happen to be exercised during the transition tour. Also, the FSM model usually just describes part of the SUT functionality, so even a huge test suite generated from the FSM is unlikely to help in finding errors that are outside the scope of the model.

> **Key Point**   Full transition coverage is a good minimum to aim for when generating tests from FSM models.

EXPLICIT TEST CASE SPECIFICATIONS

It may seem a bit cold and mechanical, or perhaps just naive, to assume that a simple algorithm like transition tour is capable of generating a good test suite. Is there no longer any need for the skill, the knowledge, the passion, and the domain expertise of an experienced test engineer?

Well, of course, the test engineer remains central to the whole process of model-based testing. He or she designed the model, must decide which test generation algorithms and heuristics to apply, and should inspect the results of testing (faults found, code coverage levels, model coverage levels, etc.) to decide how much more testing is necessary.

But it can also be useful for test engineers to directly use their domain knowledge and testing intuition to help the model-based testing tools to choose certain interesting tests. One way to do this is for the test engineer to supply *explicit test case specifications*, which ask for a particular kind of test to be generated. This means that the high-level design and the rationale for the test come from the engineer, while the low-level details of the test and the expected SUT outputs come from the model.

For example, we may have the goal of testing whether the Qui-Donc system can be used by disabled or elderly people, who are slow at entering numbers and frequently fail to complete the input before the timeout expires. We could specify these kinds of tests by asking a tool to generate a test that traverses the Star3, Enter3, and Info3 states. We could specify this as a regular expression [Fri97] over the sequence of states that will be visited (here, * is a wildcard that means "any sequence of transitions"):

```
*,Star3,*,Enter3,*,Info3,*
```

The shortest test case that this would generate is

```
dial/WELCOME, wait/WELCOME, wait/WELCOME, */ENTER,
wait/ENTER, wait/ENTER, num2/NAME,
wait/INFO, wait/INFO, wait/BYE.
```

Or we might decide that we want to test the emergency numbers more thoroughly than other numbers, so we ask for tests that go through the Emerg state many times and exercise all the transitions in and out of that state. For example, we could specify this with the regular expression (over the states visited)

```
*,Enter1,Emerg,*,Enter2,Emerg,*,Enter3,Emerg,*
```

The shortest test that satisfies this explicit test case specification is

```
dial/WELCOME, */ENTER, 18/FIRE, */ENTER,
wait/ENTER, 18/FIRE, */ENTER,
wait/ENTER, wait/ENTER, 18/FIRE, wait/BYE.
```

The same specification would give a larger, more varied test suite if we added the other emergency numbers to our model because it would explore the alternative paths between the Enter$_i$ and Emerg states. As models become larger, explicit test case specifications become more useful for focusing attention on particular parts of the model. Regular expressions are not a very expressive notation for explicit test case specifications, so it is common to use more sophisticated notations to give more control over the generated test sets.

This illustrates that model-based testing does not have to be fully automatic. It is sometimes useful for the test engineer to direct the tools explicitly to generate a certain style of test, to follow a specific path through the model, or to test one part of the model more intensively than others. Model-based testing is not intended to be a tool that replaces human skill and ingenuity; rather it should be a tool that amplifies human skills.

> **Key Point**   Explicit test case specifications give an engineer precise, low-level control over which tests are generated from a model.

5.1.4 Complete Testing Methods

In this section we look at more powerful FSM test generation techniques that can guarantee to find all SUT errors.

Researchers have been working on FSM test generation algorithms for 50 years, since Moore started the field with his *Gedanken experiments on sequential machines* [Moo56]. During the 1960s through the 1980s, several *complete* test generation methods for FSMs were invented, such as the D-method [Hen64], W-method [Vas73, Cho78], the Wp-method [FvBK$^+$91], the U-method [SD88, YU90], as well as the transition-tour or T-method [NT81], which we used earlier (which can be a complete method for some SUTs, as we shall see).

These algorithms are quite impressive in that they generate a set of tests that *guarantees* that the SUT implements the identical FSM as the model. However, to make this possible they must make some strong assumptions: they assume that the specification FSM model is *deterministic, minimal, complete, strongly connected* (or initially connected with a *reset* operation), and *has the same complexity as the SUT*. This last assumption means that if we view the actual behavior of the SUT as also being a finite state machine, then that finite state machine must have the same number of states as the FSM model. This is a very strong assumption, which is usually impossible to verify in real-world situations, especially when the SUT is a black box. However, in the Further Reading section of this chapter we discuss how some of these assumptions can be weakened.

The basic idea behind these methods is that, for every transition $s \xrightarrow{i/o} s'$ in the FSM model, we want to:

1. force the SUT into state s (by resetting and starting from the initial state, if necessary),
2. send the input i to the SUT and check that it produces the expected output o, and
3. check that the SUT is now in the expected state s'.

Step 3 is the difficult one—how can we check what state the SUT is in if the SUT is a black box?

The transition-tour method takes a simplistic approach to this: it assumes that the SUT provides a reliable[5] status() operation that tells us its

---

[5]If the status() operation is not known to be reliable, then it may be useful to call it *twice* after each transition to check that the status() operation itself does not change the state of the SUT.

current state. This means that it is sufficient to test all the transitions, calling the status() operation after each transition. If you are lucky enough to be testing an SUT that does have a trustworthy status() operation, then a transition tour of your complete FSM model is guaranteed to find all SUT errors (though we still must assume that the SUT and our model FSM have the same number of states). Of course, many SUTs do *not* provide a status() operation, like our Qui-Donc example. In this case, the transition-tour method is not guaranteed to find all *transfer* faults (where the SUT moves into the wrong state), but if there are no transfer faults, then it will find all *output* faults in the SUT.

If we do not have a status() operation, could we perhaps use one of the other methods to test the SUT, such as the D-/W-/Wp-/U-methods? They check that the destination state is correct by applying various cleverly chosen sequences of transitions and observing the outputs of the SUT.

Yes, in principle we could use one of those algorithms, but in practice they are not always useful because they produce very long test cases that contain up to $O(pn^3)$ transitions in the worst case, where n is the number of states and p is the size of the input alphabet. Our small Qui-Donc example has 11 states and 10 input symbols, so these methods could generate test suites containing up to $10 \times 11^3 = 13,310$ transitions, which is not really practical. Assuming that each transition takes an average of 15 seconds, a test suite of this magnitude would take more than 55 hours of nonstop testing, or about 1.5 person-weeks. This would be an excessive test length for such a simple system. In practice, most FSMs are better than the worst case and the D-method and U-method can generate a reasonable size test suite for many FSM models (usually the size of the test suites is T-method < U-method < D-method < Wp-method < W-method [Yu90]). The D-method and U-method test suites are usually much smaller than the Wp-method and W-method test suites.

Unfortunately, the D-method is not applicable to our Qui-Donc FSM because it does not have a *distinguishing sequence* (a sequence of inputs that gives different output behavior when applied to each state of the FSM). The U-method is also not applicable because the Info3 state does not have a UIO sequence (a sequence of inputs that gives different results when we are in the Info3 state than when we are in any other state). If it did have a UIO sequence, then the U-method would generate a test suite of about 110 tests (one for each transition in the complete FSM), with an average length of around 6 transitions.[6] So this test suite would contain 600 to 700

---

[6]This estimate is based on an average of 3 transitions to get to a given state, followed by a test of one transition and then applying the UIO sequence (average length 2) for the resulting state.

transitions, which is five times larger than our transition tour but still small enough to be practical. Optimized versions of the U-method could reduce the test suite size further by overlapping test sequences [ADLU91].

A comparative study by Sidhu [SkL89] shows that when the SUT does not provide a reliable status() method, the transition-tour method (over the complete FSM) has weaker fault-detection power than the U-method, D-method, and W/Wp-methods, which all have similar fault-finding power. The transition-tour method over just the explicit FSM is weaker still and may fail to detect sneak paths (extra transitions) in the SUT. However, transition tours are still very useful, because they exercise every state and every transition of the FSM model and produce a test suite whose total length is proportional to the number of transitions.

In the second case study of this chapter, we will explore further test generation techniques and metrics (e.g., random walks, greedy random walks, and transition-pair coverage) that can produce practical test suites that are stronger than just transition coverage.

5.2 EFSMS AND THE MODELJUNIT LIBRARY

In this section, we introduce *extended finite state machines* (EFSMs), which make it possible to model more complex SUTs than are possible with FSMs. Then, we describe the ModelJUnit library, which can be used to write EFSMs in Java and for simple kinds of test generation.

5.2.1 Extended Finite State Machines

An EFSM looks similar to an FSM (states and transitions), but it is more expressive because it has internal variables that can store more detailed state information. For example, in the Qui-Donc model, rather than have three separate Enter$_i$ states as in Figure 5.1, an EFSM model might have just one Enter state, plus a timeouts variable that counts how many times a timeout has occurred.

So an EFSM can appear to have a small number of visible states, while it actually has a much larger number of internal states. Mapping the large set of internal states down into the smaller set of visible states is a kind of *abstraction*. Deciding how to do this abstraction (i.e., how to partition the internal state space) is an important design decision because it strongly influences the kinds of test that can be generated from the EFSM.

Figure 5.2 illustrates this abstraction process. Imagine that we have an SUT with an infinite state space (lots of integer variables), and we have decided to model it by an EFSM whose internal state space contains just two

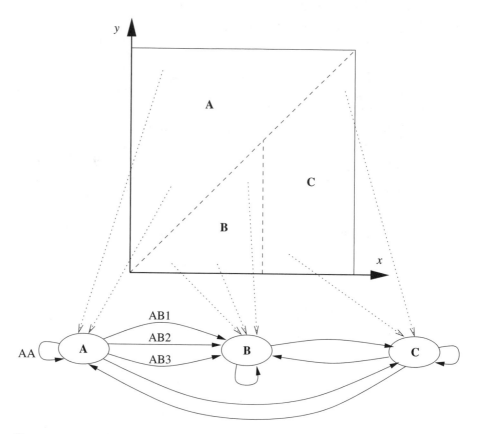

FIGURE 5.2   Abstraction of the large internal state space of an EFSM into three visible states.

integer variables, $x, y \in 0..9$. This means that the EFSM has $10 \times 10 = 100$ internal states, which we decide is still more than we need for testing the SUT. Based on our test objectives and on what we know about the SUT behavior, we decide to partition this state space into three areas: area **A** is all the states where $y \geq x$, area **B** is all the states where $y < x$ and $x < 5$, and area **C** is all the states where $y < x$ and $x \geq 5$. The three visible states of the EFSM represent these three areas, respectively.

The transitions of an EFSM sometimes need to update the EFSM state variables (e.g., x and y in Figure 5.2, or the `timeouts` variable in a Qui-Donc EFSM), so we often attach some code to each transition to perform these state updates. For example, the

$$\text{Enter1} \xrightarrow{\text{wait/ENTER}} \text{Enter2}$$

and

$$\text{Enter2} \xrightarrow{\quad\text{wait/ENTER}\quad} \text{Enter3}$$

transitions in Figure 5.1 would both be modeled by a single EFSM transition, from state `Enter` to itself, that contained code to increment the `timeouts` variable.

A transition in an EFSM can also have a *guard*, which is a boolean expression that can enable or disable the transition. It must evaluate to true for the transition to be taken. For example, the transition just discussed that increments `timeouts` would also need the guard `[timeouts<2]` to ensure that the `timeouts` variable is not incremented too many times. A separate transition, with the guard `[timeouts==2]` would handle the `wait/BYE` transition from state `Enter` to state `Start`.

Returning to the example in Figure 5.2, the transition labeled AA models an operation that, when called in a state within region A (where $y \geq x$), will stay in region A. For example, it might be an operation that increments y. The transitions labeled AB1, AB2, and AB3 model three operations that change the (x, y) variables from region A to region B. For example, they might be defined as follows:

AB1: $x, y := 1, 0$ (with no guard)

AB2: $y := 0$ with the guard $[x < 5]$

AB3: $y := y - 1$ with the guard $[x = y$ and $0 < x < 5]$

The advantage of using an EFSM model rather than a simple FSM model is that it allows us to take a complex SUT (with billions of states or infinite states) and build a more detailed model of it (perhaps with hundreds or thousands of states) than would be possible with an FSM. Then by defining the visible states of the EFSM carefully (typically just a few dozen of them), we can reduce the test generation task to something practical and focus on the interesting transitions between different areas of the model. The two levels of abstraction give us better control than one level would because they are used for different purposes.

- The medium-size state space of the EFSM and the code in its transitions are used to model the SUT behavior more accurately than is possible with just an FSM, and thus generate more accurate inputs and oracles for the SUT.
- The smaller number of *visible* states of the EFSM defines an FSM that can be used to drive the test generation. For example, we can use graph

algorithms such as transition tours to generate tests. These would not be practical on a larger EFSM state space that has thousands of states and more transitions.

> **Key Point**   An EFSM can model an SUT more accurately than an FSM, and its visible states define a second layer of abstraction (an FSM) that drives the test generation.

5.2.2 The ModelJUnit Library

The ModelJUnit library is a set of Java classes that is designed to be used as an extension of JUnit for model-based unit testing of Java classes. JUnit[7] is a widely used Java library for writing unit tests for Java classes. ModelJUnit was developed by one of the authors (Utting) as a *simple, open-source* framework for exploring FSM-based testing. It allows the FSM models to be written in Java, which is familiar to programmers, and because it is an extension of JUnit, the tests are run in the same way as other JUnit tests.

Most commercial and research model-based testing tools use sophisticated notations and theories that take some time to learn, whereas with the ModelJUnit library, one can start with an extremely simple FSM model and begin testing immediately, and then progress to slightly more sophisticated EFSM models as desired. The ModelJUnit library is based on ideas from Harry Robinson[8] and from Spec Explorer [VCST05], but it has only a small subset of the functionality of Spec Explorer. ModelJUnit is available from the website associated with this book.

The basic philosophy of ModelJUnit is to take advantage of the expressive power of Java (procedures, parameters, inheritance, annotations, etc.) to make it easier to write EFSM models, and then provide a collection of common traversal algorithms for generating tests from those models. It is typically used for *online* testing, which means that the tests are executed while they are being generated. The EFSM usually plays a dual role: it defines the possible states and transitions that can be tested, and it acts as the *adaptor* that connects the model to the SUT (which is usually another Java class).

Each EFSM model is written as a Java class, which must have at least the following methods:

---

[7] See *http://www.junit.org*.

[8] The C# login model from his STAR East 2005 presentation [Rob05] shows one way to express an FSM as a C# class. See *http://www.geocities.com/harry_robinson_testing/stareast2005.htm*.

Object getState(): This method returns the current visible state of the EFSM. So this method defines an *abstraction function* that maps the internal state of the EFSM to the visible states of the EFSM graph. Typically, the result is a string, but it is possible to return any type of object.[9]

void reset(boolean): This method resets the EFSM to its initial state. When online testing is being used, it should also reset the SUT or create a new instance of the SUT class. The boolean parameter can be ignored for most unit testing applications.[10]

@Action void *name$_i$*(): The EFSM must define several of these *action* methods, each marked with an @Action annotation. These action methods define the transitions of the EFSM. They can change the current state of the EFSM, and when online testing is being used, they also send test inputs to the SUT and check the correctness of its responses.

boolean *name$_i$***Guard():** Each action method can optionally have a *guard*, which is a boolean method with the same name as the action method but with "Guard" added to the end of the name. When the guard returns true, then the action is enabled (so may be called), and when the guard returns false, the action is disabled (so will not be called). Any action method that does not have a corresponding guard method is considered to have an implicit guard that is always true.

Each action method typically defines a short, straight-line sequence of JUnit code that tests one aspect of the SUT by calling one or more SUT methods and checking the correctness of their results. The effect of applying model-based testing to the EFSM is to make a traversal through the EFSM graph, and this weaves those short sequences of test code into longer sequences of more sophisticated tests that dynamically explore many aspects of the SUT.

Using Java as the notation for writing EFSMs has benefits and limitations. The benefits include the familiarity of Java, having the expressiveness of a full programming language available, and the ability to quickly change the structure of the EFSM graph simply by redefining the getState() abstraction function or by modifying the guards and actions.

Some of the limitations are that the guards and transitions are defined as executable methods rather than as symbolic formulae. So graph exploration

---

[9]The objects that are returned must correctly implement the Java equals and hashCode methods, since these are used to compare states.

[10]The boolean parameter can be set to false in order to explore the FSM model without testing the underlying SUT. This can be useful if the SUT operations are very slow and we want an algorithm to quickly explore the FSM before testing starts.

and test generation algorithms can execute guards and transitions and inspect their results (true/false from a guard or a new EFSM state after a transition), but they cannot inspect the internal structure of the guards or transitions. To create the EFSM graph, ModelJUnit is limited to exploring it dynamically by executing enabled transitions. This means that it can be difficult to obtain the whole graph if some guards are rarely true. On the other hand, even if the EFSM graph is too large to explore completely, some forms of test generation are still possible, so the EFSM approach is still useful.

Another limitation is that the SUT interactions are handled internally within each transition, so the SUT input and output values are not explicitly represented in the EFSM graph as they are in a Mealy machine FSM model.[11] This places some small limitations on the test generation algorithms and coverage metrics that we can use in ModelJUnit. For example, we can measure action coverage and state coverage but not input coverage or output coverage. We can use transition-tour test generation algorithms but not some other test generation methods, such as the W-method, that analyze the output part of transitions. However, in practice this limitation is outweighed by the benefit of being able to generate rich SUT inputs dynamically and perform more sophisticated checking of the SUT outputs than the simple equality check of a Mealy machine FSM.

5.2.3 An EFSM Model of Qui-Donc

As an example of writing an EFSM in the ModelJUnit style, let's convert our Qui-Donc model into an EFSM. Since we cannot automate the execution of the Qui-Donc tests (JUnit is not yet smart enough to understand the spoken responses from Qui-Donc), the tests that we generate with ModelJUnit will simply print out test sequences (input-output pairs) that a human can execute later. That is, here we are using ModelJUnit to generate offline tests, whereas in the next section we use it for online testing.

Listing 5.3 shows the state-related parts of the model and Listing 5.4 shows the actions. We use the same set of input symbols as in Figure 5.1, but we have put the full output messages into our model rather than just their names, to show how we can use Java string concatenation to reduce the duplication of strings. The "wait/..." output message means that the previous message is repeated.

The interesting thing about this EFSM model is that it has only 5 states (Start, Star, Enter, Emerg, Info) rather than the 11 states of our

---

[11] Technically, this means that ModelJUnit models are *labeled transition systems* (LTS) rather than traditional FSMs.

LISTING 5.3   Qui-Donc EFSM model in Java: the internal state variables
and the getState() and reset() methods.

```java
/** A simple EFSM model of the Qui-Donc service.
 *  Qui-Donc is a service of France Telecom that allows you
 *  to ring up, enter a telephone number, and find who
 *  owns that telephone number and what is their address.
 */
public class QuiDonc implements FsmModel
{
  public enum State
    { Start, // not yet connected to the Qui-Donc service.
      Star,  // waiting for the initial '*'.
      Enter, // waiting for a telephone number to be entered.
      Emerg, // after explaining the emergency number, waiting for '*'.
      Info   // ready to give information about the subscriber.
    };
  private State currState; // the current state of the system.
  private int timeouts;    // on the third timeout, we hang up.

  public String WELCOME  = "Welcome to Qui-Donc.  Please ...";
  public String NOTALLOW = "Your telephone does not allow...";
  public String ENTER    = "Please enter the 10-digit tel...";
  public String ERROR    = "Invalid number entered.  Plea...";
  public String FIRE     = "18 is the emergency number fo...";
  public String SORRY    = "Sorry.The number 03 81 12 3..."+ENTER;
  public String INFO     = "Press 1 to spell the name, pr...";
  public String NAME     = "The number 03 81 12 34 56 cor..."+INFO;
  public String SPELL    = "Renard is spelled R, E, N, A, R..."+INFO;
  public String ADDR     = "The address of Renard, K. J. ..."+INFO;
  public String BYE      = "Thank you for using the Qui-D....";

  public QuiDonc()
  {
    timeouts = 0;
    currState = State.Start;
  }

  public String getState()
  {
    return currState.toString(); // + (timeouts+1);
  }

  public void reset(boolean testing)
  {
    timeouts = 0;
    currState = State.Start;
  }
```

LISTING 5.4 Qui-Donc EFSM model: actions and guards.

```
public boolean dialGuard()                      public boolean num18Guard()
{return currState==State.Start;}                {return currState==State.Enter;}
public @Action void dial()                      public @Action void num18()
{                                               {
  out.println("dial/"+WELCOME);                   out.println("18/"+FIRE);
  currState = State.Star;                          currState = State.Emerg;
  timeouts = 0;                                    timeouts = 0;
}                                               }


// No guard -- always enabled.
//  We call this wait_, to avoid            public boolean num1Guard()
//  a clash with Object.wait().             {return currState==State.Enter;}
public @Action void wait_()                 public @Action void num1()
{                                           {
  timeouts++;                                 out.println("num1/"+SORRY);
  if (timeouts >= 3                           // state is unchanged.
     || currState==State.Emerg                timeouts = 0;
     || currState==State.Start)            }
  {
    if (currState==State.Star)
      out.println("wait/"+NOTALLOW);
    else                                    public boolean num2Guard()
      out.println("wait/"+BYE);            {return currState==State.Enter;}
    currState = State.Start;               public @Action void num2()
    timeouts = 0;                          {
  }                                           out.println("num2/"+NAME);
  else                                        currState = State.Info;
    out.println("wait/...");                  timeouts = 0;
}                                           }


public boolean starGuard()                  public boolean key1Guard()
{return currState==State.Star               {return currState==State.Info;}
     || currState==State.Emerg             public @Action void key1()
     || currState==State.Info;             {
}                                             out.println("1/"+SPELL);
public @Action void star()                    // state is unchanged.
{                                             timeouts = 0;
  out.println("*/"+ENTER);                  }
  currState = State.Enter;
  timeouts = 0;
}                                           public boolean key2Guard()
                                            {return currState==State.Info;}
public boolean badGuard()                   public @Action void key2()
{return currState==State.Enter;}           {
public @Action void bad()                     out.println("2/"+ADDR);
{                                             // state is unchanged.
  out.println("bad/"+ERROR);                  timeouts = 0;
  // state is unchanged.                    }
  timeouts = 0;
}
```

original Qui-Donc model because our getState() method returns only the currState variable and ignores the timeouts counter. For example, this collapses the original three states (Star1, Star2, and Star3) into a single state, Star. This smaller set of states means that some of the transitions in the original model (e.g., the three */ENTER transitions from the Star_i states to the Enter1 state) also collapse into a single transition. So our EFSM model is significantly smaller, even though it models exactly the same functionality. Figure 5.3 shows the EFSM graph that is generated by ModelJUnit with the getState() method shown in Listing 5.3.

If we redefine the getState() method so that it also puts the value of timeouts into the state string (as shown in the comment), then we get a larger EFSM graph that is almost identical to the original Qui-Donc graph in Figure 5.1. The only significant difference is that we have an extra wait_ loop on the Start state because our wait_ action has no guard, so it is enabled in *every* state. This extra transition could easily be removed by adding a guard

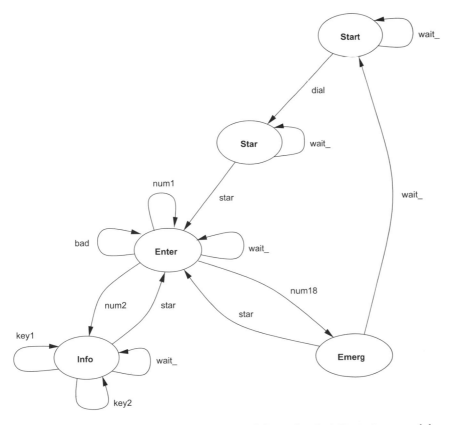

FIGURE 5.3   Qui-Donc EFSM, generated from the Qui-Donc Java model.

(currState!=State.Start) to the wait_ action, but we wanted to leave it without a guard to illustrate that a missing guard is interpreted as always true.

An interesting aspect of the FSM in Figure 5.3 is that it does not include all the wait transitions back to the Start node. This is because the wait transitions are actually nondeterministic and the random graph exploration did not follow the wait loops enough times to find the alternative path. In this case, the missing transitions could be discovered automatically if we traversed the EFSM graph using an *all-loops* heuristic, going around each loop at least three times. But in general, the EFSM notation is expressive enough to define large or infinite graphs, so when we try to take a finite projection of such a graph (to create an FSM) by traversing it randomly or using heuristics, it is quite common that we miss some transitions. This can slightly weaken the test suites generated from that FSM. It illustrates the fact that testing is often incomplete.

One last point about this EFSM model is that although we wrote only 9 action methods, these generate the 15 transitions in Figure 5.3, or the 36 transitions in the larger EFSM of Figure 5.1 if we use the alternative getState() method. This illustrates the power of using Java and the EFSM approach—a single EFSM method can define many transitions, and the full power of Java coding can be used within that action to update the state appropriately. This can dramatically reduce the time required to write a complex model. But it also means that writing the model becomes a programming task, which requires programming skills, whereas the simpler FSM models can sometimes be designed by nonprogrammers using a graphical drawing tool or by writing a transition table in a spreadsheet.

VALIDATING THE MODEL

To validate this model, we wrote a simple main method that allowed methods to be called interactively; then we did a manual traversal through the model, using the transition tour from Figure 5.1 as a guide. This exposed three errors in the model: one typo (the dial action ended in the Start state rather than the Star state, and two cut-and-paste errors (the key1 and key2 guards were true in the Enter state rather than in the Info state). Using the transition tour was a bit excessive for the validation of this simple model; a shorter informal tour that just covered all 9 actions would have exposed the same errors (which is just as well, because we don't usually have an existing transition tour before the model is built, and it would not be useful to use a tour generated from the model to validate the same model!). In fact, it would not have been a disaster if we had done *no* validation of the model—the errors might have remained in the model and we would have generated some incorrect tests, but those errors would almost certainly be exposed when the tests were executed; the chance of having an identical error in the model and in the SUT is quite low.

GENERATING TESTS FROM THE MODEL

If we take this Qui-Donc model and generate a *random walk*, which randomly calls any enabled action method, we get a test sequence that starts like this:

```
dial/Welcome to Qui-Donc.  Please press the star key.
wait/...
*/Please enter the 10-digit telephone number of the
  subscriber you are looking for, followed by the hash key.
wait/...
bad/Invalid number entered.  Please enter another number,
  followed by the hash key.
18/18 is the emergency number for the Fire Brigade.
  If you want to do another search, press star.
wait/Thank you for using the Qui-Donc service.
etc.
```

This output could be used as a manual test script. We could generate a random walk test sequence of a fixed length to match our testing budget (say 240 transitions, which would be about 1 hour of manual test execution), and then measure the model coverage to see what percentage of states, actions, or transitions we have tested. Alternatively, we might choose to use a more sophisticated generation algorithm, such as a transition tour, that achieves a certain kind of coverage (e.g., transition coverage) with a minimal test suite.

5.3 UNIT TESTING ZLIVE WITH EFSMS

In this section, we go through another case study using a parameterized EFSM model to do model-based unit testing of a hierarchy of Java classes. The concepts that we illustrate include:

- EFSM models in Java, with state variables, and guards and state updates within the transitions.
- *online* testing, where the SUT is tested while the tests are being generated, rather than later.
- a simple kind of *adaptor*, which links the model to the SUT.
- several structural model coverage criteria for FSMs/EFSMs.

5.3.1 The System under Test: ZLive `FlatPred`

ZLive is an animator for the Z specification language, developed by one of the authors (Utting). It is part of the open-source Community Z Tools project,[12] which has developed support tools for ISO Standard Z [ISO02] and several extensions of Z. ZLive can evaluate simple Z expressions and predicates and can execute some Z specifications that have small state spaces (in general, the Z specification language is not executable [HJ89, Spi92]). It is typically used to test parts of specifications, to generate instances of schemas, or to search for counterexamples. The implementation of ZLive contains about 8000 lines of commented Java.

Inside ZLive, the Z specification is translated into a sequence of `FlatPred` objects, reordered for more efficient evaluation, then evaluated using backtracking search. There are over 20 kinds (subclasses) of `FlatPred` objects, and each `FlatPred` object represents a constraint among several variables. The `FlatPred` class hierarchy is the most significant part of ZLive and accounts for about two-thirds of its source code. Here are a few examples of `FlatPred` objects and the constraints that they represent:

`FlatMult(x,y,z)`	:	$x * y = z$
`FlatPlus(x,y,z)`	:	$x + y = z$
`FlatConst(x,k)`	:	$x = k$ (k is a constant)
`FlatMember(s,x)`	:	$x \in s$
`FlatRangeSet(a,b,s)`	:	$s = (a..b)$
`FlatSetComp(decls,pred,expr,s)`	:	$s = \{decls \mid pred @ expr\}$

For example, the following sequence of `FlatPred` objects will return all the factors of 24, one by one, in the variable `answer`.

`FlatRangeSet(1,24,range),`	// $range = (1..24)$
`FlatMember(range, factor1),`	// $factor1 \in range$
`FlatMult(answer, factor1, 24)`	// $answer * factor1 = 24$

How does it do this? The `FlatMember` constraint iterates through the set `range`, setting the `factor1` variable first to 1, then to 2, then to the successive integers up to 24. For each value of `factor1`, the `FlatMult` constraint tries to find a value of `answer` that satisfies `answer` $* $ `factor1` $= 24$; if it fails then we backtrack to the previous constraint and try the next value of `factor1`; but if it succeeds, then the correct value is assigned to the `answer` variable and a solution is returned to the caller.

---

[12] See *http://czt.sourceforge.net*.

This illustrates that each `FlatPred` object can be used in several different *modes*, with inputs or outputs. The example used `FlatMult` in the mode OII, meaning that its first parameter was an output, while the second and third parameters were inputs. But `FlatMult` can also be used in the mode IIO (which multiplies $x \times y$ and sets z to the result, so it never fails), in mode IOI (which sets y to a number that satisfies $x \times y = z$ or fails if there is no such number), or in mode III (which takes all three parameters as inputs and fails if their values do not satisfy $x \times y = z$).

The behavior of a typical `FlatPred` object is reasonably sophisticated, so it needs to be tested thoroughly. We decided to apply model-based unit testing to the `FlatPred` subclasses, to try to improve the quality of the unit tests and to see how convenient it was to use an FSM approach to test a hierarchy of Java classes.

ZLive has a system test suite of over 600 tests, which tests the `FlatPred` subclasses in many ways but does not generally exercise all modes. In addition, 17 out of 23 of the `FlatPred` subclasses already had a reasonable set of manually designed JUnit tests (2500 lines of commented Java), which tested every mode of those subclasses. The remaining six `FlatPred` implementations had no unit tests (prior to adopting model-based testing), mostly because they implemented only one mode (III), so they were tested reasonably well by the system tests.

5.3.2 A Family of Models

In this section, we gradually develop a parameterized EFSM model for `FlatPred`, using `FlatMult` as an example but taking care to keep the model general enough that we can use it for all the subclasses of `FlatPred`. This means that the overhead of creating the model can be amortized over the testing of more than 20 classes.

Before we can design a model, we must describe the `FlatPred` API a little more to see which methods change the state of the `FlatPred` object under test, when each method can be called, and so on. So here is a brief summary of the main `FlatPred` methods (we ignore the constructors because they are different for each subclass).

Mode chooseMode(Envir): This is the key method that allows us to find out which evaluation modes a `FlatPred` object supports. For example, if we have a `FlatMult(x,y,z)` object and call its `chooseMode(env)` method with env containing just x, the result will be null because it is not possible to solve the $x \times y = z$ constraint knowing only x. But if env contains x and y, then a `Mode` object will be returned, indicating that mode IIO is allowed. The returned `Mode` object contains an updated environment which includes the output variable z, plus some other statistical information about the expected number of solutions of this constraint.

void setMode(Mode): After we have called `chooseMode(..)` one or more times to find out what modes are possible, we can use this method to select one of those modes. This fixes it as the mode that will be used during evaluation.

void startEvaluation(): After an evaluation mode has been set with `setMode`, this method can be called to start a new evaluation. This is similar to requesting an iterator from a collection object in order to iterate through all the solutions. Note that we typically perform a sequence of several evaluations using the same mode—each evaluation usually has different values for the input variables.

boolean nextEvaluation(): This calculates the next solution and returns true if there is a valid solution, false otherwise. When it returns true, it updates the values of the output variables in the current environment so that following `FlatPred` constraints can access those new values. This method can be called only after `startEvaluation()`.

boolean inferBounds(Bounds): This is an optional static analysis method for inferring information about integer bounds and allowing more efficient evaluation. It is usually called before `chooseMode()`. The `Bounds` parameter is a repository for the currently known lower and upper bounds of all the integer variables in scope. This method returns true if it has tightened those bounds. Some of the bounds information may be saved within the `FlatPred` object, so calling this method may change the state of the `FlatPred object`, as well as change the `Bounds` repository.

So this is the typical life cycle of a `FlatPred` object:

1. [*optional*] Call `inferBounds` to do some static analysis.
2. Call `chooseMode` one or more times to see which modes are possible, and then call `setMode` to select one of those modes.
3. Call `startEvaluation`, followed by a series of calls to `nextEvaluation` to get each solution until it returns false.

The last step is usually repeated several times for each evaluation that we want to perform. This life cycle shows that the `FlatPred` object changes state quite a few times and that some methods can be called only in certain states.

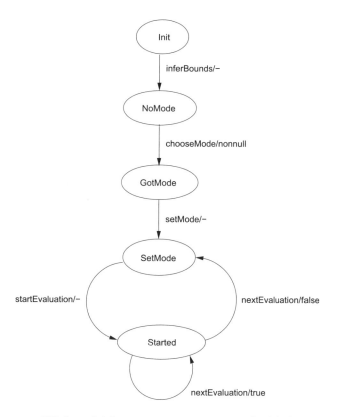

FIGURE 5.4   FSM model for FlatMult, version 1. The labels on the transitions are the names of the FlatMethods to call, with the expected result of the method shown after the slash (– means void or "don't care").

It is this state-based behavior of FlatPred that makes it suitable to model with an FSM/EFSM.

> **Key Point**   If you have a class that changes state and has different behavior in each state, then an FSM/EFSM model is a good choice for testing that class.

This typical life cycle suggests that we could use an FSM model of FlatPred like the one shown in Figure 5.4.

But in fact, this is not a good model, for the following reasons:

Not enough loops and choices: The model is too simplistic! The power of model-based testing comes from having lots of paths to explore. But this model has only two loops and very few alternative paths. We need to add more paths, to explore all the different modes that are possible, to try restarting a new evaluation before the last one is complete, to try choosing a new mode after or during an evaluation, and so on. Without these alternatives, the generated tests will repeat the same sequences of methods over and over again, with little variation.

Not deterministic: Once we reach the Started state, there are two transitions that leave that state, but both of them are labeled with the same input value, nextEval. This means that both transitions involve calling the nextEvaluation() method, but we expect a response of true from the SUT in one case and a response of false in the other case. This makes it impossible for the FSM traversal algorithms to *control* which transition will be followed. In this chapter, we require our FSM models to be deterministic so that the test generation algorithms can control the SUT.

Not a strong enough oracle: This model describes the behavior of almost every FlatPred and does not have strong enough checks to ensure that each subclass has the correct behavior. For example, if a FlatMult(x,y,z) object returned *two* solutions for *z* (say, 12 and 13) when $x = 3$ and $y = 4$, the model would happily follow the nextEval/true transition two times, then the nextEval/true transition once, and would agree that this is the correct behavior! We need some way of having stronger checking on the behavior of each FlatPred object. Since the behavior varies between FlatPred subclasses, and even between different input values, this means we need to *parameterize* our generic FlatPred model to tell it the specific behavior to expect for each particular SUT.

> **Key Point**   Whenever possible, make your FSM model deterministic. This simplifies test generation and means that the generated tests can control the SUT.

To fix the first of these problems, we add more transitions to our model. For example, we add some separate transitions to try each mode, plus some newMode transitions that go back from the evaluation states and start using a new mode. This allows us to test the effect of jumping out of an evaluation and switching to a different mode. Figure 5.5 shows some of these new transitions (it shows only the 000 and III modes).

To fix the second and third problems, we switch from a simple FSM model to a more sophisticated extended finite state machine (EFSM) model. We write our EFSM as a Java class, following the ModelJUnit style. So the

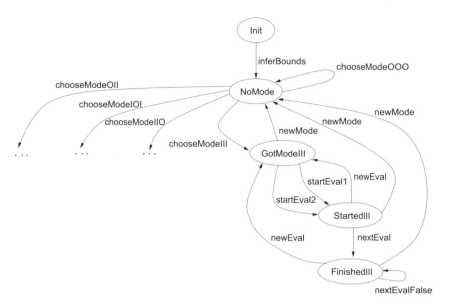

FIGURE 5.5   EFSM model for FlatMult, showing only the OOO and III modes. The labels on the transitions are the names of the @Action methods in the ModelJUnit class.

names on the transitions of Figure 5.5 are actually the names of the Java @Action methods in our ModelJUnit class, which we develop over the next few pages. Each of these methods is responsible for updating the current state of the EFSM as well as interacting with the SUT.

We will use the internal variables of the EFSM to record more precise information about the expected behavior of the current FlatPred that is being tested, such as the mode that we are testing and the values of each input variable. Also, to permit more accurate testing of each subtype of FlatPred, we will parameterize our general FlatPred model with some values that are specific to the particular FlatPred object under test so that our EFSM can use those parameters to check the correctness of the SUT behavior. For example, here is the Java code that constructs an EFSM model for FlatMult(x,y,z) (the full graph of this model is shown in Figure 5.6):

```
FlatPredModel model = new FlatPredModel(sut,
    new ZRefName[] {x,y,z},
    "OII,IOI,IIO,III",
    new Eval(1, "???", i3, i4, i12),
    new Eval(0, "I?I", i2, i5, i11) // 11 is prime
 );
```

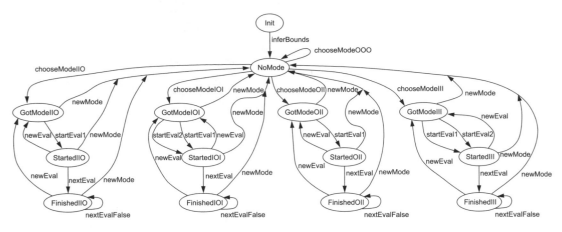

FIGURE 5.6   FSM model for FlatMult, final version.

Let us explain these parameters to give some examples of how it is possible to parameterize an EFSM. We will always create the same type of model, a FlatPredModel, but the parameters to its constructor can change the structure and the meaning of the EFSM model dramatically.

The first parameter, sut, will be discussed in Section 5.3.3—it has to do with test execution, not with the EFSM model. The second parameter informs the EFSM model about all the variables used by the SUT. In this case, our SUT implements the constraint $x \times y = z$, so the free variables are x, y, and z.

The third parameter lists all the modes that are supported by the SUT. Modes that are in this list are expected to give a non-null result when chooseMode is called, while any modes that are not in the list are expected to give a null result. The FlatPredModel class uses this parameter to determine the gross structure of the EFSM: each mode in the list generates a transition that leads to a separate subgraph of the EFSM that tests evaluations using that mode (e.g., the chooseModeIII transition); each mode not in the list generates a transition that loops back to the NoMode state (e.g., the chooseModeOOO transition).

The fourth and fifth parameters are two evaluation examples to use when testing the SUT. The first of these examples is used by the startEval1 transition to start an evaluation, and the second example is used by the startEval2 transition. We use two examples rather than one because we want to swap between *different* evaluations during the test runs to check that one evaluation does not corrupt the other. It would be possible to parameterize the model with more than two examples, but we usually do this by creating multiple models instead.

Each of these evaluation examples is encapsulated into an object that contains a value for each of the free variables (e.g., the first example sets $x = 3$, $y = 4$, and $z = 12$), plus the number of solutions expected. This enables us to strengthen the oracle checking within the `startEval1` and `startEval2` transitions so that they check that `nextEvaluation()` returns true the correct number of times, as well as telling us what values to use for the inputs and what values to expect in the outputs. It turns out that the number of solutions sometimes depends on the mode used, which is why each evaluation example has a string like I?I to say which parameters must be inputs (I), which must be outputs (O), and which can be either inputs or outputs (?). Since the second example restricts the evaluation modes to I?I, the `startEval2` transition is disabled in the OII and IIO modes, where x and z are not inputs, respectively. This is another example of how these parameters change the shape of the EFSM graph.

Having designed our EFSM model, the next section describes how this model is written as a Java class, and then we look at how we can use the ModelJUnit library to explore the model, generate tests from it, and measure the coverage of the generated tests.

5.3.3 Encoding `FlatPredModel` in Java

The ZLive `FlatPred` example is a more complex EFSM model than the Qui-Donc model. The `FlatPredModel` class contains around 350 lines of commented Java, which is 230 noncomment source lines of Java, or 120 executable statements. In this section we briefly make a few comments about some interesting features of this model before we show the results of using it for test generation.

DEFINING THE EFSM STATES
Like the Qui-Donc model, the `FlatPred` model defines an enumeration of its five main states.

```
/** The possible main states of the FlatPred. */
enum State {Init, NoMode, GotMode, Started, Finished};
private State state_;
```

However, we want to distinguish the states of the different modes (to encourage the test generation algorithms to explore all the modes), so we define our `getState()` method to add the mode string (III, IIO, etc.) to the end of the state, but only when we are in one of the GotMode, Started, or Finished states. Note that the following `getState()` method makes use of several other private variables of the EFSM: `names_` is the array of free variables of the SUT, and `env_` is the current evaluation environment, which is null in the `Init` and `NoMode` states and contains the values of the input variables in the other states.

```
public String getState()
{
  StringBuffer result = new StringBuffer();
  result.append(state_.toString());
  if (env_ != null) {
    // add the mode to the end of the state.
    for (int i=0; i<names_.length; i++)
      if ( ! env_.isDefined(names_[i]))
        result.append('O');
      else
        result.append('I');   // an input
  }
  return result.toString();
}
```

Note that if we have an SUT with five free variables, we will have EFSM states like `GotModeIIIIO` and `GotModeIIIII`, whereas if we have an SUT with just one free variable, we will have EFSM states like `GotModeI` and `GotModeO`. The `getState()` method gives us tremendous power to control the set of states in our EFSM, and this in turn helps to determine how many states of the SUT will be tested and which states will be tested. Effectively, the `getState()` method is performing the crucial *abstraction* function, mapping the huge or infinite number of possible SUT states down into a small set of interesting EFSM states that will be tested.

> **Key Point**   The abstraction function (the `getState()` method in ModelJUnit) is the key to controlling the number of states and transitions in your EFSM.

PARAMETERIZED EFSM ACTIONS

Figure 5.6 shows that we have several transitions going out of the `NoMode` state, each trying a different mode. The Java code for these transitions is very similar, so we define a parameterized helper method that contains all the common code. Then each transition can be defined in just a few lines:

```
/** Tries chooseMode with all names except the last being inputs. */
public boolean chooseModeIIOGuard() {return state_==State.NoMode;}
@Action public void chooseModeIIO() {chooseMode("IIO");}
```

The helper method (chooseMode(String)) is written to handle SUTs with any number of free variables—its parameter is always a three-character string, but the first and last characters control the first and last inputs, respectively, while the middle character controls all the remaining inputs (when *freevars* ≥ 3). This is another example of abstraction or simplification—we decided that it would be sufficient to test all the middle inputs in the same way. These kinds of decision are easy to code up into the EFSM because the full power of Java (loops, conditionals, parameterized methods, etc.) is available for use in each action method.

DEFINING THE EFSM GRAPH STATICALLY AND DYNAMICALLY

The chooseMode(String) helper method also uses a validModes_ list, which is the second parameter to the FlatPredModel constructor, to determine the destination state of each chooseMode transition. This is an example of how a construction-time parameter can change the static structure of the EFSM.

It is always safe to use parameters and conditionals to define the static structure of the EFSM, but one must be careful when using conditionals that change the structure of the EFSM dynamically (that is, on-the-fly, during a traversal of the EFSM). It is okay to use guards to disable or enable transitions (though this can make it more difficult to discover the shape of the EFSM graph). But it is undesirable to define a transition that sometimes leads from state A to state B and at other times leads from state A to state C. This is a *nondeterministic* transition, and it can make the model coverage metrics misleading and confuse some of the graph traversal algorithms.

A better approach is to split that nondeterministic transition into two or more deterministic transitions with different names. If necessary, this can be done by introducing a new state A2, then writing a transition from A to A2 that stores a flag in an internal EFSM variable, followed by two separate transitions, $A2 \xrightarrow{AB} B$ and $A2 \xrightarrow{AC} C$, that have guards to enable them when the flag is true or false, respectively. This is the technique that we used to handle the nondeterministic nextEval transition in Figure 5.4—it has been split into separate nextEval and nextEvalFalse transitions in Figure 5.5.

ONLINE TESTING WITH MODELJUNIT

We now briefly review the responsibilities of the various parts of the EFSM model when it is being used for online testing with ModelJUnit. Recall that with online testing, the EFSM model has two roles: it defines the model and it acts as the adaptor that connects the model to the SUT.

The EFSM model must maintain a pointer to the SUT object as part of its internal state so that it can communicate with the SUT as testing progresses. In fact, the SUT is the first parameter to our `FlatPredModel` constructor, so the `sut` parameter shown on page 173 would actually be an instance of `FlatMult` class, such as:

```
new FlatMult(x,y,z)
```

The guards of the action methods are responsible for saying when each action method is enabled; this may require querying the SUT to determine whether it is ready to perform some operation.

Each action method is responsible for:

1. changing the state of the EFSM (or leaving it unchanged, in the case of a loop transition);
2. sending test inputs to the SUT;
3. checking any SUT outputs to make sure they are correct (this is typically done via JUnit assert methods, which check some given condition and generate a test failure if it is false); and
4. (if possible) checking that the SUT is now in the correct state that agrees with the new EFSM state.

Responsibility 1 defines the shape of the EFSM graph. Responsibilities 2 and 3 are the *adaptor* part of the EFSM, which links the model to the SUT and implements the oracle checking. Responsibility 4 gives a stronger form of oracle checking that is not always possible to achieve if the SUT is a black box with not enough query methods to determine its state. However, when the classes that are being tested are well designed, they will often provide query methods that allow the SUT state to be determined. In this case, note that the transition-tour method is as powerful as the D-/W-/Wp-/U-methods of test generation. That is, in theory a simple transition tour is sufficient to find all differences between the model and the SUT (assuming that the SUT does not have more states than the model).

EXAMPLES OF ACTION METHODS

To illustrate how action methods can fulfill these responsibilities, here are some simple action methods from the `FlatPredModel`. The `nextEvalFalse` action calls the SUT `nextEvaluation()` method and checks its result, but it does not need to change the state of the EFSM (it loops back to the same state). The `println` message is just for debugging the model—it is sometimes useful to see the internal state of the EFSM as it is traversed.

```
public boolean nextEvalFalseGuard()
{ return state_ == State.Finished; }
```

```
/** Checks that nextEvaluation() returns false. */
public @Action void nextEvalFalse()
{
  boolean result = pred_.nextEvaluation();
  System.out.println("nextEvalFalse gives "
      +result+" with env="+env_);
  Assert.assertFalse(result);
}
```

The newMode action is the opposite. It does no testing of the SUT; it just changes the state of the EFSM and resets some of the EFSM internal variables. Note that this action is enabled in all the GotModeXXX, StartedXXX, and FinishedXXX states, so this one action method generates the 12 newMode transitions in Figure 5.6.

```
public boolean newModeGuard()
{ return state_ == State.Started
  || state_ == State.Finished
  || state_ == State.GotMode;
}
/** Go back and try a new mode. */
@Action public void newMode()
{
  System.out.println("newMode with env="+env_);
  mode_ = null;
  env_  = null;
  data_ = null;
  state_ = State.NoMode;
}
```

Other actions in FlatPredModel are more complex in that they test the SUT as well as change the EFSM state. Some of them use conditionals and loops to perform more comprehensive testing of the SUT. Now let's use this model to do some testing.

5.3.4 Test Results

We will take the simplest possible approach to test generation—a random walk through the model. This will allow us to see how the various model coverage metrics change as we generate longer and longer tests. We have also recorded the SUT code coverage metrics so that we can see how they are correlated with the model coverage.

Since we are using online testing, each transition that we take in the model is immediately testing the SUT. Note that a random walk of the model is more powerful than just generating random SUT inputs because each transition of the model not only generates SUT inputs but also runs the oracle code that checks the correctness of the outputs. So with random input generation, the only oracle you get is crash/no-crash, whereas with a random walk of the model, you get the powerful oracle checking that you have (we hope!) included in the action methods of your model adapter.

What happens when an error is detected by this oracle code? Usually, JUnit just gives you a one-line message that says how the expected and actual values differed and which assert statement detected the error. ModelJUnit gives that same information, but it can also display the current state of the EFSM model and the complete path through the model that led to the error, if desired.

One interesting possibility of online testing, which ModelJUnit does not yet support, is the BeeLine approach to minimizing the test sequence that leads to a given error.[13] Let's say that we find an error when we are deep into a random walk through the model. The BeeLine algorithm repeatedly cuts out random segments of that sequence (replacing them with shorter paths through the EFSM) until it finds the shortest sequence that leads to the error. This can make it easier to analyze the cause of the failure.

For our FlatMult application, we just set the random walk going and let it do a few thousand transitions. One of the nice features of random walks is that you can ask for any length test suite. We use a fixed seed for the random number generator so that the random walk takes the same path each time we run our unit tests and we get repeatable results from successive runs.

Figure 5.7 shows how several common model coverage metrics increase as we let the random testing continue for longer and longer. Notice that the simple state coverage metric increases very quickly and reaches 90 percent after just 30 transitions and 100 percent after 86 transitions. The action coverage metric is similar and reaches 100 percent after 104 transitions. Transition coverage takes a little longer—it reaches 90 percent after 121 transitions and 100 percent after 299 transitions. The transition-pair coverage rises even more slowly—it reaches 50 percent after 132 transitions, 90 percent after 628 transitions, and 100 percent after 1211 transitions.

Recall that before we did this model-based testing of the FlatMult implementation, we already had a set of manually written JUnit tests for FlatMult. These were a typical set of 8 JUnit tests that tested all the modes of FlatMult and contained 72 executable statements, of which 43 were JUnit assert statements. These JUnit tests had achieved 68 percent branch coverage and 89

---

[13]This is another idea taken from Harry Robinson's STAREast 2005 Model-Based Testing Tutorial.

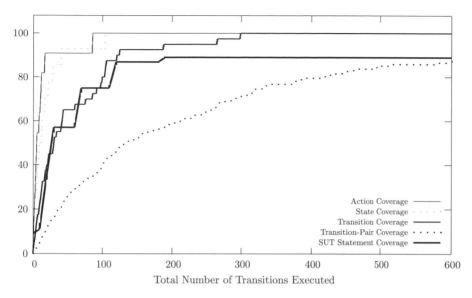

FIGURE 5.7   Coverage metrics for one random walk over the FlatPredModel, testing the FlatMult implementation.

percent statement coverage of the FlatMult code (which contained 62 executable statements). The random walk of the model-based testing improved the SUT branch coverage slightly. It reached the same level of coverage as the JUnit tests after 190 transitions and then increased the branch coverage to 73 percent after 370 transitions. Figure 5.7 shows that the statement coverage remained the same at 89 percent.

Figure 5.8 shows a logarithmic view of how these coverage metrics increase with the length of the test sequence. Rather than show percentages, this graph shows the raw numbers of items (States, Actions, Transitions, and Transition-Pairs) that have been covered as the length of the test increases.

Overall, the use of model-based testing on the FlatPred classes was very successful. It took about 8 hours to design (and redesign twice!) FlatPredModel and apply it to the FlatMult implementation. This is probably four to eight times longer than the time required to develop the original JUnit tests, but they were just for FlatMult, whereas the model was general enough to test most FlatPred subclasses. When we reused the model to test another FlatPred subclass, it took less than 15 minutes to parameterize the model and invoke a random walk, which is much less than the time required to write six to ten JUnit tests, so the overhead of the model development is cost-effective when spread across more than 20 subclasses.

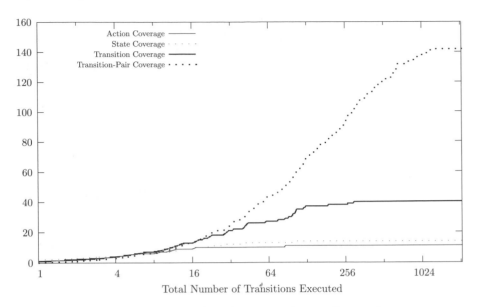

FIGURE 5.8 Raw coverage numbers for one random walk over the FlatPredModel, testing the FlatMult implementation (logarithmic view).

During the development of FlatPredModel, the random walk testing of FlatMult found 4 adaptor errors (errors in the parts of the FlatPredModel actions that communicate with the SUT), 1 model error (which was obvious when we looked at the graph of the EFSM), and 1 SUT error (to our surprise!). The error was in the IOI mode of FlatMult(x,y,z), with the data $x = 2$ and $z = 11$. The implementation of that mode correctly did a division to calculate $y = z/x = 11/2 = 5$, but then it immediately assigned 5 to y and returned true rather than rechecking the multiplication first, and finding that $2 \times 5 \neq 11$, so returning false. This error was detected by the random walk test generation, but it had not been detected by the JUnit tests or by the 600 ZLive system tests, 36 of which used multiplication.

5.4 LABELED TRANSITION SYSTEMS MODELS

Finite state machines and extended finite state machines can be viewed as special cases of *labeled transition systems* (LTS). The main difference between LTS and FSM is that an LTS is allowed to have an infinite set of states and/or an infinite set of labels, whereas an FSM must have a finite set of states and a finite input alphabet.

LTSs were defined by Keller [Kel76] and have become widely used for modeling data-intensive systems, such as sequential and concurrent programs and hardware circuits [BJK$^+$05, 113]. There are many kinds of LTS, including the Input/Output Automata of Lynch and Tuttle [LT87] and the Input/Output Transition Systems of Tretmans [Tre96].

Most of the research on test generation from LTS models has been theoretical, but some of the research has resulted in model-based testing tools being implemented. One of the most well-known theories is Tretman's *Input/Output Conformance* relation (ioco), which has been the basis for several model-based testing tools, such as TGV [JJ05] and TorX[14] [TB03].

LTS models are good at modeling nondeterministic *reactive systems*, where the generated tests must cope with events coming from the SUT spontaneously rather than as a direct response to the test inputs. We will see examples of this approach in the next two chapters (Sections 6.5 and 7.3).

5.5 SUMMARY

An FSM model has a finite set of *states*, plus a collection of *transitions* that lead from one state to another. Each transition is labeled with an input value i and an expected output value o and is sometimes written $s \xrightarrow{i/o} s'$, where the transition goes from state s to state s'.

An EFSM is similar to an FSM but is more expressive because it has internal variables that can store more detailed state information. Its actions can update those variables and can also have guards that enable or disable the action.

FSM and EFSM models can be used for system testing or for unit testing. The generated tests can be executed manually or automatically either online or offline.

If you have a system that changes state and has different behavior in each state, then a finite state model (FSM or EFSM) is a good choice for modeling that system.

The key step in designing a finite state model is abstraction—deciding which aspects of the SUT to ignore and which aspects to view as separate states or separate transitions. These design decisions determine the size and shape of the finite state model, which in turn determines the tests that are generated.

---

[14]The TorX tool is available for noncommercial use from the University of Twente. See *http://fmt.cs.utwente.nl/tools/torx* or *http://www.purl.org/net/torx*.

In the ModelJUnit library, the `getState()` method defines this abstraction function. It is the key to controlling the number of states and transitions in your EFSM. Small changes to this method can produce EFSMs of radically different shapes and sizes.

When generating tests from a finite state model, full transition coverage is a recommended minimum goal. The Chinese postman algorithm [Thi03] generates a minimum-length test sequence that satisfies 100 percent transition coverage. Transition-pair coverage is much more demanding, but the percentage of transition-pair coverage is a useful measure of how many interactions between adjacent transitions you have tested.

Random walks are the easiest way to generate test suites from an FSM model, and those test suites are surprisingly effective. Random walks have the nice properties that (1) you can easily generate a test suite of any desired length, and (2) the test suite gives more and more sophisticated coverage of the model as it grows longer and longer. With online testing, random walks can generate an infinite sequence of constantly changing tests that can be useful for overnight testing, perhaps even on multiple machines, each with a different seed for the random walk.

Explicit test specifications can be useful when you want to force a particular kind of test to be generated from a model.

5.6 FURTHER READING

Chapter 7 of Binder [Bin99] contains lots of practical advice on how to design various kinds of finite state systems. His Section 7.4.5 discusses how to choose among the test generation strategies for finite state systems. For each strategy he gives examples of the size of the generated test suite (his Table 7.12) and the fault-revealing power (his Figure 7.40) of the strategy.

Harry Robinson's entertaining introduction to the use of graph theory in model-based testing [Rob99] gives an overview of Euler tours, the Chinese postman problem, the New York street sweeper problem, the de Bruijn sequence for combinations of length 2 (also called safecracker sequences), the parallel street sweeper problem, random walks, and Markov chains.

The first four chapters of [BJK+05] give a more thorough and theoretical coverage of test generation from FSMs and describe a variety of test generation algorithms and their complexity. Chapters 5 through 9 of the same book give a comprehensive survey of model-based testing techniques for various kinds of labeled transition system. Also, see [Pet01, BT01] for brief annotated bibliographies of some of the main research papers and books in the LTS field.

Bochmann and Petrenko [BP94] and Lee and Yannakakis [LY96] give surveys of FSM and EFSM testing methods. The 1989 paper by Sidhu and Leung [SL89] describes four test generation algorithms for FSMs and gives some experimental results on their fault-detection capability and the size of the test suites that they generate. The 1991 paper by Fujiwara and colleagues [FvBK⁺91] adds some more algorithms and discusses assumptions and limitations of the various methods.

In Section 5.1.4 we note that many of the complete FSM test generation methods such as the D-method [Hen64], the W-method [Vas73, Cho78], the Wp-method [FvBK⁺91], and the U-method [SD88] place strong requirements on the FSM (it must be deterministic, minimal, complete, strongly connected, and have the same number of states as the SUT). More recent research allows many of these requirements to be relaxed. The minimal, complete, and strongly connected requirements can be satisfied reasonably easily by transforming the FSM into an equivalent minimal FSM, by adding transitions, and by adding a reset operation, respectively. There has been some research on generating tests from nondeterministic FSMs [LvBP94, Hie03, Hie04, MCLH05], and there are some FSM test generation algorithms that can weaken the assumption on the number of states, but the length of the tests grows exponentially with each additional SUT state [LY96, Section 4.7.2].

At MBT 2004 [GKP05], Kervinen and Virolainen [KV05] described an experimental evaluation (on 45 variants of a distributed conference chat system) of the fault-detection speed of seven test generation algorithms for EFSMs, ranging from purely random to sophisticated adaptive algorithms. They found that a *greedy random algorithm* (which gives higher priority to unused transitions) worked surprisingly well, but the highest fault-detection was with adaptive or pessimistic algorithms that give high priority to sending new inputs or receiving new outputs from the SUT.

The ModelJUnit library is available for download from this book's website, and the Qui-Donc model is included as one of the examples.

## CHAPTER 6

TESTING FROM PRE/POST MODELS

This chapter shows how to write pre/post models for testing and how to generate tests from those models. The main goals of the chapter are for you to understand the test generation process and become familiar with alternatives and options that you can use to control the generation of your tests. We also introduce *test targets*, which help you to control and measure the effectiveness of your test generation, *traceability* techniques for relating the informal requirements to the generated tests, and techniques for designing *nondeterministic models* of nondeterministic systems.

To make it easy to understand the generated tests and relate them to the models, we use three small examples:

- A process scheduler for a simple uniprocessor machine. We use this example to illustrate several kinds of test selection criteria, including *all-values*, *boundary-values*, and *transition-pair* testing.

- The classic *triangle* program [Mye79], which takes the lengths of three sides of a triangle and classifies it as equilateral, isosceles, scalene, or invalid. We use this example to illustrate the common test selection criteria for complex decisions, such as DC, D/CC, MC/DC, and MCC (see Chapter 4) and to show why it is sometimes useful to have multiple testing models.

- A simple online chat system that allows clients to enter and exit a single chat room and send messages to one another. This example illustrates techniques for testing a nondeterministic system under test (SUT). We use the Spec Explorer tool [CGN+05] to do online testing of an implementation of the chat system.

Before working through the examples, we discuss specific strategies and techniques for writing pre/post models for testing purposes.

6.1 HOW TO WRITE PRE/POST MODELS FOR TESTING

This section gives some detailed guidelines to write a pre/post model that is suitable for test generation.

We use the B abstract machine notation for our pre/post models because it is a typical example of a pre/post notation, it has good tool support, and it is easily learned by programmers since many of its constructs are similar to programming languages (assignment, if-then-else, etc.). However, most of the principles that we cover in this chapter can be applied to any pre/post style of model (e.g., in Z, VDM, Spec#, Java Modeling Language, or UML with OCL pre/postconditions).

There are four main steps to writing a pre/post model:

1. Choose a high-level test objective.
2. Design the signatures of the operations in the model.
3. Design the state variables of the model and choose their types.
4. Write the preconditions and postconditions of each operation.

As we discuss each of these steps, we will see that the central theme that runs through them all is how to choose a good level of abstraction for the model. The goal is to have just enough detail in the model to be able to generate test inputs and check the correctness of outputs while avoiding unnecessary detail that would make the model larger and more complex.

The first step is to choose a high-level test objective that says which aspects of the SUT we want to test. For example, if we are testing the software for a GPS navigation system in a vehicle, we might decide that we want to test just its position tracking capabilities (including its interaction with the GPS satellites, the car speedometer, and the gyroscope). Alternatively, we might decide that we want to test just its route planning capabilities.

The models for these two alternatives would be quite different since they would be modeling different aspects of the navigation system. The generated tests would also be quite different since they would use different subsets of the control and observation ports of the GPS navigation system.

Although it would be possible to write a single model to test both these aspects at once, this would be undesirable because the model would be much more complex. Test generation would be more difficult, and we could get a useless combinatorial explosion between the position tracking and route planning functions when computing test cases. Whenever possible, it is preferable to use separate models to test different aspects of a system.

The second step is to decide which control and observation ports of the SUT we need to use to satisfy our high-level test objective and how those ports should be mapped into operations of the model. As well as choosing a name for each model operation, we must decide what input and output parameters it will have. The input parameters will correspond to the inputs to the SUT control ports, and the output parameters will correspond to the output from the SUT observation ports.

Typically, the operations of the model will match the control and observation ports of the SUT quite closely. However, it is interesting to consider the possible relationships between the model operations and the SUT ports. Here are the four possibilities, in decreasing order of importance:

One-to-one: A model operation represents exactly one port of the SUT. The inputs of the model operation must be able to be mapped (by the adapter code) into inputs of the SUT port, and the outputs of the model operation should be useful for checking the correctness of the outputs from the SUT port.[1]

Many-to-one: A single SUT port is decomposed into several simpler model operations. For example, if the SUT port has quite complex behavior (it can perform several different actions depending on the input values, or it may throw several different exceptions), then each model operation may correspond to one case of this SUT behavior.

One-to-many: A model operation corresponds to *several* SUT control or observation ports. This can be a useful way of reducing the complexity

---

[1] If the interaction with the SUT is via procedure calls, then we view a procedure call with inputs and outputs as being both an observation port and a control port.

of the model, by packaging a sequence of SUT operations into a single model operation. For example, a sequence of N SUT operations that add N values into a buffer could be modeled as a single operation in the model. During the concretization stage of model-based testing, each use of this operation would be expanded back into the appropriate sequence of lower-level SUT operations.

Many-to-many: One could imagine combining the one-to-many and many-to-one strategies and ending up with a many-to-many relationship between the SUT ports and model operations. However, such a complex relationship does not arise often and should perhaps be avoided because it is more difficult to explain.

We use mainly the simplest one-to-one relationship in the examples in this chapter. However, when modeling real applications, the one-to-many and many-to-one modes can be very useful tools for mastering the complexity of complex operations.

The third step is to design the data structures that will be used within the model. This involves choosing some state variables for the model with an appropriate data type for each variable. In the case of the B notation, each variable can be boolean, integer, enumerated type, set, relation, function, or sequence. The goal is for the model to record just enough of the internal state of the SUT to make it possible to check the correctness of its outputs.

The fourth step is to write the preconditions and postconditions of each operation. We start by putting the typing conditions of the inputs into the preconditions. In B, *all* the typing information goes into the precondition. In other languages, the basic type information is already in the signature of the operation, but any additional constraints on the inputs should go into the precondition. For example, the signature may define `size:int`, but we actually want to limit the inputs to `size < 100` or say that `size` must be less than the length of some other input. These kinds of constraints go into the precondition so that we generate only test inputs that satisfy these constraints.

> **Key Point**   Model-based testing usually generates tests *within* the preconditions of each operation. So you can use strong preconditions to restrict your testing to the "normal" behavior of an operation or weaker preconditions to test the "exception" cases of its behavior. The weakest precondition is true, which means that *all* input values can be tested.

We also write the postcondition, or the body of the operation, which says how the operation will update the state variables. In B, this typically has an IF-ELSE structure, with some parallel assignments to update all the necessary state and output variables. As we write the body of the operation, we are using the input variables, which often exposes the need for additional preconditions, and we are reading and updating the state variables. This is where we find out how good our choice of data structure was—a good choice makes the operations simpler to write, while a bad choice makes them rather more difficult.

6.1.1 Adding Requirements Tags

A common objective of functional testing is to cover the requirements expressed in the informal requirements documents. To know which requirements have been tested, we first need to define the relationship between the requirements and the model. Then the model-based testing tool can use those relationships plus the generated connection between the model and the tests to create a traceability matrix from the requirements to the tests.

To define the relationship between the requirements and the model, we give each requirement a unique identifier and add these as *tags* to various elements of the model. For example, we might tag one assignment statement, or postcondition, or precondition, to say which requirement it relates to.

Key Point Traceability from requirements to tests is based on a well-structured informal requirements document and a model that is annotated with requirements identifiers.

The exact syntax for requirements traceability is quite tool dependent. However, to illustrate how it works, we use the LEIRIOS Test Generator (LTG/B) tag notation within the B machines of this chapter. The LTG/B tag notation for B uses several types of tag, but we use only two of them in this chapter.

An LTG/B requirement tag is written

```
/*@REQ: IDLIST @*/
```

The IDLIST part is simply a semicolon-separated list of requirements identifiers, which can be integers or alphanumeric names. This requirement tag is an annotation on the statement that precedes it. Note that the tags are written inside B comments so that they will be ignored by other B tools.

It often happens that an adjacent group of statements all have the same requirements tag. Rather than write a separate tag on each statement, a pair of tags, BEGIN..END, can be used to tag the whole group. For example, instead of writing

```
size := size + 1        /*@REQ: req1;req44 @*/ ||
val(size) := size       /*@REQ: req1;req44 @*/ ||
total := total + size   /*@REQ: req1;req44 @*/ ||
result := OK
```

we can group the three tagged statements and use the BEGIN..END form of the REQ tag:

```
/*@BEGIN_REQ: req1;req44 @*/
size := size + 1        ||
val(size) := size       ||
total := total + size
/*@END_REQ: req1;req44 @*/ ||
result := OK
```

6.2   THE SYSTEM PROCESS SCHEDULER EXAMPLE

In this section, we go through the complete model-based testing process, starting from the informal requirements and ending with several test suites of different sizes. We use a simple uniprocessor scheduler as an example.

6.2.1   Functional Requirements

A process executing on a CPU is defined by its code, or program, and by the contents of its working space (data, stack, ...). When several processes can be executed at the same time, they are activated in turn, with each process following the life cycle shown in Figure 6.1. At any one time, the system may have some processes *ready* to be scheduled; some processes *waiting* for some external action before they become ready; and, optionally, a single *active* process.

The system must respect the following requirements (to make it easy to refer to these requirements later, we label each requirement with a name such as [REQ1]):

- Each process is identified by a unique *process identifier* (PID) [REQ1].
- The only time there is no active process is when there are none ready to be scheduled [REQ2].
- The initial state of the system is idle and empty of processes [REQ3].

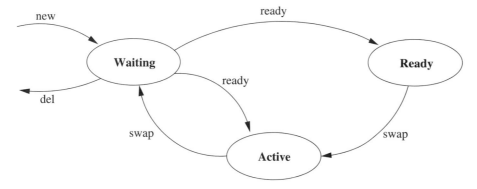

FIGURE 6.1   Life cycle of each process within the scheduler.

The scheduler has five operations:

1. new(pp) introduces a new process into the system, putting that process into a waiting state [NEW1]. This operation may throw the following exceptions:

   - MemoryFull when all the possible processes have already been created [NEW2]

   - AlreadyExists when the process pp already exists in the system [NEW3]

2. del(pp) erases a waiting process from the system [DEL1]. This operation may throw the following exceptions:

   - UnknownProcess if pp is not a known process [DEL2]

   - BusyProcess if process pp is active or ready [DEL3]

3. ready(pp) is called when a process has finished waiting and is now ready to execute—for example, when a disk read request has been satisfied or a user input event becomes available. It moves the waiting process into a ready state if there is already another process active [READY1], or directly into the active state if the system is idle [READY2].

   It may throw the following exceptions:

   - UnknownProcess if process pp is not known by the scheduler [READY3]

- BusyProcess if process pp is in an active or ready state rather than a waiting state [READY4]

4. swap is called regularly by a system timer [SWAP1] (each 100 milliseconds by default [SWAP2]) in order to provide preemptive scheduling. It swaps the currently active process out and replaces it by a ready one [SWAP3] or leaves the system idle if there are no ready processes [SWAP4]. If swap is called when there is no active process (which means that there are also no ready processes), it does nothing [SWAP5].

5. A status(pp) operation can be called to determine the status of a known process (pp) [STATUS].

6.2.2 Modeling the Scheduler

To model the scheduler, our main task is to choose a good level of abstraction for the model. We must decide on the scope of the model and which aspects are important to test and which should be omitted. The preceding requirements are much simpler and shorter than is usually the case in a real application, but they still contain some details that we do not wish to test or some details that are handled better in the concretization phase of test generation, rather than adding them to the model and making the model more complex.

To help us choose a good level of abstraction for the model, we use the four steps discussed in Section 6.1:

1. Choose a high-level test objective.
2. Design the signatures of the operations in the model.
3. Design the state variables of the model and choose their types.
4. Write the preconditions and postconditions of each operation.

For the first step, we decide that our high-level test objective is to test just the functional correctness of the scheduler, leaving the real-time aspects to be tested elsewhere. This means that requirements SWAP1 and SWAP2 are outside the scope of our testing, so we do not need to model the passage of time and the 100 millisecond requirement does not appear in the model.

For the second step, the signatures of the model operations, we decide that we want to test all five of the scheduler operations but generalize the status operation so that we can test the status of all the processes with a single call. That is, instead of a signature of st<--status(pp), which returns an Active, Ready, or Waiting status for a given process pp, we model the status operation as returning three sets of processes: the active, ready, and waiting processes. This will make it a little easier to generate the oracle part of tests since a single call of this `status` operation can check that *all* processes have the correct status. Note that the concretization phase of test generation transforms this powerful `status` operation of the model into some code that checks the status of all the processes by iterating through each set and using the lower-level `status(pp)` operation provided by the scheduler implementation. This is an example of using a one-to-many relation between model and SUT operation calls to simplify the test generation.

We also decide to model exceptions by adding an output parameter to each operation that may throw an exception. This output parameter will be `OK` when the operation does a normal return (no exception) or the name of the exception thrown otherwise (e.g., `UnknownProcess`).

A radically different approach to exceptions would be to decide not to test the exception handling because it is less interesting than the normal behavior. In this case we would have added the negation of the exception conditions as *preconditions* of the operations. Since the generated tests will call operations only when their preconditions are true, this would mean that the exception-handling cases would not be exercised by the generated tests. We can now start to write a B model with these five operations:

OPERATIONS
```
    excep <-- new(pp) =
    excep <-- del(pp) = ...
    excep <-- ready(pp) = ...
    swap = ...
    act,rdy,wtg <-- status = ...
```

The third modeling step is to design the data structures of our model. We decide to model each process simply by its process identifier—the detailed contents of its code and data are not needed for testing the correctness of the scheduling algorithm. We also decide that six process identifiers will be plenty to exercise all the behaviors of the scheduler (e.g., 1 process `Active`, 2 processes `Ready`, 2 processes `Waiting`, and 1 process unused). For many test generation tools, making the state space of the model as small as possible helps to make the test generation task faster and more tractable.

These decisions mean that our model simply needs to record the current status of each process. We could model this in B by three sets of processes (for active, ready, and waiting processes) or by a relation or function that associates a status with each process. Since each process has a unique status, we use a function from process identifiers to status. In fact, both representations work quite well, and the three-sets model is often used for this scheduler example. We choose the function model because it may seem more natural to engineers who are familiar with UML associations or programming language arrays.

We can now design the data parts of our B model, by defining sets, constants, and variables, plus their types. These are shown in full in Listing 6.1. The most important data structure is the proc variable, which is a *partial function* from PID to STATE. We make it a partial function because only the known processes need to have a status—processes that have not yet been created with new will not appear in the proc data structure.

```
SETS
    PID = {p1,p2,p3,p4,p5,p6};
    STATE = {Waiting, Ready, Active}
VARIABLES
    proc
INVARIANT
    proc : PID +-> STATE
```

We also add an invariant to restrict the number of active processes to at most one; (the proc |> {Active} operator extracts just the Active processes out of the proc function):

```
card(proc |> {Active}) <= 1
```

and another invariant to make sure that the CPU is kept busy (recall that REQ2 says if there are no active processes, then there must be no ready processes):

```
(proc|>{Active}={} => proc|>{Ready}={}) /*@REQ: REQ2@*/
```

The last modeling step is to write the body of each operation. That is, we design the functionality of each operation by transforming the informal requirements for the operation into more precise preconditions and postconditions in B.

In the new operation, the requirements do not make it clear which exception should be thrown when both error conditions are true. The designers of the system tell us that in this case, the MemoryFull exception should take priority over AlreadyExists. Similarly, in the delete and ready operations, the UnknownProcess should take priority over the BusyProcess exception. Alternatively, if the answer had been that there was no particular priority between those exceptions, we could have used the SELECT statement of B to write a nondeterministic model that allowed either exception when both conditions are true.

LISTING 6.1   Process scheduler: state variables and new operation.

```
MACHINE
    PID
SETS
    PID = {p1,p2,p3,p4,p5,p6}; /*? Set of all processes ?*/
    STATE = {Waiting, Ready, Active}; /*? Process States ?*/
    EXCEPTION = {OK,MemoryFull,AlreadyExists,BusyProcess,
                 UnknownProcess,NoActiveProcess}
VARIABLES
    proc
INVARIANT
    /*? The state of each process ?*/
    proc : PID  +-> STATE /*@REQ: REQ1@*/ &
    /*? Only one process can be active ?*/
    card(proc |> {Active}) <= 1 &
    /*? The only time there is no active process is
        when there are none ready to be scheduled ?*/
    (proc|>{Active}={} => proc|>{Ready}={}) /*@REQ: REQ2@*/

INITIALISATION
    /*? Initially the system is idle, with no processes ?*/
    proc := {} /*@REQ: REQ3@*/

OPERATIONS
/*? Introduce a new process (in waiting state).
    pp is the new process to be introduced.
    excep is: OK or MemoryFull or AlreadyExists ?*/
excep <-- new(pp) =
    PRE pp : PID
    THEN
        /*? Is memory already full? ?*/
        IF dom(proc) = PID THEN
            excep := MemoryFull /*@REQ: NEW2@*/
        ELSE
            /*? pp must not already exist ?*/
            IF pp : dom(proc) THEN
                excep := AlreadyExists /*@REQ: NEW3@*/
            ELSE
                /*@BEGIN_REQ: NEW1@*/
                excep := OK ||
                proc(pp) := Waiting
                /*@END_REQ: NEW1@*/
            END
        END
    END
END;
```

This is a small example of the kinds of requirements issues (lack of precision, ambiguities, omissions, contradictions) that almost always arise during the modeling process. In fact, the feedback from the modeling process can often result in clarifying or simplifying the requirements, which is a beneficial side effect of using model-based testing.

LISTING 6.2   Process scheduler: del and ready operations.

```
/*? Delete a waiting process (pp) from the system.
    excep is: OK or BusyProcess or UnknownProcess ?*/
excep <-- del(pp)=
    PRE pp : PID
    THEN
        IF pp /: dom(proc) THEN
            excep := UnknownProcess /*@REQ: DEL2@*/
        ELSE
            IF proc(pp) /= Waiting THEN
                excep  := BusyProcess /*@REQ: DEL3@*/
            ELSE
                /*@BEGIN_REQ: DEL1@*/
                excep := OK ||
                proc  := proc - {pp |-> Waiting}
                /*@END_REQ: DEL1@*/
            END
        END
    END;

/*? Move a waiting process (pp) into a ready/active state.
    If there are no active processes, then pp becomes active.
    excep is: OK or BusyProcess or UnknownProcess ?*/
excep <-- ready(pp) =
    PRE pp : PID
    THEN
        IF pp /: dom(proc) THEN
            excep := UnknownProcess /*@REQ: READY3@*/
        ELSE
            IF proc(pp) /= Waiting THEN
                excep := BusyProcess /*@REQ: READY4@*/
            ELSE
                excep := OK ||
                /*? Is there an active process? ?*/
                IF Active : ran(proc) THEN
                    proc(pp) := Ready   /*@REQ: READY1@*/
                ELSE
                    proc(pp) := Active  /*@REQ: REQ1, READY2@*/
                END
            END
        END
    END;
```

The resulting B model is shown in Listings 6.1, 6.2, and 6.3, complete with requirements tags to relate each part of the model to the corresponding requirement label. We will briefly explain a few of the less obvious features.

LISTING 6.3   Process scheduler: swap and status operations.

```
/*? Swap the currently active process for a ready one.
    Leaves the system idle if there are no ready processes. ?*/
swap =
    IF Active : ran(proc) THEN
        ANY   current   /*? Find the active process ?*/
        WHERE current : PID &
            (current|->Active) : proc
        THEN
            /*? Are there any ready processes?  ?*/
            IF Ready : ran(proc) THEN
                /*@BEGIN_REQ: SWAP3@*/
                ANY pp WHERE pp:PID & (pp|->Ready):proc THEN
                    proc := proc <+ {pp |-> Active,
                                     current |-> Waiting}
                END /*@END_REQ: SWAP3@*/
            ELSE
                /*@BEGIN_REQ: SWAP4@*/
                proc(current) := Waiting
                /*@END_REQ: SWAP4@*/
            END
        END
    ELSE
        skip /*@REQ: SWAP5@*/
END;

/*? Display all the active, ready, and waiting processes. ?*/
act, rdy, wtg <-- status =
    PRE
        act <: PID &
        rdy <: PID &
        wtg <: PID
    THEN
        /*@BEGIN_REQ: STATUS@*/
        act := dom(proc |> {Active}) ||
        rdy := dom(proc |> {Ready})  ||
        wtg := dom(proc |> {Waiting})
        /*@END_REQ: STATUS@*/
    END
END
```

In the new operation in Listing 6.1, the condition dom(proc)=PID checks if all processes are in use by checking if the set of already created processes (the domain of proc) is equal to the set of all processes PID.

In the del operation in Listing 6.2, the subtraction of {pp |-> Waiting} completely removes the pp process from proc, which means that process is free to be reused later by new.

In the swap operation in Listing 6.3, we start by using the B construct, ANY current WHERE..., to search through proc, find the currently active process, and put it into the variable current. We could have avoided this search by having an additional state variable that keeps track of the active process, but we prefer to keep our state variables as minimal as possible and avoid adding redundant variables because they might increase the chance of errors in our model. Then, if there are some processes ready to execute, we use the ANY...WHERE... construct again to nondeterministically choose one of those ready processes to become the new active process. Since we have to change the state of *two* processes simultaneously (sequential composition is not allowed within a B operation), we update both the pp and current entries of proc using the *relational override* operator <+ (see Section 3.4.4).

6.2.3 An Introduction to Test Targets

To make the test generation process easier to understand and control, we break up the test generation step of the model-based testing process into two substeps:

Test selection: We give our test selection criteria, plus our model, to the model-based testing tool and it generates a set of *test targets*, one for each desired test. Each test target is a detailed test specification for testing a particular path through one of the operations of our model. For example, one test target for the new operation might be dom(proc)=PID because this will test the MemoryFull case.

Test case generation: For each test target, the model-based testing tool tries to generate a path though the model that reaches the desired operation (new in this case), sets up the state variables to satisfy the conditions in the test target (this means we want proc to be full of processes), and chooses input values that satisfy the test target (our example test target has no constraints on the pp input of new, so any value will do). For example, one test case that satisfies the dom(proc)=PID test target would be the sequence

new(p1);new(p2);new(p3);new(p4);new(p5);new(p6);new(p1)

> **Key Point**   A test target is a detailed specification of a desired test case. It is usually generated from applying your test selection criteria to the model.

Since a test target is a *specification* of a desired test case, there may be zero, one, or many tests that satisfy that specification. Also, it is possible that

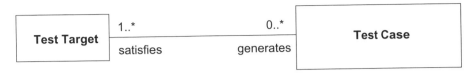

FIGURE 6.2 UML class diagram showing the relationship between test targets and generated test cases.

a single test case satisfies many test targets because it contains a long sequence of operations that exercise many different parts of the model. Some model-based testing tools try to generate very long test cases to satisfy as many test targets as possible, and others try to generate many small test cases so that each test target is tested independently. There are advantages to both approaches: the *long-tests* approach gives fewer tests, which may be faster to execute and exercise the SUT in more interesting ways, whereas the *short-tests* approach generates more tests, which are shorter and easier to analyze when they fail.

The relationship between test targets and the generated test cases is shown as a UML class diagram in Figure 6.2. It is a many-to-many relationship in both directions. Note that it is possible to have a test target that is related to zero test cases (in a moment we will discuss why this can happen), but it is not useful for a test case to be related to zero test targets since this means that there would be no rationale for generating that test case.

When many possible test cases satisfy a given test target, the test case generation tool is free to choose any one of those test cases. When there are no possible test cases for a test target, we say that the test target is either *unsatisfiable* or *unreachable*. Let us discuss these two possibilities in more detail.

Unsatisfiable means that the test target contains some contradictory conditions, such as $x : 10..20 \& x \times x < 40$. Typically, each condition has come from a different part of the model, so having a contradiction between them is not an error; it simply means that this path through the model is not possible. When a test target is as simple as this example, the contradiction can usually be detected automatically and the test target can be discarded or classified as unsatisfiable. But in general, knowing whether a test target is satisfiable or not is a difficult problem that is not always decidable, so it is not always possible to detect all unsatisfiable test targets. When the satisfiability of a test target is unclear, the best thing to do is simply to pass that test target on to the test case generation step, to see if it is possible to find a test case that satisfies it. If a test case is found, then we know that the test target was satisfiable!

Unreachable means that there is no sequence of operations that starts from the initial state and reaches the test target. For example, we might have the test target $x : 10..20 \ \& \ x \times x \geq 400$. This is satisfiable, when $x = 20$, but imagine that the initial value of x is 10 and the operations of the system never allow the value of x to get as high as 20. In this case, there would be no sequence of operations that starts from the initial state and reaches a state that satisfies this test target, so this test target would be unreachable. It is worth reporting unreachable test targets to the test engineer because it often exposes some problems in the model. In this case, it tells us that we could tighten the invariant of the model from $x : 10..20$ to $x : 10..19$ since the operations never allow x to become 20. Or we may be rather surprised to hear that x cannot reach 20, and after investigating our model a little more, find that this is due to an off-by-one error in one of the operations of the model.

Unreachable test targets are detected during the test case generation step. This step uses sophisticated search algorithms to search for test cases (sequences of B operations) that satisfy the test targets. If our model has a large or infinite state space, then the search space may be huge and it will not be possible to search it all. In this case, there are three possible outcomes for each test target:

Reached: One or more test cases were generated for this test target.

Unreachable: It is impossible to generate a test case for this target, so it has been proven to be unreachable (or unsatisfiable).

Unknown: The tool cannot find a suitable test case but is not certain that the test target is unreachable. In this case, we may want to try a different search algorithm or manually inspect the test target to see if it is reachable or unreachable. Typically, we use an interactive animation tool to find a sequence of operations that reach the test target. If we are successful, then that sequence can be turned into a test case that satisfies that test target. If we are not successful, then we have found a weakness in the model and may choose to improve the model.

One major benefit of splitting test generation into two steps and introducing test targets is that it makes our detailed test objectives visible and explicit. That is, each test target is a high-level and concise specification of a test case that we want to generate. Each test target is usually expressed as a boolean formula over the state and input variables or a fragment of a path through the model, but we will see that it is also possible to translate each test target into English to give a more readable interpretation of the desired test. Section 6.2.5 illustrates this on our scheduler example.

A second benefit of introducing test targets is that it gives us a clear way to measure coverage. Each test target specifies a desired test case, so we can measure coverage simply as the percentage of test targets that have been covered by a test case. More precisely, the test case generation phase will tell us the number of test targets in each of the three categories: reached, unreachable, or unknown. The unreachable targets give us useful feedback about our model but are not testable, so we can define the coverage as

$$coverage = reached / (reached + unknown) \times 100$$

This is the coverage percentage for whatever kind of coverage we asked for in our test selection criteria. For example, if we asked for decision coverage, this tells us the percentage of feasible (satisfiable) decision outcomes that have been tested. If we asked for MC/DC coverage or requirements coverage or some other kind of coverage, then the percentage will be for that kind of coverage. Now let us put this into practice on our scheduler example.

6.2.4 Test Selection for the Scheduler

To start testing the scheduler, we choose decision coverage (defined in Section 4.1.1) as our test selection criteria. This means that we want each boolean decision in our B model (e.g., each decision within an IF-THEN-ELSE) to be tested with a true outcome and also with a false outcome. This is a simple kind of coverage, which will generate a small number of test targets, roughly proportional to the number of cases in the model. Since decision coverage implies statement coverage, we will get at least one test target for each assignment statement, but we will also get test targets for any empty else statements (none in this example).

Using decision coverage, we obtain 14 test targets for the scheduler. These are shown in Table 6.1, grouped by the operation name. To save space, we omit the obvious typing condition, pp:PID, from the condition column because this appears in almost every row. Note that the test targets do not specify the exact values of every variable. Rather, they leave some variables unspecified so that there is more freedom to find a test case that satisfies the test target.

Section 6.2.8 addresses several ways to generate more test targets than just these 14. But first we show how these 14 targets can be transformed into English explanations and how they can be transformed into test cases.

TABLE 6.1   Test Targets for Scheduler, Using Decision/Condition Coverage

Target	Condition Path	Expected Output Value
TGnew1	dom(proc) = PID	excep = MemoryFull
TGnew2	dom(proc) /= PID & pp : dom(proc)	excep = AlreadyExists
TGnew3	dom(proc) /= PID & pp /: dom(proc)	excep = OK
TGdelete1	pp /: dom(proc)	excep = UnknownProcess
TGdelete2	pp : dom(proc) & proc(pp) /= Waiting	excep = BusyProcess
TGdelete3	pp : dom(proc) & proc(pp) = Waiting	excep = OK
TGready1	pp /: dom(proc)	excep = UnknownProcess
TGready2	pp : dom(proc) & proc(pp) /= Waiting	excep = BusyProcess
TGready3	pp : dom(proc) & proc(pp) = Waiting & Active : ran(proc)	excep = OK
TGready4	pp : dom(proc) & proc(pp) = Waiting & Active /: ran(proc)	excep = OK
TGswap1	Active : ran(proc) & current|->Active:proc & Ready : ran(proc) & pp |-> Ready : proc	
TGswap2	Active : ran(proc) & current|->Active:proc & Ready /: ran(proc)	
TGswap3	Active /: ran(proc)	
TGstatus1		act=dom(proc|>Active)& rdy=dom(proc|>Ready) & wtg=dom(proc|>Waiting)

6.2.5 Understanding the Test Targets

To make the test targets easier to understand, particularly for nontechnical people who are not programmers or are not familar with B notation, it is useful to be able to explain each test target in English.

TABLE 6.2   Explanation Phrases for Scheduler Conditions

Atomic Condition	Explanatory Phrase
`dom(proc) = PID`	All process identifiers are used
`dom(proc) /= PID`	There is an unused process identifer
`pp : dom(proc)`	pp is a known process
`pp /: dom(proc)`	pp is an unknown process
`proc(pp) = Waiting`	pp is `Waiting`
`proc(pp) /= Waiting`	pp is not `Waiting`
`Active : ran(proc)`	There is an `Active` process
`Active /: ran(proc)`	There is no `Active` process
`Ready : ran(proc)`	There is at least one process `Ready`
`Ready /: ran(proc)`	There are no processes `Ready`
`current|->Active : proc`	Process current is `Active`
`pp |-> Ready : proc`	pp is `Ready`

To do this, we give a short English phrase to explain each condition in our B model (see Table 6.2), and then a tool can easily combine these phrases to give an English explanation of each test target. Table 6.3 shows the explanations that are generated by a direct translation of each condition into English. A more sophisticated translation tool might remove redundant conditions to obtain more concise English explanations (e.g., "There is an unknown process" can be removed when we have the stronger statement, "pp is an unknown process").

6.2.6 Test Case Generation Using LTG/B

For each test target, we now try to generate one or more test cases. For this simple example, it turns out that all of the 14 test targets are reachable, so we can generate tests for all of them.

Each generated test case is a sequence of operation calls. Following the ISO 9646-1 standard terminology [96494], we often talk about a test case as the concatenation of four subsequences:

Preamble sets test up, getting the SUT into the correct state to run the test.

Body is the test's main part, often a single call to the operation being tested.

Observation (also called the *verification* or *identification* sequence) checks the test results and tries to ensure that the SUT is in the correct state.

Postamble takes the SUT back to some standard state, ready to start the next test.

TABLE 6.3   English Explanations of Scheduler Test Targets

Test Target	English Explanation
TGnew1	All process identifiers are used
TGnew2	There is an unused process identifer and pp is a known process
TGnew3	There is an unused process identifer and pp is an unknown process
TGdelete1	pp is an unknown process
TGdelete2	pp is a known process and pp is not Waiting
TGdelete3	pp is a known process and pp is Waiting
TGready1	pp is an unknown process
TGready2	pp is a known process and pp is not Waiting
TGready3	pp is a known process and pp is Waiting There is an Active process
TGready4	pp is a known process and pp is Waiting There is no Active process
TGswap1	There is an Active process Process current is Active There is at least one process Ready and pp is Ready
TGswap2	There is an Active process Process current is Active There are no processes Ready
TGswap3	There is no Active process
TGstatus1	

Since the status operation returns the status of all the processes, we define it to be an observation operation. This means that the observation part of the generated tests will call the status operation to check the correctness of the internal state of the scheduler.

Table 6.4 shows the 14 test cases that are generated by the LTG/B tool when we ask for one test case per test target, use status as an observation operation, and ask for postambles that return the scheduler to its initial state. The body part of each test case is highlighted in bold. To save space in the table, we show the expected return values of the body operations but omit the return values of all other calls. In reality, the generated tests include all return values, and they also record the values of the state variables of the model after each call; this can be used in the concretization phase to do additional

TABLE 6.4   Generated Test Cases for Scheduler

Test Target		Test Case
TGnew1	T1	new(p1); new(p2); new(p3); new(p4); new(p5); new(p6); **new(p1)=MemoryFull**; status; del(p1); del(p2); del(p3); del(p4); del(p5); del(p6)
TGnew2	T2	new(p1); **new(p1)=AlreadyExists**; status; del(p1)
TGnew3	T3	**new(p1)=OK**; status; del(p1)
TGdelete1	T4	**del(p1)=UnknownProcess**; status
TGdelete2	T5	new(p1); ready(p1); **del(p1)=BusyProcess**; status; swap; del(p1)
TGdelete3	T6	new(p1); **del(p1)=OK**; status
TGready1	T7	**ready(p1)=UnknownProcess**; status
TGready2	T8	new(p1); ready(p1); **ready(p1)=BusyProcess**; status; del(p1)
TGready3	T9	new(p1); ready(p1); new(p2); **ready(p2)=OK**; status; swap; del(p1); swap; del(p2)
TGready4	T10	new(p1); **ready(p1)=OK**; status; swap; del(p1)
TGswap1	T11	new(p1); ready(p1); new(p2); ready(p2); **swap**; status; del(p1); swap; del(p2)
TGswap2	T12	new(p1); ready(p1); **swap**; status; del(p1)
TGswap3	T13	**swap**; status
TGstatus1	T14	**status=({},{},{})**

validation on the state of the SUT. So the full version of the abstract test case for the TGnew3 test target would be

```
/* initial state */    [proc = {}]
new(p1) = OK;          [proc = {p1|->Waiting}]
status = ({},{},{p1}); [proc = {p1|->Waiting}]
del(p1) = OK           [proc = {}]
```

6.2.7 Traceability between Requirements and Test Cases

Since we tagged our B model with requirements identifiers, we can generate traceability matrices that show the relationships between the informal requirements and the generated tests in Table 6.4.

The matrix of the requirements to test cases in Table 6.5 shows us how well each requirement is tested (the invar and init entries mean that every

TABLE 6.5   Traceability Matrix from
Requirements to Tests

Requirements ID	Generated Test Cases
NEW1	T3
NEW2	T1
NEW3	T2
DEL1	T6
DEL2	T4
DEL3	T5
READY1	T9
READY2	T10
READY3	T7
READY4	T8
SWAP1	
SWAP2	
SWAP3	T11
SWAP4	T12
SWAP5	T13
STATUS	T14, T1..T13
REQ1	T10, invar
REQ2	invar
REQ3	init

test is exercising those requirements). This matrix is useful for identifying requirements that have not been tested adequately. In our example, SWAP1 and SWAP2 have not been tested because they are outside the scope of our model. So the requirements traceability matrix reminds us that they need testing by some separate means. It is also possible to generate an inverted matrix that maps test case names to all the related requirements. This can act as a rationale for each test, and when a test fails, it tells us which requirements were being tested. This can help us to determine whether the failure is due to incorrect requirements or a fault in the SUT.

6.2.8 Generating More Tests

In this section, we experiment with several ways of generating more tests by choosing different model coverage criteria for our test selection criteria. We investigate

- *all-values coverage* on the inputs of the operations,
- *boundary-value coverage* of our test targets, and
- *transition-pair coverage* of the model.

Most of these model coverage criteria can be viewed as *refinements* of the 14 test targets that we generated earlier. That is, we expand each of those 14 test targets into several more detailed test targets in order to ask for more tests.

ALL-VALUES FOR THE INPUT PARAMETERS

The meaning of the "all-values" coverage criterion is pretty obvious—we want to test all the possible values of a given variable. This can be a good strategy to apply to variables with a small range of possible values, such as enumerations, booleans, small integer ranges, and finite sets of objects.

For our scheduler example, we decide to apply the all-values coverage criterion to all the input variables—that is, to the pp inputs of the new, ready, and delete operations. This is a bit artificial because there is little semantic difference between processes p_i and p_j in our model, but it does enable us to illustrate the effect of the all-values criterion.

Applying all-values increases our set of test targets from 14 to 64 because each test target for the new, ready, and delete operations is expanded into 6 test targets, one for each possible process identifier (p1..p6). For example, the TGready1 test target,

```
TGready1: pp /: dom(proc) & excep=UnknownProcess
```

is expanded into 6 test targets:

```
TGready1_1:  pp=p1 & pp /: dom(proc) & excep=UnknownProcess
TGready1_2:  pp=p2 & pp /: dom(proc) & excep=UnknownProcess
TGready1_3:  pp=p3 & pp /: dom(proc) & excep=UnknownProcess
TGready1_4:  pp=p4 & pp /: dom(proc) & excep=UnknownProcess
TGready1_5:  pp=p5 & pp /: dom(proc) & excep=UnknownProcess
TGready1_6:  pp=p6 & pp /: dom(proc) & excep=UnknownProcess
```

When we generate tests from these test targets, instead of just one test case for the original TGready1 target

```
TGready1:   ready(p1)=UnknownProcess; status,
```

we get six test cases:

```
TGready1_1:   ready(p1)=UnknownProcess; status
TGready1_2:   ready(p2)=UnknownProcess; status
TGready1_3:   ready(p3)=UnknownProcess; status
TGready1_4:   ready(p4)=UnknownProcess; status
TGready1_5:   ready(p5)=UnknownProcess; status
TGready1_6:   ready(p6)=UnknownProcess; status
```

BOUNDARY-VALUE TESTING

The next variation we explore is to ask for *boundary-value* tests for each of our original 14 test targets. Rather than look for a single arbitrary test case that satisfies a test target, we now want to find several test cases that satisfy it, and each of those test cases must exercise a boundary value of the test target. That is, one or more of the variables in the test must have the maximum (or minimum) value that is allowed by the test target.

There are many possible variants of boundary value testing, as we discussed in Section 4.2.1. The LTG/B tool allows the test engineer to choose which variables should have boundary values and whether their maximal values or the minimal values should be tested, or both.

For our scheduler application, we will use a typical *min&max* heuristic and ask for two boundary values for each test target, one that minimizes all the variables and the other that maximizes all the variables. The inputs of type PID will be unordered because PID is an enumeration, but the proc function will be ordered by its size (the number of tuples it contains). This means that our 14 test targets become 28 more specific test targets. For example, the TGnew3 test target (the normal case of the new operation), which was

```
TGnew3 = dom(proc) /= PID & pp : dom(proc)
         & excep = AlreadyExists,
```

is split into two test targets (maximal([X,Y]) means maximize X and then maximize Y, and similarly for minimal([X,Y])):

```
TGnew3_max = dom(proc) /= PID & pp /: dom(proc)
             & excep = OK & maximal([proc,pp])
TGnew3_min = dom(proc) /= PID & pp /: dom(proc)
             & excep = OK & minimal([proc,pp])
```

The maximal solutions for dom(proc) /= PID & pp /: dom(proc) all have card(proc)=5 because proc must be as big as possible, but it must not contain pp. The minimal solutions have card(proc)=0. So some typical test cases generated from these two targets are

```
TGnew3_max: new(p1); new(p2); new(p3); new(p4); new(p5);
            new(p6)=OK; status;
            del(p1);del(p2);del(p3);del(p4);del(p5);del(p6)
TGnew3_min: new(p1)=OK; status
```

As you can see, the difference between the min and the max case is that the max case puts as many processes as possible in the system (to maximize the size of the proc function) before doing a successful new operation. This means that proc is completely full after the test body. In contrast, the min case executes the new operation in a minimal context, when proc is empty. So, the minimized and maximized test targets generate quite different tests that test significantly different situations.

For some other test targets, such as TG_new1, the minimal and maximal solutions happen to be equal, so in practice we do not always get twice as many tests generated when we apply this min&max heuristic. If we use LTG/B to generate min&max tests from the 14 test targets, we actually get the 25 tests shown in Table 6.6 (to save space in this table, the expected output of each operation is not shown).

TRANSITION-PAIR COVERAGE

The *transition-pair* coverage criterion is aimed at testing all the possible combinations of *two* operations. Since we have already broken down each operation into a set of test targets (corresponding to the different behaviors of the operation), a good way of exploring all the combinations of behaviors is to take all pairs of test targets. That is, we want to generate all the test bodies of the form $Test_i; Test_j$, where $Test_i$ and $Test_j$ are test cases generated from one of our 14 test targets.

An obvious name for this coverage criterion would be "test-target-pair coverage," but it is usually called *transition-pair coverage* because it is widely used when generating tests from transition-based models (see Chapters 5 and 7). Obviously, one can generalize the idea of transition pairs to longer sequences of k transitions. This is called *transition k-tuples coverage*, but it is rarely used with $k > 2$ because it generates too many tests.

If we apply the transition-pair criterion to all the scheduler operations except for the status operation (because it will appear in each test case as an observation operation anyway), then we might expect to get $13 \times 13 = 169$ test cases. But many of these pairs turn out to be unsatisfiable because the first operation puts the scheduler into a state where the second operation is not allowed. For example, target TGnew1 immediately followed by target TGnew3 (that is, new(_)=MemoryFull; new(_)=OK) is not satisfiable because the first call to new requires the memory to be full, so the second call to new cannot possibly succeed. So in practice, we get only 84 test cases rather than 169. Table 6.7 shows all the transition-pair test cases that start with the TGnew3 case of the new operation—in this case, all the possible pairs are satisfiable.

TABLE 6.6 Min&max (Boundary-Value) Tests for the Scheduler

Test Target	Test Case
TGnew1	new(p1); new(p2); new(p3); new(p4); new(p5); new(p6); **new(p1)**; status; del(p1); del(p2); del(p3); del(p4); del(p5); del(p6)
TGnew2_min	**new(p1)**; status; del(p1)
TGnew2_max	new(p1); new(p2); new(p3); new(p4); new(p5); **new(p6)**; status; del(p1); del(p2); del(p3); del(p4); del(p5); del(p6)
TGnew3_min	new(p1); **new(p1)**; status; del(p1)
TGnew3_max	new(p1); new(p2); new(p3); new(p4); new(p5); **new(p1)**; status; del(p1); del(p2); del(p3); del(p4); del(p5)
TGdel1_min	**del(p1)**; status
TGdel1_max	new(p1); new(p2); new(p3); new(p4); new(p5); **del(p6)**; status; del(p1); del(p2); del(p3); del(p4); del(p5)
TGdel2_min	new(p1); **del(p1)**; status
TGdel2_max	new(p1); new(p2); new(p3); new(p4); new(p5); new(p6); **del(p1)**; status; del(p2); del(p3); del(p4); del(p5); del(p6)
TGdel3	new(p1); ready(p1); **del(p1)**; status; swap; del(p1)
TGready1_min	**ready(p1)**; status
TGready1_max	new(p1); new(p2); new(p3); new(p4); new(p5); **ready(p6)**; status; del(p1); del(p2); del(p3); del(p4); del(p5)
TGready2_min	new(p1); ready(p1); new(p2); **ready(p2)**; status; swap; del(p1); swap; del(p2)
TGready2_max	new(p1); new(p2); new(p3); new(p4); new(p5); new(p6); ready(p1); **ready(p2)**; status; swap; del(p1); swap; del(p2); del(p3); del(p4); del(p5); del(p6)
TGready3_min	new(p1); **ready(p1)**; status; swap; del(p1)
TGready3_max	new(p1); new(p2); new(p3); new(p4); new(p5); new(p6); **ready(p1)**; status; swap; del(p1); del(p2); del(p3); del(p4); del(p5); del(p6)
TGready4_min	new(p1); ready(p1); **ready(p1)**; status; swap; del(p1)
TGready4_max	new(p1); new(p2); new(p3); new(p4); new(p5); new(p6); ready(p1); **ready(p1)**; status; swap; del(p1); del(p2); del(p3); del(p4); del(p5); del(p6)
TGswap1_min	new(p1); ready(p1); **swap**; status; del(p1)
TGswap1_max	new(p1); new(p2); new(p3); new(p4); new(p5); new(p6); ready(p1); **swap**; status; del(p1); del(p2); del(p3); del(p4); del(p5); del(p6)
TGswap2_min	new(p1); ready(p1); new(p2); ready(p2); **swap**; status; del(p1); swap; del(p2)
TGswap2_max	new(p1); new(p2); new(p3); new(p4); new(p5); new(p6); ready(p1); ready(p2); **swap**; status; del(p1); swap; del(p2); del(p3); del(p4); del(p5); del(p6)
TGswap3_min	**swap**; status
TGswap3_max	new(p1); new(p2); new(p3); new(p4); new(p5); new(p6); **swap**; status; del(p1); del(p2); del(p3); del(p4); del(p5); del(p6)
TGstatus1	**status**

TABLE 6.7   Transition-Pair Tests for the Scheduler (Just the Subset That Starts
with TGnew3)

Test Targets	Test Case
TGnew3;TGnew1	new(p1); new(p2); new(p3); new(p4); new(p5); **new(p6)=OK**; **new(p1)=MemoryFull**; status; del(p1); del(p2); del(p3); del(p4); del(p5); del(p6)
TGnew3;TGnew2	**new(p1)=OK**; **new(p1)=AlreadyExists**; status; del(p1)
TGnew3;TGnew3	**new(p1)=OK**; **new(p2)=OK**; status; del(p1); del(p2)
TGnew3;TGdelete1	**new(p1)=OK**; **del(p2)=UnknownProcess**; status; del(p1)
TGnew3;TGdelete2	new(p1); ready(p1); **new(p2)=OK**; **del(p1)=BusyProcess**; status; del(p2)
TGnew3;TGdelete3	**new(p1)=OK**; **del(p1)=OK**; status
TGnew3;TGready1	**new(p1)=OK**; **ready(p2)=UnknownProcess**; status; del(p1)
TGnew3;TGready2	new(p1); ready(p1); **new(p2)=OK**; **ready(p1)=BusyProcess**; status; del(p1)
TGnew3;TGready3	new(p1); ready(p1); **new(p2)=OK**; **ready(p2)=OK**; status; del(p2); swap; del(p1)
TGnew3;TGready4	**new(p1)=OK**; **ready(p1)=OK**; status; swap; del(p1)
TGnew3;TGswap1	new(p1); ready(p1); new(p2); ready(p2); **new(p3)=OK**; **swap**; status; del(p1); del(p2); del(p3)
TGnew3;TGswap2	new(p1); ready(p1); **new(p2)=OK**; **swap**; del(p1); del(p2)

The transition-pair criterion generally produces $O(N^2)$ tests, where N is the number of individual test targets. For large models, this is far too many tests to be practical, so it is useful to look for ways to reduce the number of pairs. The problem is that the transition-pair generation often puts together two test targets that are quite unrelated, and testing such sequences of two operations is unlikely to be more useful than testing each operation independently.

We want to generate just the pairs where there is some *semantic link* between the two test targets in the pair. Here are two techniques (*filters*) for selecting interesting pairs:

Common-variables: This filter selects only pairs of test targets that mention some common variables. That is, there must be at least one variable that is read or written by the first test target and also read or written by the second test target.

Cause-effect: This stronger filter selects only those pairs of test targets T_1; T_2 where T_1 *writes* to some variable, and then T_2 *reads* that same variable. This is derived from the *def-use* relationship discussed in Chapter 4.

These two filters are supported by the LTG/B tool and are quite effective in reducing the number of generated transition-pair tests to more manageable proportions. It is not very useful to apply them to our scheduler example because its model has only one variable, which is read by all paths through the operations and written by about half the paths. So the common-variables filter has no effect, but the cause-effect filter reduces the number of transition pairs from 84 to 46 because it generates only the cases where the first operation updates the proc variable and then the second operation reads it.

On larger models with many variables, these filters can reduce the number of generated tests even more dramatically. In fact, once models have more than a few dozen test targets, it is not practical to use the transition-pair criterion without such filters.

6.3 THE TRIANGLE EXAMPLE

Our second example is the triangle classification program [Mye79], which is frequently used as a small example in testing books and papers. Our two main reasons for using this example are (1) that it nicely illustrates the different test selection criteria for complex decisions and (2) it shows how it can be useful to have two separate models for testing at different levels of abstraction.

6.3.1 Informal Specification and Formal Models

The informal specification of the triangle program was originally given by Myers in his classic 1979 book on testing [Mye79]:

> The program reads three integer values from a card. The three values are interpreted as representing the lengths of the sides of a triangle. The program prints a message that states whether the triangle is scalene, isosceles, or equilateral. (p. 1)

Reading input from a deck of cards is a distant memory for us, so to update this by a few decades, we interpret *card* as meaning one line of text input.

These informal requirements are not very precise, so we must also recall some elementary school facts about triangles.

1. A *triangle* is a polygon with three sides.
2. The *vertices* of the triangle (the points where the sides meet) must not be in a straight line.

3. An *equilateral* triangle has three sides of equal length.

4. An *isosceles* triangle has two sides of equal length.

5. A *scalene* triangle has three sides of different lengths.

Thinking a little more thoroughly about the requirements, we realize that a significant part of this program is going to be checking that the input line of text contains the correct data. What should it do when the input line contains only two integers, or four integers, or noninteger values, or negative values?

If we write one single model that deals with the mathematical aspects of the requirements (equilateral, isosceles, etc.) as well as all the low-level input format details, that model will be quite complex and will be a mixture of high-level and low-level aspects.

It is better to have *two* models at different levels of abstraction and dealing with different kinds of error. One model deals with the low-level input format details (i.e., the input line must contain three positive integer values), and the other model takes those three positive integers and deals with the high-level triangle classification problem.

We deal with the more interesting, high-level model in the next few sections. Then in Section 6.4 we develop the low-level model and show how it can be used to generate additional tests for the triangle program.

> **Key Point**   It is often useful to have more than one model of your SUT, such as one for the normal functional behavior and one for robustness testing.

6.3.2 The High-Level Triangle Model

To write the high-level test model for the triangle program, let's follow the four modeling steps in Section 6.1. We have already done the first step (choosing a high-level test objective) by deciding that the goal of this model is to test the correctness of the mathematical aspects of the triangle program.

For the second step (signatures of the model operations), we decide to have a single operation that takes the three positive integer values as input and returns an enumerated value (scalene, isosceles, equilateral, notriangle, or badside) as output.

OPERATIONS
```
kind <-- classify(s1,s2,s3)
```

Note that this is a much more abstract view of the triangle program than the low-level approach of taking a line of characters as input. We have abstracted away from all the details of checking the input format and parsing strings into numbers.

The third step (choosing the state variables) is trivial because this model is stateless—the only variables are the inputs and output of the classify operation.

LISTING 6.4   High-level triangle model.

```
MACHINE
    triangle1
SETS
    KIND = {scalene,isosceles,equilateral,notriangle,badside}
OPERATIONS
kind <-- classify(s1,s2,s3) =
    PRE
        s1:INT & s2:INT & s3:INT
    THEN
        IF s1<=0 or s2<=0 or s3<=0
        THEN
            kind := badside
        ELSE
            IF s1+s2<=s3 or s2+s3<=s1 or s1+s3<=s2
            THEN
                kind := notriangle
            ELSE
                IF s1=s2 & s2=s3
                THEN
                    kind := equilateral
                ELSE
                    IF s1=s2 or s2=s3 or s1=s3
                    THEN
                        kind := isosceles
                    ELSE
                        kind := scalene
                    END
                END
            END
        END
    END
END
```

The fourth step is to write the detailed preconditions and postconditions of the `classify` operation. The preconditions are just the input typing conditions. The postconditions are more complex because they must encode the rules about equilateral, isosceles, and scalene triangles and also check that we have a valid triangle with its three vertices not on the same line. The three vertices form a line when the sum of two sides is the same as the third side (for example, $s1 + s2 = s3$). So a valid triangle must have $s1 + s2 > s3$, and this must be true for all permutations of the sides.

Listing 6.4 shows the resulting high-level triangle model.

6.3.3 Test Generation for Compound Decisions

Our triangle model contains some *compound decisions*, which are conjunctions or disjunctions of several conditions. For example, the decision `s1=s2 & s2=s3` is the conjunction of the two conditions `s1=s2` and `s2=s3`. This means that there are several ways to make this condition false: we could make `s1=s2` false, or we could make `s2=s3` false, or we could make both equalities false.

When a model or code contains compound decisions like this, it is good practice (to say the least!) to test the interactions between the conditions within the decision rather than just have one or two tests for the whole decision. For example, it is a legal requirement that all flight control code within an aircraft be tested with at least MC/DC coverage of the conditions within each decision [RTC92].

In this section, we use this triangle model to illustrate several widely used test selection criteria for compound decisions: decision coverage (DC), condition/decision coverage (C/DC), modified decision/condition coverage (MC/DC), and multiple condition coverage (MCC).

If your model has no compound decisions, there will be no differences among these coverage criteria—they will all generate the same set of tests. But when your model does contain compound decisions, we will see that DC gives you the minimum number of tests and C/DC, MC/DC, and MCC give you increasingly larger and more sophisticated test suites.

DECISION COVERAGE

The goal of decision coverage (DC), also called branch coverage, is to make sure that each decision is tested with a true outcome and also with a false outcome.

Our triangle model contains four decisions, so we need at most $2 \times 4 = 8$ tests to test every decision with a true and false value. However, some paths through the `classify` operation cover more than one decision, so in this example, five tests are sufficient to obtain decision coverage.

Table 6.8 shows the test targets that result from choosing decision coverage as our test selection criteria (each test target also includes the precondition, which gives the typing conditions of the input variables, but we omit these throughout this section, to save space). Note that there is one test target for each kind of output. Decision coverage (or branch coverage) has simply exercised all the control-flow paths through the classify operation, treating each decision as an atomic true/false switch. This illustrates the general

TABLE 6.8   Triangle Test Targets Using Decision Coverage

	Test Target	kind=
DC1	s1>0 & s2>0 & s3>0 & s1+s2>s3 & s1+s3>s2 & s2+s3>s1 & s1=s2 & s2=s3	equilateral
DC2	s1>0 & s2>0 & s3>0 & s1+s2>s3 & s1+s3>s2 & s2+s3>s1 & (s1/=s2 or s2/=s3) & (s1=s2 or s2=s3 or s1=s3)	isosceles
DC3	s1>0 & s2>0 & s3>0 & s1+s2>s3 & s1+s3>s2 & s2+s3>s1 & (s1/=s2 or s2/=s3) & s1/=s2 & s2/=s3 & s1/=s3	scalene
DC4	s1>0 & s2>0 & s3>0 & (s1+s2<=s3 or s1+s3<=s2 or s2+s3<=s1)	notriangle
DC5	(s1<=0 or s2<=0 or s3<=0)	badside

TABLE 6.9   Triangle Tests Using Decision Coverage

Target	Test Case
$DC1_{min}$	classify(1,1,1)=equilateral
$DC1_{max}$	classify(1000,1000,1000)=equilateral
$DC2_{min}$	classify(2,2,1)=isosceles
$DC2_{max}$	classify(1000,1000,999)=isosceles
$DC3_{min}$	classify(2,3,4)=scalene
$DC3_{max}$	classify(998,999,1000)=scalene
$DC4_{min}$	classify(1,1,2)=notriangle
$DC4_{max}$	classify(1,999,1000)=notriangle
$DC5_{min}$	classify(-1000,-1000,-1000)=badside
$DC5_{max}$	classify(0,1000,1000)=badside

principle: with decision coverage, the number of test targets is proportional to the number of decisions in the model.

Table 6.9 shows the test cases that are generated by LTG/B for each test target. We use boundary coverage and ask for a minimal solution and a maximal solution for each test target. We also limit integers to $-1000..1000$ to make the tests easier to read. Note that there is no need for preamble, observation, or postamble calls because our triangle model has no internal state. Decision coverage is a good coverage criterion to start with when you want a minimal number of tests and you are happy to use a test suite that does not exercise the logic of complex decisions within your model.

CONDITION/DECISION COVERAGE

Condition/decision coverage is an enhancement of decision coverage. In addition to requiring each decision to be tested with a true outcome and with a false outcome, it requires each *condition* to be tested with a true outcome and with a false outcome.

At first, this looks quite trivial to satisfy: if we have a decision, such as A & B & C & D, then two tests should be enough—one test with all the conditions (A,B,C,D) true and the other test with all the conditions false. This would give us at most $2 \times D$ tests, where D is the number of decisions in our operation.

However, in practice we often have dependencies between the conditions within a decision as well as dependencies between the conditions in different decisions; so a naive algorithm, such as making all the conditions true, then false, is not sufficient. For example, in the first decision of our triangle model, we can easily make all the conditions (s1+s2<=s3, s2+s3<=s1 and s1+s3<=s2) false, but trying to make them all true at the same time gives a contradiction. So a danger of using a naive algorithm like this is that it may generate some unsatisfiable test targets, and this may cause us to omit important tests and fail to get C/DC coverage. This example also shows that it is not always possible to satisfy the C/DC criteria with just $2 \times D$ tests; sometimes we need more tests.

There are many possible approaches to generating a set of tests that satisfy the C/DC criteria. We will briefly describe an algorithm used in the LTG/B tool before we apply it to the triangle model. This algorithm generates a maximum of $2 \times C$ tests, where C is the number of conditions in the operation (and in typical applications, the number of tests is usually closer to $1 \times C$ than $2 \times C$).

The basic idea is that for each boolean operator like $C_1 \& C_2 \& \ldots \& C_n$, we still generate one test with all of the C_i conditions true, but rather than generate a single negative test target with all of the C_i conditions false, we generate n separate negative test targets. Each of these negative test targets has the form $not(C_i)$, with a *don't care* attitude toward all the remaining conditions. So each negative test target $not(C_i)$ is the *weakest* possible constraint that will falsify C_i. More precisely, the rules for generating C/DC tests from conjunctions and disjunctions are:

$$C_1 \;\&\; C_2 \;\&\; \ldots \;\&\; C_n \longrightarrow C_1 \;\&\; C_2 \;\&\; \ldots \;\&\; C_n,$$

$$not(C_1),$$

$$not(C_2),$$

$$\vdots$$

$$not(C_n)$$

$$C_1 \text{ or } C_2 \text{ or } \ldots \text{ or } C_n \longrightarrow C_1,$$

$$C_2,$$

$$\vdots$$

$$C_n,$$

$$not(C_1) \;\&\; not(C_2) \;\&\; \ldots \;\&\; not(C_n)$$

The rules for nested boolean operators and negations are an extension of this idea and are described fully elsewhere [LPU04]. The important point is that this approach minimizes the possibility of losing tests that have dependencies between conditions.

It is also important to decide whether we want to test interactions among the conditions in *different* decisions. For example, we might have a path through an operation that contains two decisions, A or B or C followed by D or E or F. Each of these decisions will generate four test targets with our C/DC algorithm (one with a false outcome and three with true outcomes). If we choose not to test the interactions between these two decisions (we call this the "without distribution" option), then we will get just $4 + 4 = 8$ test targets in total. If we choose to test the interactions between the two decisions (we call with the "with distribution" option), then we will try to test all combinations of these test targets, so we will get up to $4 \times 4 = 16$ test targets in total. In practice, some of those combined test targets will be unsatisfiable, so we will get fewer than 16. However, the "with distribution" option still produces a much larger number of test targets in general and an exponential number in the worst case.

So for small operations with only a few decisions, the "with distribution" option is practical and can give more thorough testing of the interactions

TABLE 6.10   Triangle Test Targets Using Condition/Decision Coverage

	Test Target	kind=
CDC1	s1>0 & s2>0 & s3>0 & s1+s2>s3 & s1+s3>s2 & s2+s3>s1 & s1=s2 & s2=s3	equilateral
CDC2	s1>0 & s2>0 & s3>0 & s1+s2>s3 & s1+s3>s2 & s2+s3>s1 & (s1=s2 or s2=s3 or s1=s3) & s2/=s3	isosceles
CDC3	s1>0 & s2>0 & s3>0 & s1+s2>s3 & s1+s3>s2 & s2+s3>s1 & (s1=s2 or s2=s3 or s1=s3) & s1/=s2	isosceles
CDC4	s1>0 & s2>0 & s3>0 & s1+s2>s3 & s1+s3>s2 & s2+s3>s1 & (s1/=s2 or s2/=s3) & s1=s2	isosceles
CDC5	s1>0 & s2>0 & s3>0 & s1+s2>s3 & s1+s3>s2 & s2+s3>s1 & (s1/=s2 or s2/=s3) & s2=s3	isosceles
CDC6	s1>0 & s2>0 & s3>0 & s1+s2>s3 & s1+s3>s2 & s2+s3>s1 & (s1/=s2 or s2/=s3) & s1=s3	isosceles
CDC7	s1>0 & s2>0 & s3>0 & s1+s2>s3 & s1+s3>s2 & s2+s3>s1 & s1/=s2 & s2/=s3 & s1/=s3	scalene
CDC8	s1>0 & s2>0 & s3>0 & s2+s3<=s1	notriangle
CDC9	s1>0 & s2>0 & s3>0 & s1+s3<=s2	notriangle
CDC10	s1>0 & s2>0 & s3>0 & s1+s2<=s3	notriangle
CDC11	s1<=0	badside
CDC12	s2<=0	badside
CDC13	s3<=0	badside

among decisions. But if you want a small test suite, or some of the paths through your operations contain many complex decisions, then it is best to use the "without distribution" option. For our triangle model, there are so many dependencies among the different decisions (such as s1=s2 & s2=s3 and s1=s2 or s2=s3 or s1=s3) that it happens to make little difference whether we generate test targets with distribution or without. We will use "without distribution" in this section so that the test targets are easier to understand because each decision is handled independently.

Table 6.10 shows the 13 test targets that LTG/B produces when it applies this condition/decision coverage algorithm to the triangle model. We

TABLE 6.11   Triangle Tests Using Condition/Decision Coverage

Target	Test Case
$CDC1_{min}$	classify(1,1,1)=equilateral
$CDC1_{max}$	classify(1000,1000,1000)=equilateral
$CDC2/CDC4_{min}$	classify(2,2,1)=isosceles
$CDC2/CDC4_{max}$	classify(1000,1000,999)=isosceles
$CDC3/CDC5_{min}$	classify(1,2,2)=isosceles
$CDC3/CDC5_{max}$	classify(999,1000,1000)=isosceles
$CDC6_{min}$	classify(2,1,2)=isosceles
$CDC6_{max}$	classify(1000,999,1000)=isosceles
$CDC7_{min}$	classify(2,3,4)=scalene
$CDC7_{max}$	classify(998,999,1000)=scalene
$CDC8_{min}$	classify(2,1,1)=notriangle
$CDC8_{max}$	classify(1000,1,999)=notriangle
$CDC9_{min}$	classify(1,2,1)=notriangle
$CDC9_{max}$	classify(1,1000,999)=notriangle
$CDC10_{min}$	classify(1,1,2)=notriangle
$CDC10_{max}$	classify(1,999,1000)=notriangle
$CDC11_{min}$	classify(-1000,-1000,-1000)=badside
$CDC11_{max}$	classify(0,1000,1000)=badside
$CDC12_{min}$	classify(-1000,-1000,-1000)=badside
$CDC12_{max}$	classify(1000,0,1000)=badside
$CDC13_{min}$	classify(-1000,-1000,-1000)=badside
$CDC13_{max}$	classify(1000,1000,0)=badside

have slightly more isosceles test targets than we need because some (CDC2 and CDC3) are designed to make s1=s2 & s2=s3 false, and the others are designed to make the s1=s2 or s2=s3 or s1=s3 decision true, so there is some redundancy among these targets.

Table 6.11 shows the tests that are generated for each test target when we request a minimal or maximal boundary-value test for each target. If we use just the minimal boundary-value tests, we get 9 tests (because the redundancy between the isosceles test targets means that 3 tests are enough to satisfy all 5 targets and because the 3 badside minimal tests are identical). These 9 test cases are sufficient to satisfy all 13 of the test targets, so they give us C/DC coverage of the model. Alternatively, if we use just the maximal boundary-value tests, we get 11 test cases, which also give us C/DC coverage of the model. Or if we prefer to have a slightly more comprehensive test suite, we could use both the minimal and maximal boundaries, giving a test suite of 20 tests.

Note that all these test suites include all three permutations of the isosceles and notriangle cases (this is a result of our stronger algorithm rather than a necessary consequence of using C/DC coverage). In addition, the maximal tests have a zero in each input position, which is rather nice.

MODIFIED CONDITION/DECISION COVERAGE

Modified condition/decision coverage is a well-known coverage criterion. There are two common variants, *unique-cause MC/DC* and the weaker *masking MC/DC*, but we concentrate solely on unique-cause modified decision–condition coverage in this chapter. This extends C/DC by adding the requirement that *each condition in a decision has been shown to independently affect that decision's outcome. A condition is shown to independently affect a decision's outcome by varying just that condition while holding fixed all other possible conditions.* [RTC92, 105].

We have four decisions in our triangle model, so we want a test suite that gives MC/DC coverage of each decision. This means that for each condition C within each decision, our test suite must contain two tests: one must make C true and the other must make C false, and both tests must have the same outcome for all the other conditions in the decision.

The decisions in our triangle model are very simple (just a disjunction or a conjunction), which makes MC/DC quite easy. Let's consider the first condition (s1=s2) within the decision s1=s2 or s2=s3 or s1=s3. Decision coverage is part of MC/DC, so we must have one test that has all of these three conditions false in order to make the whole decision false. Then to get an MC/DC pair for the s1=s2 condition, we must have another test that switches s1=s2 to true, while leaving the other conditions unchanged (so s2=s3 and s1=s3 remain false). We have to do this for each of the three conditions in this decision, so in total we need four tests that satisfy the following criteria.

	s1=s2	s2=s3	s1=s3
1	false	false	false
2	**true**	false	false
3	false	**true**	false
4	false	false	**true**

This looks easy, but remember that we must also *reach* this decision, which means that the three preceding decisions,

```
s1<=0 or s2<=0 or s3<=0,
s1+s2<=s3 or s1+s3<=s2 or s2+s3<=s1,
s1=s2 & s2=s3,
```

must all be false. So Table 6.12 shows the test targets for our MC/DC pairs for this decision. The pair of test targets MCDC4/5 will generate a pair of MC/DC tests for the condition s1=s2, the pair MCDC4/6 gives an MC/DC pair of tests for s2=s3, and the pair MCDC4/7 gives an MC/DC pair of tests for s1=s3.

It is interesting to compare each of these MC/DC test targets with the corresponding C/DC targets in Table 6.10. If you look closely, you will see that they are very similar, but the MC/DC targets are slightly more specific because they constrain all the conditions in the disjunction, whereas the C/DC targets constrain just one of the conditions.

Since the MC/DC test targets are so similar to the C/DC ones, we do not list them all. For this triangle example, it turns out that the Max C/DC tests shown in Table 6.11 already satisfy MC/DC coverage of each decision.

TABLE 6.12   Unique-Cause MC/DC Test Targets for the Decision
                s1=s2 or s2=s3 or s1=s3

	Test Target	kind=
MCDC4	s1>0 & s2>0 & s3>0 & s1+s2>s3 & s1+s3>s2 & s2+s3>s1 & (s1/=s2 or s2/=s3) & s1=s2 & s2/=s3 & s1/=s3	isosceles
MCDC5	s1>0 & s2>0 & s3>0 & s1+s2>s3 & s1+s3>s2 & s2+s3>s1 & (s1/=s2 or s2/=s3) & s1/=s2 & s2=s3 & s1/=s3	isosceles
MCDC6	s1>0 & s2>0 & s3>0 & s1+s2>s3 & s1+s3>s2 & s2+s3>s1 & (s1/=s2 or s2/=s3) & s1/=s2 & s2/=s3 & s1=s3	isosceles
MCDC7	s1>0 & s2>0 & s3>0 & s1+s2>s3 & s1+s3>s2 & s2+s3>s1 & (s1/=s2 or s2/=s3) & s1/=s2 & s2/=s3 & s1/=s3	scalene

TABLE 6.13   Example of MC/DC Test Pairs for the Triangle Model

Condition and Decision	True Test/False Test	
s1<=0 or s2<=0 or s3<=0	$CDC11_{max}$	(0,1000,1000)
	$CDC1_{max}$	(1000,1000,1000)
s1<=0 or **s2<=0** or s3<=0	$CDC12_{max}$	(1000,0,1000)
	$CDC1_{max}$	(1000,1000,1000)
s1<=0 or s2<=0 or **s3<=0**	$CDC13_{max}$	(1000,1000,0)
	$CDC1_{max}$	(1000,1000,1000)
s1+s2<=s3 or s2+s3<=s1 or s1+s3<=s2	$CDC10_{max}$	(1,999,1000)
	$CDC1_{max}$	(1000,1000,1000)
s1+s2<=s3 or **s2+s3<=s1** or s1+s3<=s2	$CDC8_{max}$	(1000,1,999)
	$CDC1_{max}$	(1000,1000,1000)
s1+s2<=s3 or s2+s3<=s1 or **s1+s3<=s2**	$CDC9_{max}$	(1,1000,999)
	$CDC1_{max}$	(1000,1000,1000)
s1=s2 & s2=s3	$CDC1_{max}$	(1000,1000,1000)
	$CDC5_{max}$	(999,1000,1000)
s1=s2 & **s2=s3**	$CDC1_{max}$	(1000,1000,1000)
	$CDC4_{max}$	(1000,1000,999)
s1=s2 or s2=s3 or s1=s3	$CDC4_{max}$	(1000,1000,999)
	$CDC7_{max}$	(998,999,1000)
s1=s2 or **s2=s3** or s1=s3	$CDC5_{max}$	(999,1000,1000)
	$CDC7_{max}$	(998,999,1000)
s1=s2 or s2=s3 or **s1=s3**	$CDC6_{max}$	(1000,999,1000)
	$CDC7_{max}$	(998,999,1000)

Table 6.13 shows how Max C/DC tests can be paired up to prove that the test suite satisfies MC/DC coverage. The left column shows the decision with one condition in bold, and the right column shows first the test that makes that condition true and then the test that makes it false. Note that the nonbold conditions have the same boolean outcome in both tests of the pair, even though the input values—s1, s2, s3—sometimes vary a little.

The Min C/DC test suite does not satisfy MC/DC because it contains only one badside Min test, which makes all three of the s1<=0, s2<=0, s3<=0 conditions false. To make the Min C/DC test suite satisfy modified condition–decision coverage, we would have to add three badside tests, such as (0,1,1), (1,0,1), and (1,1,0), that each change just one of the conditions—these would each pair up with one of the equilateral test cases, giving us an MC/DC test suite.

MC/DC coverage becomes more complex when decisions contain a mixture of logical operators. For example, in decision A & (B or C), one must be careful to keep B and C unchanged while changing A from true to false. In this example, we can satisfy C/DC coverage with just two tests.

	A	B	C	A & (B or C)
1	true	true	false	true
2	false	false	true	false

These do not satisfy MC/DC because the outcomes of B and C are not constant while A is changing. To get MC/DC coverage, we must have the following four tests. Tests 1 and 2 form an MC/DC pair for A, tests 1 and 4 form an MC/DC pair for B, and tests 3 and 4 form an MC/DC pair for C.

	A	B	C	A & (B or C)
1	true	true	false	true
2	false	true	false	false
3	true	false	true	true
4	true	false	false	false

In general, the number of tests required to satisfy MC/DC is proportional to the number of conditions. More precisely, for a decision with N conditions, MC/DC coverage requires between $N + 1$ and $2 \times N$ tests. MC/DC is a good choice when you have complex decisions that you want to test thoroughly while limiting the number of tests.

MULTIPLE CONDITION COVERAGE

The goal of multiple condition coverage (MCC) is to explore *all* the possible combinations of true and false for all the conditions within a decision. That is, it exhaustively tests the complete truth table for all those conditions. In general, this requires an exponential number of tests for the number of conditions. For example, a conjunction (or disjunction) of N conditions requires 2^N tests to achieve MCC coverage. But in practice, many of these combinations are unsatisfiable, so they cannot be tested.

Consider the decision s1=s2 or s2=s3 or s1=s3 in our triangle model. This contains three conditions, so we have $2^3 = 8$ potential test targets. However, the context of this decision within the triangle model means that s1+s2>s3, s1+s3>s2, and s2+s3>s1 must all be true, and that s1=s2 & s2=s3 must be false. So our eight assignments of truth values give us only four interesting cases.

	s1=s2	s2=s3	s1=s3	Comment
1	true	true	true	*Contradicts* not(s1=s2 & s2=s3)
2	true	true	false	*Unsatisfiable*
3	true	false	true	*Unsatisfiable*
4	true	false	false	Isosceles case—e.g., $(2, 2, 1)$
5	false	true	true	*Unsatisfiable*
6	false	true	false	Isosceles case—e.g., $(1, 2, 2)$
7	false	false	true	Isosceles case—e.g., $(2, 1, 2)$
8	false	false	false	Scalene case—e.g., $(2, 3, 4)$

On the other hand, in the decision s1<=0 or s2<=0 or s3<=0, the conditions are independent and we have no other constraints, so all eight combinations produce satisfiable test targets.

Table 6.14 shows the 18 satisfiable test targets that we get from LTG/B when we choose the MCC coverage criteria. Table 6.15 shows the resulting test cases, 15 Min tests and 15 Max tests. Note how these tests explore all the various combinations of good and bad inputs in the badside cases. MCC coverage is a good choice when you have complex decisions, you want to test the logic of these decisions thoroughly, and it is acceptable to execute a larger number of tests.

6.3.4 Evaluation of the Generated Test Suites

The triangle example was used by Myers [Mye79] as a self-assessment test to illustrate how difficult it is to design a good test suite. He gave 14 questions that can be used to evaluate the quality of a test suite for this simple triangle example.

In Myers's experience, the average score for highly qualified programmers was 7.8; this was back in 1979, but in 2000–2005 our classes of computer science graduate students consistently obtained a class average of around 7 to 8 (before we taught them model-based testing!), which confirms Myers's average. This illustrates that manually designing good test suites is still a difficult job, even for such a simple example.

Table 6.16 shows the score for the various coverage-based test suites that we generated in the previous section. We merge the C/DC and MC/DC columns, since the Max C/DC test suite generated by the LTG/B algorithm satisfies MC/DC in this example. The last column (labeled as [M]C/DC$_2$) is the C/DC and MC/DC test suite for a variant triangle model that we describe in a moment.

TABLE 6.14   Triangle Test Targets Using Multiple Condition Coverage

	Test Target	kind=
MCC1	s1>0 & s2>0 & s3>0 & s1+s2>s3 & s1+s3>s2 & s2+s3>s1 & s1=s2 & s2=s3	equilateral
MCC2	⋯ (first 2 lines of MCC1) & s1=s2 & s2/=s3 & (s1=s2 or s2=s3 or s1=s3)	isosceles
MCC3	⋯ & s1/=s2 & s2=s3 & (s1=s2 or s2=s3 or s1=s3)	isosceles
MCC4	⋯ & s1/=s2 & s2/=s3 & (s1=s2 or s2=s3 or s1=s3)	isosceles
MCC5	⋯ & (s1/=s2 or s2/=s3) & s1=s2 & s2/=s3 & s1/=s3	isosceles
MCC6	⋯ & (s1/=s2 or s2/=s3) & s1/=s2 & s2=s3 & s1/=s3	isosceles
MCC7	⋯ & (s1/=s2 or s2/=s3) & s1/=s2 & s2=s3 & s1=s3	isosceles
MCC8	⋯ & s1/=s2 & s2/=s3 & s1/=s3	scalene
MCC9	s1>0 & s2>0 & s3>0 & s1+s2>s3 & s2+s3>s1 & s1+s3<=s2	notriangle
MCC10	s1>0 & s2>0 & s3>0 & s1+s2>s3 & s2+s3<=s1 & s1+s3>s2	notriangle
MCC11	s1>0 & s2>0 & s3>0 & s1+s2<=s3 & s2+s3>s1 & s1+s3>s2	notriangle
MCC12	s1<=0 & s2>0 & s3>0	badside
MCC13	s1>0 & s2<=0 & s3>0	badside
MCC14	s1>0 & s2>0 & s3<=0	badside
MCC15	s1<=0 & s2<=0 & s3>0	badside
MCC16	s1<=0 & s2>0 & s3<=0	badside
MCC17	s1>0 & s2<=0 & s3<=0	badside
MCC18	s1<=0 & s2<=0 & s3<=0	badside

Key Point   The DC, C/DC, MC/DC, and MCC coverage criteria are useful for specifying how thoroughly you want to test interactions between the conditions in complex decisions. They give a roughly increasing number of tests.

TABLE 6.15   Triangle Tests Using Multiple Condition Coverage

Target	Test Case
$MCC1_{min}$	classify(1,1,1)=equilateral
$MCC1_{max}$	classify(1000,1000,1000)=equilateral
$MCC2/MCC5_{min}$	classify(2,2,1)=isosceles
$MCC2/MCC5_{max}$	classify(1000,1000,999)=isosceles
$MCC3/MCC6_{min}$	classify(1,2,2)=isosceles
$MCC3/MCC6_{max}$	classify(999,1000,1000)=isosceles
$MCC4/MCC7_{min}$	classify(2,1,2)=isosceles
$MCC4/MCC7_{max}$	classify(1000,999,1000)=isosceles
$MCC8_{min}$	classify(2,3,4)=scalene
$MCC8_{max}$	classify(998,999,1000)=scalene
$MCC9_{min}$	classify(1,2,1)=notriangle
$MCC9_{max}$	classify(1,1000,999)=notriangle
$MCC10_{min}$	classify(2,1,1)=notriangle
$MCC10_{max}$	classify(1000,1,999)=notriangle
$MCC11_{min}$	classify(1,1,2)=notriangle
$MCC11_{max}$	classify(1,999,1000)=notriangle
$MCC12_{min}$	classify(-1000,1,1)=badside
$MCC12_{max}$	classify(0,1000,1000)=badside
$MCC13_{min}$	classify(1,-1000,1)=badside
$MCC13_{max}$	classify(1000,0,1000)=badside
$MCC14_{min}$	classify(1,1,-1000)=badside
$MCC14_{max}$	classify(1000,1000,0)=badside
$MCC15_{min}$	classify(-1000,-1000,1)=badside
$MCC15_{max}$	classify(0,0,1000)=badside
$MCC16_{min}$	classify(-1000,1,-1000)=badside
$MCC16_{max}$	classify(0,1000,0)=badside
$MCC17_{min}$	classify(1,-1000,-1000)=badside
$MCC17_{max}$	classify(1000,0,0)=badside
$MCC18_{min}$	classify(-1000,-1000,-1000)=badside
$MCC18_{max}$	classify(0,0,0)=badside

The highest score of our test suites so far is 10/14, which is obtained by MCC with Min&Max values. This score is better than the average score for highly qualified programmers! But is this the best that we can do? Why doesn't this test suite get 14/14? There are two reasons:

1. In the notriangle tests, we have no test cases with three positive integers where the sum of two of the numbers is strictly *less* than the third number (questions 9 and 10).

TABLE 6.16   Evaluation of Functional Test Suites for Triangle

Question	DC min	DC min& max	[M]C/DC min	[M]C/DC min& max	MCC min	MCC min& max	[M]C/DC$_2$ min	[M]C/DC$_2$ min& max
Number of tests	5	10	9	20	15	30	12	26
1 Do you have a test case that represents a valid scalene triangle?	✓	✓	✓	✓	✓	✓	✓	✓
2 Do you have a test case that represents a valid equilateral triangle?	✓	✓	✓	✓	✓	✓	✓	✓
3 Do you have a test case that represents a valid isosceles triangle?	✓	✓	✓	✓	✓	✓	✓	✓
4 Do you have at least three test cases that represent valid isosceles triangles such that you have tried all three permutations of two equal sides?	×	×	✓	✓	✓	✓	✓	✓
5 Do you have a test case in which one side has a zero value?	×	✓	×	✓	✓	✓	×	✓
6 Do you have a test case in which one side has a negative value?	✓	✓	✓	✓	✓	✓	✓	✓
7 Do you have a test case with three integers greater than zero such that the sum of two of the numbers is equal to the third?	✓	✓	✓	✓	✓	✓	✓	✓
8 Do you have at least three test cases in category 7 such that you have tried all three permutations where the length of one side is equal to the sum of the lengths of the other two sides?	×	×	✓	✓	✓	✓	✓	✓
9 Do you have a test case with three integers greater than zero such that the sum of two of the numbers is less than the third?	×	×	×	×	×	×	✓	✓
10 Do you have at least three test cases in category 9 such that you have tried all three permutations?	×	×	×	×	×	×	✓	✓
11 Do you have a test case in which all sides are zero?	×	×	×	×	×	✓	×	×
12 Do you have at least one test case specifying noninteger values?	—	—	—	—	—	—	—	—
13 Do you have at least one test case specifying the wrong number of values (two rather than three integers, for example)?	—	—	—	—	—	—	—	—
14 For each test case did you specify the expected output from the program in addition to the input values?	✓	✓	✓	✓	✓	✓	✓	✓
Total Score/14	6	7	8	9	9	10	10	11

Note: The [M]C/DC column is for C/DC coverage and MC/DC coverage, while the [M]C/DC$_2$ column is the same but using a modified model that produces the tests in Table 6.18. — means *outside the scope of the model*; × means *No*; ✓ means *Yes*.

2. In the badside tests, we have no tests with noninteger values or with the wrong number of input values (questions 12 and 13).

The second reason is understandable because noninteger values and missing/extra values are outside the scope of our triangle1 model. In Section 6.4, we use a different model to allow us to generate these kinds of test.

The first reason is more interesting. Questions 9 and 10 are asking for tests like (5,5,11), where the sum of the first two sides is strictly less than the third side. This seems a strange request to us, since this is not a boundary test; if we gradually increase the value of the third side,

```
classify(5,5,7)=isosceles
classify(5,5,8)=isosceles
classify(5,5,9)=isosceles
classify(5,5,10)=notriangle
classify(5,5,11)=notriangle
classify(5,5,12)=notriangle
```

we see that (5,5,9) and (5,5,10) are the boundaries. The Min&Max strategy computes test data at the boundaries of conditions like s1+s2<=s3, which is why we got tests that satisfied s1+s2=s3 and s1+s2=s3+1.

It seems to us that any reasonable errors in our triangle implementation that give the wrong results for (5,5,11) are also likely to give wrong results for (5,5,10). This is an example of a *uniformity assumption*.

However, Myers believes that these extra tests are useful, and he even says that all of these questions are important because he has observed incorrect behavior relating to each one of them in real implementations of the triangle problem. So, let's accept that, or imagine that our boss insists on having these tests in our test suite. We could write the tests manually, of course, but is it possible to generate them using model-based testing?

Yes! If we believe that the s1+s2<s3 case is important, then we should change our model to reflect this. The easiest way to do this is to change the notriangle decision in our model (refer to Listing 6.4) from

```
IF s1+s2<=s3 or s2+s3<=s1 or s1+s3<=s2
THEN
    kind := notriangle
ELSE
    ...
```

to

```
IF (s1+s2<s3 or s1+s2=s3) or
   (s2+s3<s1 or s2+s3=s1) or
   (s1+s3<s2 or s1+s3=s2)
THEN
    kind := notriangle
ELSE
        ...
```

Table 6.17 shows how the C/DC test targets for the notriangle cases change when we use this model. The original three test targets, CDC8...CDC10, are split into six test targets because each <= predicate is split into the strictly less and the equal cases. The remaining test targets are unchanged.[2] Table 6.18 shows the Min&Max tests that are generated from

TABLE 6.17   Test Targets for the notriangle Case of the Modified
              Triangle Model Using the C/DC Criteria

	Test Target	kind=
CDC8a	s1>0 & s2>0 & s3>0 & s2+s3<s1	notriangle
CDC8b	s1>0 & s2>0 & s3>0 & s2+s3=s1	notriangle
CDC9a	s1>0 & s2>0 & s3>0 & s1+s3<s2	notriangle
CDC9b	s1>0 & s2>0 & s3>0 & s1+s3=s2	notriangle
CDC10a	s1>0 & s2>0 & s3>0 & s1+s2<s3	notriangle
CDC10b	s1>0 & s2>0 & s3>0 & s1+s2=s3	notriangle

TABLE 6.18   Tests for the notriangle Case of the Modified
              Triangle Model Using the C/DC Criteria

Target	Test Case
CDC8a$_{min}$	classify(3,1,1)=notriangle
CDC8a$_{max}$	classify(1000,1,998)=notriangle
CDC8b$_{min}$	classify(2,1,1)=notriangle
CDC8b$_{max}$	classify(1000,1,999)=notriangle
CDC9a$_{min}$	classify(1,3,1)=notriangle
CDC9a$_{max}$	classify(1,1000,998)=notriangle
CDC9b$_{min}$	classify(1,2,1)=notriangle
CDC9b$_{max}$	classify(1,1000,999)=notriangle
CDC10a$_{min}$	classify(1,1,3)=notriangle
CDC10a$_{max}$	classify(1,998,1000)=notriangle
CDC10b$_{min}$	classify(1,1,2)=notriangle
CDC10b$_{max}$	classify(1,999,1000)=notriangle

---

[2]Actually, equilateral, isosceles, and scalene targets now contain predicates like not(s1+s2<s3) & not(s1+s2=s3)—but this is semantically equivalent to the original form—not(s1+s2<=s3).

these targets by LTG/B. The whole test suite now contains 12 Min C/DC tests and 14 Max C/DC tests, giving 26 tests in total. The test cases CDC8a, CDC9a, and CDC10a satisfy questions 9 and 10, so our evaluation scores for C/DC and MC/DC increase by 2 with this model, giving 10/14 for the Min test suite and 11/14 for the Min&Max test suite.

6.4 ROBUSTNESS TESTING FROM A PRE/POST MODEL

Robustness testing means using *negative test cases* (or *dirty tests*). The goal of these tests is to invoke the system operations with some bad input values or bad operation calls to check how resistant the implementation is.

Informal requirements usually define the expected, positive behavior of the SUT. Typically, only a few requirements, if any, specify the illegal inputs or unauthorized calls and what the response of the system should be in such cases. One reason is that even if the set of authorized inputs is large or infinite, the set of negative inputs is, in general, much bigger; there are a huge number of possibilities and therefore it is difficult to describe them all.

So, for robustness testing, the tester has to choose which kinds of invalid input data or which illegal call sequences he or she wants to test. Beizer [Bei95] notes that in mature test suites, negative tests typically outnumber positive tests in a ratio of 4:1 or 5:1.

We consider two kinds of robustness testing:

Format testing: Each command of the SUT is invoked with all conceivable erroneous inputs; this corresponds to systematically testing the resistance of each command to bad input parameter values.

Context testing: Unauthorized sequences of commands are tested inside a regular usage of the system; it differs from format testing in that the input parameters of each command have correct values, but the commands are called in an invalid order.

To manage these kinds of robustness testing with model-based testing, a good methodology is to develop a specific model for format testing but to include context testing in the functional model by using a *defensive style* of modeling.

The model developed for format testing is called a *syntactic model*. It is necessary to separate the syntactic model from the functional model because in the syntactic model, the purpose is really to introduce exotic data: all the *unauthorized* input values that we want to test. To put these specific input variable domains in the syntactic model helps to avoid the "pollution" of the functional model. With a dedicated syntactic model, one can test a large variety of illegal input parameter values.

In context testing, the purpose is to test some unauthorized calls (but with in-domain input variables) during the execution and to check if the system produces the right results. Therefore, the functional model must include all these in a defensive modeling style. This means that all possible answers of the system, including exceptions, are defined in the functional model.

To sum up:

- The syntactic model defines all the bad input values.
- The functional model defines just the authorized input values but models all the possible functional errors during execution.

A good example of context testing can be seen in the scheduler example earlier in this chapter. For each operation we modeled the exceptional cases (`MemoryFull`, `AlreadyExists`, `BusyProcess`, `UnknownProcess`, `NoActiveProcess`) as well as the normal case. This was a defensive style of modeling, where most of the operations were robust (their preconditions were true), and they returned an exception if they were called at the wrong time or called with an input that was not acceptable even though it was correctly typed.

The next section illustrates format testing, using the triangle example.

6.4.1 Syntactic Modeling and Format Testing

We want to develop a separate model of the triangle for robustness testing of the `classify` operation. Our previous, functional model (Listing 6.4) modeled the input of `classify` as being three integer values. But in fact, the input is a line of text, so it may contain fewer than three values, more than three values, some noninteger values, and so on.

We decide that we want to test the following kinds of illegal input:

- Zero integers (a boundary value, adjacent to the smallest correct input of 1)
- Floating point numbers, like 2.5, because their first characters look like an integer, but on reading further, an error should be reported
- A completely noninteger value, like the alphabetic character a
- Fewer than three input values
- More than three input values

LISTING 6.5   Low-level syntactic triangle model for format testing.

```
MACHINE
    triangle2
SETS
    KIND = {scalene,isosceles,equilateral,notriangle,badside};
    INPUT = {none,one,zero,flot,char}
OPERATIONS
kind <-- classify(s1,s2,s3) =
    PRE
        s1 : INPUT & s2 : INPUT & s3 : INPUT
    THEN
        IF s1=one & s2=one & s3=one
        THEN
            kind := equilateral
        ELSE
            kind := badside
        END
    END
END
```

The `triangle2` model shown in Listing 6.5 models the first three kinds of illegal input values explicitly, uses none to mean the empty string (missing values), and has one correct value (one) so that we can test combinations of correct and incorrect inputs. This model will not generate tests with *more* than three inputs, but one such test will suffice, so we decide to write it manually rather than make the model larger.

The input values are defined symbolically, as an enumeration, because B is a strongly typed language, so we cannot combine different types of value in the same set. However, here is our intended mapping from the model's abstract constants to the concrete strings that will be used in the test cases.

Model Constant	Concrete String
none	""
one	"1"
zero	"0"
flot	"2.5"
char	"a"

With such a restricted set of inputs, and almost all of them bad inputs, the oracle part of this model is extremely simple: if all three inputs equal one, then the response is equilateral; otherwise, it is badside.

From this syntactic triangle model, if we use DC or C/DC coverage, with Min boundary-value testing, we get just two tests by default (LTG/B arbitrarily chooses char as the minimum value). The right column shows the concrete input line that is the concatenation of the three inputs.

```
classify(one,one,one)=equilateral    "1 1 1"
classify(char,char,char)=badside     "a a a"
```

This is a rather inadequate test suite for robustness testing, which is not unexpected, since DC and C/DC coverage produce a small number of tests, and our model is also very small. However, if we try DC or C/DC coverage, with *all-values* coverage of the three input variables, 125 tests cases are produced (one equilateral test and the rest all badside tests). This is *all* the 5^3 possible combinations of the five input values for the three input parameters. This is *exhaustive* testing of the erroneous values chosen for these inputs, which is useful in some situations. However, when there are more inputs or more values to try, this combinatorial explosion would produce an impractical number of tests, so let us try MC/DC.

With MC/DC coverage, we get four tests by default because it forces each of the three conditions to change while holding the other two conditions true (with value one).

```
classify(one,one,one)=equilateral    "1 1 1"
classify(char,one,one)=badside       "a 1 1"
classify(one,char,one)=badside       "1 a 1"
classify(one,one,char)=badside       "1 1 a"
```

This looks promising, so now let us try MC/DC coverage with all-values coverage of the three input variables. This produces 13 tests: the equilateral case, plus a systematic exploration of the four invalid inputs in each of the three positions. This is our favorite test suite for this model—with just 13 tests (11 after we map the abstract values into concrete strings), it tries all the bad inputs at all three input positions.

```
classify(one,one,one)=equilateral    "1 1 1"

classify( none, one, one)=badside    "1 1"
classify( zero, one, one)=badside    "0 1 1"
classify( flot, one, one)=badside    "2.5 1 1"
classify( char, one, one)=badside    "a 1 1"

classify( one, none, one)=badside    "1 1"
classify( one, zero, one)=badside    "1 0 1"
classify( one, flot, one)=badside    "1 2.5 1"
classify( one, char, one)=badside    "1 a 1"
```

```
classify( one,  one,  none)=badside    "1 1"
classify( one,  one,  zero)=badside    "1 1 0"
classify( one,  one,  flot)=badside    "1 1 2.5"
classify( one,  one,  char)=badside    "1 1 a"
```

Just to complete the picture, let us finish with MCC coverage. We get eight tests by default:

```
classify( one,  one,  one)=equilateral  "1 1 1"
classify( one,  one, char)=badside       "1 1 a"
classify( one, char,  one)=badside       "1 a 1"
classify( one, char, char)=badside       "1 a a"
classify(char,  one,  one)=badside       "a 1 1"
classify(char,  one, char)=badside       "a 1 a"
classify(char, char,  one)=badside       "a a 1"
classify(char, char, char)=badside       "a a a"
```

This is all eight combinations of char or one for each of the three inputs. If we request all-values for the three inputs, we again get the maximum size exhaustive test suite of 125 tests.

To conclude, Table 6.19 evaluates these format-testing test suites using Myers's 14 questions. The "Both" column is the result of combining the test suites from both triangle models, the MC/DC (or C/DC) tests from the enhanced functional model, plus our favorite test suite from the format testing model (MC/DC with all-values coverage). Once we combine the test suites from both models, we get a small but comprehensive test suite (32 tests) that thoroughly tests illegal inputs as well as the interesting logical combinations of legal inputs, and we achieve the near perfect score of 13/14. If we use the slightly larger MCC Min&Max test suite from the enhanced functional model, which has the (0,0,0) test, with our favorite suite from the format testing model, then we have 42 tests and we do achieve 14/14.[3]

6.5 TESTING A CHAT SYSTEM WITH SPEC EXPLORER

This section shows a different approach to using pre/post models for test generation. Rather than analyze the syntax and structure of the preconditions and postconditions and use that as the basis for test generation, we treat the model as an EFSM. By executing the model in various ways, we can

---

[3]Of course, it helped that we knew the examination questions before we entered the exam!

TABLE 6.19 Evaluation of Syntactic Test Suite for Triangle

Question	DC C/DC		MC/DC		MCC		Both	
	min	*all*	*min*	*all*	*min*	*all*	*min*	*all*
Number of abstract tests	2	125	4	13	8	125	12	32
1 Do you have a test case that represents a valid scalene triangle?	×	×	×	×	×	×	✓	✓
2 Do you have a test case that represents a valid equilateral triangle?	✓	✓	✓	✓	✓	✓	✓	✓
3 Do you have a test case that represents a valid isosceles triangle?	×	×	×	×	×	×	✓	✓
4 Do you have at least three test cases that represent valid isosceles triangles such that you have tried all three permutations of two equal sides?	×	×	×	×	×	×	✓	✓
5 Do you have a test case in which one side has a zero value?	×	✓	×	✓	×	✓	×	✓
6 Do you have a test case in which one side has a negative value?	×	×	×	×	×	×	✓	✓
7 Do you have a test case with three integers greater than zero such that the sum of two of the numbers is equal to the third?	×	×	×	×	×	×	✓	✓
8 Do you have at least three test cases in category 7 such that you have tried all three permutations where the length of one side is equal to the sum of the lengths of the other two sides?	×	×	×	×	×	×	✓	✓
9 Do you have a test case with three integers greater than zero such that the sum of two of the numbers is less than the third?	×	×	×	×	×	×	✓	✓
10 Do you have at least three test cases in category 9 such that you have tried all three permutations?	×	×	×	×	×	×	✓	✓
11 Do you have a test case in which all sides are zero?	×	×	×	×	×	✓	×	×
12 Do you have at least one test case specifying noninteger values?	✓	✓	✓	✓	✓	✓	✓	✓
13 Do you have at least one test case specifying the wrong number of values (two rather than three integers, for example)?	×	✓	×	✓	×	✓	✓	✓
14 For each test case, did you specify the expected output from the program in addition to the input values?	✓	✓	✓	✓	✓	✓	✓	✓
Total Score/14	3	5	3	5	3	6	12	13

Note: The first three columns are for test suites generated from the syntactic model only, and the Both column is for the combined test suite generated from the syntactic and functional models.

either build up an FSM graph of the SUT behavior and use that to drive test generation, or we can just explore the model dynamically while doing online testing.

This approach treats the preconditions and postconditions as executable *black boxes* (the only thing one can do with them is execute them in a given state to get a true or false result), whereas the test generation techniques earlier in this chapter treated the preconditions and postconditions as *white boxes* and analyzed the internal syntax and structure of the predicates to determine what tests should be generated. The white-box approach has the advantage of allowing deeper analysis of the predicates that define each model operation, which may make it possible to generate more sophisticated tests. The black-box approach is simpler and has the advantage that the test generation depends only on the preconditions and postconditions semantics rather than on their syntax, so the generated test suite depends only on the meaning of the model rather than on its syntax. Note that regardless of whether we take a black-box or white-box view of the preconditions and postconditions in the model, we are still generating black-box tests of the SUT.

The following are the key aspects of model-based testing illustrated in this section.

- The importance of classifying model actions/transitions as *controllable* or *observable*. This distinction is necessary when testing nondeterministic reactive SUTs like the Chat system (by *reactive* we mean that the SUT can spontaneously generate events, so it is not limited to just returning a response for each test input).

- Online testing, where test generation and test execution are done simultaneously. This allows the test generator to observe the SUT response to each test step before generating more test steps. This makes it much easier to test nondeterministic SUTs.

- An EFSM approach to modeling, where each action of the model is an executable method plus a (black-box) guard predicate that says when the action is enabled. This is similar to the modeling style used by ModelJUnit in Section 5.2.

To illustrate this approach, we test a simple conference chat system with the Spec Explorer tool [CGN+05], which is a prototype tool from Microsoft Research. We gave an overview of some uses of Spec Explorer within Microsoft in Section 2.6.2. Here we describe the test generation approach of Spec Explorer in more detail and show how it can be used to test reactive systems like the Chat system. The Chat system is one of the examples that is included in the Spec Explorer distribution, with a test model and a sample implementation.

6.5.1 An Overview of Spec Explorer

Spec Explorer[4] is a model-based testing tool that supports both online and offline testing, is integrated with the Microsoft .NET architecture, and uses pre/post models that are usually written in an extended version of C#, called Spec#.[5]

Spec# is used more widely than just in Spec Explorer—it is a general-purpose language that is intended to strengthen C# to support a more cost-effective way of developing and maintaining high-quality software. The Spec# programming system is fully integrated into Microsoft Visual Studio and supports runtime checking of assertions as well as static checking of program correctness. The following are the main extensions that Spec# adds to C# [BLS04].

- A stronger type system that can specify which object references must be non-null (for each object type T, there is a corresponding non-null type T!)
- Method specifications using preconditions (`requires`), postconditions (`ensures`), frame conditions (`modifies`), and exception specifications (`throws`)
- Extensive support for object invariants and class invariants, with fine-grained control over which methods are allowed to break these invariants while updating an object
- Executable quantifiers and comprehension expressions for data structures. These make it much easier to specify complex properties of data structures within specifications. For example, the expression `Map{d in Members; <d,Seq{}>}` creates a new `Map` object that maps every element in the `Members` set to an empty sequence.

The Spec# models that are used by Spec Explorer for test generation use most of these Spec# features, such as preconditions, object invariants, non-null types, quantifiers, and comprehension expressions. Preconditions on methods are interpreted as *guards*, saying whether or not the methods are enabled. The bodies of the methods are written as C# code rather than as

---

[4] See *http://research.microsoft.com/SpecExplorer*.

[5] See the Spec# homepage at *http://research.microsoft.com/specsharp*.

postconditions and frame conditions. This makes it easier for programmers to write models because the transitions of the model are just like normal C# methods; the main new concept is the addition of a precondition to each method.

Spec Explorer uses a theory of *interface automata* to generate tests from Spec# models. Test generation is viewed as a game between the test generation process and the SUT. To enable this game approach to test generation, each method in the model can be annotated as either an *Action* method (which is under the control of the test generator) or an *Observation* method (which is under the control of the SUT).

The online testing algorithm (OLT) works as follows (see [VCST05] for a more detailed description). The test generation starts from the initial state of the model and can end whenever execution reaches an *accepting state* of the model (the modeler can specify which states are accepting states). In each state, Spec Explorer first waits for a state-dependent timeout period to see if an observable event arrives from the SUT. If one does arrive, Spec Explorer checks that the event is allowed by the model, and then takes that transition so that the model follows the SUT behavior. If no observable events arrive before the timeout, Spec Explorer executes one of the controllable methods in the model whose precondition is true, sends the corresponding event to the SUT, and checks that this transition is allowed by the SUT.

This raises the question of how Spec Explorer interacts with the SUT to capture the observable events and to trigger and check the controllable events. The SUT is simply another C# class and is typically an adapter class that gives an abstract view of the real system that is being tested. Spec Explorer instruments this SUT class at the binary level so that all calls to its observable methods are logged (these calls typically come from within the SUT, which may be multithreaded or distributed). Because these observable methods may be called at arbitrary times, the instrumentation code that is injected into the SUT class buffers the calls, queues them in the order that they occur, and makes that queue available for inspection by the OLT algorithm.

Whenever Spec Explorer takes an event $m(v)$ off that queue (where m is the name of an observable method and v is the vector of argument values), it checks that the observed event is legal by checking the precondition of $m(v)$ in the current state of the model; then it executes the $m(v)$ method in the model and checks that no postcondition or invariant failures occur.

When Spec Explorer decides to execute a controllable method m, it generates some input parameters v_{in} so that $m(v_{in})$ satisfies the precondition of the model method m. Then it executes the method $m(v_{in})$ in both the model and the SUT class and obtains their respective outputs, v_{out} from the model and *w* from the SUT (*w* includes the return result, which may be void or may be an exception). Finally, it checks that $v_{out} = w$.

This OLT algorithm is a bit like a game of cards: each time it is your turn to play, you select a card from your hand and put it on the table (an event you have control over); then you watch the table to see which cards opponents (the SUT!) play. Generation of offline tests uses a similar algorithm. Now we will apply this testing technique to online testing of the Chat system.

> **Key Point**   Distinguishing between controllable and observable events in the model is necessary when testing nondeterministic reactive systems, which may produce events spontaneously.

6.5.2   The Chat System

The Chat system allows members to enter and leave chat rooms and to send and receive messages. Our top-level testing goal is to check that the order of messages is preserved between a particular sender and each receiver. That is, we want to check that if sender S sends two messages, such as "hi" then "bye," then all members who receive those messages receive them in the correct order. For testing purposes, we restrict our testing to a single chat room.

The API of the Chat SUT is:

```
class Client
{
  Client();     // constructor for new clients
  void Enter();     // this member enters the chat room
  void Exit();       // this member exits the chat room
  void Send(Message msg); // this member sends a message
  void Receive(Message msg, Client! sndr);
}
```

Next we give a Spec# model of the desired behavior. Since we are primarily interested in testing the message sending and receiving, we model the ability to create clients, have them enter the chat room, and have them send and receive messages, but we omit the Exit action.

6.5.3   The Spec# Model

We model each member of the Chat system as an instance of the Client class shown in Listing 6.6. This contains a boolean flag called entered that records whether the member is currently in the chat room, plus several queues of messages that have been sent to this member but have not yet been read

LISTING 6.6   Spec# model of the client actions of the Chat system.

```
class Client
{
  bool entered = false;
  Map<Client, Seq<string>> unreceivedMsgs = Map{};

  [Action] Client()
  {
    this.unreceivedMsgs = Map{};
    entered = false;
    foreach (Client s in enumof(Client), s != this)
    {
        s.unreceivedMsgs[this] = Seq{};
        this.unreceivedMsgs[s] = Seq{};
    }
  }

  [Action] void Enter()
    requires !entered;
  {
    entered = true;
  }

  [Action]
  void Send(string message)
    requires entered;
  {
    foreach (Client c in enumof(Client), c != this, c.entered)
      c.unreceivedMsgs[this] += Seq{message};
  }

  [Action(Kind=ActionAttributeKind.Observable)]
  void Receive(Client! sender, string message)
    requires sender != this &&
             unreceivedMsgs[sender].Length > 0 &&
             unreceivedMsgs[sender].Head == message;
  {
    unreceivedMsgs[sender] = unreceivedMsgs[sender].Tail;
  }
}
```

(the `unreceivedMsgs` map contains one queue for each other member of the Chat system). The model takes a global view of the whole Chat system, so it puts messages on to the `unreceivedMsgs` queues of all members in the chat room instantaneously, as part of the `Send` method. This ability to take a global view makes the model dramatically simpler than a real implementation because a real implementation would be distributed and would have to cope with sending the messages across communication channels with delays and possible loss of messages. This is an example of how abstraction (such as hiding the distributed nature of the implementation) can make models simpler.

The constructor of the `Client` class creates a new member and uses the `enumof` operator of Spec# to iterate through all existing instances of the `Client` class and add an empty message queue in both directions between the new member and all existing members. The `Enter` method is called to make a member join the chat room. Once the member has joined, he or she can use the `Post` method to send a message to all other members who are currently in the chat room. These three methods are marked as `Action` methods, which means that they are under the control of the test generation process.

In contrast, the `Receive` method is marked as an `Observable` method, which means that the test generator cannot call it. Instead, the SUT will call it whenever a message is actually delivered to the receiving member, and the instrumentation code injected by Spec Explorer into the SUT assembly (the binary code of the SUT class) will log that call and report it to Spec Explorer. The precondition of the `Receive` method defines when this event is allowed, and the body of the method updates the state of the model to reflect the changes that should have occurred within the implementation. Note that the precondition checks that the received message is the *first* message in the `unreceivedMsgs` queue—this is how the model checks that messages are delivered in the same order that they are sent.

In addition to the `Client` class shown in Listing 6.6, the model contains several global definitions that set up the starting state of our test scenario and define the *accepting states* of the model (that is, the final state of each test sequence). To make these definitions easier to write, we first define the set of members who are currently in the chat room. The following `Members` property is computed by iterating through all instances of the `Client` class and selecting just those members whose `entered` field is true.

```
Set<Client!> Members
{
    get { return Set{c in enumof(Client), c.entered; c}; }
}
```

LISTING 6.7   The test initialization action for the Chat model.

```
[Action] void Start(int nrOfMembers)
  requires enumof(Client) == Set{};
{
  Seq<Client!> clients = Seq{};

  // 1: The given number of clients are created
  for (int i = 0; i < nrOfMembers; i++)
    clients += Seq{new Client()};

  // 2: all clients enter the session
  for (int i = 0; i < nrOfMembers; i++)
    clients[i].Enter();
}
```

Using this Members property, we can easily define the special boolean function, IsAcceptingState(), to be true only when all members in the chat room have received all their messages. This means that the test generator will not terminate a test sequence until the SUT has delivered all messages.

```
bool IsAcceptingState()
{
  return Forall{m in Members, q in m.unreceivedMsgs.Values;
                q.Length == 0};
}
```

Finally, the Start action shown in Listing 6.7 sets up the initial state of our testing scenario by creating a given number of members, and then putting them all into the chat room. After this Start action has been performed, some of the actions in the Client class will be enabled, so testing can continue.

6.5.4 Test Generation with Spec Explorer

Spec Explorer supports a wide range of test selection criteria, including the following:

- Choice of actions. You can choose which controllable actions can be generated and which observable actions will be observed.
- Choice of a set of possible values for each parameter type.

- Filters that restrict the state space of the model.

- State grouping expressions, which partition the states into equivalence classes to make the model's FSM smaller.

- Search order (e.g., depth-first to produce long test sequences, breadth-first to produce short test sequences, or user-defined priority expressions).

- The timeout expression, for the length of time to wait for observable events in each state.

- An AcceptingState condition, which says which states are accepting states (where testing may terminate).

- The maximum number of steps per test sequence or in total. When one of these counters is exceeded during online testing, Spec Explorer goes into cleanup phase, trying to reach an accepting state.

- The choice of the seed that controls the random number generator used during test generation. Note that even using a fixed seed does not guarantee that the same test sequence will occur since the nondeterminism of the SUT is not under the control of Spec Explorer.

To illustrate the online testing capabilities of Spec Explorer, we test a sample implementation of the Chat system using the following test selection criteria:

- The input parameter of the Start action is set to 2, so that the chat room will contain two members.

- The Start, Send, and Receive actions are chosen for use during testing, while the Client constructor and Enter actions are disabled. This ensures that all testing will focus on the two members added by Start rather than try to create or enter other members.

- The message parameter of the Send action is restricted to be either "hi" or "bye".

- Two filters are used to restrict the number of states that will be tested: one restricts the total number of pending deliveries to be less than 3, and the other prevents the sending of duplicate messages.

- The search order is arbitrary, where all states have equal priority.

- The AcceptingState condition is set to the IsAcceptingState() boolean method so that test sequences will terminate only after all messages are delivered.

- The timeout is 0, which means that at any state that has both a controllable action and an observable action enabled, the controllable action will be taken immediately, unless there happens to be an observable action already waiting, in which case that observable action will be taken. For states that have only observable actions enabled, the timeout is 10 seconds, which gives the Chat implementation sufficient time to pass messages around a network.

- The maximum number of states and steps for online test is set to several hundred.

Figure 6.3 shows a screenshot of Spec Explorer running with these test selection criteria just after it has found an error in the sample implementation. The randomly generated online test sequence was the following (the observed events are prefixed by a question mark):

```
Client()=c0; Client()=c1; c0.Enter(); c1.Enter();
c1.Send("hi"); c0.Send("bye"); c1.?Receive(c0,"bye");
c1.Send("bye"); c0.?Receive(c1,"hi"); c0.Send("hi");
c0.?Receive(c1,"bye"); c1.?Receive(c0,"hi");
c1.Send("bye"); c1.Send("hi"); c0.?Receive(c1, "hi")
```

The SUT error (which was intentionally inserted!) can be seen in the last line of this sequence—two messages were sent from c1 to c0, first "bye" then "hi", but the "hi" message was received first. So the implementation does not satisfy the requirement of delivering messages to each client in the order that they were sent, and the online testing has correctly detected this violation.

The graph in the screenshot shows the part of the model that was explored during the online testing up to the point where the error occurred. Note that states S0 and S1 are accepting states (shown as dark gray in Figure 6.3) because in those states there are no messages that have been sent but not yet received. S2, S3, and S4 are also accepting states, but were not marked as such because they were internal to the Start action. S8 is the state in which the only undelivered message is a "bye" sent from c1 to c0. So after the c1.Send("hi") transition to S11, the client c0 has two messages waiting and should receive the "bye" message first, but the transition from S11 to S12 shows that it incorrectly received the "hi" message first.

This example illustrates the power of Spec Explorer and of online testing. The model is used not only to control which actions should be sent to the SUT but also to model enough of the internal state of the SUT (the undelivered messages) to make it possible to know exactly which observed events from the SUT are valid and which are not. The separation of actions into

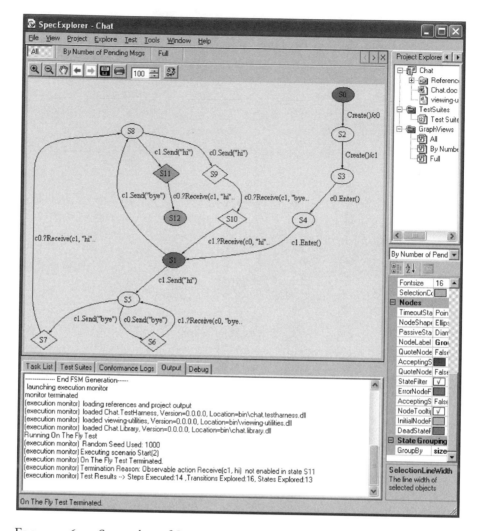

FIGURE 6.3   Screenshot of Spec Explorer showing an error detected during on-the-fly testing.

controllable and observable actions tells Spec Explorer when to wait for the SUT to respond and allows it to handle nondeterministic responses, which can occur due to network delays and concurrency within the SUT.

6.6 SUMMARY

It is often useful to have more than one model of your SUT. In particular, it can be useful to have a high-level model of the normal behavior of the SUT and also a low-level syntactic model that models the good and bad values of each input and is used for robustness testing.

These are the four main steps to writing a pre/post model:

1. Choose a high-level test objective (*what* to model).
2. Design the *signatures* of the operations in the model.
3. Choose the state variables of the model and their types.
4. Write the preconditions and postconditions of each operation.

Model-based testing usually generates tests *within* the preconditions of each operation. So you can use strong preconditions to restrict your testing to the "normal" behavior of an operation or weaker preconditions to test the "exception" cases of its behavior.

It is possible to generate a traceability matrix that links the generated tests to the informal requirements, but this requires well-structured requirements documents, a model that is annotated with requirements identifiers, and support for traceability in the model-based testing tool that is used for test generation.

One way of making the test generation process more transparent is to first generate formal *test targets* from the model and then generate one or more tests to satisfy each test target. A test target is a formal *specification* of a desired test case. The model coverage can then be defined as the percentage of test targets for which a test has been generated.

Unsatisfiable test targets are usually quietly discarded—they correspond to impossible (contradictory) paths through the model. *Unreachable* test targets are those for which no test can be found. These are usually worth investigating because they can expose issues in the model, such as an error in an operation or an invariant that is not as tight as it could be.

For models that contain complex decisions, the number of tests for those decisions can be controlled using coverage criteria such as decision coverage, condition/decision coverage, modified condition/decision coverage, and multiple condition coverage. These give an increasing number of tests that exercise the logical connections between the conditions within each decision.

To test nondeterministic reactive systems, which may generate events spontaneously or in arbitrary orders, it is necessary to classify each model action as either a controllable event or an observable event. Based on this distinction, the test generation process can generate a sequence of controllable events, send them to the SUT, and observe the observable events produced by the SUT. This is typically done as an online testing process, where test generation and SUT observation are interleaved.

6.7 FURTHER READING

A description of the test generation process used in the LEIRIOS Test Generator and discussion of some techniques for controlling the number of generated tests can be found in [LPU04]. The challenge of searching for the preamble is discussed in [CLP04].

The Spec Explorer home page[6] has several papers about the theory and practical application of Spec Explorer, plus instructions on how to obtain Spec Explorer for academic use and for noncommercial evaluation. The Chat system is one of the examples included in the Spec Explorer distribution, and some of the papers available from the Spec Explorer home page [CGN+05, VCST05] discuss testing the Chat system. The Chat system is similar to the Conference Protocol case study,[7] which has been used to illustrate the capabilities of several kinds of model-based testing tool [dBRS+00, HFT00].

---

[6] See *http://research.microsoft.com/SpecExplorer.*
[7] See *http://fmt.cs.utwente.nl/ConfCase.*

## CHAPTER 7

TESTING FROM UML TRANSITION-BASED MODELS

This chapter describes several approaches to model-based testing from UML models. UML 2.0 [RJB05] contains a large set of diagrams and notations that are defined in a flexible and open-ended way using a metamodel[1] and have some freedom allowed for different interpretations of the semantics of the diagrams by different UML tools. So for practical model-based testing it is necessary to select a subset of UML and clarify the semantics of the chosen subset so that model-based testing tools can interpret the UML models.

Each model-based testing tool takes a different approach to this by supporting several kinds of diagram and defining a safe subset of those diagrams that can be used in models. It is necessary to define both the data part of the model (class diagrams are typically used for this) and the dynamic behavioral aspects of the model. In this chapter we focus on state machine models of the dynamic behavior, but Section 7.1 discusses a variety of UML diagrams and how useful they are in modeling systems for testing.

---

[1]A metamodel is a notation for describing other notations. See *http://www.omg.org* for lots of details.

More specifically, this chapter illustrates the following approaches and tools:

- Section 7.2 addresses testing a web-based system for buying movie tickets using a UML state machine model with OCL to express guards and actions, and the LEIRIOS LTG/UML tool for test generation.

- Section 7.3 discusses testing a nondeterministic bidirectional transport protocol using online testing, driven by multiple state machines, using the Conformiq Qtronic Test Generator tool.

7.1 UML MODELING NOTATIONS

This section discusses UML from the perspective of automated generation of black-box tests from UML models. This perspective means that we want to use UML to model the *behavior* of systems rather than their physical structure (e.g., deployment diagrams) or the design of their implementation (e.g., component diagrams, collaboration diagrams, or internal structure diagrams).

Table 7.1 gives a summary of the role of the main UML diagrams that are relevant for modeling for testing.

Invariably, a test model starts with a class diagram, which defines an abstract view of the SUT class, the data fields within that class that are useful for testing purposes, and the relationships with other classes that are needed to generate tests. Note that this class diagram is usually much simpler than the class diagram for the *design* of the SUT. We discuss the relationship between the design process and the testing model in Section 11.5.

The class diagram is not enough by itself because it does not model the dynamic behavior of the SUT. There are many possible ways of modeling the SUT behavior in UML, but the following are most common:

- Use UML state machines to define the behavior of the SUT object and perhaps also the behavior of other objects in the model.

- Use UML activity diagrams to define complex operations that spread across several classes.

- Use OCL preconditions and postconditions to define the behavior of the methods declared in the class diagram.

The examples in this chapter illustrate mostly the first approach (state machines), but Section 7.2 also briefly illustrates the use of OCL for modeling behavior. None of the examples here use activity diagrams, but modeling

TABLE 7.1   UML Diagrams and Their Use for Modeling for Testing

View	Diagram	Role in Modeling for Testing
Static	Class Diagram	Excellent for describing the static structure of a system, the data within each class, and the associations between classes.
	Object Diagram	Good for defining initial states of the model for test generation.
Reqs	Use Case Diagram	Gives an overview of the system requirements but does not give enough detail to be useful for test generation. However, each textual use case can act as a high-level informal test goal, which guides the choice of test selection criteria.
Dynamic	State Machine Diagram	Ideal for modeling the behavior of an SUT for testing purposes. Each transition describes one fragment of behavior that we want to test.
	Activity Diagram	Good for modeling a process or workflow and a good basis for test generation.
	Sequence Diagram	Good for describing an abstract test case, that is, for viewing the *output* of the test generation process. Also useful as a test selection notation that can specify a desired path through a separate behavioral model.
	Communication Diagram	Similar role to sequence diagrams.

with activity diagrams is not too dissimilar from modeling with state machines, so many of the principles we discuss carry over.

7.2   TESTING AN ETHEATER WITH LTG/UML

In this section we develop a UML model for a web-based system for buying movie tickets. This is a typical transaction-oriented web system that includes both data-oriented aspects (ticket prices, movie titles, session times) and control-oriented aspects (the sequence of web events required to log in, select a movie, and purchase a ticket).

7.2.1   Requirements

The eTheater application allows moviegoers to buy movie tickets online before they go to the theater. For popular movies, this avoids having to wait in

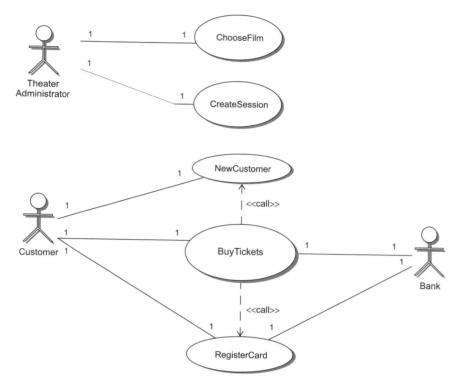

FIGURE 7.1 eTheater use case diagram.

a queue to buy tickets and means that you can arrive at the movie just before it starts.

Figure 7.1 shows the main use cases for this system. There are two main actors: the customer who buys tickets and the theater administrator who chooses the films to show, decides on session times, sets the price of tickets, and so on. There is also the bank, which is a secondary actor, handling the validation of credit cards and payments. Use Cases 7.1, 7.2, and 7.3 describe the details of the three customer-oriented use cases. Here are the use cases for the theater administrator:

ChooseFilm: The administrator enters the name and details of a film that will be shown at the theater.

CreateSession: The administrator creates a new session by choosing a film (which must be showing at the theater), a session time, the number of seats available in that session, and the price of the tickets for those seats.

USE CASE 7.1   eTheater use case for a customer buying tickets.

Use Case: BuyTickets
Scope: eTheater
Primary Actor: Customer
Secondary Actor: Bank
Goal: The customer wants to buy one or more tickets for a given session of a movie.
Precondition: The customer is an existing customer of the eTheater system and has registered a valid payment card.

Main Success Scenario

1. Customer enters her username and password.
2. Customer is shown a welcome page, which shows all the tickets she has previously bought (and not yet used) and offers two links: "Buy Tickets" and "Register Payment Card."
3. Customer clicks the Buy Tickets link and is taken to the buying page, which displays information about the films that are showing, the date and time of each session of those films, and the number of available tickets. It also displays the current contents of her shopping basket at the top of the page.
4. Customer selects the desired number of tickets for a particular session of a particular film. She may repeat this for several films, adding more tickets to her shopping basket each time.
5. Customer confirms her selection.
6. A payment is made using a credit card, via the bank.
7. A receipt is displayed showing payment details, film name, and the session time.
8. Customer logs out from the eTheater system.

Extensions

1a. If the customer username or password is wrong, then an error message is displayed and the same login page remains onscreen.
4a. In the buying page, the customer can also delete tickets from the shopping basket if she changes her mind.
6a. If there are not enough tickets for a given session, an error message is displayed and customer is returned to the buying page.
6b. If the payment fails, an error message is displayed and the customer is returned to the welcome page. From there she can choose to register a different payment card or go back into the buying page to delete some tickets.

USE CASE 7.2   eTheater use case for creating a new customer.

Use Case: NewCustomer
Scope: eTheater
Primary Actor: Customer
Goal: The customer wants to create an account with the eTheater system.

Main Success Scenario
1. Customer chooses a username.
2. Customer enters his full name and address details.
3. Customer confirms his details.
4. The customer is added to the customer database and the welcome page is displayed.

Extensions
1a. If the customer username is already in use, an error message is displayed and he remains in the same login page and must choose a new username.

USE CASE 7.3   eTheater use case for registering a payment card.

Use Case: RegisterCard
Scope: eTheater
Primary Actor: Customer
Secondary Actor: Bank
Goal: The customer wants to register a credit card or payment card to purchase movie tickets.
Precondition: The customer is an existing customer of the eTheater system and is currently logged in with the welcome page displayed.

Main Success Scenario
1. Customer clicks on the Register Payment Card link.
2. The register card page is displayed.
3. Customer chooses a card type and enters the card details.
4. The credit card is validated with the bank.
5. A confirmation message is displayed.

Extensions
4a. If the card type is a PRIVILEGE card, no bank validation is required because it is a prepaid card issued by the theater and tickets are deducted from the card each time they are purchased.
4b. If the credit card is refused by the bank, then an error message is displayed and the customer can continue from step 2.

7.2.2 Assumptions for the Test Model

The primary goal of our testing is to test the web-based transaction process for choosing films, buying tickets, and paying for them. We will reuse an existing web service for registering and validating payment cards. It has been thoroughly tested in other applications, so we decide not to test the details of this subsystem but to take a simplified view of it in our test model.

We decide not to model all the customer details that are stored in the database, only the login name. Similarly, we do not model the database of tickets that the customer has already bought. We also abstract away from the password checking since this is a standard feature of our web server, which is tested elsewhere.

On the buying page, the customer can add a desired number of tickets (1 to 10) from a drop-down menu next to a given session. However, to keep the model simple, we will break this down into separate "addTicket" and "delTicket" transitions in the model, with each transition taking just one ticket object as a parameter.

7.2.3 A UML Model of eTheater

Figure 7.2 shows a class diagram for the eTheater system. The main class is the eTheater class, so we mark this with the ≪SUT≫ stereotype to indicate that we want to test an instance of this class. This is typical of a class diagram for testing purposes: the central object is the SUT, which contains lots of events and methods, and around this SUT object are just those classes and attributes that are needed to support the SUT testing.

Note that we make a clear distinction between the *methods* and the *events* of classes, as shown by the ≪events≫ stereotype in the eTheater class. These play different roles in our model. The events, which are written below the ≪events≫ stereotype, are allowed to appear only within the state machine for that class, where they are used as the triggering events of transitions. The methods, which are written above the ≪events≫ stereotype, are the usual kinds of method used in object-oriented development. They can be called from outside the class if they are public or called from within the class (typically from within the *action* part of a transition in the state machine). So the meaning of a method is usually defined using OCL preconditions and postconditions, whereas the meaning of an event is defined by the transitions in the state machine.

The class diagram also shows that we use enumeration classes quite heavily to define small sets of users, times, and payment cards for testing purposes. A design model of the eTheater system would have much more sophisticated

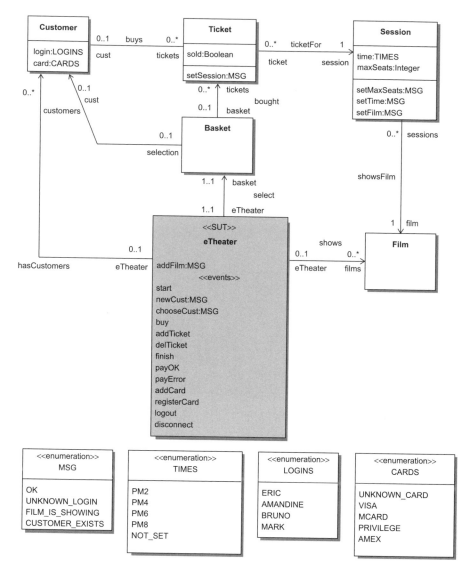

FIGURE 7.2   eTheater class diagram.

models of these types. To define the behavior of this class, we use a state machine, as shown in Figure 7.3.

Transitions have the form *Event*[*Guard*]/*Action*, where *Event* must be one of the events listed in the SUT class, *Guard* is an OCL predicate, and *Action* is either an OCL postcondition or a call to a method in the SUT class (which must be specified with an OCL precondition and postcondition). When the *Action* part contains a method call, we require that the precon-

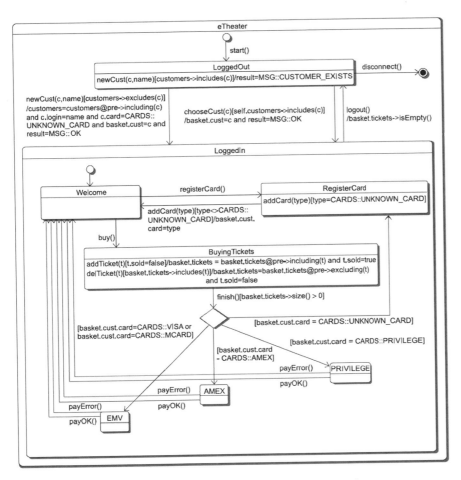

FIGURE 7.3 State machine for the eTheater class.

dition of the method be satisfied (for example, it follows from *Guard*), and then we define the semantics of the method call to be the postcondition of the method. So the method calls within the *Action* part of transitions are simply a convenient procedural abstraction mechanism that allows large chunks of OCL to be moved out of the class diagram and given a method name.

Any of the *Event*, *Guard*, or *Action* parts may be omitted. When the *Event* part (the trigger) is omitted, the transition is automatically fired whenever the machine is in the right state and the guard is true. For example, after the finish() transition is taken in Figure 7.3, one of the four outgoing transitions is automatically taken, depending on which guard is true. To avoid nondeterministic behavior, the guards of the four outgoing transitions must be mutually disjoint. An omitted guard is equivalent to true, so the transition is fired whenever the machine is in the right state and the *Event* occurs. An omitted *Action* is equivalent to leaving all attributes unchanged.

To be able to execute transitions, we need to take an operational interpretation of OCL postconditions. This is necessary to overcome an inadequacy of OCL: unlike a programming language, where variables that are not assigned retain their original value, OCL does not provide a way to say precisely which variables in a class are changed by an operation and which are not. For example, OCL allows postconditions such as

```
self.attr1 = self.attr2
```

but does not specify whether this means that `attr1` has changed, `attr2` has changed, or both or neither of them have changed.

LTG/UML gives OCL postconditions an operational interpretation by classifying all their atomic predicates as either *active* or *passive*. A passive predicate is one that can only read attributes, whereas an active predicate may write to attributes. Any equality that is active and whose left side is either an attribute (without a `@pre` modifier) or an output variable is interpreted as an assignment. That is, an active equality `attr1=E` is interpreted as an assignment to `attr1`, so the final value of `attr1` will be equal to `E`. To avoid ambiguities, the expression `E` must refer only to input values and the previous state (using `@pre`). So, if we wanted the previous postcondition to mean that `attr2` is assigned the original value of `attr1`, we must write it as

```
self.attr2 = self.attr1@pre
```

On the other hand, if we wanted the postcondition to mean that `attr1` and `attr2` are both set to the same value, such as 0, we must write it as

```
self.attr1 = 0 and self.attr2 = 0
```

This interpretation makes it possible to determine the *frame* of an OCL postcondition (all the variables that may change value) by syntactic inspection of that postcondition.

The classification of predicates as active or passive is based on the semantics of each OCL operator. For example, the condition part of an `if-then-else` is passive, while the `then` and `else` parts are active (if the whole `if-then-else` is active). Preconditions and transition guards are always passive. In `P1 implies P2`, `P1` is passive and `P2` is active; in `E->select(P)`, `P` is passive; while in `E->forall(P)` and `E->exists(P)`, `P` is active.

7.2.4 Generating Tests Using LEIRIOS LTG/UML

To get a first version of a small test suite, we decide to use the following test selection criteria:

- Explicit-transition coverage of the UML state machine. This means that we only need to test the `logout` transition in Figure 7.3 once rather than seven times (once for each of the atomic states with the `LoggedIn` superstate).

- Decision coverage (DC) of the complex decisions within transitions, preconditions, and postconditions. This is the simplest kind of coverage for complex decisions, but in this example, there is only one condition that contains an `or` operator, so choosing more sophisticated coverage of the complex decisions would generate only one or two more tests.

- *Any one value* for the input parameters of the events and methods. This means that we are happy to test just one input value for each parameter, within each path chosen by the test selection criteria. In some cases, an event may appear in several paths, and the constraints of these paths will require different input values for an input parameter. But within each path, we test just one input value for each parameter.

With these test selection criteria, we get one test target for each of the 22 transitions (including the internal transitions), plus six additional test targets from the five methods in the class diagram that do not appear in the state machine. The behavior of these methods was defined via OCL preconditions and postconditions, which are not shown here because we want to focus on the tests generated from the UML state machine.

Next we define an initial state for the tests, as shown in Figure 7.4. This has several films, sessions, and tickets set up ready for sale. The main `sut` object (an instance of the `eTheater` class) has a basket and two films showing, with just one session per film and a very small number of tickets for each session. It also has the film *Sissi*, which is not yet showing in any sessions, and three customers who have no payment cards registered. This is not exactly a picture of a thriving eTheater, but it is a useful scenario for testing.

The next step is to generate tests from these test targets. The strategy used to generate the tests is to first search for a *preamble* sequence from the initial state to the transition mentioned in a test target, then to take that transition, and then to search for a *postamble* sequence that goes from that transition to the final state. However, the search for the preamble and postamble sequences is more than a simple graph traversal because the constraints associated with a path (the guards and postconditions, etc.) mean

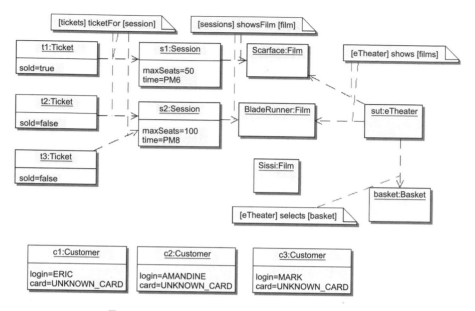

FIGURE 7.4 eTheater initial state for testing.

that some paths through the graph are not feasible, so alternative paths must be taken. In addition, to find a feasible path it is often necessary to choose suitable input values for the parameters of events along that path.

For example, if we are searching for a preamble for the chooseCust(c) transition (from the LoggedOut state to the LoggedIn state), then it looks from the graph as though we can just use the following sequence (where *Cust* stands for any instance of the Customer class):

start(); chooseCust(*Cust*)

But the guard [customers->includes(c)] on the chooseCust(c) transition prevents this because in our initial state the set of customers is empty. So it is necessary to do a loop around the LoggedOut and LoggedIn states in order to create a new customer before we can choose that customer as an existing customer. The path that we need to take is actually

start(); newCust(*Cust,Name*); logout(); chooseCust(*Cust2*)

and *Cust* and *Cust2* must be the same instance of the Customer class, so that the guard of chooseCust is true.

Using this approach, with search algorithms like best-first search plus a proprietary constraint analysis engine to solve the constraints associated with each path, the LTG/UML tool generates the test suite shown in Table 7.2. The number of tests generated from the state machine (T1–T13) is smaller than the number of transitions (22) because some of the test targets were satisfied by the preambles of another test. The calls in bold show the transition that is the body of each test. Some transitions along the main payment path (start, newCust, registerCard, addCard with a card that is not UNKNOWN_CARD, buy and addTicket) are covered by the preambles of other tests, so are not shown in bold.

Chapter 8 shows how the abstract tests of Table 7.2 can be transformed into executable test scripts and executed on an implementation of the eTheater web server.

7.2.5 Generating Better Test Suites

In this section, we discuss how we could test our eTheater system more thoroughly by choosing different test selection criteria. We focus just on the buying of tickets, as modeled by the eTheater state machine and as tested by tests T1 to T13 of Table 7.2.

As we explained in Section 4.1.3, testing just the *explicit transitions* of a UML state machine with nested states is not really sufficient. The test suite in Table 7.2 does not even test the behavior of our eTheater system when a customer logs out in the middle of paying for tickets! We prefer to define all-transitions as meaning that each transition out of a superstate should be expanded into all its implicit transitions, that is, expanded into a set of transitions from all the atomic states within its source superstate. In our eTheater state machine, this means that the logout() transition is split into six transitions so that every state within the LoggedIn superstate has a logout() transition to the LoggedOut state. So instead of having 22 transitions to cover, we now have $22 - 1 + 6 = 27$ transitions.

If we ask LTG/UML to generate an independent test for each transition (including implicit transitions), it generates exactly 27 test sequences, each one leading from the start state to the desired transition. However, many of these tests are prefixes of other tests, so they can be removed to make the test suite smaller. This leaves 18 distinct tests: six of them test the payOK and payError transitions with three kinds of payment card, six of them test what happens when a customer logs out at various stages of a transaction, and the remaining six test other interesting cases:

- Immediate disconnect. (start(); disconnect()).
- A customer tries to create a new account twice. This checks that the first try succeeds and that the second try gives a CUSTOMER_EXISTS message.

TABLE 7.2 Generated Test Cases for eTheater

No.	Test Case
T1	sut.start(); sut.newCust(c1,AMANDINE); sut.registerCard(); sut.addCard(PRIVILEGE); sut.buy(); sut.addTicket(t3); sut.finish(); **sut.payOK();** sut.logout(); sut.disconnect()
T2	sut.start(); sut.newCust(c1,AMANDINE); sut.registerCard(); sut.addCard(VISA); sut.buy(); sut.addTicket(t3); sut.finish(); **sut.payOK();** sut.logout(); sut.disconnect()
T3	sut.start(); sut.newCust(c1,AMANDINE); sut.registerCard(); sut.addCard(AMEX); sut.buy(); sut.addTicket(t3); sut.finish(); **sut.payOK();** sut.logout(); sut.disconnect()
T4	sut.start(); sut.newCust(c1,AMANDINE); sut.registerCard(); sut.addCard(PRIVILEGE); sut.buy(); sut.addTicket(t3); sut.finish(); **sut.payError();** sut.logout(); sut.disconnect()
T5	sut.start(); sut.newCust(c1,AMANDINE); sut.registerCard(); sut.addCard(VISA); sut.buy(); sut.addTicket(t3); sut.finish(); **sut.payError();** sut.logout(); sut.disconnect()
T6	sut.start(); sut.newCust(c1,AMANDINE); sut.registerCard(); sut.addCard(AMEX); sut.buy(); sut.addTicket(t3); sut.finish(); **sut.payError();** sut.logout(); sut.disconnect()
T7	sut.start(); sut.newCust(c1,AMANDINE); sut.buy(); sut.addTicket(t2); **sut.finish();** sut.logout(); sut.disconnect()
T8	sut.start(); sut.newCust(c1,AMANDINE); sut.logout(); **sut.newCust(c1,AMANDINE)=MSG::CUSTOMER_EXISTS;** sut.logout(); sut.disconnect()
T9	sut.start(); sut.newCust(c1,AMANDINE); sut.registerCard(); **sut.addCard(UNKNOWN_CARD);** sut.logout(); sut.disconnect()
T10	sut.start(); sut.newCust(c1,AMANDINE); sut.buy(); sut.addTicket(t2); **sut.delTicket(t2);** sut.logout(); sut.disconnect()
T11	sut.start(); sut.newCust(c1,AMANDINE); sut.logout(); **sut.chooseCust(c1);** sut.logout(); sut.disconnect()
T12	sut.start(); sut.newCust(c1,AMANDINE); **sut.logout();** sut.disconnect()
T13	sut.start(); **sut.disconnect()**
T14	sut.addFilm(Sissi)=MSG::OK
T15	sut.addFilm(BladeRunner)=MSG::FILM_IS_SHOWING
T16	s1.setMaxSeats(1)=MSG::OK
T17	s1.setFilm(BladeRunner)=MSG::OK
T18	s1.setTime(PM2)=MSG::OK
T19	t3.setSession(s2)=MSG::OK

Note: What is shown here is with explicit transition coverage of the state machine, decision coverage of the OCL decisions, and one-value coverage of input parameters.

- An existing customer logs in. (That is, a customer creates a new account, then logs out, and then logs back in again.)

- A customer who changes his or her mind (adds a ticket to the shopping basket and then deletes that ticket).

- A customer tries to buy tickets without a payment card. This tests that when customer who clicks `finish()` he or she is taken to the `RegisterCard` state to enter card details.

- A customer tries to register an unknown kind of payment card.

This is a reasonable test suite, but it contains only 18 tests. If we wanted to test our eTheater system much more thoroughly, how might we do it?

One easy ("push-button") strategy would be to use all-transition-pairs coverage of the state machine. Table 7.3 shows the number of ingoing and outgoing transitions of each state and the number of transition pairs that result (the product of the two numbers). The left columns show these numbers when we consider explicit transitions only (so there's only one `logout` transition), while the right columns show the numbers when we want to test all the implicit transitions. With explicit transitions only, we test 62 transition pairs, while with implicit transitions, we test 92 transition pairs. On larger models, transition-pair coverage can rapidly become impractical.

How useful would these test suites be? Well, they do test a few extra useful scenarios, such as buying some tickets and then going back into the `BuyingTickets` page, testing all possible actions of a customer immediately after logout, and all combinations of adding and deleting tickets. But it is a bit of a shotgun approach: some tests are useful and some are not.

Another push-button technique for doing more thorough testing would be to generate random traversals of the state machine. This just chooses tran-

TABLE 7.3   Transition-Pair Coverage of eTheater State Machine

State	Explicit Transitions			All Transitions		
	In	Out	Pairs	In	Out	Pairs
LoggedOut	3	4	12	8	4	32
Welcome	8	2	16	8	3	24
RegisterCard	2	2	4	2	3	6
BuyingTickets	3	6	24	3	7	21
EMV	1	2	2	1	3	3
AMEX	1	2	2	1	3	3
PRIVILEGE	1	2	2	1	3	3
Total Pairs			62			92

sitions randomly, but because we are traversing a model of the expected eTheater behavior, we can still perform accurate checking of the SUT response to each transition. As an example of using random generation, we could generate two hours of tests, using online testing, between 1am and 3am every night during the final stages of development of the eTheater implementation. Random testing generates many unusual test sequences that a human tester would probably not consider, but these can be useful for finding errors in the less frequently used parts of the system and for testing interactions between features.

To get more sophisticated test suites, rather than just larger ones, requires more detailed test selection criteria than just pushing a button. For example, we could write an explicit test case specification that tests one common scenario of a customer using the eTheater system. Then we could use Harry Robinson's GAWAIN algorithm [Rob05] to explore all the minor variations of that sequence. It uses probabilities to generate dozens or hundreds of test sequences that are similar to the original sequence but contain a few mutations or alternative paths. This is a good way of using model-based test generation to amplify the insight and expertise of a human tester because the human can choose a realistic scenario, and then the model-based testing tool can generate many variations on that scenario to test that the SUT implements them correctly.

7.3   TESTING A PROTOCOL WITH QTRONIC

In this section we develop a UML model for a small bidirectional transport protocol and use it to test an implementation of the protocol.

The model includes data, timing constraints, and concurrency. It consists of a set of UML state machine models that have actions written in extended Java. (In the previous section we used a different language, OCL, as the action notation within state machine transitions.) Conformiq Qtronic, the tool used to generate tests in this section, provides this extended Java as an action notation. The extensions to Java include value records (e.g., struct in C#) and type inference (which allows you to omit variable and type declarations when their types can be inferred from the context).

We perform online model-based testing using Conformiq Qtronic.[2] This tool supports multithreaded and concurrent models, timing constraints, and testing of nondeterministic systems. The model we present here contains two kinds of nondeterminism: it consists of multiple threads that

---

[2] See *http://www.conformiq.com* for more information about Qtronic.

are scheduled nondeterministically, and it has explicit nondeterminism in the time domain.

7.3.1 Protocol

The transport protocol we test in this section is very simple. It is used to relay data packets via a router node that has an internal buffer. The router node works bidirectionally. It has four ports: two input ports and two output ports. Transported data items are integers.

The protocol keeps track of a sequence number in both directions. Data is sent into the router in a packet that contains the data item and a sequence number. If the sequence number in a packet is the next sequence number expected by the router, the router answers with an acknowledgment and stores the data item in a central buffer. If it is the same number as in the previously received message, the router answers with an acknowledgment but does not modify the buffer (it is a resend from the client). Packets with any other sequence numbers are discarded. The exception to this behavior is that if the central buffer is full, then the router drops any incoming data and does not provide an acknowledgment.

Similarly, when the router sends a packet out of its central buffer, it expects to get an acknowledgment from the client who receives the packet. The router must periodically resend the data until it receives an acknowledgment. In the model there is a timing constraint that there must be at most 10 seconds between two resends.

The two directions of data are not completely independent because they use the same internal buffer memory. When the central buffer gets full, no data will be accepted in either of the directions until some data is succesfully received by clients (and removed from the buffer).

7.3.2 Model

The model for this protocol has four active objects, one active object for each of the four ports of the router. There is also one important passive object: the central buffer that is shared by the four port handlers. Because the buffer is shared, access to it is serialized using a mutex (*mutual exclusion*) lock.

The behavior of the port handlers is specified using UML state machines (see Figures 7.6 and 7.7 later in this chapter). The port handlers and the buffer object also have some methods that are written textually inside their class declarations and called from within the state machines. No class diagram is required, but it could be derived from the class declarations if desired.

SYSTEM DECLARATION

The system has four external ports. The external interface of the system is declared with a system block (if a more graphical approach were desired, this could be expressed as a UML component diagram).

```
system
{
    Inbound ain : AnyRecord;
    Outbound aout : AnyRecord;
    Inbound bin : AnyRecord;
    Outbound bout : AnyRecord;
}
```

In the Qtronic approach, ports can be declared without restricting the type of data that can be sent to them because the set of valid data types handled by the system can be inferred from the behavior of the objects managing the ports.

MESSAGE DATA TYPES

The system uses only two record types for external communication: Send, a data item in an envelope, and ACK, which is used for communication acknowledgment in both inbound and outbound directions. The last two records, Expected and BufferContainsData, are used for communication *within* the model but not externally.

```
record Send { public int seq, data; }
record ACK { public int ack; }
record Expected { public int ack; }
record BufferContainsData { }
/* We use one global instance of BufferContainsData */
BufferContainsData gBufferContainsData;
```

TEST SCENARIO

To define the scenario that we wish to test, we write a main method for the preceding system class. This main method creates four active objects (one for each port); one main passive object (the shared buffer) connects them all together using several CQPort objects for communication and then starts the active objects by giving them threads to run. Figure 7.5 shows an alternative view of the resulting test scenario as a UML object diagram. Note that gBufferSize is a global constant that defines the size of the FIFO queues.

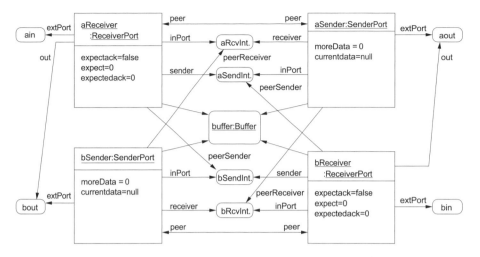

FIGURE 7.5   Test scenario as a UML object diagram.

Since the SUT is allowed to drop data when its buffers are full, gBufferSize must be defined to match the amount of buffer memory in the actual SUT so that the behavior of the model matches the expected SUT behavior.

The CQPort objects are synchronous rendezvous points that support synchronous message passing without buffering. Sending a message to a CQ-Port, written as port.send(msg) or msg->port, blocks the sender until someone is ready to receive the data.

```
void main()
{
    /* Global mutex for accessing buffers. */
    Lock mutex = new Lock();

    /* Protocol buffer. */
    Buffer buffer = new Buffer(gBufferSize, mutex);

    /* Traffic from a to b. */
    aRcvInternal = new CQPort();
    ReceiverPort aReceiver =
    new ReceiverPort(buffer, aRcvInternal, ain);
    aSendInternal = new CQPort();
    SenderPort aSender =
    new SenderPort(buffer, aSendInternal, aout);
    aSender.SetPeer(aReceiver);
    aReceiver.SetPeer(aSender);
```

```
/* Traffic from b to a. */
bRcvInternal = new CQPort();
ReceiverPort bReceiver =
new ReceiverPort(buffer, bRcvInternal, bin);
bSendInternal = new CQPort();
SenderPort bSender =
new SenderPort(buffer, bSendInternal, bout);
bSender.SetPeer(bReceiver);
bReceiver.SetPeer(bSender);

aReceiver.SetOutput(bout);
bReceiver.SetOutput(aout);

/* "Glue" them together. */
aReceiver.SetSender(aSendInternal);
aReceiver.SetPeerSender(bSendInternal);
aSender.SetReceiver(aRcvInternal);
aSender.SetPeerReceiver(bRcvInternal);

bReceiver.SetSender(bSendInternal);
bReceiver.SetPeerSender(aSendInternal);
bSender.SetReceiver(bRcvInternal);
bSender.SetPeerReceiver(aRcvInternal);

buffer.Register(aReceiver);
buffer.Register(bReceiver);
/* Start state machines.. */
Thread t;
t = new Thread(aSender);
t.start();
t = new Thread(aReceiver);
t.start();
t = new Thread(bSender);
t.start();
t = new Thread(bReceiver);
t.start();
}
```

BUFFER

The central buffer is defined here as a generic class (TemplateBuffer), plus an instance (Buffer) of that type for Send messages. The buffer uses a mutex lock to control access to it. To keep the model simple, this class uses a separate buffer for the FIFO queue in each direction (abuffer and bbuffer). However, it uses a single counter (mSize) for the total number of buffered messages in *both* queues to model the fact that the SUT is expected to use a more space-optimal design with a single buffer.

```
/** FIFO buffer for protocol testing */
class GenericBuffer<T>
{
    /** Exceptions. */
    class BufferException { }

    /** Construct a new buffer of the given size. */
    public GenericBuffer(int size, Lock mutex)
    {
        mSize = size;
        abuffer = new T[mSize];
        bbuffer = new T[mSize];
        mMutex = mutex;
    }

    /** Push a new item to the buffer. */
    public void PushBuffer(Runnable caller, T data)
    {
        if (IsFull() || IsFull(caller))
            throw new BufferException();
        if (caller == aowner)
        {
            if (aEnd == mSize)
                aEnd = 0;
            abuffer[aEnd++] = data;
            mItemsA++;
        }
        else if (caller == bowner)
        {
            if (bEnd == mSize)
                bEnd = 0;
            bbuffer[bEnd++] = data;
```

```
            mItemsB++;
        }
        else
        {
            throw new BufferException();
        }
    }

    /** Pop one item from buffer. */
    public T PopBuffer(Runnable caller)
    {
        if (IsEmpty(caller))
            throw new BufferException();
        T retval;
        if (caller == aowner)
        {
            if (aStart == mSize)
                aStart = 0;
            retval = abuffer[aStart++];
            mItemsA--;
        }
        else if (caller == bowner)
        {
            if (bStart == mSize)
                bStart = 0;
            retval = bbuffer[bStart++];
            mItemsB--;
        }
        else
        {
            throw new BufferException();
        }
        return retval;
    }

    public void Lock() { mMutex.lock(); }

    public void UnLock() { mMutex.unlock(); }

    public boolean IsFull() { return Size() >= mSize; }
```

```java
private boolean IsFull(Runnable r)
{
    if (r == aowner)
        return mItemsA >= mSize;
    else if (r == bowner)
        return mItemsB >= mSize;
    else
        throw new BufferException();
}

private boolean IsEmpty(Runnable r)
{
    if (r == aowner)
        return mItemsA == 0;
    else if (r == bowner)
        return mItemsB == 0;
    else
        throw new BufferException();
}

public int Size() { return mItemsA + mItemsB; }

public void Register(Runnable owner)
{
    if (aowner == null)
        aowner = owner;
    else if (bowner == null)
        bowner = owner;
    else
        throw new BufferException();
}

int mSize = 0;
int mItemsA = 0, mItemsB = 0;

int aStart = 0;
int aEnd = 0;

int bStart = 0;
int bEnd = 0;
```

```
        Runnable aowner = null;
        Runnable bowner = null;

        Lock mMutex = null;

        T[] abuffer;
        T[] bbuffer;
}
typedef GenericBuffer<Send> Buffer;
```

INBOUND PORTS

Inbound ports are managed by ReceiverPort active objects. The constructor
and method variables for ReceiverPort are defined by the following code:

```
class ReceiverPort extends StateMachine
{
    public ReceiverPort(Buffer buffer, CQPort inport,
                        CQPort extport)
    {
        this.buffer = buffer;
        inPort = inport;
        extPort = extport;
    }
    public void SetPeer(Runnable peer) { this.peer = peer; }
    public void SetSender(CQPort s) { sender = s; }
    public void SetPeerSender(CQPort s) { peerSender = s; }
    public void SetOutput(CQPort out) { this.out = out; }

    CQPort sender = null, peerSender = null;
    CQPort inPort = null, extPort = null, out = null;

    Runnable peer = null;
    Buffer buffer = null;

    int expectedack = 0, expect = 0;
    boolean expectack = false;
}
```

The behavior of `ReceiverPort` objects is modeled by the state machine shown in Figure 7.6. Recall that `gBufferContainsData` is a global constant that is an instance of a `BufferContainsData` message.

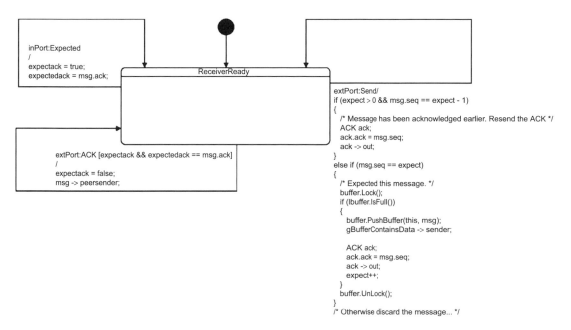

FIGURE 7.6   State machine for `ReceiverPort` active object.

OUTBOUND PORTS

Outbound ports are managed by `SenderPort` active objects. The constructor and method variables for `SenderPort` are defined by the following code:

```
class SenderPort extends StateMachine
{
    public SenderPort(Buffer buffer, CQPort inport,
                      CQPort extport)
    {
        this.buffer = buffer;
        inPort = inport;
        extPort = extport;
    }
    public void SetPeer(Runnable peer) { this.peer = peer; }
    public void SetReceiver(CQPort r) { receiver = r; }
    public void SetPeerReceiver(CQPort r) { peerReceiver = r; }
```

```
        CQPort receiver = null, peerReceiver = null;
        CQPort inPort = null, extPort = null;

        Runnable peer = null;
        Buffer buffer = null;
        Send currentdata;

        int moreData = 0;
}
```

The behavior of `SenderPort` objects is modeled by the state machine shown in Figure 7.7.

The test scenario set up by our `main()` procedure contains objects—two `SenderPort` and two `ReceivedPort` (see Figure 7.5). These are active objects, which is illustrated in the model by the fact that a `SenderPort` can spontaneously take a transition after some period of time (0 to 10 seconds, as shown in Figure 7.7). So our final model is the parallel composition of four state machines:

- Two instances of the `SenderPort` state machine (Figure 7.7).
- Two instances of the `ReceiverPort` state machine (Figure 7.6).

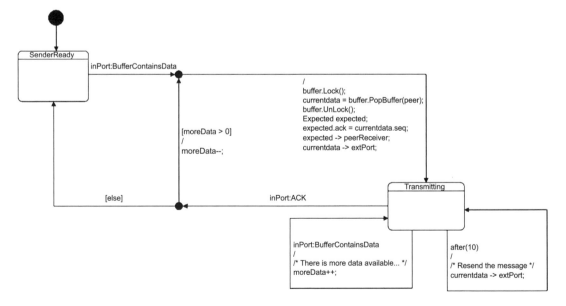

FIGURE 7.7   State machine for `SenderPort` active object.

There is also the passive Buffer object, but this is effectively just a (shared) state variable of the four state machines, and it is updated via method calls within the transitions of those state machines.

The possible behaviors of our test scenario are defined by this compound state machine, which is highly nondeterministic because of the random delays before resending lost messages and because each active object has the freedom to proceed at a different rate. It is the job of the Qtronic test generation algorithms to explore this nondeterministic model in a way that covers as many different behaviors as possible.

7.3.3 Importing the Model into Qtronic

Before we can generate tests, we must import the model from the UML tool used to develop the model into the model-based testing tool Qtronic. This is typically done by exporting the model in XMI format and then using the EMF (Eclipse Modeling Framework) transformation engine to transform the model into the form used by Qtronic.

Depending on which UML tool is used, sometimes this process includes additional steps such as exporting the UML model into a tool-specific format, then translating into XMI, translating the model from a MOF (Meta Object Facility) metamodel to the EMF metamodel, and parsing the action parts of the state machines.

7.3.4 Connecting Qtronic to the SUT

Qtronic is a tool for online (on-the-fly) testing. This means that the tool does not generate a test script that would have to be compiled and later executed. Rather, it directly executes tests against the SUT as it generates the tests. This is the only sensible approach when the model allows a large degree of internal nondeterminism (which models the fact that the SUT can make many internal, autonomous choices), because an offline test script that covered all the possible continuations could be enormous.

The online connectivity between Qtronic and the SUT is provided via a C++ plug-in architecture. In the simplest configuration, Qtronic connects to the SUT by loading a user-defined C++ plug-in that works as middleware between Qtronic and the SUT. Figure 7.8 shows some of the configurations that are possible: (1) An adapter that can talk with the SUT is connected directly to Qtronic as a plug-in and hence runs in the same process. (2) The same adapter is run on a host other than Qtronic, employing a general adapter that provides distribution over TCP/IP. (3) A filter is plugged into the pipeline, providing a way to log and modify data when it flows between Qtronic and the SUT. (4) Two components of the SUT are connected

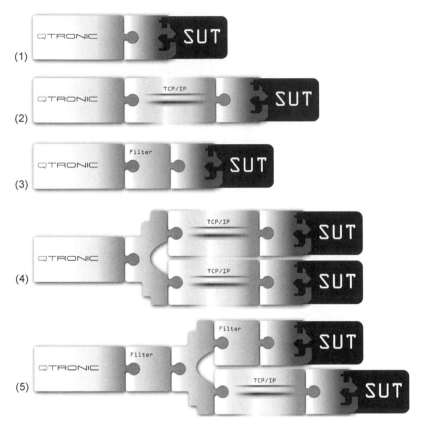

FIGURE 7.8   Connecting Qtronic to the SUT via a C++ plug-in architecture for adapters.

to Qtronic on two hosts using a chain of adapters that contains a programmable multiplexing component. (5) A more complex configuration shows that the same adapter components can be reused in complex chains.

For example, the fourth scenario in the figure can be used to test a distributed implementation of the SUT, with Qtronic sending messages to the SUT on one computer and checking that they are correctly received from the SUT on the other computer. Note that the multiplexing middleware component in scenarios (3) and (4) is responsible not only for routing messages from Qtronic to the appropriate SUT, but also for merging the response streams that the SUT processes are sending back to Qtronic while respecting the timing behavior of those messages. This merging of response streams is necessary whenever we are testing a distributed or multitasking system.

7.3.5 Generating and Running Tests

Qtronic guides test generation using model-based coverage criteria, for example, transition coverage or state coverage. In practice, however, these simple coverage criteria are usually satisfied quite quickly, and it is usual to continue testing long after they are satisfied. This is because on-the-fly testing is very cheap to run for a long time, once the model and the testing infrastructure have been created.

Therefore the Qtronic tool uses model-based coverage criteria as heuristics and guidance for selecting tests but does not stop testing when the criteria are fulfilled. A Qtronic user can control testing either by using coverage criteria (e.g., transition sequence or data-driven coverage) or by employing abstract use cases to guide testing. In the latter approach, the user gives a set of partial or high-level use cases (e.g., as sequence diagrams) that are used to guide the test generation.

An example of one test run is shown in Table 7.4. In this run, the SUT was an implementation of the transport protocol with an internal buffer size of four messages.

The → lines show the stimuli generated by Qtronic from the model and sent to the SUT, and the ← lines show the responses observed from the SUT. As the test sequence was generated, the responses from the SUT

TABLE 7.4   An Example Run of Qtronic Testing the SUT

Step	Time (secs)	Data	Direction and Port
1	0.0	[Send 0 0]	→ ain
2	0.0	[ACK 0]	← bout
3	0.0	[Send 0 0]	← aout
4	1.7	[Send 0 0]	← aout
5	1.7	[ACK 1]	→ bin
6	3.3	[Send 0 0]	← aout
7	4.3	[Send 0 0]	→ bin
8	4.3	[ACK 0]	← aout
9	4.3	[Send 0 0]	← bout
10	5.4	[Send 0 0]	← aout
11	7.8	[Send 0 0]	← bout
12	8.2	[Send 0 0]	→ bin
13	8.2	[ACK 0]	← aout
14	8.4	[Send 0 0]	← aout
15	9.2	[Send 0 0]	← aout
16	9.5	[Send 0 0]	← bout

were checked against the current state of the model and were all found to be correct.

Note that since the SUT is nondeterministic, another test run with identical SUT inputs at identical times may produce different SUT responses. For example, this may be caused by different random delays in the resend mechanism or by different scheduling behavior of the tasks, which depends on the current machine load. Determining the correctness of the responses from a nondeterministic SUT like this is normally an extremely difficult task, but since Qtronic has the behavioral model and knows the current state of that model, it can perform accurate oracle checking automatically.

We give a brief commentary on the first few steps of the test run in Table 7.4 to show the roles of Qtronic and the SUT.

Qtronic started by sending a message with a sequence number of zero and data value zero (SEND 0 0) to the ain port of the SUT. The SUT acknowledged this immediately (within a few milliseconds) on its bout port and propagated the message to its aout port. Qtronic then decided not to acknowledge that message in order to test the resend facility of the SUT. A resend was observed after 1.7 seconds, which was well within the maximum allowable time of 10.0 seconds.

Qtronic then sent the ACK 1 message to the bin port, which was the correct message and port but a different sequence number from the zero that was expected by the SUT. Since this was not the desired acknowledgment, the SUT resent the SEND 0 0 message again at time 3.3.

In the remainder of the test sequence, Qtronic sends the same message (SEND 0 0) over the protocol in the reverse direction twice (steps 7 and 12) but does not acknowledge receipt of that message from port bout. This tests the resend facility quite thoroughly, with resends happening in both directions in parallel.

7.4 SUMMARY

A UML model can be a good basis for model-based testing, provided that it is precise enough. In addition to a class diagram, we must have some description of the dynamic behavior of the classes, such as state machines, activity diagrams, or preconditions and postconditions for the methods. Use cases are useful as high-level test goals, but they must be formalized (e.g., into state machines or activity diagrams) before they can be used for model-based test generation.

The UML models that are suitable for model-based testing are typically quite different from the UML models that are used during the system development. As we saw in the eTheater model, the test model usually takes a limited view of the system, replaces some classes by simple enumerations of test values, and omits many of the details that would be needed for implementation.

UML state machines are one kind of statechart notation. They support state variables (as do EFSMs) as well as nested states, orthogonal states, and broadcast communication.

When state machines are used to model the behavior of a class, the transitions of that state machine define the change of state and may also update the state variables of the class. These updates can be specified using a programming language notation (as in Section 7.3), using OCL as a postcondition notation (as in Section 7.2) or using UML action semantics [FGDTS06].

7.5 FURTHER READING

Chapter 8 of Binder [Bin99], *A Tester's Guide to the UML*, goes through each kind of UML diagram and notation, describing how they can be used to express test-ready models. Chapter 6 of the same book describes some practical test generation techniques for UML state machines and gives guidelines about features of the state machine notation that should be avoided.

Chapter 3 of the book *Component-based testing with UML* by Gross [Gro05] also gives a general overview of each kind of UML diagram and how it could be used for model-based testing.

Offutt and Abdurazik [OA99] describe and compare four kinds of coverage of UML state machines: *all-transitions*, *full predicate coverage* (which is similar to masking MC/DC), *all-transition-pairs*, and *complete sequence testing* (where the test engineer supplies sequences of states that should be tested). They performed an experimental comparison of the fault-finding power of several of these criteria on a small cruise control system and concluded that full predicate coverage found more errors than transition-pair coverage, which found more errors than a manually designed test suite with 100 percent statement coverage of the SUT.

Briand and colleagues [BLL05] show that the use of data-flow criteria to analyze the OCL preconditions and postconditions in a UML state machine can strengthen Binder's *round-trip paths* test generation algorithm [Bin99] and increase its fault-finding ability. They comment that all-transitions coverage of UML state machines has weak fault-finding ability, all-transitions pairs is much stronger but often too expensive, and that the round-trip paths is a good compromise.

The European research project AGEDIS[3] (2001–2003) developed a suite of model-based testing tools that used UML models: class diagrams and state machines. In addition to simple structural test selection criteria, they used state machines as a notation for explicit test case specifications to guide the test generation. Hartman's final report [Har04] gives an overview of the project, describes five industry trials, and discusses the lessons learned. It discusses the two questions: "What would we do the same?" and "What would we do differently?". He reports that the use of UML as the modeling language was a wise decision, but that instead of using a custom language called IF as the action language for transitions, they should have used OCL or a subset of Java. These are the two action languages that we illustrate in this chapter. He also notes the importance of providing "instant gratification" test selection criteria, such as using random generation as an immediate "smoke test" option.[4]

---

[3] See *http://www.agedis.de*.

[4] A *smoke test* is a rudimentary test intended to quickly check a few basic features of the SUT functionality. The name comes from electronics, where the first test of a new device is sometimes to turn on the power and check that it does not start smoking or sparking.

CHAPTER 8

MAKING TESTS EXECUTABLE

This chapter deals with the practical issues of how to take a suite of abstract tests, generated from an abstract model, and make them executable on the real SUT. This *concretization* phase is an important part of the model-based testing process, and it can take a significant amount of effort. In some applications of model-based testing, the amount of time spent on concretization can be the same as the time spent on modeling; in other applications concretization is less time-consuming (for example, between 25 and 45 percent of the modeling time in the case studies in Section 2.6.3).

Section 8.1 discusses the challenges that can arise, gives an overview of the various approaches, and briefly discusses some examples. Section 8.2 gives an extended example of how these approaches work. It shows how the test suite generated for the eTheater case study in Section 7.2 can be transformed into executable test scripts, written in the Ruby scripting language, and executed on an implementation of the eTheater system.

Note: A Viking battle axe, such as the one shown above, was the height of fashion during the tenth century (*http://www.wealddown.co.uk/gransfors-bruks-axes-ancient-collection.htm*). Photo courtesy of *www.gransfors.us*.

8.1 PRINCIPLES OF TEST ADAPTATION

Having used model-based testing to generate a nice test suite, we almost always want to automate the *execution* of that test suite. The Qui-Donc example in Chapter 5 was one exception to this, where we decided it was better to execute the generated tests manually because the test execution involved interacting with a telephone system with voice output. But in most cases, we want to automate the execution of the generated tests so that our whole test process is automated and so that we can execute more tests, execute tests more often for regression testing, reduce our test execution costs, reduce the overall testing time, and so on.

The problem that we face in trying to execute tests generated from a model is that the generated tests are highly abstract, just like the model, so they usually do not contain enough concrete detail to be directly executable. In other words, the API of the model does not exactly match the API of the SUT. Recall from Section 3.1 some of the kinds of abstraction that are commonly used when designing a model for testing purposes:

- Model only one aspect of the SUT, not all its behavior.
- Omit inputs and outputs that are not relevant to the test goals.
- Take a simplified view of complex data values, such as enumerating a few typical values.
- Assume that the SUT has already been initialized to match a particular testing scenario.
- Define a single model operation that corresponds to a sequence of SUT operations, or to just one part of an SUT operation.

To execute the generated tests, we must first initialize the SUT so that it is ready for our test suite, add the missing details into the tests, and fix any mismatches between the API of the model and the SUT so that our tests can connect to the SUT interface.

We also have to manage the relationships among abstract values in the model and real-world values or objects in the SUT. This requires expanding the abstract model values into more complex concrete values that can be used as SUT inputs. For example, an enumerated constant in the model might have to be expanded into a complex data value such as a record that contains several fields.

To be able to check SUT outputs against the model, we must either transform the expected outputs from the model into concrete values or get concrete outputs from the SUT and transform them back into abstract values

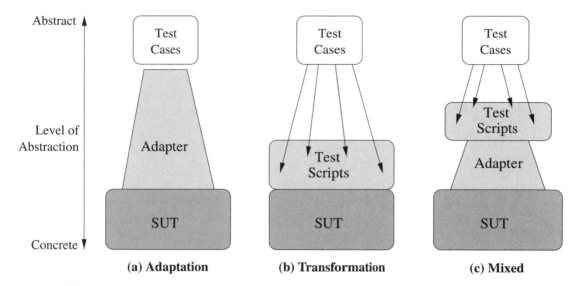

FIGURE 8.1   Three approaches to bridging the semantic gap between abstract tests and the concrete SUT.

so that we can check them against the model. If the model is deterministic, we can use either approach; but if it is nondeterministic, then the latter approach is better.

If the SUT creates new objects during the testing process, it is often necessary to keep track of the *identity* of those objects, not just their values. This requires maintaining a mapping table from the abstract objects in the model to the corresponding concrete objects that have been created by the SUT. Each time the model creates a new abstract value A, the SUT performs the corresponding operation and creates a concrete object C; then we add the pair (A, C) into the mapping table so that future uses of A in the model can be translated into uses of C in the SUT.

These techniques are all examples of the difference in abstraction levels between the model and the SUT. Figure 8.1 shows the main approaches to bridging this abstraction gap.

- The *adaptation* approach, (a), is to manually write some adapter code that bridges the gap. This is essentially a wrapper around the SUT that provides a more abstract view of the SUT to match the abstraction level of the model.

- The *transformation* approach, (b), is to transform the abstract tests into concrete test scripts.

• The *mixed* approach, (c), is a combination of the other two approaches. It is sometimes useful to add some adapter code around the SUT to raise its abstraction level part of the way toward the model and make testing easier, and then transform the abstract tests into a more concrete form that matches the adapter interface. Some benefits of this mixed approach are that the transformation can be easier, since the levels of abstraction are closer, and the adapter can be less model-specific, which may allow it to be reused for several different models or different testing scenarios.

We explore the adaptation and transformation alternatives more in the next two subsections and then discuss which approach is best for each kind of application. As an analogy, the transformation approach is like compiling the abstract tests down into some lower-level language, while the adaptation approach is like interpreting the abstract test sequences. The mixed approach is like a bytecode system, which compiles the input language down to byte-codes, and then interprets those bytecodes.

8.1.1 The Adaptation Approach

The adaptation approach involves writing some adapter code that wraps around the SUT, manages the low-level details of interacting with the SUT, and presents a more abstract view of the SUT to the model. Essentially, this adapter code acts as an interpreter for the abstract operation calls of the model, executing them with the help of the SUT.

More specifically, the adapter code is responsible for the following tasks:

Setup: Set up the SUT so that it is ready for testing. This may involve configuring and initializing the SUT so that it reflects the test scenario assumed by the model.

Concretization: Translate each model-level abstract operation call and its abstract input values into one or more concrete SUT calls with the appropriate input values.

Abstraction: Obtain the SUT results from those concrete calls (e.g., catching exceptions and turning them into result values), and translate them back into abstract values, and then pass them back to the model for comparison with the expected results in order to produce the test verdict.

Teardown: Shut down the SUT at the end of each test sequence or at the end of each batch of tests.

There are many possible architectures for connecting the model-based testing tool, the adapter, and the SUT. Most of the test harness architectures invented over the last decades for automating the execution of manually designed tests can be applied to model-based testing as well. Earlier in this book, we discussed two examples of the adaptation approach that nicely illustrate some typical solutions.

ZLIVE (SECTION 5.2)

Here the SUT is a passive Java library (the ZLive classes), so the adapter code is simply another layer of Java code that imports the ZLive library, calls the various methods that the model-driven testing requests, and checks the results of those method calls for correctness using JUnit Assert calls. In fact, since ModelJUnit is a very simple model-based testing tool and the model is also written as a Java class, the adapter code and the model-updating code are mixed together in the methods of that class.

One example of abstraction in this adapter code is that some of the ZLive SUT implementations of the FlatPred interface actually return a sequence of results, but the adapter code ignores the values of those results and simply counts the length of the sequence; then it checks that against the number of results predicted by the model.

CHAT (SECTION 6.5)

The Chat system is a nondeterministic, distributed system with multiple tasks running in parallel. The adapter code is responsible for sending input events to the appropriate task, monitoring each task, recording all observable events, and putting them into a queue for the Spec Explorer tool to read. So the adapter hides the complexity of the network communication and presents a simple sequential log of the communication between clients.

This adapter code includes a manually written wrapper class (ClientWrapper) around each distributed client implementation plus another manually written class (Global) that contains a *Setup* method (which creates the Chat server and the desired number of clients) and a *Teardown* method (which kills all the processes).

In addition to these manually written classes, Spec Explorer automatically generates some code to support communication with the instances of these classes. It injects this code into the binary form of each class. The code modifies each observation method in the class so that every call to the method (from within the class or elsewhere) is logged. The injected code within each ClientWrapper and Global process communicates with Spec Explorer via the network. When the Spec Explorer online test generation algorithm decides to call a controllable action, it sends the details (including parameter values) for that action over the network to the injected code of the desired wrapper class, which then calls the appropriate method. Similarly, when the injected code traps a call to an observation method, it sends the details over the network to Spec Explorer, which merges all such events into a single queue that can be inspected by the online test generation algorithm.

These two examples and the protocol testing example in Section 7.3 illustrate that the adaptation approach can be used for a wide variety of test setups, ranging from simple cases where the model-based testing tool, the adapter code, and the SUT are all bound together in one process, to more complex distributed situations. Figure 7.8 shows a variety of adapter configurations for testing local, remote, and distributed SUTs.

> **Key Point**   The adapter code transforms each abstract operation call into low-level SUT operations on-the-fly, as the abstract test sequence is interpreted.

8.1.2 The Transformation Approach

The transformation approach involves transforming each abstract test into an executable test script. The resulting test scripts are typically in one of the following notations:

- A standard programming language, such as Java or C
- A scripting language, such as TCL, JavaScript, or VBScript
- A standard test notation, such as TTCN-3 [WDT+05]
- A proprietary test notation, such as the TSL (Test Script Language) of Mercury WinRunner or some company-specific test notation

The transformation process may be performed by a single-purpose translation program that always produces output in a particular language or by a more generic engine that is capable of transforming abstract tests into several languages because it is parameterized by various templates and mappings for each output language. For example, we might define a TCL template for each abstract operation, which contains the TCL code for calling that operation in the SUT, with placeholders for the parameter values. This would allow a generic transformation engine to build a concrete test script by transforming the calls in an abstract test sequence into a sequence of these TCL templates, with actual parameter values replacing the placeholders.

In reality, the transformation process is likely to be more complex than this because the following factors must be taken into account.

- Some concrete setup and teardown code will be needed. This could be written manually (for example, in TCL) and then inserted automatically by the transformation engine at the beginning and end of each test sequence or test run.

- The template for each operation may be quite complex because there is not necessarily a one-to-one mapping between the signature of the abstract operation and the SUT operations. For example, it may have to call several SUT operations to implement the abstract operation; it typically has to generate any missing input parameters; it must trap exceptions produced by the SUT and check if they were expected or not; and it may have to call some SUT query operations to check that the internal state of the SUT agrees with the expected state from the model. Note that some of the oracle checking may be done within the template for each operation, and other parts of the oracle checking may be done by separate query operations in the abstract test sequence.

- The model uses abstract constants and values—these must be translated into the concrete values used by the SUT. This can often be done by defining a mapping from each abstract value to a corresponding concrete value or into a concrete expression that generates a suitable value. For example, we might map the enumeration type {*BadPIN*, *GoodPIN*} into the two concrete PINs 1111 and 2593 or map *BadPIN* into an expression like rand.Next(2000), which randomly generates a different incorrect PIN on each call.

- When testing nondeterministic SUTs, an abstract test may have a tree structure rather than being a simple sequence. This requires the transformation engine to be more sophisticated to handle such structures. It must generate an executable test script that includes conditional statements to check the SUT outputs and then take the appropriate branch through the tree to the next part of the test.

- Traceability between the concrete test scripts and the abstract tests must be maintained, and it is often desirable to directly record within each generated test script the traceability links back to the model and the informal requirements. This can be done by inserting these traceability links as comments within the test scripts or as executable statements so that the traceability information can be displayed whenever a test fails.

The *structure* of the transformed test suite is almost as important as the code within each test script. When you have hundreds or thousands of tests, their naming conventions and organization into hierarchies of folders become very important. Most companies that have a mature testing process have standards for the organization and version management of their test suites, and it is desirable for the executable test suites generated via model-based testing to follow the same standards.

For example, in addition to generating the executable code of the test scripts, it may be desirable to generate a *test plan*, which describes, in English, the structure of the test suite, the rationale for each test in the suite, the settings used to generate the tests, who generated the tests, when they were generated, and so on.

Another important issue is version management of the tests. Typically, each generated test suite is put into a version control system so that it can be recorded, managed, and used for regression testing. But with the transformation approach, we have the abstract test suite as well as the concrete (executable) test scripts, so it is necessary to decide which artifacts to put under version control. Just the executable test scripts? Or the abstract test suite as well? Or should we instead store the model and the test selection criteria that were used to generate the tests? The answers depend on the culture and practice of your company, but deciding on the answers to these questions is an important part of adopting model-based testing into an existing testing process.

> **Key Point**   The transformation approach can produce test scripts that fit smoothly into your existing test management practices, with similar language, structure, and naming conventions as manually written test scripts.

We will see some examples of the transformation approach later in this chapter and other examples in Sections 9.5 and 10.4. Before looking at those examples, we give some guidelines for choosing between the transformation and adaptation approaches.

8.1.3 Which Approach Is Better?

For online testing, it is almost always better to use the adaptation approach because online testing requires a tightly integrated, two-way connection between the model-based testing tool and the SUT. This is easiest to achieve when the model-based testing can directly connect to the adapter API and the adapter is in turn directly connected to the SUT interface.

For offline testing, we can choose between the adaptation approach or the transformation approach, or use a mixture of the two. If we use the transformation approach, then we obtain a suite of executable test scripts that can be executed directly on the SUT. If we use the adaptation approach, then our suite of abstract tests effectively becomes executable because the adapter acts as an interpreter, mapping each abstract call into SUT operations and translating the SUT results back to the abstract level. With the mixed approach, we transform the abstract tests into executable test scripts that call an adapter layer to handle the low-level details of SUT interaction.

The transformation approach has the advantage that it can produce test scripts in the same language and with the same naming and structuring conventions that are already used for manually written tests. This can make the adoption of model-based testing less disruptive on the overall testing process by allowing existing test management tools, test repositories, test execution platforms, and test reporting processes to remain unchanged. Essentially, model-based testing is replacing the test design and test scripting stages of the testing process by new techniques and tools, but the rest of the testing process remains the same.

For these reasons, we suggest that you generally consider the adaptation approach first when you are doing online testing and consider the transformation approach first when doing offline testing. However, this is not a hard-and-fast rule—other combinations are possible, and it is quite common to use the adaptation approach for offline testing as well as for online testing. The best approach for your project depends on political, technical, and human factors as well as on the available tools and the nature of the project.

> **Key Point**   For online testing, use the adaptation approach. For offline testing, the transformation approach has some advantages (less disruption), and it is often useful to combine it with the adaptation approach.

8.2 EXAMPLE: THE ETHEATER SYSTEM

In this section, we take the eTheater test cases that we generated in Section 7.2 and turn them into executable test scripts. We use a mixed approach that illustrates both the transformation and adaptation techniques for making tests executable.

We execute the tests on a simple implementation of the eTheater system that was developed by one of our colleagues, Eric Torreborre. The implementation was developed using "Ruby on Rails,"[1] which is a popular open-source web development framework built on top of the Ruby scripting language.[2] So we want our executable test scripts to be written in Ruby as well.

Ideally, we would like to take each generated abstract test, like test T12 shown at the top of Listing 8.1 (one of the eTheater tests generated in Section 7.2.4), and transform it into an executable Ruby test script, like the one shown at the bottom of Listing 8.1. However, this is rather a big transformation step, and in practice, we find it is better to use a mixture of transformation and adaptation. That is, we will transform our abstract test cases into a set of Ruby test scripts like the one shown in the bottom half of Listing 8.2 in Section 8.2.1.

Each test method (e.g., `test_T12`) implements one of the abstract tests and does this by calling a sequence of Ruby adaptation procedures that we write manually in Ruby. Each of these Ruby adaptation procedures provides an interface similar to one of the abstract operations in the model and implements that interface using the lower-level calls to the eTheater web server. The advantages of this mixed approach include:

- The generated test scripts are more readable because they are shorter and the names of the Ruby adaptation procedures act as high-level comments to tell us what is happening at each step.

- It is easier to relate the generated test scripts to the UML state machine model. To make this relationship more obvious, we add the names of the UML states as parameters of our Ruby adaptation procedures. That is, the first parameter of each adaptation procedure is the name of the expected UML model state after the transition.

- There is less duplication of code in the generated test scripts. This would make maintenance of those scripts easier if we wanted to modify the test scripts in some way. (But in practice, we usually prefer to regenerate the test scripts than modify them directly.)

- The transformation step is smaller so it is easier to define the template files that perform the transformation.

In the next few subsections, we show the abstract tests can be transformed into Ruby code, give examples of the Ruby adaptation procedures, and discuss the results of executing the tests on our eTheater implementation.

---

[1] See *http://www.rubyonrails.org* for information on Ruby on Rails.

[2] See *http://www.ruby-lang.org* for information on the Ruby scripting language.

LISTING 8.1   Abstract test_T12 and its corresponding Ruby test script.

```
# Generated e-Theater test T12
sut.start();
sut.newCust(c1,AMANDINE);
sut.logout();
sut.disconnect()
```

```
# Ruby code that implements e-Theater test T12
require 'test/unit'
require File.dirname(__FILE__) + '/../../test_helper'

class ETheater_T12 < Test::Unit::TestCase

  fixtures :customers

  def setup
    @controller = CustomersController.new
    @request    = ActionController::TestRequest.new
    @response   = ActionController::TestResponse.new
  end

  def test_T12
    # start();
    post :register
    # newCust(c1,AMANDINE);
    customer = @customers["AMANDINE"]
    post :save_new_customer, :customer =>
      {:login => customer["login"],
       :password => customer["password"]}
    assert_response :redirect
    assert_redirected_to :action => "list"
    # logout();
    post :logout
    assert_redirected_to :action => "login"
    # disconnect()
  end
end
```

LISTING 8.2   Generating the Ruby test scripts.

```
require 'test/unit'
require File.dirname(__FILE__) + '/../../test_helper'

class ETheater_${test.name}_Test < Test::Unit::TestCase

  ${conf.evaluateFragment('fixturesFragment', this)}

  def setup
    adaptation_setup
  end

  def test_${test.name}
<%  for (message in test.behavior.messages)
  {%>     ${conf.evaluateFragment('messageFragment', this)}<%}%>
  end
end
```

```
require 'test/unit'
require File.dirname(__FILE__) + '/../../test_helper'

class ETheater_T12 < Test::Unit::TestCase

  fixtures :customers

  def setup
    adaptation_setup
  end

  def test_T12
    e_start  "LoggedOut"
    e_newCust  "Welcome", "AMANDINE"
    e_logout  "LoggedOut"
    e_disconnect  "LoggedOut"
  end
end
```

8.2.1 Transforming Tests into Ruby

In this section we look at several ways to transform abstract test sequences into concrete test scripts. The end point of our transformation is a collection of executable Ruby test scripts, nicely organized into directories. But what is our starting point? What representation of the abstract tests do we have?

The abstract test T12 is shown in a textual form at the top of Listing 8.1, but this is just a summary form that is human-readable. The generated tests actually contain much more information than is shown there because after each operation call, we know the updated state of each object in the system, the relationships between objects, and so on. Also, it would be inconvenient to have to parse that textual form when we could instead have arranged for the test generator to produce the tests in a more computer-friendly format.

A common approach is to generate the abstract tests into an XML format and then use a transformation language such as XSLT[3] to transform that XML format into Ruby syntax. This has the advantage that one starts with a tree-structured XML document, and XSLT is good at selecting parts of XML documents and transforming them.

The LTG tools take a slightly different approach so that the transformations can be written in an object-oriented language rather than in XSLT. (XSLT is written in XML, so it is very verbose and its style of programming is rather different from most object-oriented languages.) Instead of generating the tests in XML format, the LTG tools provide a Java API that can be used to directly query the generated tests' structure. This allows the transformations to be written in any object-oriented language that can access the Java API.

For the examples in this book, we use the Groovy scripting language, which is very Java-like but provides higher-level facilities that make it easy to write transformations. For example, `suite.each{test->C}` applies the code `C` to each test in the Java collection called `suite`, with the variable `test` bound to the current test. This is similar to using a Java `for` loop to iterate over the collection, but it is more concise and untyped. The engineers at LEIRIOS who write transformation scripts prefer Groovy to XSLT.

The top half of Listing 8.2 shows the template file that is used to transform each test case, and the bottom half of the figure shows the Ruby test script that is produced when this template is applied to the abstract test T12. We will briefly explain the contents of this template and the others in this chapter. However, the details of these template files are not important to

---

[3]XSLT is the transformation language for the Extensible Stylesheet Language (XSL). It is typically used to transform XML documents into a viewable form such as HTML. See *http://www.w3.org/Style/XSL* for information about XSL and XSLT.

understand; our goal in showing them is simply to illustrate the kinds of techniques that can be used to transform abstract tests into a concrete test scripting language and how it can be useful to use several templates to generate a structured suite of test scripts.

In LTG, a *transformation configuration* defines how a suite of generated tests can be transformed into a structured collection of test script files. It is common to apply several transformation configurations to a given test suite: one transformation configuration might be used to transform the test suite into a set of HTML web pages, another transformation configuration to transform the test suite into a hierarchy of Ruby test scripts, and a third transformation configuration to generate a detailed test plan to document the rationale and test suite structure. Each transformation configuration contains one or more transformation templates that define the directory structure of the generated test suite, the file naming conventions, and the various output files such as the individual test scripts and test suite driver scripts.

Each transformation template contains a mixture of literal Ruby code, which is output unchanged, plus Groovy commands within <%...%> brackets and Groovy expressions within $(...) brackets. In the figures, we show the Groovy parts in bold italics and the literal Ruby code in normal nonbold font. When a transformation template is applied to a test case or a test suite, it is given several parameters that can be used within the Groovy code:

- conf refers to the whole transformation configuration that contains this transformation template.
- suite refers to the current test suite that is being transformed.
- tests refers to the set of tests in the current test suite.
- test refers to the current test case that is being transformed.

> **Key Point**   The transformation templates are a mixture of two languages: the test script language that is being output (Ruby in this case) and the language that is defining the transformation (Groovy in this case).

Our Ruby transformation configuration will apply the transformation template in Listing 8.2 to each abstract test case in turn, with the variable test referring to that test case. Each Groovy expression within the template will be evaluated, and the result of the expression will be inserted into the output file, replacing the expression. Similarly, each Groovy command will be executed, and the output it produces will be inserted into the output file at that point. The Groovy code in Listing 8.2 makes use of two auxiliary Groovy fragments: fixturesFragment generates Ruby code to define the location of the *fixtures* (Ruby-talk for the sample data used by the tests) and messageFragment generates a Ruby method call from a given operation call in the abstract test (Listing 9.8 shows a similar template to messageFragment that generates C function calls rather than Ruby method calls).

When test suites contain hundreds or thousands of tests, it is desirable to structure the generated test scripts into a hierarchy of directories. This is usually designed to follow the existing manual test-design practices of your company so that the adoption of model-based testing causes as little disruption as possible to your existing test process.

Our Ruby adapter configuration is set up to put each test suite into a separate directory, with a file called suite.rb in each directory to run all the tests within that directory. The top of Listing 8.3 shows the transformation template that generates this suite.rb file, and an example of the resulting file is shown at the bottom of the figure.

When we generate multiple test suites, it is useful to have another suite.rb script at the top level of the generated directories, which runs all of the test suites. Listing 8.4 shows the transformation template and the resulting suite.rb file that does this. In this example, there is only one test suite, but in general there are several, so this top-level suite.rb file gives a convenient way of running several generated test suites at once.

The last transformation template that we show (see Listing 8.5 on page 300) is used to transform the initial state of our test scenario into Ruby *.yml fixture files. This template is applied to each class C in our initial-state object diagram (see Figure 7.4) and produces a file C.yml that defines all the objects of that class. This shows how we can use transformation templates to generate test data files as well as executable code.

8.2.2 Writing a Ruby Adapter for eTheater

Before we can execute the Ruby test scripts produced by the preceding transformation process, we need to define the adapter procedures that they call, such as e_start, e_newCust, and e_login. Listing 8.6 (see page 301) shows these three adapter procedures. They interact with the eTheater web server using HTTP post and get commands.

After each interaction with the eTheater web server, these adapter procedures typically call the assert_state method to check that the eTheater system has given the correct response. The name of the UML model state is passed into this method, and the state_template function translates that abstract state into part of the expected URL of the eTheater system so that an

LISTING 8.3 Generating suite.rb for the TicketSale test suite.

```ruby
require 'test/unit'
require 'test/unit/ui/tk/testrunner'
<%tests.each{test ->%>require '${test.name}'
<%}%>

class ${suite.name}Suite

  def initialize()
    @suite = Test::Unit::TestSuite.new('${suite.name}')
<%tests.each{ test ->
  %>    @suite << ETheater_${test.name}.suite<%}%>
  end

  def start
    runner = Test::Unit::UI::Tk::TestRunner.new @suite
    runner.start
  end

  def suite
    @suite
  end
end
```

```ruby
require 'test/unit'
require 'test/unit/ui/tk/testrunner'
require 'startRegistration_0'
require 'ETheater_T1'
require 'ETheater_T2'
...

class TicketSaleSuite

  def initialize()
    @suite = Test::Unit::TestSuite.new('TicketSale')
    @suite << ETheater_T1.suite
    @suite << ETheater_T2.suite
    ...
  end

  def start
    runner = Test::Unit::UI::Tk::TestRunner.new @suite
    runner.start
  end

  def suite
    @suite
  end
end
```

LISTING 8.4   Generating the top-level `suite.rb` file.

```
require 'test/unit'
require 'test/unit/ui/tk/testrunner'
<% project.testSuites.each{suite ->
  %>\$: << File.dirname(__FILE__) + '/${suite.name}'<%}%>
<% project.testSuites.each{suite ->
%>require '${suite.name}/suite.rb'<%}%>

class ProjectSuite < Test::Unit::TestSuite

  def suite
    <% project.testSuites.each{suite ->
      %>${suite.name}Suite.new.suite<%}%>
  end
end
```

```
require 'test/unit'
require 'test/unit/ui/tk/testrunner'
$: <<File.dirname(__FILE__) + '/TicketSale'
require 'TicketSale/suite.rb'

class ProjectSuite < Test::Unit::TestSuite

  def suite
    TicketSaleSuite.new.suite
  end
end
```

accurate oracle check can be done. The `assert` and `assert_template` methods are part of the usual Ruby testing framework for checking test results.

The detailed code in the `post` calls and the translation of abstract state names into concrete eTheater URLs are examples of how the adapter code must add the concrete details that were abstracted away during the modeling process.

To save a little time when writing these adapter procedures, we actually used a transformation template to generate skeleton versions of the adapter procedures from the model, and then we manually fill in the bodies of the procedures. We do not show the template here because it is similar to the transformation templates in the previous section.

LISTING 8.5   Translation of initial state into Ruby .yml fixtures.

```
<% def i = 1;
   invariants = instances.value;
   invariants.each{ inv -> if (conf.map( 'known', inv))
                               {%>${inv.name.toUpperCase()}:
     id: ${i++}
     <% inv.slots.each{s ->
       %>${conf.map( 'attributes',
           s.definingFeature.name)}: ${s.value.value}
     <%}%>
<%}}%>
```

```
ERIC:
    id: 1
    login: ERIC
    card: UNKNOWN_CARD

AMANDINE:
    id: 2
    login: AMANDINE
    card: UNKNOWN_CARD

MARK:
    id: 3
    login: MARK
    card: UNKNOWN_CARD
```

8.2.3   Executing the eTheater Tests

What happens when we execute our beautiful suite of model-based tests, which have been generated automatically from the UML model and transformed into Ruby test scripts? We get the results shown in Listing 8.7: three tests fail!

On further investigation, it turns out that Eric had made some improvements to the eTheater implementation! We didn't know about these and had not incorporated them into our model. So in fact, the model-based testing was successful in finding the differences between the implementation and the model.

LISTING 8.6 Some of the adapter code for the Ruby tests.

```ruby
require 'models/customer'
  def adaptation_setup
    @controller = CustomersController.new
    @request    = ActionController::TestRequest.new
    @response   = ActionController::TestResponse.new
  end
  def e_start state
    post :login
  end
  def e_newCust state, c
    customer = @customers[c]
    post :save_new_customer, :customer =>
      {:login => customer["login"],
        :password => customer["password"]}
    assert_state state, "e_newCust"
  end
  def e_login state, l, p
    customer = @customers[l]
    @@customer = Customer.find(customer["id"])
    post :authenticate,
        :customer => {:login => customer["login"], :password => p}
    assert_state state, "e_login"
  end
  def assert_state state, op
    if @response.redirect?
      action = state_action(state)
      assert @response.redirect_url_match?(action)
    else
      template = state_template(state)
      assert_template(template, op + " should use " + template)
    end
  end
  def state_template state
    case state
      when "WAITING" : 'login'
      when "BuyingTickets" : 'showtimes_selection'
      when "RegisterCard" : 'register'
      when "PAYING" : 'buy'
    end
  end
  def state_action state
    case state
      when "BuyingTickets" : 'order'
      else state_template(state)
    end
  end
```

LISTING 8.7   Results of executing the eTheater tests.

```
E:>test\ generated_tests.rb
Loaded suite E:/test/generated_tests
Started
...EEE............
Finished in 1.282 seconds.

  1) Error:
test_T4(ETheater_T4):
NoMethodError: You have a nil object when you didn't expect it!
You might have expected an instance of Array.
The error occurred while evaluating nil.[]
    E:/test/model_adaptation/eTheaterAdaptation.rb:39:in 'e_payError'
    E:/test/generated/TicketSale/eTheater_T4.rb:17:in 'test_T4'

  2) Error:
test_T5(ETheater_T5):
NoMethodError: You have a nil object when you didn't expect it!
You might have expected an instance of Array.
The error occurred while evaluating nil.[]
    E:/test/model_adaptation/eTheaterAdaptation.rb:39:in 'e_payError'
    E:/test/generated/TicketSale/eTheater_T5.rb:17:in 'test_T5'

  3) Error:
test_T6(ETheater_T6):
NoMethodError: You have a nil object when you didn't expect it!
You might have expected an instance of Array.
The error occurred while evaluating nil.[]
    E:/test/model_adaptation/eTheaterAdaptation.rb:39:in 'e_payError'
    E:/test/generated/TicketSale/eTheater_T6.rb:15:in 'test_T6'

19 tests, 30 assertions, 0 failures, 3 errors
```

In this case the differences were caused by intentional improvements to the SUT, so we model-based testers should get busy and update our model (and the informal requirements). In other cases, the failed tests might point to errors in the SUT, which means that the developers should correct the system under test.

> **Key Point**   This is a case of where we needed better communication between testers and developers!

8.3 SUMMARY

Since we use an abstract model as the input for test generation, the generated tests are also abstract. This means that they are not directly executable on the SUT, and we have to add detail to make them executable.

There are two main ways to make the abstract tests executable. With the *adaptation approach*, a wrapper is added around the SUT to lift the SUT interface up to the abstract level so that the abstract tests can be interpreted at that level. With the *transformation approach*, the abstract tests are transformed into executable test scripts by adding the necessary details and translating them into some executable language.

Generally, online testing requires the use of the adaptation approach, and offline testing may use either approach or a combination of the two.

8.4 FURTHER READING

There is a vast literature on automated test execution, and much of this is relevant to the execution of the tests generated via model-based testing. Two good books for practical advice about automated test execution are *Software Test Automation*, by Fewster and Graham [FG99], and *Just Enough Test Automation*, by Mosley and Posey [MP02].

Barnett and Schulte [BS03] describe some of the techniques and challenges of injecting monitoring code into .NET classes for runtime verification of the SUT against a model, similar to how Spec Explorer works.

Bouquet and Legeard [BL03] describe an early version of the transformation approach used by LTG/B, which transformed the abstract tests into JavaCard code.

9

THE GSM 11.11 CASE STUDY

This chapter describes a case study of applying model-based testing to a smart card application based on the GSM 11.11 standard. This standard is managed by the European Telecommunication Standard Institute. It defines the intended behavior of the *Subscriber Identification Module* (SIM) card embedded in phone mobiles. So there is a good chance that while you are reading this chapter about testing the GSM protocol, your mobile phone will actually use the protocol.

This case study uses the B notation as a modeling language. The model is a purely functional model developed for the purpose of testing. The LEIRIOS Test Generator (LTG/B version 2.2) is used to generate the test cases, the requirements traceability matrix, and the executable test scripts. The test execution environment used for this application offers interfaces in the C language.

We start with an overview of the GSM 11.11 standard. Then we follow the four major steps of the model-based testing process.

Model: Design and write a behavior model of the GSM 11.11 (including requirements traceability annotations)—Sections 9.2 and 9.3.

Generate: Choose test selection criteria (we focus on model coverage criteria in this case study) and then use the model-based testing tool to generate an abstract test suite—Section 9.4.

Concretize: Transform the generated test cases into executable test scripts. For this case study we use a mixture of transformation and adaptation (see Section 8.1), with the test cases being transformed into executable tests in C, and an adaptation layer bridging the gap between the C API and the smart card hardware—Section 9.5.

Execute: Execute the generated test cases on the platform and report bugs and discrepancies between expected results and actual execution results—Section 9.6.

For this case study, we consider an imaginary smart card manufacturer with an R&D team that has developed an implementation of the GSM 11.11 standard. The technical context includes an existing test execution environment for automated test execution and a configuration management system for storing and managing the test cases.

9.1 OVERVIEW OF THE GSM 11.11 STANDARD

GSM (Global System for Mobile communication) was the first of the second-generation mobile phone systems—that is, the first system involving fully digital features. It was launched in 1979 by the World Administrative Radio Conference and evolved technically for many years before the official opening of the first commercial GSM networks in Europe around 1993. Since 1991 it has been adapted to create several similar new systems (DCS 1800 and then DCS 1900 in which only the radio interface differs). Nowadays, GSM is a worldwide standard and is used in almost all countries. In 2005 it was used by about 70 percent of mobile phones in the world and was dominant in Europe, Africa, and the Middle East [Wik06]. Its evolution is managed by a consortium of telecommunications standards bodies under the 3rd Generation Partnership Project (3GPP).[1]

Security and mobility are important features of mobile networks. To ensure security, GSM features an optimized radio interface with digital communications that are secured by cryptographic algorithms. The SIM card

---

[1] See *http://www.3gpp.org*.

contains the ciphering keys, authentication algorithms, and information about the subscriber's identity and available services, as well as space for text messages and phone book information, and so on. It is a card belonging to and preset by the GSM operator but remaining in the user's mobile phone. Since it contains all the user's details, it is possible to move the SIM card from one ME (*mobile equipment*) to another and retain the user's data, identity, and security keys. The GSM 11.11 standard [Eur99] specifies the physical and electrical characteristics of the SIM card, as well as the logical structure of the data within it and the security features that protect that data.

The GSM 11.11 standard also defines the software interface between the SIM and the ME. During communication, the SIM is passive: it only answers the requests sent by the ME. The applications in the ME access and modify the files of the SIM through defined commands, which enforce the access conditions of each file. The abstraction level of the tested kernel concerns only the commands of the GSM 11.11, without formalizing the upper layer (the application layer) or the lower layer (the communication protocol between the SIM and the ME).

The files of the SIM and the selected commands are now described. These commands make it possible to select a file and insert a personal identification number (PIN). Depending on the validity of this code and the relevant access of files, the user may read the currently selected file. The rights corresponding to the PIN code may be blocked if the authentication process fails three times and can be unblocked if a corresponding personal unblocking key (PUK) is entered.

9.1.1 Selected Files

Here we consider two kinds of file defined in the GSM 11.11 standard:

- The transparent *elementary files* (EF) are files that contain data only. An EF file with a transparent structure consists of a sequence of bytes. The GSM 11.11 standard also includes sequences of records and cyclic EF, but these are not considered in this study.
- The *dedicated files* (DF) are directories that can contain other DF or EF. They define the tree structure of the files. A special DF file, called the *master file* (MF), defines the root of the tree.

For testing purposes, we decide to limit the file structure of this case study to two DFs (of which MF is one) and four EFs, with the tree structure shown in Figure 9.1. The current directory of the system is always a DF. The currently selected file is always an EF within the current directory, except

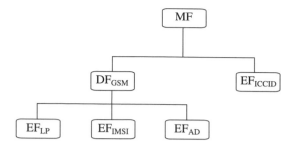

FIGURE 9.1   Tree structure of the SIM files used for testing.

in the case where no file is selected. For example, after a new directory is selected, there is no current file selected. Initially, the current directory of the system is an MF and no current file is selected. The selection of a file (DF or EF) is performed according to the following rules:

- Any file that is a child of the current directory can be selected.
- Any DF file that is a sibling of the current directory can be selected.
- The parent of the current directory can be selected.
- The current directory can be selected.
- The MF can always be selected.

9.1.2 Security Aspects

Each EF has specific read access conditions (no file access conditions are currently assigned by GSM to the DF). The relevant access condition must be fulfilled before the requested action can take place. These conditions are described in Table 9.1. Four types of access condition can be found in the standard:

- ALWays: The action can be performed without restrictions.
- NEVer: The action cannot be performed over the SIM/ME interface (the SIM may perform the action internally).
- CHV (card holder verification): The action is possible only if one of the following conditions is fulfilled:
  – A correct PIN code has been presented to the SIM during the current session
  – The PUK code has been successfully presented during the session

TABLE 9.1   Read Access Conditions

File Name	Read Access Conditions
ef_iccid	NEVer
ef_lp	ALWays
ef_imsi	CHV
ef_ad	ADM

The CHV access condition, once satisfied, remains valid until the end of the GSM session, as long as the corresponding PIN code remains unblocked. That is, after three consecutive wrong attempts, not necessarily in the same session, the access rights previously granted by the PIN or PUK code are lost immediately.

- ADM: Allocation of these levels and respective requirements for their fulfilment are the responsibility of the appropriate administrative authority. In the kernel of the standard that we are testing, ADMinistrator access is always denied.

9.1.3 Selected Commands

We present six commands from the larger set of commands defined in the GSM 11.11 standard. This selection is enough to have a clear view of the modeling style that can be used for this kind of application with a pre/post notation.

RESET: This function selects MF as the current file and suppresses the access conditions granted since the beginning of the session. This function makes it possible to simulate consecutive card sessions.

SELECT_FILE: This function selects a new file according to the conditions defined in Section 9.1.1.

READ_BINARY: This function reads the data from the current EF. This function can be performed only if the read access condition for this EF is satisfied.

VERIFY_CHV: This function verifies the PIN code presented by the ME by comparing it with the relevant one stored in the SIM. The verification process is allowed only if CHV is not blocked.

If the presented PIN code is correct, the number of remaining CHV attempts is reset to its initial value of 3 and the CHV access condition is satisfied.

TABLE 9.2   Potential Response Codes Returned by SIM Commands

Responses Codes	Descriptions
9000	- Normal return of the command
9400	- No EF selected
9404	- File not found
9804	- Access condition not fulfilled - Unsuccessful CHV verification, at least one attempt left - Unsuccessful UNBLOCK CHV verification, at least one attempt left
9840	- Unsuccessful CHV verification, no attempts left - Unsuccessful UNBLOCK CHV verification, no attempts left - CHV blocked - UNBLOCK CHV blocked

If the presented PIN code is false, the number of remaining CHV attempts is decremented. After three consecutive false PIN attempts, not necessarily in the same card session, the CHV is blocked and the CHV access condition is blocked until the UNBLOCK_CHV function has been successfully performed.

UNBLOCK_CHV: This function, by verifying the presented PUK code, unblocks a CHV that has been blocked by three consecutive wrong PIN code attempts. This function may be performed whether or not CHV is blocked, but it is not allowed if UNBLOCK CHV is itself blocked.

If the presented PUK code is correct, the value of the PIN code, presented with the PUK code, replaces the current CHV PIN value; the number of remaining UNBLOCK CHV attempts is reset to its initial value of 10 and the number of remaining CHV attempts is reset to its initial value of 3. After a successful unblocking attempt, the CHV access condition level is satisfied.

If the presented PUK code is incorrect, the number of remaining UNBLOCK CHV attempts shall be decremented. After 10 consecutive incorrect PUK code attempts, not necessarily in the same card session, the UNBLOCK CHV will be blocked. This leaves the card permanently unusable. An incorrect PUK code will have no effect on the status of the CHV itself.

STATUS: This function gives a view of the state of the SIM, including which directory is selected, which file is currently selected (if any), and the current values of the CHV counter and the UNBLOCK CHV counter.

Each function, except the STATUS operation, always returns a status word. This response, which has the form of a hexadecimal code, takes one of the values described in Table 9.2.

9.2 MODELING GSM 11.11 IN B

The purpose of the following model is generating functional test cases. By functional, we mean testing the normal behavior of the SIM, including its error responses, within the normal operating context of a typical ME. For example, one functional test case might be a call to the VERIFY_CHV command with a good PIN code, in the context where the PIN is already blocked and checking that the command returns an error status-word of 9840. In this case study, we are not interested in testing syntactic robustness, such as the invocation of a command with errors in the parameter formats. In other words, we consider that all commands are syntactically well formed, and we focus on the functional behavior of this application.

Next we discuss the abstraction level of our model, including the signatures of the B operations. The following subsections go through the data and the operation parts of the model, describing the major features and design decisions.

9.2.1 Abstracting the Behavior

We have already made some abstraction decisions by deciding to focus on testing just the transparent elementary files (EF) and leave the testing of record-oriented and cyclic elementary files for another time. This allows us to model just six commands and ignore the other dozen or so commands in the GSM 11.11 standard. This keeps the case study small enough for this chapter. Another abstraction decision we make is to test just one kind of CHV (the GSM standard has two kinds of CHV, CHV1 and CHV2, where CHV1 is the normal PIN for using the phone and CHV2 is a separate PIN that may be required to access advanced features of the phone).

In the GSM 11.11 standard, each command is coded as a hexadecimal signature with five single-byte parameters (CLASS, INS, P1, P2, and P3) plus a variable-length data region. The CLASS parameter is always hexadecimal A0 for GSM applications, the INS byte determines which command is being invoked, and the P1, P2, and P3 bytes contain the parameters for that command. For example, for the VERIFY_CHV command, the various input parameters are shown in Table 9.3. For this command, only the parameter DATA is interesting from a functional point of view because it contains the PIN code given by the user for authentication. The parameters CLASS, INS,

TABLE 9.3   Encoding of the VERIFY_CHV Command

CLASS	INS	P1	P2	P3	DATA
'A0'	'20'	'00'	CHV Number	'08'	CHV Value

P1, and P3 are fixed data for this command; and for the parameter P2 (CHV number), we consider only CHV1 so its value is always 1. During the adaptation step, these parameter values will be used to complete the call to the VERIFY_CHV command.

Notice that for *format testing* of the GSM 11.11 commands, we would use a lower-level syntactic model that includes a complete list of parameters in the signatures of each command. This would make it possible to test the commands with invalid values for robustness testing.

Key Point   The definition of the operation signatures in the model should focus on just the input and output parameters that are useful for the current test objectives. The operation signatures give an abstract view of the points of control and observation of the SUT.

9.2.2 The Data Model

The B data model consists of a static part, shown in Listing 9.1, which defines the sets and constants used in the model, and a dynamic part, shown in Listing 9.2, which defines the state variables of the model and their invariant properties and initial values. Next we explain each section of the model.

SETS
Seven sets are defined to model the simplified kernel:

- FILES defines the set of SIM files and directories to be considered.
- PERMISSION represents the various read access rights.
- VALUE defines the two boolean values true and false.
- BLOCKED_STATUS models the various blocking states.
- CODE represents the potential PIN codes, which can be used to verify an access condition. The codes were limited to four possible values to make it easier to read the generated test sequences.

LISTING 9.1   Sets and constants of the GSM 11.11 model.

```
MACHINE GSM

SETS
    FILES = {mf,df_gsm,ef_iccid,ef_lp,ef_imsi,ef_ad};
    PERMISSION = {always,chv,never,adm};
    VALUE = {true, false};
    BLOCKED_STATUS = {blocked, unblocked};
    CODE = {c1,c2,c3,c4};
    DATA = {data1,data2,data3,data4};
    STATUS_WORDS={sw_9000,sw_9400,sw_9404,sw_9804,sw_9840}

CONSTANTS
    FILES_CHILDREN,
    PERMISSION_READ,
    MAX_CHV,
    MAX_UNBLOCK,
    PUK

DEFINITIONS
    MF == {mf};
    DF == {df_gsm};
    EF == {ef_iccid,ef_lp,ef_imsi,ef_ad}

PROPERTIES
    FILES_CHILDREN : (MF \/ DF) <-> FILES &
    FILES_CHILDREN = {(mf,df_gsm), (mf,ef_iccid),
        (df_gsm,ef_lp), (df_gsm,ef_imsi), (df_gsm,ef_ad)} &
    PERMISSION_READ : EF --> PERMISSION &
    PERMISSION_READ = {(ef_iccid,never),(ef_lp,always),
        (ef_imsi,chv),(ef_ad,adm)} &
    MAX_CHV = 3 &
    MAX_UNBLOCK = 10 &
    PUK : CODE &
    PUK = c3
```

- DATA is the abstract set of all the data that can be written in the files. For testing purposes, it is not necessary to model the file contents as a sequence of bytes—we take a more abstract view, simply declaring four different file contents as four constants.

- STATUS_WORDS is the set of all status words that can be returned from the various operations.

LISTING 9.2 Data part of the GSM 11.11 model.

VARIABLES

```
    current_file,
    current_directory,
    counter_chv,
    counter_unblock_chv,
    blocked_chv_status,
    blocked_status,
    permission_session,
    pin,
    data
```

INVARIANT

```
    current_file <: EF &
    card(current_file) <= 1 &
    current_directory : DF \/ MF &
    counter_chv : 0..MAX_CHV &
    counter_unblock_chv : 0...MAX_UNBLOCK_CHV &
    pin : CODE &
    permission_session : PERMISSION --> VALUE &
    (always,true) : permission_session &
    (adm,false) : permission_session &
    (never,false) : permission_session &
    blocked_chv_status : BLOCKED_STATUS &
    blocked_status : BLOCKED_STATUS &
    data : EF --> DATA &
    (blocked_chv_status=blocked => (chv,false):permission_session) &
    (counter_chv=0 => blocked_chv_status=blocked) &
    (counter_unblock_chv=0 => blocked_status=blocked) &
    (current_file = {} or
       (dom(FILES_CHILDREN |> current_file) = {current_directory}))
```

INITIALISATION

```
    current_file := {} ||
    current_directory := mf ||
    counter_chv := MAX_CHV ||
    counter_unblock_chv := MAX_UNBLOCK ||
    blocked_chv_status := unblocked ||
    blocked_status := unblocked ||
    permission_session := {(always,true),(chv,false),
                           (adm,false),(never,false)} ||
    pin := c1 ||
    data := {(ef_iccid,data1),(ef_lp,data2),(ef_imsi,data3),(ef_ad,data4)}
```

CONSTANTS AND PROPERTIES

Five constants are defined in the B machine. The *Constants* clause lists the constant data, and the *Properties* clause defines their types and values.

- FILES_CHILDREN is the relation used to define the tree structure of the file hierarchy. It contains several (*parent*, *child*) pairs.
- PERMISSION_READ is the function that describes the read access condition for each file.
- MAX_CHV is the maximum number of consecutive unsuccessful PIN attempts that will be tolerated.
- MAX_UNBLOCK is the maximum number of consecutive unsuccessful PUK attempts that will be tolerated.
- PUK defines the constant value of the PUK code.

DEFINITIONS

Three definitions complete the sets and constants already defined. These are defined to make the model more readable and maintainable.

- MF is a set that contains just the master file.
- DF is a sct that contains all the directories except the master file.
- EF is a set that contains all the transparent files.

VARIABLES

Nine state variables are used in the formal model:

- current_file indicates the current file. It is modeled by a set that is empty when no file is currently selected or a singleton set when a file is selected.
- current_directory indicates the current directory.
- counter_chv defines the remaining number of incorrect PIN attempts that will be allowed before the card is blocked.
- counter_unblock_chv defines the remaining number of incorrect PUK attempts that will be allowed before the card is permanently blocked.
- blocked_chv_status defines whether the CHV status is currently blocked.
- blocked_status defines whether the card is permanently blocked after too many incorrect PUK attempts.

- permission_session maps each PERMISSION level to a boolean, to indicate whether the user is currently allowed to access all the files that have that permission level.
- pin defines the correct CHV PIN code.
- data defines the contents of each elementary file.

> **Key Point**   The state variables give an abstract view of the current state of the SUT. The choice of state variables depends on what is necessary to control and observe the behavior of the SUT.

The INVARIANT and INITIALISATION clauses introduce, respectively, the invariant properties of the state of the machine and the initialization of the state variables. The invariant properties are mostly typing conditions, but the last four invariants describe consistency conditions that we expect should always be true—if we made a mistake in one of the operations that violated these conditions, these invariants could help us to detect that mistake (see Section 9.3). The meaning of these four invariant formulae is the following:

- If a PIN is blocked, then the corresponding permissions are denied.
- If the PIN try counter is equal to 0, then the PIN is blocked.
- If the unblock try counter is equal to 0, then the card is completely blocked.
- The current file is either a child of the current directory or empty.

9.2.3 The Operational Model

SIGNATURE OF THE OPERATIONS
The six operations described earlier are modeled in the OPERATIONS clause. Table 9.4 summarizes the input and output parameters of each operation.

REQUIREMENTS TRACEABILITY
To make it possible to track requirements through the test generation process, we define a requirements table that lists all the requirement identifiers with a corresponding description. This explicit description of requirements does not exist in the original GSM 11.11 specification, but it has been created as a summary of that specification so that we can give a short name to each informal requirement. Table 9.5 shows just the part of this table that relates to the VERIFY_CHV command.

The link from requirements to the model is supported by the tagging notation of the LTG/B tool (see Section 6.1).

TABLE 9.4   Input and Output Parameters of GSM 11.11 Operations

Operation	Input Parameters	Output Parameters
RESET	none	none
SELECT_FILE	ff: selected file	sw: status word
READ_BINARY	none	dd: read data sw: status word
VERIFY_CHV	code: PIN code	sw: status word
UNBLOCK_CHV	code_unblock: PUK code new_code: new CHV code	sw: status word
STATUS	none	cd: current directory cf: current file cc: CHV counter cuc: UNBLOCK CHV counter

TABLE 9.5   Requirements for the VERIFY_CHV Command

Requirement ID	Description of Requirements
VERIFY_CHV0	If the access solution for a function to be performed on the last selected file is CHV1 or CHV2, then a successful verification is required prior to the use of the function on this file.
VERIFY_CHV1	If the CHV presented is correct, the number of remaining CHV attempts for that CHV will be reset to its initial value MAX_CHV.
VERIFY_CHV2	If the CHV presented is false, the number of remaining CHV attempts for that CHV will be decremented.
VERIFY_CHV3	After MAX_CHV consecutive false CHV presentations, not necessarily in the same card session, the respective CHV will be blocked and the access condition can never be fulfilled until the UNBLOCK_CHV function has been successfully performed on the respective CHV.
VERIFY_CHV4	The verification process is subject to the following condition: CHV is not blocked.

Key Point   Traceability from functional requirements to test case is an important output of model-based testing techniques. If the original informal specification is not well structured with requirements identifiers, it is worth adding this structure before modeling for test generation, to support traceability.

MODEL OF THE OPERATIONS

Listings 9.3, 9.4, and 9.5 give the operational part of the B machine. For each operation, the precondition gives the typing of input variables, and the postcondition specifies the various effects of the operation. The output

LISTING 9.3   The GSM 11.11 operations (part 1 of 3).

```
OPERATIONS
    RESET =
        BEGIN
            /*@BEGIN_REQ: RESET@*/
            current_file := {} ||
            current_directory := mf ||
            permission_session := {(always,true),(chv,false),
                (adm,false), (never,false)}
            /*@END_REQ: RESET@*/
        END;

    sw <-- VERIFY_CHV(code) =
        PRE
            code : CODE
        THEN
            IF (blocked_chv_status = blocked)
            THEN
                sw := SW_9840              /*@REQ: VERIFY_CHV4@*/
            ELSE
                IF (pin = code)
                THEN
                    counter_chv := MAX_CHV ||    /*@REQ: VERIFY_CHV1@*/
                    permission_session(chv) := true || /*@REQ: VERIFY_CHV0@*/
                    sw := SW_9000
                ELSE
                    IF (counter_chv = 1)
                    THEN
                        /*@BEGIN_REQ: VERIFY_CHV3@*/
                        counter_chv := 0 ||
                        blocked_chv_status := blocked ||
                        permission_session(chv) := false ||
                        sw := SW_9840
                        /*@END_REQ: VERIFY_CHV3@*/
                    ELSE
                        /*@BEGIN_REQ: VERIFY_CHV2@*/
                        counter_chv := counter_chv - 1 ||
                        sw := SW_9804
                        /*@END_REQ: VERIFY_CHV2@*/
                    END
                END
            END
        END;
```

LISTING 9.4   The GSM 11.11 operations (part 2 of 3).

```
sw <-- UNBLOCK_CHV(code_unblock, new_code) =
    PRE
        code_unblock : CODE &
        new_code : CODE &
        sw : STATUS_WORDS
    THEN
        IF (blocked_status = blocked)
        THEN
            sw := SW_9840              /*@REQ: UNBLOCK_CHV4@*/
        ELSE
            IF (PUK = code_unblock)
            THEN
                /*@BEGIN_REQ: UNBLOCK_CHV1@*/
                pin := new_code ||
                blocked_chv_status := unblocked ||
                counter_chv := MAX_CHV ||
                counter_unblock_chv := MAX_UNBLOCK ||
                permission_session(chv) := true ||
                sw := SW_9000
                /*@END_REQ: UNBLOCK_CHV1@*/
            ELSE
                IF (counter_unblock_chv = 1)
                THEN
                    /*@BEGIN_REQ: UNBLOCK_CHV2@*/
                    counter_unblock_chv := 0 ||
                    blocked_status := blocked ||
                    sw := SW_9840
                    /*@END_REQ: UNBLOCK_CHV2@*/
                ELSE
                    counter_unblock_chv := counter_unblock_chv-1 ||
                    sw := SW_9804    /*@REQ: UNBLOCK_CHV3@*/
                END
            END
        END
    END;

cd,cf,cc,cuc <-- STATUS =
    BEGIN
        /*@BEGIN_REQ: STATUS@*/
        cd := current_directory ||
        cf := current_file ||
        cc := counter_chv ||
        cuc := counter_unblock_chv
        /*@END_REQ: STATUS@*/
    END;
```

LISTING 9.5 The GSM 11.11 operations (part 3 of 3).

```
sw <-- SELECT_FILE(ff) =
    PRE
        ff : FILES &
        sw : STATUS_WORDS
    THEN
        IF (ff : (DF \/ MF))
        THEN
            IF (((ff,current_directory) : FILES_CHILDREN)
              or ((current_directory,ff) : FILES_CHILDREN)
              or (ff = mf)
            THEN
                /*@BEGIN_REQ: SELECT_FILE1@*/
                sw := SW_9000 ||
                current_directory := ff ||
                current_file := {}
                /*@END_REQ: SELECT_FILE1@*/
            ELSE
                sw := SW_9404          /*@REQ: SELECT_FILE2@*/
            END
        ELSE
            IF ((current_directory,ff) : FILES_CHILDREN)
            THEN
                /*@BEGIN_REQ: SELECT_FILE4@*/
                sw := SW_9000 ||
                current_file := {ff}
                /*@BEGIN_REQ: SELECT_FILE4@*/
            ELSE
                sw := SW_9404          /*@REQ: SELECT_FILE3@*/
            END
        END
    END;


sw,dd <-- READ_BINARY =
    IF (current_file = {})
    THEN
        sw := SW_9400              /*@REQ: READ_BINARY4@*/
    ELSE
        IF (#file . file : current_file &
            permission_session (PERMISSION_READ[file]) = true)
        THEN
            sw := SW_9000 ||
            ANY ff WHERE ff : current_file
            THEN
                dd := data(ff)    /*@REQ: READ_BINARY2@*/
            END
        ELSE
            sw := SW_9804          /*@REQ: READ_BINARY3@*/
        END
    END
END;
```

parameters are not typed in the precondition (because it is a *pre*condition) but implicitly by their assignments in the postcondition.

We briefly explain here the VERIFY_CHV operation. Its input parameter is the PIN code given by the user, the output is the status word, and the goal of this operation is to verify the PIN value and to give the permission rights for the session. If the personal identification number is already blocked, the VERIFY_CHV returns a status word with the appropriate error code, else the given input value is compared with the real PIN value. If the user gives the correct PIN value, the PIN try counter is initialized to MAX_CHV, the permissions are given, and status word success is returned. Otherwise, the last IF_THEN_ELSE blocks access to the SIM card or decrements the number of remaining PIN attempts.

9.3 VALIDATION AND VERIFICATION OF THE B MODEL

Before generating the test cases, it is useful to check the quality of the model by applying some validation and verification procedures to it:

- "Validate the model" means check that it agrees with the informal requirements; this is usually done by model review and by animating the model on some use cases.
- "Verify the model" consists of checking its internal correctness; for example, verifying that all the operations respect the invariant properties of the model.

9.3.1 Validation by Animation

The formal nature of the B model makes it possible to simulate its execution—we call this animation. LTG provides an animation tool that allows us to call a sequence of operations and either choose specific input values for each operation or leave their values unconstrained so that we can test all possible input values. After each operation, the animation tool displays the output values and updated state variables and verifies that the invariant is still true.

Figure 9.2 shows a screenshot of an animation sequence with the LTG animator. This sequence is a typical use case with a sequence of VERIFY_CHV commands, each with a wrong PIN parameter, in order to block the personal identification number, then some SELECT_FILE commands, and finally an UNBLOCK_CHV command to unblock the PIN. This animation step can be

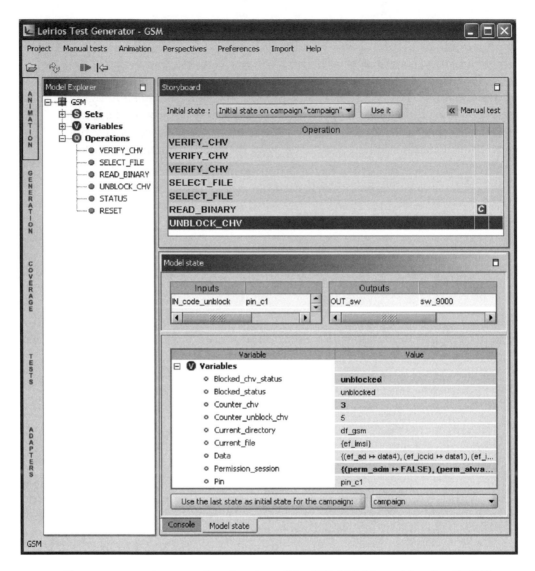

FIGURE 9.2 An example animation of the GSM 11.11 model, using LTG/B.

seen as a "model debugging" step, which interactively validates the model against the requirement specifications (that is, the informal specifications of the GSM 11.11 standard).

9.3.2 Model Verification

Checking the consistency of a B model involves two kinds of verification.

First, it must be proved that the model initial state is consistent with respect to the invariant properties. This is done by proving that the initialization establishes the invariant:

$$Static \Rightarrow [Initialization]\,Invariant$$

The *Static* predicate contains all the information about the static aspects of the model, such as the sets and constants and all their properties. *[Initialization]Invariant* means that the initialization values are substituted into the invariant. This checks that the initialization verifies the invariant formulae.

Second, it must be proved that each operation preserves the invariant. In this case, for each operation body *OP* with precondition *PRE*, there is a verification of the following form:

$$Static \wedge Invariant \wedge PRE \Rightarrow [OP]\,Invariant$$

These two verification procedures make it possible to prove the consistency of the whole model (and the underlying reachability graph). This ensures that every possible state of the model satisfies the invariant.

Verification is an automated or semi-automated process. For this case study, we use a proof tool for B called Atelier B.[2] The GSM 11.11 B model was automatically proved without detecting errors. Notice that for a larger model, verifying it can be more labor intensive. Therefore, there is a clear tradeoff between the time spent verifying the model and the added value of that formal verification.

Verifying all these consistency conditions can help to detect errors in the model and improve its quality, but still does not guarantee that the model has correctly captured all the informal requirements. Fortunately, it is not a disaster if a few errors remain in the model, since they usually will be detected and corrected when the generated tests are executed on the SUT.

Key Point   Model validation and verification help to raise confidence that the model agrees with the informal specifications. But don't spend too much time on it because test execution will detect errors in the model as well as the SUT.

9.4 GENERATING TESTS WITH LTG/B

The model-based test generation process with the LTG tool proceeds through the following three main steps:

---
[2] See *http://www.atelierb.societe.com/index_uk.htm*.

1. The Tester configures the model coverage criteria.
2. LTG computes test targets.
3. Using test generation parameters, LTG computes the test cases, the requirements traceability matrix, and a coverage report.

9.4.1 Model Coverage Criteria and Test Generation Parameters

We consider three kinds of model coverage criteria:

1. Operation coverage criteria
2. Decision coverage criteria
3. Data coverage criteria

For our GSM 11.11 model, we define a test generation configuration with the following settings:

- All operations are selected for test generation.
- The decision coverage criterion for all operations is condition/decision coverage.
- The data coverage for input parameters is 'all values' for the SELECT_FILE operation and 'several values' for both the UNBLOCK_CHV and the VERIFY_CHV operations.
- The observation operation for UNBLOCK_CHV and VERIFY_CHV operations is STATUS; for SELECT_FILE, the observation operation is READ_BINARY.

> **Key Point**   Defining **test selection criteria** is an iterative process. A first set of test criteria gives a first set of tests, which you can analyze using requirements coverage and model coverage metrics, or even SUT coverage metrics. Then, you can update your test criteria to increase the coverage and reach your test objectives for that test generation configuration.

9.4.2 Computing Test Targets

In LTG, a test target is a set of statements that precisely specifies a desired test. Each test target specifies:

TABLE 9.6   The Test Targets Generated for VERIFY_CHV

Target ID	Context	Requirement ID
tt1	blocked_chv_status = blocked	VERIFY_CHV4
tt2	blocked_chv_status /= blocked	VERIFY_CHV1
	& pin = code	VERIFY_CHV0
tt3	blocked_chv_status /= blocked	VERIFY_CHV3
	& pin /= code & counter_chv = 1	
tt4	blocked_chv_status /= blocked	VERIFY_CHV2
	& pin /= code & counter_chv /= 1	

- the activation of a given path through an operation (we call each path an *effect* of the operation),
- the given input arguments (if the operation has inputs),
- the given state of the model,
- the expected return values of the operation (if any), and
- the expected updates of the model variables.

The test targets are computed by LTG from the specification of each operation in the model and based on the test selection criteria chosen to configure the test generation. With the test selection criteria that we chose in the previous section, the LTG tool generates 22 test targets.

A test target is divided into three parts: the *precondition*, the *context*, and the *effect*. Table 9.6 shows the context part of the four test targets generated for the VERIFY_CHV operation, plus their associated requirements identifiers.

The context part contains the conditions that must be true in order to activate the effect (which is a particular path through the operation). For example, in the tt1 test target, the context condition is blocked_chv_status = blocked, the effect is sw:=SW_9840, and the precondition is code:CODE.

A test target may be related to zero, one, or several requirements. A requirement may be covered by no target: either it is not applicable to model or there may be a lack of coverage. A requirement may be related to several targets: in this case the requirement is covered by all related test targets together.

Key Point   The test targets are test case specifications generated from the model with respect to the test selection criteria. They make it possible to see which parts of the model should be covered before generating the complete test cases, and they provide the basis for model coverage metrics.

TABLE 9.7   Number of Generated Test Cases per Command

Operation	Number of Test Cases
VERIFY_CHV	5
SELECT_FILE	8
READ_BINARY	6
STATUS	1
UNBLOCK_CHV	5
RESET	1

TABLE 9.8   Generated Test Cases for the VERIFY_CHV Operation

Target	Test ID	Test Sequence
tt1	test1	VERIFY_CHV(pin_c2)=sw_9804; VERIFY_CHV(pin_c2)=sw_9804; VERIFY_CHV(pin_c2)=sw_9840; **VERIFY_CHV(pin_c1)=sw_9840;** STATUS=mf,{},0,5; UNBLOCK_CHV(pin_c1,pin_c1)=sw_9000; RESET
	test2	VERIFY_CHV(pin_c2)=sw_9804; VERIFY_CHV(pin_c2)=sw_9804; VERIFY_CHV(pin_c2)=sw_9840; **VERIFY_CHV(pin_c2)=sw_9840;** STATUS=mf,{},0,5; UNBLOCK_CHV(pin_c1,pin_c1)=sw_9000; RESET
tt2	test3	**VERIFY_CHV(pin_c1)=sw_9000;** STATUS=mf,{},3,5; RESET
tt3	test4	VERIFY_CHV(pin_c2)=sw_9804; VERIFY_CHV(pin_c2)=sw_9804; **VERIFY_CHV(pin_c2)=sw_9840;** STATUS=mf,{},0,5; UNBLOCK_CHV(pin_c1,pin_c1)=sw_9000; RESET
tt4	test5	**VERIFY_CHV(pin_c2)=sw_9804;** STATUS=mf,{},2,5; UNBLOCK_CHV(pin_c1,pin_c1)=sw_9000; RESET

9.4.3 Generating Test Cases

For each test target, the LTG tool computes, if possible, one or more test cases, depending on which data coverage criteria are chosen for the input parameters. With the test selection criteria configured in Section 9.4.1, 26 test cases are generated (see Table 9.7). These 26 test cases cover 100 percent of the 22 test targets and also give 100 percent coverage of the requirements.

Table 9.8 shows the five test cases that are generated for the VERIFY_CHV operation. Notice that the two test cases generated for test target tt1 (test1 and test2) come from the several values coverage criteria assigned to the input parameter "code": test1 tries the correct PIN after CHV is blocked, while test2 tries an incorrect PIN.

Figure 9.3 shows test1 displayed within the LTG/B tool.

9.5 GENERATING EXECUTABLE SCRIPTS

As usual, our generated test cases are somewhat abstract: the sequences involve operations and symbols defined in the model. So, as explained in Chapter 8, they cannot be executed directly on the SUT until they have been either transformed into lower-level test scripts or linked to some adapter code that translates the high-level calls into SUT operations.

For this GSM 11.11 smart card application, we use a Windows test execution environment with a C language interface. So each executable test script will be a C program that makes calls to the GSM 11.11 interface via a DLL (dynamically linked library).

Given this test execution environment, we decide to use a combination of the transformation and adaptation approaches. We transform (in Section 9.5.1) the abstract test cases into medium-level C code that calls a separate C procedure for each SIM command, such as VERIFY_CHV(pin,sw). We also define an adaptation layer (in Section 9.5.2) that implements these C procedure calls by adding the various fixed parameters for each SIM command (as illustrated in Table 9.3 for the VERIFY_CHV command) and calling the low-level SIM communication procedures provided by the DLL.

To transform the generated test cases into executable C code, we use the LTG test script generator. It takes as input a test script template and some mappings from abstract names to concrete names, then it transforms each abstract test case into an executable test script in C. The generated test scripts can be compiled and linked against the GSM 11.11 interface DLL, then executed to test a particular SIM card.

Listing 9.6 shows the generated test script corresponding to test case test1.

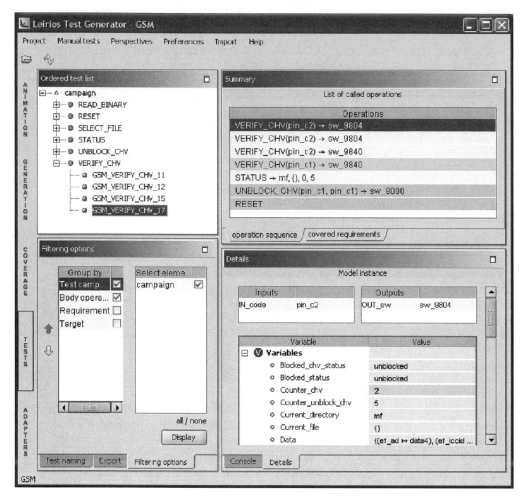

FIGURE 9.3   An example of a generated test case in LTG/B.

9.5.1 LTG Test Script Generator

In this section, we show the details of how the abstract test cases can be transformed into executable test scripts in C, using the LTG test script generator. The conversion involves several actions, as follows:

- Filter and sort test cases from LTG's internal repository.
- Map abstract symbols into matching symbols in the test environment.
- Compose a concrete sequence of operations from the abstract sequence.
- Generate test scripts that have the desired directory structure.

LISTING 9.6   Generated test script for VERIFY_CHV test case test1.

```c
/* Operation    : VERIFY_CHV
 * Test         : test1
 * Requirements: VERIFY_CHV4
 */
#include <stdio.h>
#include "AdaptationLayer.h"

int main(int argc, char *argv[])
{
    int OUT_sw, OUT_cd, OUT_cc, OUT_cuc;
    PRINT_LOG("Test objective for %s : %s",
        "test1",
        "VERIFY_CHV4");
    INIT_LIB(argc, argv);
    POWER_ON(argc, argv);

    // Preamble
        OUT_sw = sw_9804;
        VERIFY_CHV(pin_c2, OUT_sw);
        OUT_sw = sw_9804;
        VERIFY_CHV(pin_c2, OUT_sw);
        OUT_sw = sw_9840;
        VERIFY_CHV(pin_c2, OUT_sw);

    // Body
        OUT_sw = sw_9840;
        VERIFY_CHV(pin_c1, OUT_sw);

    // Observation
        OUT_cd  = mf;
        OUT_cc  = 0;
        OUT_cuc = 5;
        STATUS(OUT_cd, OUT_cc, OUT_cuc);

    // Postamble
        OUT_sw = sw_9000;
        UNBLOCK_CHV(pin_c1, pin_c1, OUT_sw);
        RESET();

    POWER_OFF();
    TERM_LIB();
    return 0;
}
```

The script generator is based on a template engine and requires one or more templates to achieve these tasks. A template file contains both static and dynamic information.

- The static information is read and printed by the engine without any transformation. It can be any type of information because it is handled transparently by the engine.
- The dynamic information is identified by <% and %> or ${ and } pairs of markers embedded in the template. These markers delimit sections of code written in the Groovy scripting language.[3] When the engine encounters such a section, it parses and runs the code that it contains. Each section marked by <% and %> contains Groovy scripting code such as loops or conditionals, and the section is replaced by the output of that Groovy code (if any). Each section marked by ${...} contains a Groovy expression, and the section is replaced by the result of evaluating that Groovy expression.

The templates are designed once at the beginning of the test project and loaded into LTG. (They can often be reused by similar test projects that use the same SIM card interface.) Their use by the test script generator is fully managed by the LEIRIOS Test Generator without further intervention by the test engineer.

The sample script generator used to generate the script shown in Listing 9.6 uses two templates: one global template describing the test script file structure (shown in Listing 9.7) and one small template describing the format of each function call in the script sequence (shown in Listing 9.8). For example, the script header will be generated as follows:

- The engine calls the getName() method of the operation object to retrieve the name of the currently tested operation.
- The name is appended to the string "/* Operation   : " to build the first header line.
- The same is done with the next header line.
- The engine calls the getRequirements() method of the testSuite object to retrieve a collection of requirements objects. An iterator then retrieves the requirement name from each object of the collection. Then names are joined to build the comma-separated list of requirement names, and output after Requirements.

---

[3] See *http://groovy.codehaus.org*.

LISTING 9.7   Template of the test script file structure.

```
/* Operation    : ${operation.getName()}
 * Test         : ${testCase.getName()}
 * Requirements: ${testSuite.getRequirements(testCase)
                      .collect{it.getName()}.join(', ')}
 */
#include <stdio.h>
#include "AdaptationLayer.h"

int main(int argc, char *argv[])
{
    int OUT_sw, OUT_cd, OUT_cc, OUT_cuc;
    PRINT_LOG("Test objective for %s : %s"),
        "${testCase.getName()}",
        "${testSuite.getRequirements(testCase)
            .collect{it.getName()}.join(', ')}");
    INIT_LIB(argc, argv);
    POWER_ON(argc, argv);

    // Preamble
    <% for (message in testCase.getBehavior().getPreambleMessages()){%>
        ${conf.evaluateFragment('message template', this)}
    <% } %>

    // Body
    <% for (message in testCase.getBehavior().getBodyMessages()){ %>
        ${conf.evaluateFragment('message template', this)}
    <% } %>

    // Postamble
    <% if (testSuite.hasPostambleBeenFoundFor(testCase))
    {
      for (message in testCase.getBehavior().getPostambleMessages())
      {%>
        ${conf.evaluateFragment('message template', this)}
      <% }
    }
    else
    {%>
    GLOBAL_CLEANUP();
    <% } %>

    POWER_OFF();
    TERM_LIB();
    return 0;
}
```

LISTING 9.8   Template "message template" for generating function calls.

```
<% for (p in message.getOperation().getReturnResults()) {
    if (message.getArgument(p).getValue() != '_') {
        %>${p.getName()} = ${message.getArgument(p).getValue()};
    <% }
    }
%>$m{message.getOperation().getName()}(${message
        .getOperation().getFormalParameters()
        .sort({p1,p2 | p1.getName().compareTo(p2.getName())})
        .collect{message.getArgument(it).getValue()}
        .plus(message.getOperation().getReturnResults()
                .sort({p1,p2 | p1.getName().compareTo(p2.getName())})
                .collect{conf.map('output', it)}
                )
        .join(', ')
    });
```

9.5.2 GSM 11.11 Adaptation Layer

The test script shown in Listing 9.6 consists mainly of calls to C functions and usage of global variables and definitions. The role of the adaptation layer is to declare and/or define everything required by these test scripts. Then it provides an interface that makes it easy to integrate the C test scripts with the test environment.

The adaptation depends partly on the test environment used to run the test scripts (language, libraries available, tests scheduler, etc.) and partly on the tested system (operation stubs specific to the model and to the SUT).

In our GSM 11.11 example each model operation matches one command. Then the goals of the VERIFY_CHV function are:

- to encode its argument and build up a command byte sequence,
- to invoke a card reader primitive that sends the command and receives the command response, and
- to decode the response into the same data format as the one used in the script.

Card reader primitives may be provided by a library that is part of the test execution environment. They do not belong to the adaptation layer itself.

LISTING 9.9   Contents of the file *AdaptationLayer.h.*

```
#ifndef ADAPTATION_LAYER
#define ADAPTATION_LAYER

/* Status words. */
#define sw_9804    0x9804
#define sw_9840    0x9840
#define sw_9000    0x9000

/* File IDs. */
#define mf      0x3f00

#define PRINT_LOG   printf

extern char pin_c1[];
extern char pin_c2[];

extern void INIT_LIB(int argc, char** argv);
extern void POWER_ON(int argc, char** argv);
extern void GLOBAL_CLEANUP();
extern void POWER_OFF();
extern void TERM_LIB();

extern void RESET();

extern void VERIFY_CHV(const char* value, int sw);

extern void STATUS(int directory, int pin_counter,
                   int puk_counter);

extern void UNBLOCK_CHV(const char* value_puk, const char*
                        value_pin, int sw);

#endif /* #ifndef ADAPTATION_LAYER */
```

They need not be implemented specifically for LTG generated tests and may be used by existing manually designed test suites.

To ease implementation and to make test scripts more readable, we also make the adapter procedures responsible for comparing the actual output values from the SIM card against the expected output values generated by LTG. In our example, VERIFY_CHV takes two arguments:

- The input CHV value for the verification, as a char array
- The status word value predicted by LTG, as an integer

The PIN code values (see Listing 9.9) are declared as global constant variables in *AdaptationLayer.h* and initialized in *AdaptationLayer.c* (see Listings 9.10 and 9.11). The status word values are defined as macros in *AdaptationLayer.h*. In this example, symbols used in the test scripts have the same names as the ones used in the model, but in the adaptation layer they have been given a C type and a concrete value.

The body of the VERIFY_CHV function can be found in *AdaptationLayer.c* (refer to Listings 9.10 and 9.11). In a few lines, the command is sent and possible communication problems with the reader library are checked. Then the status word read from the card is compared with the one computed by LTG (the ref_sw parameter); in the case of a value mismatch, an error message is written into the test log.

> **Key Point**   The adaptation layer makes the link between the model operation signatures and the real interface of the SUT. The design of the adaptation layer must start at the same time as the design of the model.

9.6 TEST EXECUTION

The C test scripts generated with the LEIRIOS Test Generator have the same format and the same syntax as manually designed test scripts. Therefore, the same process and the same tools are used for test execution and version control.

In the context of this case study, three main tools are used during the test execution process:

- An off-the-shelf configuration management tool manages software configurations, software and test versioning, building and deployment, and management dashboard.

- A proprietary test execution environment makes it possible to automatically execute the test cases both on a simulator and on the real card. This tool manages the test verdict assignment for each test and also gives a global report on the success of the whole test suite.

- An off-the-shelf bug-tracking system allows management of bug reports and tracking of their status and resolution.

LISTING 9.10   Contents of the file *AdaptationLayer.c* (part 1 of 2).

```c
#include <string.h>
#include <stdio.h>
#include "Reader.h"
#include "AdaptationLayer.h"

char pin_c1[] = {0x31, 0x31, 0x31, 0x31, 0xff, 0xff, 0xff, 0xff};
char pin_c2[] = {0x32, 0x32, 0x32, 0x32, 0xff, 0xff, 0xff, 0xff};

#define FID_INDEX           4
#define PIN_COUNTER_INDEX   18
#define PUK_COUNTER_INDEX   19
#define COUNTER_MASK        0x0f

static reader_t* reader = NULL;

void INIT_LIB(int argc, char** argv)
{
  if ((reader = allocate_reader()) == NULL) {
      fprintf(stderr, "Reader allocation error.\n");
      exit(-1);
    }
}

void POWER_ON(int argc, char** argv)
{
  if(power_on(reader) == -1) {
      fprintf(stderr, "Reader error.\n");
      exit(-1);
    }
}

void GLOBAL_CLEANUP()
{
}

void POWER_OFF()
{
  if(power_off(reader) == -1)
      fprintf(stderr, "Reader error.\n");
}

void TERM_LIB()
{
  if(free_reader(reader) == -1)
      fprintf(stderr, "Reader error.\n");
}
```

LISTING 9.11   Contents of the file *AdaptationLayer.c* (part 2 of 2).

```
void RESET()
{
  reset(reader);
}

void VERIFY_CHV(const char* value, int ref_sw)
{
  int command_sw;

  /*                      CLA  INS  P1   P2   Lc    DATA  SW */
  if(send_command3(reader,0xa0,0x20,0x00,0x01,0x08,value,&command_sw)==-1)
      fprintf(stderr, "Reader error");
  else if(command_sw != ref_sw)
      PRINT_LOG("test failed");
}

void UNBLOCK_CHV(const char* value_puk, const char* value_pin, int ref_sw)
{
  int   command_sw;
  char data[16];

  memcpy(data,    value_puk, 8);
  memcpy(data+8, value_pin, 8);

  /*                      CLA  INS  P1   P2   Lc    DATA SW */
  if(send_command3(reader,0xa0,0x2c,0x00,0x00,0x08,data,&command_sw)==-1)
    fprintf(stderr, "Reader error");
  else if(command_sw != ref_sw)
    PRINT_LOG("test failed");
}

void STATUS(int directory, int pin_counter, int puk_counter)
{
  int   command_sw;
  char data[24];

  /*                      CLA  INS  P1   P2   Le    DATA SW */
  if(send_command2(reader,0xa0,0xf2,0x00,0x00,0x24,data,&command_sw)==-1)
      fprintf(stderr, "Reader error");
  else if(
    ((data[FID_INDEX] << 8) + data[FID_INDEX+1] != directory)   ||
    ((data[PIN_COUNTER_INDEX] & COUNTER_MASK)    != pin_counter) ||
    ((data[PUK_COUNTER_INDEX] & COUNTER_MASK)    != puk_counter))
      PRINT_LOG("test failed");
}
```

In the smart card industry, the automation of test execution has been solved for more than 10 years. The test execution environment includes hardware that controls the card during test execution, as well as software that supports the communication protocol used to exchange information with the card using Application Protocol Data Units (APDU)—that is, the commands to the card and the responses from the card. The test execution environment provides a language and a library of services to make it easier to develop customized execution environments.

Therefore, in our GSM 11.11 case study, the generated test scripts are stored in our configuration management system and then executed using the test execution environment. At this stage, each test execution that fails has to be analyzed. As you already know, the problem can come from the adaptation layer (with some syntactic errors that are generally easy to analyze) or from a functional discrepancy between the SUT and the model. In the second case, model animation can help to decide if the failure is due to a fault in the model or in the implementation. If it is a model fault, then the model will be corrected. If it is an implementation fault, then a bug issue will be opened in the bug-tracking system.

> **Key Point**   Automated test execution is generally a prerequisite for model-based testing. It makes it possible to repeatedly execute your generated test suites for regression testing purposes.

9.7 SUMMARY

In this chapter, we present a complete case study of applying model-based testing to a simplified version of an actual smart card application. The following are the main lessons learned from this case study.

- The definition of the operation signatures and the state variables in the model depends on what is necessary to control and observe the behavior of the system under test—this is linked to the testing objectives of the project.
- It can be useful to have several test models of the SUT at different levels of abstraction, to fulfill different test objectives. For example, we discussed the option of developing a syntactic model of the GSM 11.11 commands for robustness testing. This would complement our functional model of the behavior of the commands (which assumes that arguments are correctly typed and formatted).

- Annotating the model with requirements makes it possible to automatically generate a traceability matrix from the functional requirements to the generated test cases. This matrix will be automatically maintained after each change to the model and regeneration of test cases.

- Using model validation and verification tools can increase confidence that the model conforms to the requirements. But the key point is that the validation of the SUT comes from the confrontation of two independent views of the requirements: the model versus the SUT implementation. Any discrepancies will be detected during the test execution analysis phase.

- The coverage of the model by the generated test suite is given by the percentage of test targets that have test cases associated with them. The test targets are generated from the model and the test selection criteria.

- Test concretization is based first on a test script generator that translates the generated test cases into the language supported by the automated test execution environment. Second, it uses an adaptation layer that bridges the gap between the abstract signatures of the model operations and the concrete APIs provided by the test execution environment.

9.8 FURTHER READING

More detail on this GSM 11.11 case study can be found in [BLLP04]. Another experience with using LTG to validate smart card software is described in [BLPT04].

## CHAPTER 10

THE ATM
CASE STUDY

This chapter uses model-based testing with UML models to test an open-source implementation of a simple automated teller machine (ATM) system.

We take the informal requirements from an example ATM system provided by Russell C. Bjork of Gordon College in Wenham, Massachusetts (see *http://www.math-cs.gordon.edu/index.html*, click the Courses tab and then CS211: Object-Oriented Software). As well as requirements, he gives detailed use cases with UML interaction diagrams, some initial functional test cases, a high-level UML analysis model, detailed UML design models, and a sample implementation of an ATM simulator in Java.

In this chapter, our modeling language is UML 2.0, and we discuss various modeling scenarios regarding abstraction choices and structure of the model. We develop our UML model by starting from a simplified version of the analysis model given by Bjork (use cases, class diagram, state machines, interaction diagrams). We model the ATM behavior using UML state machines that are more detailed than the state machines discussed by Bjork. This is a good example of how it is often possible to reuse some parts of a

UML analysis model but with considerable abstraction and formalization to make the model suitable for model-based testing.

We use the LTG/UML tool from LEIRIOS Technologies to generate the test cases. We discuss the relationship between the test model and the analysis and design model of the application and use several model coverage criteria to obtain good functional coverage of the test model. Finally, executable scripts are generated using a mixed transformation and adaptation approach and are then executed on the ATM simulator provided by Bjork.

10.1 OVERVIEW OF THE ATM SYSTEM

Bjork introduces the ATM requirements as follows (indented paragraphs in this section are quotes from the requirements and use case pages of his web page).

The software to be designed will control a simulated automated teller machine (ATM) having a magnetic stripe reader for reading an ATM card, a customer console (keyboard and display) for interaction with the customer, a slot for depositing envelopes, a dispenser for cash (in multiples of $20), a printer for printing customer receipts, and a key-operated switch to allow an operator to start or stop the machine. The ATM will communicate with the bank's computer over an appropriate communication link.

The ATM will service one customer at a time. A customer will be required to insert an ATM card and enter a personal identification number (PIN), both of which will be sent to the bank for validation as part of each transaction. The customer will then be able to perform one or more transactions. The card will be retained in the machine until the customer indicates that he/she desires no further transactions, at which point it will be returned, except as noted below.

The ATM must be able to provide the following services to the customer:

1. A customer must be able to make a cash withdrawal from any suitable account linked to the card, in multiples of $20.00. Approval must be obtained from the bank before cash is dispensed.

2. A customer must be able to make a deposit to any account linked to the card, consisting of cash [no coins] and/or checks in an envelope. The customer will enter the amount of the deposit into the ATM, subject to manual verification when the

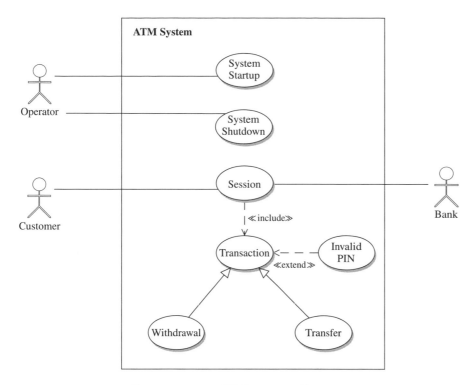

FIGURE 10.1   ATM use case diagram.

envelope is removed from the machine by an operator. Approval must be obtained from the bank before physically accepting the envelope.

3. A customer must be able to make a transfer of money between any two accounts linked to the card.

4. A customer must be able to make a balance inquiry of any account linked to the card.

Figure 10.1 shows the main use cases for this example ATM system (just the withdraw and transfer use cases).

There are two main actors: the operator who starts up and shuts down the system and replenishes cash and paper and the customer who may perform several *transactions* at the ATM during one *session*. Here is an informal description of each use case, also from Bjork's web page.

System Startup: The system is started when the operator turns the operator switch to the "on" position. The operator will be asked to enter the amount of money currently in the cash dispenser, and a connection to the bank will be established. Then the servicing of customers can begin.

System Shutdown: The system is shut down when the operator makes sure that no customer is using the machine, then turns the operator switch to the "off" position. The connection to the bank will be shut down.

Session: A session is started when a customer inserts an ATM card into the card reader slot of the machine. The ATM pulls the card into the machine and reads it. (If the reader cannot read the card due to improper insertion or a damaged [magnetic] stripe, the card is ejected, an error screen is displayed, and the session is aborted.) The customer is asked to enter his/her PIN, and is then allowed to perform one or more transactions, choosing from a menu of possible types of transaction in each case. After each transaction, the customer is asked whether he/she would like to perform another. When the customer is through performing transactions, the card is ejected from the machine and the session ends. If a transaction is aborted due to too many invalid PIN entries, the session is also aborted, with the card being retained in the machine. The customer may abort the session by pressing the Cancel key when entering a PIN or choosing a transaction type.

Transaction: Transaction is an abstract generalization. Each specific concrete type of transaction implements certain operations in the appropriate way. The flow of events given here describes the behavior common to all types of transaction. The flows of events for the individual types of transaction (withdrawal, deposit, transfer, inquiry) give the features that are specific to that type of transaction. A transaction use case is started within a session when the customer chooses a transaction type from a menu of options. The customer will be asked to furnish appropriate details (e.g., account(s) involved, amount). The transaction will then be sent to the bank, along with information from the customer's card and the PIN the customer entered. If the bank approves the transaction, any steps needed to complete the transaction (e.g., dispensing cash or accepting an envelope) will be performed, and then a receipt will be printed. Then the customer will be asked whether he/she wishes to do another transaction. If the bank reports that the customer's PIN is invalid, the Invalid PIN extension will be performed and then an attempt will be made to continue the transaction. If the customer's card is retained due to too many invalid PINs, the transaction will be aborted, and the customer will not be offered the option of doing another. If a transaction is cancelled by the customer, or fails for any reason other than repeated entries of an invalid PIN, a screen will be displayed informing the customer of the reason for the failure of the transaction, and then the customer will be offered the opportunity to do another. The customer may cancel a transaction by pressing the Cancel key as described for each individual type of transaction below.

Invalid PIN Extension: An invalid PIN extension is started from within a transaction when the bank reports that the customer's transaction is disapproved due to an invalid PIN. The customer is required to re-enter the PIN and the original request is sent to the bank again. If the bank now approves the transaction, or disapproves it for some other reason, the original use case is continued; otherwise the process of re-entering the PIN is repeated. Once the PIN is successfully re-entered, it is used for both the current transaction and all subsequent transactions in the session. If the customer fails three times to enter the correct PIN, the card is permanently retained, a screen is displayed informing the customer of this and suggesting he/she contact the bank, and the entire customer session is aborted. If the customer presses Cancel instead of re-entering a PIN, the original transaction is cancelled.

In the original ATM specifications, four transactions were considered (Withdrawal, Transfer, Deposit, and Inquiry), but we will model just the first two in order to keep this example short.

Withdrawal: A withdrawal transaction asks the customer to choose a type of account to withdraw from (c.g., checking) from a menu of possible accounts, and to choose a dollar amount from a menu of possible amounts. The system verifies that it has sufficient money on hand to satisfy the request before sending the transaction to the bank. (If not, the customer is informed and asked to enter a different amount.) If the transaction is approved by the bank, the appropriate amount of cash is dispensed by the machine before it issues a receipt. A withdrawal transaction can be cancelled by the customer pressing the Cancel key any time prior to choosing the dollar amount.

Transfer: A transfer transaction asks the customer to choose a type of account to transfer from (e.g., checking), from a menu of possible accounts, to choose a different account to transfer to, and to type in a dollar amount on the keyboard. No further action is required once the transaction is approved by the bank before printing the receipt. A transfer transaction can be cancelled by the customer pressing the Cancel key any time prior to entering a dollar amount.

10.2 MODELING THE ATM SYSTEM IN UML

Our ATM UML model uses two class diagrams (main classes and enumeration classes), a state machine that formalizes the expected behavior of the SUT, and an object diagram to set up the initial state for test generation. The dynamic behavior of the system is specified mainly by the ATM state machine, with some OCL preconditions and postconditions specifying the behavior of a few internal ATM actions.

10.2.1 Class Diagrams

Figure 10.2 shows our ATM class diagram. To make diagrams more readable, we use a few naming conventions throughout this chapter: acct is an abbreviation for *account* and tran or trans is an abbreviation for *transaction*.

The ATM class models the points of control and observation of the application. The points of observation are the various public fields shown in the class diagram, such as the message on the console of the ATM, the balance of each bank account, and the amount of cash remaining in the machine (this would not be public in an ATM implementation, but it is important for it to be available for testing purposes).

The points of control are modeled as *events* that come from the customer or the operator and cause changes in the ATM state. These events are the *public*[1] operations that are shown in the ATM class beneath the ≪ events≫ stereotype. These events are the input commands that will appear in our generated test cases to control the ATM. We define the following abstract events:

switchOn: Switch on the ATM and display a message on the console for the operator to replenish the cash.

switchOff: Switch off the ATM.

setCash(in initialCash): Replenish the cash supplies of the ATM so that it contains a given number of 20-dollar bills.

custInsertCard(in card): Insertion of a magnetic card by the customer. The *card* parameter is the card number that is detected by the card reader (zero means an unreadable card).

custEnterPin(in pin): Action of entering the PIN code with the pin code value.

---

[1]In UML 2.0 class diagrams, the public operations are graphically preceded by a + character.

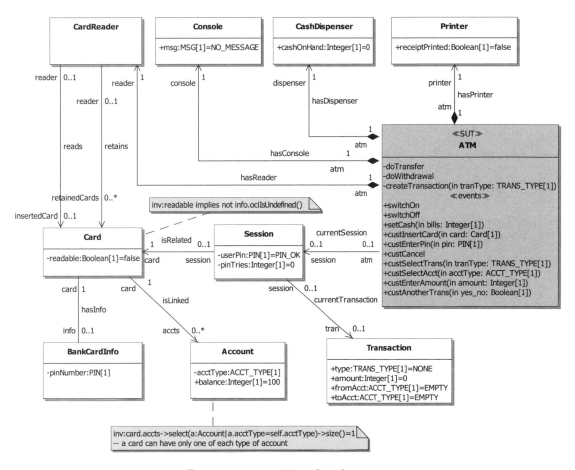

FIGURE 10.2   ATM class diagram.

custCancel: Press the Cancel key to cancel the session.

custSelectTrans(in transactionType): Choice of a particular kind of transaction within a session.

custSelectAcct(in accountType): Select an account for the transaction.

custEnterAmount(in amount): Enter an amount for the selected transaction. In the original ATM model, this involves a series of key presses, but we take a more abstract view and treat this input as a single integer.

custAnotherTrans(in yes_no): This action says whether or not a customer wants to do another transaction within the same session. If the yes_no parameter is true, a new transaction is started; otherwise, the current session is terminated and the card is ejected.

To help us model some of the more complex aspects of transactions, we also define several *internal actions* within the ATM class. These are called from within the action part of some of the transitions in the ATM state machine (see Figures 10.5 and 10.8 later) and are simply helper methods that allow us to move a few complex OCL postconditions out of the state machine diagram and into separate methods. We define three of these internal actions and model them as *private*[2] operations within the ATM class:

doTransfer: Performs the transfer transaction.

doWithdrawal: Performs the withdrawal transaction.

createTransaction(in tranType): This internal action creates the association between the ATM object and the current transaction.

The other classes model several physical components of the ATM. Our example ATM contains four main components: the printer, the cash dispenser, the customer console, and the card reader. Each component appears as a class that is associated with the ATM class using a *composition* link (solid black diamond), which means that these components are viewed as part of the ATM and they are created and destroyed at the same time as the ATM object.

Printer: This class has an attribute that records whether a receipt is printed during the transaction or not.

CashDispenser: This class has an attribute that indicates the amount of cash in the ATM. This is initialized by the setCash event and updated by the withdrawal transaction.

Console: This class models the message that is currently displayed on the ATM display.

CardReader: This class models the physical handling of cards, such as inserting and retaining cards.

The other classes concern the information on the card, the bank information for the card, the accounts, the session, and the transactions.

---

[2]In UML 2.0 class diagrams, private operations are preceded by a − character.

Card: This class has an attribute that determines if the card is readable or not. When this is false, it models a card that is very scratched or belongs to a different bank.

Session: A session is opened when a readable card is read. Several transactions (transfer or withdrawal) can be realized in the same session. This class records the PIN code given by the customer, and its pinTries variable counts the number of unsuccessful PIN code tries.

BankCardInfo: This class stores the PIN code associated with the card. Remember that the card is not a smart card but an old-fashioned magnetic card, so the PIN code is stored at the bank.

Account: This class stores the account information for each account that is associated with a card.

Transaction: This class stores information about one transaction.

Notice that in this class diagram, the ATM class representing the SUT defines all the user events, but all the data attributes are distributed over the associated classes.

Two class invariants have been added to this class diagram to place some constraints on the data model. One is linked to the Card class:

```
Inv:  readable implies not info.oclIsUndefined()
```

This says that if the card is readable, then there must be an association to some bank information (more precisely, if the card is readable, then its association to the BankCardInfo class is not undefined). The second invariant is written in the context of the Account class:[3]

```
Inv:  card.accounts
      ->select(a:Account|a.accountType=accountType)
      ->size() = 1
```

This says that a card can own at most one of each type of account. These invariants constrain the class diagram to be more precise so that we do not generate tests for bizarre scenarios that are outside the scope of the requirements or are not possible in the real world.

---

[3]It could also be written in the context of the Card class, but then the OCL predicate becomes a little more complex.

> **Key Point**   Class invariants can place constraints on the classes and associations to ensure that the data model conforms to the requirements.

Figure 10.3 shows the enumeration classes that we use for messages, transaction types, account types, and PINs:

MSG: This enumerates the messages that can be displayed on the ATM console.

TRANS_TYPE: This enumerates the various kinds of ATM transaction (Withdrawal and Transfer), plus a NONE value for the initial state.

ACCT_TYPE: This enumerates the three types of account: Checking, Savings, and MoneyMarket.

PIN: This enumerates some abstract PIN values: PIN_OK for the correct PIN value and PIN_KO for a wrong PIN.

These enumeration classes provide the value domains for the main variables. This includes values for the initial state. Notice also that some domains are purely symbolic like the PIN_OK and PIN_KO values. These will be concretized when the abstract tests are transformed into executable test scripts.

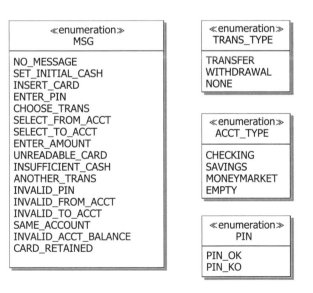

FIGURE 10.3   ATM enumerations.

10.2.2 Modeling Behavior with State Machines and OCL

The behavior of the ATM system is defined by a complex layered state machine. To display this large state machine in this book, we have split it up over five diagrams, but when space allows, it can be displayed as a single large diagram. Figure 10.4 shows the top level of this state machine. This state machine models the following behavior:

- From an initial state where the ATM is off, the operator can switch on the ATM and then replenish the cash dispenser.
- To replenish the cash dispenser, the operator provides from 1 to 100 $20 bills; the ATM then enters the idle state with the message "Insert card" on the user display.
- In the idle state, the operator can switch off the ATM, or the user can insert a card, which may be readable or unreadable.
- If the user inserts a readable card, the ATM asks for a PIN code, a session is created, and the PIN try counter is incremented. Then the system enters the doTransactions state (defined in Figure 10.5), which allows the user to perform a series of withdrawal and transfer transactions.
- From the doTransactions state, the output transitions are either a retained card situation or no more transactions followed by an ejection of the card. If the card is retained, the OCL expression

```
reader.insertedCard.oclIsUndefined()
```

deletes the link between the card reader and the current card.
- In the waitingUserPIN and doTransaction states, the customer may cancel the transactions. This causes the card to be ejected.

Figure 10.5 shows the state machine for the doTransaction nested state, which models the behavior of one session. This state machine defines the following behavior:

- After entering the doTransaction state, the system prompts the user to choose a type of transaction (withdrawal or transfer). If the user chooses a transaction type, the transition calls an internal action:

```
createTransaction(in tranType: TRANS_TYPE)
```

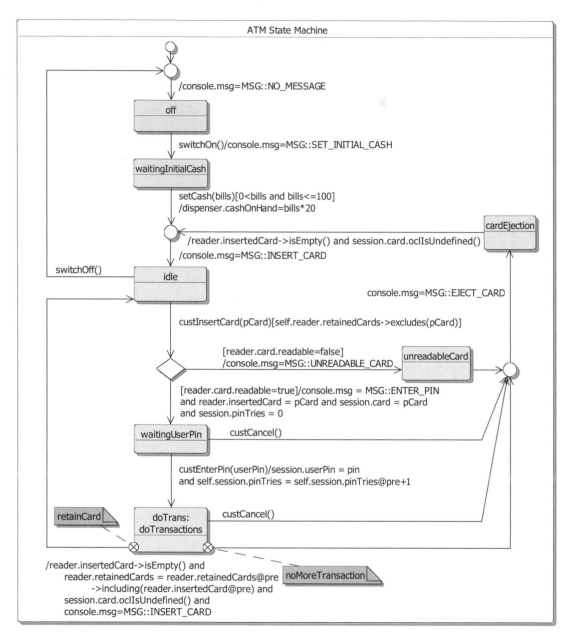

FIGURE 10.4   The top-level ATM state machine.

This internal action is defined by an OCL postcondition that finds an unused transaction (type=NONE), initializes it to the user's choice of transaction, links it to the session, and resets the receiptPrinted attribute in the Printer class to false:

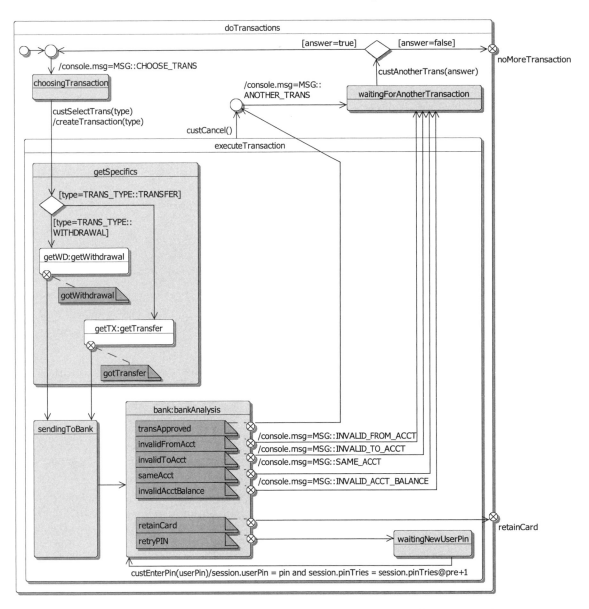

FIGURE 10.5   UML state machine for a session (a sequence of transactions).

```
let tr = Transaction.allInstances()
        ->any(t:Transaction | t.type=TRANS_TYPE::NONE)
in  self.session.tran = tr
    and tr.type = tranType
    and printer.receiptPrinted = false
```

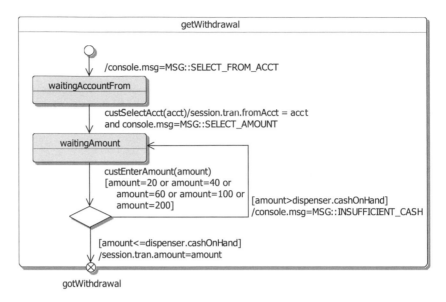

FIGURE 10.6 UML state machine for getting Withdrawal details.

- Next, the system interacts with the customer to get specific information for a withdrawal transaction (the getWithdrawal state machine is shown in Figure 10.6) or a transfer transaction (the getTransfer state machine is shown in Figure 10.7), and then sends all the information to the bank (card, PIN code, and the transaction-specific details).

- The bank state models the expected behavior of the bank (the bankAnalysis state machine is shown in Figure 10.8). This has seven possible outcomes: transApproved indicates a successful transaction, and the other six outcomes are the unsuccessful cases.

- After any of the above outcomes, except for retrying a PIN and retaining the card, the system asks if the customer wishes to perform another transaction. If the customer wants to do so, then the state machine loops back to the beginning of a new transaction.

Figure 10.8 shows the bankAnalysis state machine that models the behavior of the bank. This has seven possible outcomes:

retainCard: The PIN code is false and this was the last possible attempt, so the card is retained.

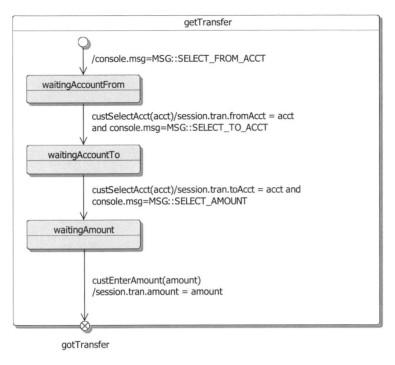

FIGURE 10.7   UML state machine for getting Transfer details.

retryPIN: The PIN code is false and the PIN try limit has not been not reached, so the user is invited to try another PIN value.

invalidFromAcct: The FromAccount of a withdrawal or transfer transaction is invalid.

invalidAcctBalance: The balance in the selected account is not sufficient to perform the transaction.

invalidToAcct: The ToAccount of a transfer transaction is invalid.

sameAcct: The same account has been chosen as both the source and destination account (fromAcct and toAcct) of the transfer transaction.

transApproved: The transaction has been approved by the bank, and funds have been transferred or withdrawn.

The transitions in the bankAnalysis state machine call two internal actions (one for each transaction type) that formalize the actions that occur when the bank authorizes the transaction. The doWithdrawal action models

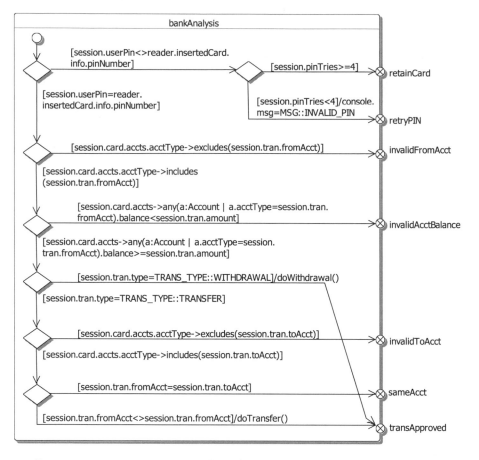

FIGURE 10.8   UML state machine for handling responses from the bank.

the effect of a successful withdrawal and is defined by the OCL postcondition:

```
let fromAcct = session.card.accts
            ->any(a:Account |
                   a.acctType=session.tran.fromAcct)
in
    printer.receiptPrinted = true and
    fromAcct.balance = fromAcct.balance@pre -
                        session.tran.amount and
    dispenser.cashOnHand = dispenser.cashOnHand@pre
                        - session.tran.amount
```

This postcondition decreases the balance of the selected account by the amount withdrawn. It also decreases the amount of cash remaining in the cash dispenser by the same amount. We do not explicitly model the bills that are output to the customer, but we do set the receipt attribute in the Printer class to true to indicate that a receipt has been printed.

The doTransfer action models the effect of a successful transfer transaction and is defined by the OCL postcondition:

```
let toAcct = session.card.accts
            ->any(a:Account | a.acctType=session.tran.toAcct),
    fromAcct = session.card.accts
            ->any(a:Account | a.acctType=session.tran.fromAcct)
in
    printer.receiptPrinted = true and
    toAcct.balance = toAcct.balance@pre
                        + session.tran.amount and
    fromAcct.balance = fromAcct.balance@pre
                        - session.tran.amount
```

This postcondition decreases the selected fromAcct balance and increases the selected toAcct balance by the amount user enters. The Printer class's receipt attribute is set to true to indicate that a receipt has been printed.

10.2.3 Comparing the Design and Test Models

It is interesting to compare our class diagrams designed for test generation purposes with the design-level class diagram by Bjork.

Figure 10.9 shows the design class diagram from Bjork's web pages. This diagram gives the class hierarchies for the example ATM implementation. Our class diagram, developed for testing purposes, is much simpler than the design class diagram (22 classes simplified down to 10). Roughly, the test model is a subset of the design model. The main differences are:

* Our diagram does not contain the classes related to the "Deposit" and "Inquiry" transactions (Envelope acceptor, Deposit, and Inquiry classes).

* Various classes have been abstracted or managed as attributes in other classes: Money, Balances, Log, NetworkToBank, and so on.

* Last but not least, in our test-oriented class diagram, class attributes are restricted to compulsory information, and the class methods concern only user actions (the "events") on the SUT class, internal actions, or operations used on the data classes to set up the context.

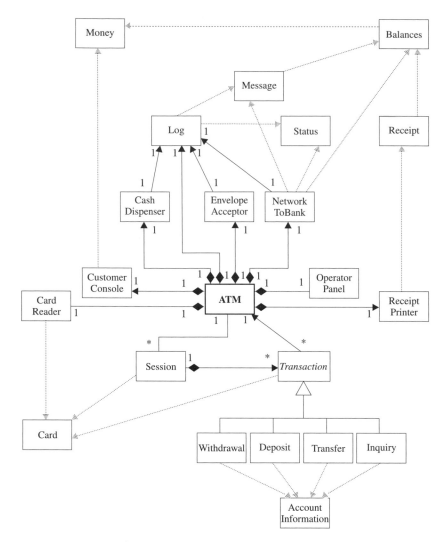

FIGURE 10.9 Design class diagram of the example ATM system.

Key Point A class diagram of a test model can be viewed as an abstraction of the design-level class diagram. This test model is focused on the SUT class, so only needs to include the attributes and associations relevant to that class.

On the other hand, our state machine for the ATM class (including all the submachines that it uses) is larger and considerably more detailed than the three simple state machines designed by Bjork. Our state machines have a total of 20 states and 50 transitions, while Bjork's three have a total of 14 states and 23 transitions.

This is because his state machines give a semiformal sketch of the behavior and do not specify the details of each kind of transaction; our state machines have to be detailed enough to be executable, so they go a little deeper into the details of each kind of transaction (just Withdraw and Transfer) and use a more formal notation to describe the effect of each transition (OCL rather than English).

> **Key Point**   The state machines of the test model formalize the expected SUT behavior that is defined informally in the state machines of the design model.

10.3 GENERATING TEST CASES

Our test objectives for this ATM validation project are to validate the implementation of the withdrawal and transfer transactions, including success and failure scenarios (e.g., unreadable cards, incorrect PINs, transactions declined by the bank). To configure our test generator (LTG/UML), we first need to set up an initial state for test generation and then to choose the model coverage criteria to be used.

10.3.1 Initial State for Test Generation

For our test campaign, we set up a test scenario with two cards that have two accounts each. Figure 10.10 shows a UML object diagram that describes all the objects used in this test scenario and the relationships among them. The test assumptions include testing one session with a readable or unreadable card, and within that session, zero or more transactions (withdrawal or transfer). This means that we need just one session instance but several transaction instances.

The object diagram is designed to give all the required test data for testing the combinations of possible behavior in the dynamic model:

1. There is one ATM object with all its components: one customer console, one printer, one cash dispenser, and one card reader.
2. There is only one session object because each test will be within one session, possibly with several transactions.
3. We consider three card instances: two are readable and one unreadable. The readable cards make it possible to test various combinations of accounts associated with those cards.

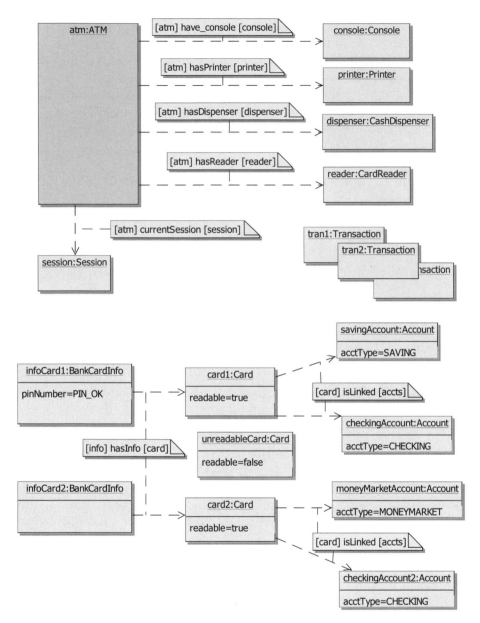

FIGURE 10.10   ATM object diagram, showing the test scenario.

4. There are three transaction instances (tran1, tran2, and tran3) in the object diagram, which make it possible to perform up to three transactions during a session.

The initial values of attributes may be set either in the ATM class diagram (see Figure 10.2) or in the instance diagram. If we want to initialize an attribute so that all instances have the same value (e.g., the attribute *type* in the class *Transaction*, which is always initialized to *NONE*), then it is best to do this in the class diagram. If we want every instance to have a different value for an attribute (e.g., the acctType field in the Account class), then this is best done in the object diagram. If most instances have the same value but a few are different, it is useful to set a default value in the class diagram and override it for those few instances in the object diagram. We require all attributes of all objects to be fully instantiated in the initial state, so it is an error to omit the initial value in both the class diagram and the object diagram.

> **Key Point**   The initial state is set up by the object diagram. The instances of each class, and the attribute values of those instances, are directly related to the project test objectives.

10.3.2 Generation of Test Cases

To generate the test cases, we decide to test all the explicit and implicit transitions of the layered state machines (all-transitions coverage). Each generated path through the state machine will be tested independently and with a preamble that starts up the ATM machine and a postamble that shuts down the ATM. For data coverage, we choose to test the maximum value of the cash parameter of the setCash user action, the minimum value (20 dollars) for the custEnteredAmount user action, and all-values for the yes_no parameter of the custAnotherTrans event.

With this test generation configuration, 31 test cases are generated by LTG to cover the 50 transitions (explicit and implicit) of the layered state machines. The generated test suite is shown in Tables 10.1, 10.2, and 10.3. All the method calls are applied to the main SUT object, atm, but we omit the atm. prefix of each call to save space.

10.3.3 Discussion

This all-transitions coverage gives an interesting test suite that fires each transaction at least once and explores most of the behavior of the model. When comparing this generated test suite with the initial functional test cases for the example ATM system manually designed by Bjork, we see that all the relevant manual test cases are covered by the model-based generated test suite. The manual test cases that are not covered are the ones that con-

TABLE 10.1   ATM Test Suite (part 1 of 3)

No.	Test Case
	Testing the ATM operator facilities
T1	switchOn(); setCash(100); switchOff()
	Testing card insertion and reading
T2	switchOn(); setCash(100); custInsertCard(card1); custCancel(); switchOff()
T3	switchOn(), setCash(100); custInsertCard(unreadableCard); switchOff()
	Testing initial PIN entry
T4	switchOn(); setCash(100); custInsertCard(card1); custEnterPin(PIN_KO); custCancel(); switchOff()
	Testing PIN reentry
T5	switchOn(); setCash(100); custInsertCard(card1); custEnterPin(PIN_KO); custSelectTrans(WITHDRAWAL); custSelectAcct(CHECKING); custEnterAmount(20); custEnterPin(PIN_OK); custAnotherTrans(false); switchOff()
T6	switchOn(); setCash(100); custInsertCard(card1); custEnterPin(PIN_KO); custSelectTrans(TRANSFER); custSelectAcct(CHECKING); custSelectAcct(SAVING); custEnterAmount(20); custEnterPin(PIN_OK); custAnotherTrans(false); switchOff()
T7	switchOn(); setCash(100); custInsertCard(card1); custEnterPin(PIN_KO); custSelectTrans(WITHDRAWAL); custSelectAcct(CHECKING); custEnterAmount(20); custEnterPin(PIN_KO); custEnterPin(PIN_OK); custCancel(); custAnotherTrans(false); switchOff()
	Testing card retention
T8	switchOn(); setCash(100); custInsertCard(card1); custEnterPin(PIN_KO); custSelectTrans(WITHDRAWAL); custSelectAcct(CHECKING); custEnterAmount(20); custEnterPin(PIN_KO); custEnterPin(PIN_KO); switchOff()
	Testing transaction chaining
T9	switchOn(); setCash(100); custInsertCard(card1); custEnterPin(PIN_OK); custSelectTrans(TRANSFER); custSelectAcct(CHECKING); custSelectAcct(SAVING); custEnterAmount(20); custAnotherTrans(true); custCancel(); switchOff()
T10	switchOn(); setCash(100); custInsertCard(card1); custEnterPin(PIN_OK); custSelectTrans(WITHDRAWAL); custSelectAcct(CHECKING); custEnterAmount(20); custCancel(); custAnotherTrans(true); custCancel(); switchOff()

cern the inquiry and deposit transactions (we omitted these from our model) and one that verifies the connection to the bank (we made an abstraction of that). So in this case, the all-transitions coverage criterion applied to our ATM state machines gives the same level of coverage as the manually designed test suite.

TABLE 10.2   ATM Test Suite (part 2 of 3)

No.	Test Case
	Testing transaction choice
T11	switchOn(); setCash(100); custInsertCard(card1); custEnterPin(PIN_OK); custSelectTrans(TRANSFER); custCancel(); custAnotherTrans(false); switchOff()
T12	switchOn(); setCash(100); custInsertCard(card1); custEnterPin(PIN_OK); custSelectTrans(WITHDRAWAL); custCancel(); custAnotherTrans(false); switchOff()
	Testing Withdrawal data gathering
T13	switchOn(); setCash(100); custInsertCard(card2); custEnterPin(PIN_KO); custSelectTrans(WITHDRAWAL); custSelectAcct(MONEYMARKET); custCancel(); custAnotherTrans(false); switchOff()
T14	switchOn(); setCash(100); custInsertCard(card2); custEnterPin(PIN_KO); custSelectTrans(WITHDRAWAL); custSelectAcct(CHECKING); custCancel(); custAnotherTrans(false); switchOff()
T15	switchOn(); setCash(100); custInsertCard(card1); custEnterPin(PIN_KO); custSelectTrans(WITHDRAWAL); custSelectAcct(CHECKING); custEnterAmount(20); custCancel(); switchOff()
T16	switchOn(); setCash(100); custInsertCard(card1); custEnterPin(PIN_OK); custSelectTrans(WITHDRAWAL); custSelectAcct(CHECKING); custEnterAmount(20); custAnotherTrans(false); switchOff()
	Testing Transfer data gathering
T17	switchOn(); setCash(100); custInsertCard(card1); custEnterPin(PIN_OK); custSelectTrans(TRANSFER); custSelectAcct(CHECKING); custCancel(); custAnotherTrans(false); switchOff()
T18	switchOn(); setCash(100); custInsertCard(card1); custEnterPin(PIN_OK); custSelectTrans(TRANSFER); custSelectAcct(SAVING); custCancel(); custAnotherTrans(false); switchOff()
T19	switchOn(); setCash(100); custInsertCard(card1); custEnterPin(PIN_OK); custSelectTrans(TRANSFER); custSelectAcct(SAVING); custSelectAcct(CHECKING); custCancel(); custAnotherTrans(false); switchOff()
T20	switchOn(); setCash(100); custInsertCard(card1); custEnterPin(PIN_KO); custSelectTrans(TRANSFER); custSelectAcct(CHECKING); custSelectAcct(SAVING); custEnterAmount(20); custCancel(); switchOff()
T21	switchOn(); setCash(100); custInsertCard(card1); custEnterPin(PIN_OK); custSelectTrans(TRANSFER); custSelectAcct(CHECKING); custSelectAcct(SAVING); custEnterAmount(20); custAnotherTrans(false); switchOff()

However, the following several points are worth discussing.

- We chose to generate single-purpose tests, which produces lots of short tests rather than a few long tests that cover many test targets. This

TABLE 10.3 ATM Test Suite (part 3 of 3)

No.	Test Case
	Testing transaction errors
T22	switchOn(); setCash(1); custInsertCard(card1); custEnterPin(PIN_OK); custSelectTrans(WITHDRAWAL); custSelectAcct(CHECKING); custEnterAmount(40); custCancel(); custAnotherTrans(false); switchOff()
T23	switchOn(); setCash(1); custInsertCard(card1); custEnterPin(PIN_KO); custSelectTrans(WITHDRAWAL); custSelectAcct(CHECKING); custEnterAmount(40); custEnterPin(PIN_OK); custAnotherTrans(false); switchOff()
T24	switchOn(); setCash(100); custInsertCard(card1); custEnterPin(PIN_OK); custSelectTrans(TRANSFER); custSelectAcct(CHECKING); custSelectAcct(CHECKING); custEnterAmount(20); custAnotherTrans(false); switchOff()
T25	switchOn(); setCash(100); custInsertCard(card1); custEnterPin(PIN_KO); custSelectTrans(TRANSFER); custSelectAcct(CHECKING); custSelectAcct(CHECKING); custEnterAmount(20); custEnterPin(PIN_OK); custAnotherTrans(false); switchOff()
T26	switchOn(); setCash(100); custInsertCard(card1); custEnterPin(PIN_OK); custSelectTrans(WITHDRAWAL); custSelectAcct(MONEY_MARKET); custEnterAmount(20); custAnotherTrans(false); switchOff()
T27	switchOn(); setCash(100); custInsertCard(card1); custEnterPin(PIN_KO); custSelectTrans(WITHDRAWAL); custSelectAcct(MONEY_MARKET); custEnterAmount(20); custEnterPin(PIN_OK); custAnotherTrans(false); switchOff()
T28	switchOn(); setCash(100); custInsertCard(card1); custEnterPin(PIN_OK); custSelectTrans(TRANSFER); custSelectAcct(CHECKING); custSelectAcct(MONEY_MARKET); custEnterAmount(20); custAnotherTrans(false); switchOff()
T29	switchOn(); setCash(100); custInsertCard(card1); custEnterPin(PIN_KO); custSelectTrans(TRANSFER); custSelectAcct(CHECKING); custSelectAcct(MONEY_MARKET); custEnterAmount(20); custEnterPin(PIN_OK); custAnotherTrans(false); switchOff()
	Testing the remaining customer cancellation options
T30	switchOn(); setCash(100); custInsertCard(card1); custEnterPin(PIN_OK); custSelectTrans(TRANSFER); custCancel(); custCancel(); switchOff()
T31	switchOn(); setCash(100); custInsertCard(card1); custEnterPin(PIN_KO); custSelectTrans(WITHDRAWAL); custSelectAcct(CHECKING); custEnterAmount(20); custCancel(); custAnotherTrans(false); switchOff()

means that the preamble operations are repeated in several test cases, so the test suite is larger than a minimal transition tour using the Chinese postman algorithm. On the other hand, an advantage of these single-purpose tests is that each test is directly linked to a particular test purpose (testing some aspect of a certain transaction) and to a small number of requirements. Also, each test is relatively independent of the other tests, which can make failure analysis easier.

- The main weakness of this generated test suite is the absence of transaction chaining. When the user asks for another transaction, the test generator takes the [answer=true] transition into the choosingTransaction state of the second transaction, but then sees that all transitions there have already been covered, so chooses the shortest path to the final state, using the custCancel() event.

Now we discuss several ways to make this generated test suite more complete.

BOUNDARY ANALYSIS

We can apply the minimum *and* maximum criteria for the custEnterAmount input parameter (only the minimum value was chosen before). This adds withdrawal tests that call custEnterAmount(200) (which tests the withdrawal limit of $200) and custEnterAmount(16777200)—the maximum integer currently managed by LTG/UML—within a transfer transaction. This maximum criterion for the amount parameter of the custEnterAmount operation adds 18 test cases because for each test where custEnterAmount(20) is called, the same test is called with either custEnterAmount(200) or custEnterAmount(16777200).

MULTIPLE TRANSACTIONS

There are several ways to generate tests that perform multiple transactions within a session, such as chaining a transfer after a withdrawal. One way to generate such tests is to use structural coverage criteria that go around loops a given number of times (this is an extension of the all-round-trips coverage criteria discussed in Section 4.1). However, this typically results in a combinatorial explosion between the various branches and error cases of each loop. For example, if we are testing a transfer followed by a withdrawal, we end up testing all combinations of transfer errors and withdrawal errors, which is too many.

A better way to control the chaining of transactions is to define some explicit test case specifications (see Chapter 4). For example, we might specify that we want a test that reaches the state where

```
savingAccount.balance=0 and checkingAccount.balance=0
```

This would force the test to withdraw all money from both the accounts associated with card1 (see Figure 10.10 in Section 10.3.1). Or we might explicitly state that we want to generate two nominal test cases: one that does a withdrawal followed by a transfer and another that does a transfer followed by a withdrawal.

Two or three explicit test case specifications like this would extend the all-transitions test suite and give us a reasonable test suite for the ATM.

> **Key Point**   Test generation is always a tradeoff between test coverage and the number of generated tests. Structural model coverage criteria are systematic and can deliver many test cases. Therefore, a good basic model coverage (all-transitions with boundary values, for example) can be complemented by a few explicit test case specifications or manually defined test cases that address specific needs.

10.4 GENERATING EXECUTABLE TEST SCRIPTS

Next we want to execute the generated tests on the simulated ATM implementation provided by Bjork. This implementation provides a Java GUI that simulates the look of a real ATM machine. Input is mostly via mouse clicks on a simulated keypad, so it is necessary to click six times to enter the transfer amount $123.45 (5 digits, followed by ENTER).

We designed our ATM model at a higher level than this, with the intention of testing it at a more abstract level. To make it easier to execute the abstract tests, we implement an alternative text-based user interface on top of the ATM simulation and use the public domain expect tool to interact with that command line interface and check the correctness of the SUT responses. The expect tool is available from NIST[4] and is basically a library of TCL procedures for sending input strings to interactive programs and searching their output for expected results.

In other words, we again use a mixed approach to concretize our test cases: we transform each abstract test sequence into an expect test script, and we add an adaptation layer around the SUT code to make it easy to interact with. The modular structure of the ATM implementation makes it reasonably easy to add the command line interface. The total ATM implementation (GUI and core functionality) comprises over 2500 noncomment lines of code, and only another 210 lines are needed to add the command line interface.

We do not go into the details of how the abstract test cases can be transformed into expect scripts because the process is similar to what we did in

---

[4] See *http://expect.nist.gov*, but we use the Windows version of expect that is included in the DejaGnu open source testing framework, available from *http://www.gnu.org/software/dejagnu*.

Sections 8.2 and 9.5.1. As well as transforming the syntax of the calls into TCL, an important step is to map each MSG constant of our model into the actual message that we expect from the ATM. For example:

```
NO_MESSAGE          →   "shut down"
SET_INITIAL_CASH    →   "number of*bills"
INSERT_CARD         →   "insert a card"
```

Listing 10.1 shows the expect test script that is produced for test T16. It starts by changing directory and starting the SUT by running java ATMCmdLine. Then it has a sequence of send and expect commands. Each send command sends some input to the SUT, such as a digit followed by a RETURN key (\r), while each expect command scans the SUT output looking for a given string or pattern. For example, the pattern "number of*bills" (the wildcard character * matches any sequence of characters) will match output like:

```
Enter number of $20 bills:
```

If an expect command does not find the expected output after waiting for 10 seconds, it calls the fail procedure, which we define to print an error message and exit with a nonzero error status.

10.5 EXECUTING THE TESTS

Listings 10.2 and 10.3 show the output produced when we execute the test script T16.exp. The inputs sent to the ATM by the expect test script are shown in bold.

The first time we executed all the tests on the ATM implementation, most of them failed. A little investigation showed that the main problem was some typos in the transformation from abstract tests into expect test scripts: the transfer command had been entered as 1 rather than 3; the unreadable card was numbered 1 rather than 0; and the string "Please enter your PIN" was expected after a PIN error, whereas the ATM implementation actually displays "Please re-enter your PIN".

We also had to correct a difference in the abstraction level of the model and the ATM implementation. In our model, the parameter of the custEnterAmount event is the number of dollars that the customer wishes to withdraw or transfer, whereas in the ATM implementation, the withdrawal amount is entered by choosing from a fixed menu of amounts (1:$20, 2:$40,

LISTING 10.1   Generated executable expect test script T16.exp.

```
$ more ATM_custEnterAmount_5.exp
# LTG Generated tests
# LTG version number : 2_2
# Export date : 30/06/06 12:31

# Define what to do when correct output is not detected
proc fail {} {send_user "\nTEST FAILED!!!\n"; exit 1}

# Start up the SUT then start testing it
cd ../bin
spawn java ATMCmdLine
expect timeout fail "Welcome to the ATM Command Line"
expect timeout fail "number of*bills"

#       setCash(100)
send "100\r"
expect timeout fail "insert a card"

#       custInsertCard(card1)
send "1\r"
expect timeout fail "card number"
send "1\r"
expect timeout fail "Please enter your PIN"

#       custEnterPin(PIN_OK)
send "42\r"
expect timeout fail "choose transaction type"

#       custSelectTrans(WITHDRAWAL)
send "1\r"
expect timeout fail "Account*from"

#       custSelectAcct(CHECKING)
send "1\r"
expect timeout fail "Amount"

#       custEnterAmount(20)
send "1\r"
expect timeout fail "another transaction"

#       custAnotherTrans(FALSE)
send "2\r"
expect timeout fail "insert a card"

#       switchOff()
send "\r"
expect timeout fail "ATM*shut down"
```

LISTING 10.2   Execution of the T16.exp ATM test script (part 1 of 2).

```
$ expect T16.exp
spawn java ATMCmdLine
Welcome to the ATM Command Line User Interface.
Enter number of $20 bills: 100
Enter 1 to insert a card, or RETURN to shut down.
Enter a number (or CANCEL): 1
Enter your card number (1..2): 1
Display Cleared.
Please enter your PIN
Then press ENTER

Enter a number (or CANCEL): 42
Display Cleared.
Display Cleared.
Please choose transaction type
1) Withdrawal
2) Deposit
3) Transfer
4) Balance Inquiry
Enter a number (or CANCEL): 1
Display Cleared.
Display Cleared.
Account to withdraw from
1) Checking
2) Savings
3) Money Market
Enter a number (or CANCEL): 1
Display Cleared.
Display Cleared.
Amount of cash to withdraw
1) $20
2) $40
3) $60
4) $100
5) $200
Enter a number (or CANCEL): 1
Display Cleared.
Display Cleared.
```

3:$60, 4:$100, and 5:$200), so the actual input number is in the range 1–5. This means that custEnterAmount(20) in our abstract tests must be translated to an input menu choice of 1, custEnterAmount(40) must be translated to 2, and so on.

LISTING 10.3   Execution of the T16.exp ATM test script (part 2 of 2).

```
LOG: Message:   WITHDRAW CARD# 1 TRANS# 1 FROM  0 NO TO $20.00
LOG: Response:  SUCCESS
Output $20.00
LOG: Dispensed: $20.00
Mon Jul 03 02:24:46 NZST 2006
First National Bank of Podunk
ATM #42 Gordon College
CARD 1 TRANS #1
WITHDRAWAL FROM: CHKG
AMOUNT: $20.00
TOTAL BAL: $80.00
AVAILABLE: $80.00
Display Cleared.
Would you like to do another transaction?
1) Yes
2) No
Enter a number (or CANCEL): 2
Display Cleared.
Card Ejected.
Enter 1 to insert a card, or RETURN to shut down.
Enter a number (or CANCEL):
ATM has been shut down.
$
```

In our first transformation of the abstract tests into expect scripts, we forgot this difference, so many tests failed. To fix this, we simply modified the transformation templates to generate numbers from 1 to 5 rather than dollar amounts and then reran the transformation process to produce an updated suite of expect scripts.

After we made these corrections to the transformation phase, all the tests passed when executed on the ATM implementation, except test T8, which tests that three bad PIN entries will cause the card to be retained. Listing 10.4 shows the relevant parts of the output from this failed test. The test fails because it is expecting the output string Card Retained after the third entry of the incorrect PIN (9999), but we can see that the SUT is actually prompting for the user to enter the PIN a fourth time.

Upon investigation of the ATM source code, we found that it allows three *retries* of the PIN entry, which means that a total of four incorrect PIN entries are required to cause the card to be retained. In contrast, our interpretation of the informal requirements was that the three PIN tries should include the initial PIN entry, so the card should be retained after the second unsuccessful retry. That is, the card should be retained after three incorrect

LISTING 10.4   Execution of the failing T8.exp ATM test script.

```
$ expect T8.exp
...
Please enter your PIN
Then press ENTER
Enter a number (or CANCEL): 9999
...
Amount of cash to withdraw
1) $20
2) $40
3) $60
4) $100
5) $200
Enter a number (or CANCEL): 1
Display Cleared.
Display Cleared.

LOG: Message:   WITHDRAW CARD# 1 TRANS# 1 FROM  0 NO TO $20.00
LOG: Response:  INVALID PIN
Display Cleared.
PIN was incorrect
Please re-enter your PIN
Then press ENTER

Enter a number (or CANCEL): 9999
Display Cleared.
Display Cleared.

LOG: Message:   WITHDRAW CARD# 1 TRANS# 1 FROM  0 NO TO $20.00
LOG: Response:  INVALID PIN
Display Cleared.
PIN was incorrect
Please re-enter your PIN
Then press ENTER

Enter a number (or CANCEL): 9999
Display Cleared.
Display Cleared.

LOG: Message:   WITHDRAW CARD# 1 TRANS# 1 FROM  0 NO TO $20.00
LOG: Response:  INVALID PIN
Display Cleared.
PIN was incorrect
Please re-enter your PIN
Then press ENTER

Enter a number (or CANCEL):
TEST FAILED!!!
```

PINs have been entered. The real banks that we use certainly follow this interpretation, as we know from bitter experience. So we conclude that the failure of test T8 does expose a real SUT error, or at least a different interpretation of the requirements. The error can easily be fixed in the ATM implementation by changing a loop in the `src/atm/Transaction.java` file to allow only two PIN retries rather than three. After this change, all tests pass.

10.6 SUMMARY

UML can be used to express test models as well as analysis models and design models. Compared with Bjork's analysis and design models, the class diagram of our ATM test model is considerably simpler because we can omit many classes and attributes that are not needed for testing. On the other hand, we make the test model more precise by adding some OCL invariants within the class diagram; this ensures that we test only the system states that conform to the requirements.

The state machines of our test model formalize the expected behavior that was defined informally by the state machines of the design model. Formalizing the behavior means that our state machines are more complex than Bjork's and use OCL guards and postconditions, rather than informal English descriptions.

We define the initial state of our test scenario with a UML object diagram. The instances of each class and the attribute values of those instances are chosen to fulfill the project test objectives.

10.7 FURTHER READING

See Bjork's ATM web page *http://www.math-cs.gordon.edu/courses/cs211/ ATMExample/index.html* for the full analysis and design UML models of the ATM system, as well as the manually designed test suite and the Java implementation of the ATM simulator.

We want to thank Russell Bjork for giving us permission to use his ATM material in this chapter.

## CHAPTER 11

PUTTING IT INTO PRACTICE

This chapter discusses several practical issues and techniques for adopting model-based testing. We start with the prerequisites of model-based testing and then go through a taxonomy of the possible approaches with the goal of helping you to choose a good approach for your needs. Section 11.3 deals with people and training issues; Sections 11.4 and 11.5 discuss how model-based testing can fit into agile development processes and the UML unified process. Section 11.6 contains some final conclusions.

11.1 PREREQUISITES FOR MODEL-BASED TESTING

We start this chapter by briefly reviewing the desirable prerequisites for the successful application of model-based testing.

Someone enthusiastic: Human factors are perhaps the most important factors for the successful adoption of any practice. It is important to have

Note: The launch of the Mars Reconnaissance Orbiter (MRO) in August 2005. The MRO successfully put itself into Mars orbit on March 10, 2006. Courtesy Lockheed Martin.

some high-level management support for the adoption of model-based testing, as well as some grassroots enthusiasm for model-based testing among the team who will put it into practice.

Test execution maturity: As discussed in Section 2.4, model-based testing tools are sophisticated testing tools since they automate the test *design* stage and this usually implies that the test execution phase is already automated. A testing team who has little experience with automated test execution might be wise to gain experience with an automated test execution approach (e.g., scripting or keyword-based testing) before using model-based testing.

Modeling skills: Model-based testing requires models! Fortunately, it is not necessary to be an expert in modeling notations before commencing with model-based testing. But it is helpful to have some experience with designing interfaces and choosing good levels of abstraction. Most programmers and system analysts exercise these skills every day, so many of them can quickly adapt to designing models.

People who are familiar with UML modeling may have a head start in this direction, but we should not assume that everyone who has designed a UML class diagram or written a UML use case can instantly write models for testing. The models for model-based testing are more precise than most UML models and require detailed modeling of the SUT behavior. Developing these kinds of models is more similar to programming than to designing UML use cases and class diagrams.

Depending upon the modeling notation chosen, some training may be required to learn the notation and to gain experience with choosing a good level of abstraction for testing purposes. This brings us to the next point.

Access to training, tools, and experts: As with all new technologies, it is important to have ready access to training and expert advice, particularly during the first pilot project stage and the first one or two real uses of model-based testing. Having a model-based testing expert who can give a little advice on the best ways to apply model-based testing to your project or review a test model and test selection criteria can make the adoption process much more efficient and effective.

At the time of writing, we are not aware of any independent training companies who offer courses specifically on model-based testing. It is usually just covered briefly as part of a more general testing course. So training in model-based testing usually comes from the vendor of whichever model-based testing tool you purchase. This has the advantage that the training can be focused on the particular notation, modeling style, and test selection criteria that you need for that tool, but the disadvantage is that it may not cover the whole field of model-based testing. One objective of this book is to give a broader overview of the field, covering a variety of approaches and styles of tools. We hope that this will be a useful background for more specific training courses.

The right kind of application: Some applications are more suited to model-based testing than others. Model-based testing is most likely to be cost-effective when the *execution* of the generated tests can also be automated. If your application has to be tested manually because the test steps require human interaction, then the cost of that manual testing may dominate any cost savings of model-based testing. If you do decide to use model-based testing in combination with manual test execution (like our Qui-Donc example in Section 5.1), your goal will usually be to minimize the costs of manual test execution by generating a *small* test suite while maintaining some measure of coverage.

The next section gives some guidelines for classifying your SUT into a model-based testing taxonomy. This can help you to decide whether model-based testing would be useful for your SUT and which approaches would be suitable.

11.2 SELECTING A MODEL-BASED TESTING APPROACH

To get an overview of the different approaches to model-based testing and an understanding of which kinds of techniques and tools are likely to suit your needs, it is useful to classify the possible approaches into a taxonomy.

Figure 11.1 shows a taxonomy of model-based testing with seven main dimensions, taken from [UPL06]. The seven dimensions are clustered into three groups according to whether they affect the model, the test generation process, or the execution of the generated tests. We will discuss each dimension in turn. Appendix C gives a list of some currently available model-based testing tools and shows how they fit into this taxonomy.

The *subject* of the model is the SUT, its environment, or a combination of the two. You must decide whether the main goal of your modeling is to describe the behavior of the SUT, to describe the external environment of the SUT (e.g., a statistical model of the expected usage of the SUT), or to model both of these. In all the case studies in this book, we use an SUT model

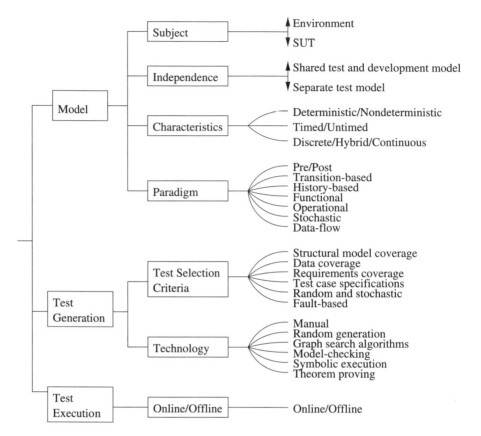

FIGURE II.I A taxonomy of model-based testing.

because this gives us strong oracle checking. But in large applications, it is often useful to use an environment model as well to direct the exploration of the SUT model. For example, the Spec Explorer tool allows you to specify a state-dependent priority expression for each action, and this allows you to define an expected usage profile of the SUT actions and focus your testing on that usage profile.

The *independence* dimension reflects the source of the test model. If it is designed directly from the informal requirements specifically for testing purposes, by a team that is independent of the SUT developers, then there will be a high degree of independence between the test model and the SUT implementation, and the testing is more likely to discover significant errors. At the other extreme, reusing too much of the SUT development models for testing purposes can weaken the independence of the test suite, as discussed in Section 2.3.

The third dimension describes the *characteristics* of the model, which are related to the characteristics of the SUT that you wish to test. When considering using model-based testing on a particular SUT, it is important to consider these questions:

- Is the SUT behavior deterministic or nondeterministic? Does the model have to be nondeterministic as well, or can you hide the system under test's nondeterminism in the adapter code?

- Does the SUT have real-time constraints that you want to test? Are these simple timeouts on each operation, which could be checked within the adapter code, or are they more complex global timing constraints that need to be included in the model?

- Will the data in the test cases be discrete or continuous or a mixture of both? Is it reasonable to discretize the continuous data in the model, or should the model reflect the continuous nature of the SUT?

The answers to these questions will determine the characteristics of your test model, which will in turn influence your choice of model-based testing tool. For example, there are more model-based testing tools available for discrete models than for continuous models because all tools handle the simpler discrete cases, whereas only some of them handle continuous variables. The case is similar for nondeterministic models and for real-time models.

The model *paradigm* is the style of the model and the notation used to write it. The various paradigms and notations are discussed in Section 3.1.1. Recall that two of the most common paradigms for SUT models are transition-based models and pre/post models. Broadly speaking, the transition-based notations are best for control-oriented applications, and the pre/post notations are best for data-intensive applications. Section 3.1.2 gives some suggestions for choosing between these.

Test selection criteria is the subject of Chapter 4. Figure 11.1 shows six kinds of test selection criteria, and a good model-based testing tool should support several of these. The more the better, because you rely on test selection criteria to help you generate the kind of test suites that you want; and the more different test selection criteria you can use, the more control you have over the test generation.

The test generation *technology* should not be of major concern to a user of model-based testing, unless it is manual, which means you must generate tests from the model by hand! The ideal is for the technology to be hidden under the hood of the model-based testing tool and to work without human intervention. However, it is worth being aware of the strengths and limitations of each technology.

Random generation is the easiest to implement, but it may take longer to reach a given level of model coverage than with more sophisticated algorithms. However, random testing is surprisingly powerful [DN84, Gut99] and is a particularly good technology to use when you want to generate a large or infinite sequence of constantly varying tests from your model—the SUT model is useful as the oracle for those tests.

The next three technologies—graph search algorithms, model-checking, and symbolic execution (or constraint systems)—rely on various kinds of exhaustive analyses of the model, so it is usually necessary to keep the graph reasonably small or limit the size of the data domains to ensure that test generation can be done within reasonable time and memory limits. The theorem-proving technology is more independent of the size of data domains, but since theorem proving is undecidable in general, an automatic prover usually has a limit on the time that it will search for a test, so it may fail to satisfy some test targets that exceed the time limit.

The last dimension is whether to do *online* or *offline* testing. Online testing is where tests are executed as they are generated, so the model-based testing tool is tightly coupled to the SUT. Offline testing decouples the generation and execution phases, so the test execution can be completely independent of the model-based test generation process.

This book contains several examples of each of these. Online testing is particularly good for testing nondeterministic SUTs and for long-running test sessions, such as overnight testing based on random traversal of a model. Offline testing has the advantage that it can perform a deeper analysis of the model to generate a small but powerful test suite, and the generated test suite is a stand-alone product that can be inspected, used repeatedly for regression purposes, put into a test management system, and so on.

Table 11.1 shows how the case studies in this book fit into this taxonomy. We omit the Model Subject column because all our case studies used SUT models, and the Model Independence column because all the case studies used a model designed specifically for testing (except that our eTheater and ATM case studies reused parts of the class diagrams from the development model).

The Qui-Donc model is deterministic, untimed, and discrete, even though the Qui-Donc system includes some timing requirements (the timeouts of 6 seconds and 20 seconds). This is because we used abstraction to hide the timing aspects. Even if we had included some of this timeout information in the model, as suggested in Section 5.1, the model would still effectively be an untimed model because the output messages, $ENTER_6$ and $ENTER_{20}$, are just symbolic constants and no special timed semantics is needed for the model. Checking that the SUT has the correct timeouts can all be

TABLE 11.1   Classification of Our Case Studies According to the Taxonomy

Case Study		Model Characteristics	Paradigm	Test Selection Criteria	Technology	Online
1.3	Smartcard	U,D,D	Transition	Struct	Graph	Off
5.1	Qui-Donc	U,D,D	Transition	Struct	Graph	Off
5.2	ZLive	U,D,D	Transition	Random	Random	On
6.2	Scheduler	U,D,ND	Pre/post	Struct+Data+Reqs	SymbExec.	Off
6.3	Triangle	U,D,D	Pre/post	Struct+Data	SymbExec.	Off
6.5	Chat	U,D,ND	Pre/post	Struct+Data	Graph+Random	On
7.2	eTheater	U,D,D	Transition	Struct	SymbExec.	Off
7.3	Protocol	T,D,ND	Transition	Struct	Graph+Random	On
9	GSM 11.11	U,D,D	Pre/post	Struct+Data	Graph+SymbExec.	Off
10	ATM	U,D,D	Transition	Struct+Data	Graph+SymbExec.	Off

Note: In the Model Characteristics column, U,D,D means that the model is "Untimed, Discrete, Deterministic"; U,D,ND means that it is "Untimed, Discrete, Nondeterministic", and T,D,ND means that it is "Timed, Discrete, Nondeterministic".

done in the adaptation layer, which in this Qui-Donc example happens to be the human who executes the test.

This illustrates that it is sometimes possible to model a timed system with an untimed model. Similarly, it is often possible to use abstraction to model a nondeterministic system with a deterministic model or a continuous system with a discrete model. If the nondeterministic aspects of the SUT, or its timed or continuous behavior, can be encapsulated and checked in the adapter code, then the model does not need to represent those aspects and can be greatly simplified. On the other hand, if the real-time aspects, the continuous behavior, or the nondeterminism, are an intrinsic part of our test objectives, then they probably should be represented in the model.

11.3 PEOPLE, ROLES, AND TRAINING

In this section, we discuss some organizational issues for a company that wishes to integrate model-based testing into its testing process: team organization, roles, training, and so on.

Recall from Chapter 2 that there are four main roles within a project in the model-based testing process.

Role 1. Develop the test model. This requires expertise in the application domain as well as good knowledge of modeling principles and tools.

Role 2. Drive the automated test generation. This role concerns mostly the translation of project test objectives into a set of test selection criteria that can be used by the model-based test generator. This requires good understanding of the application and some validation experience to know where it is important to focus the test generation and where it is not.

Role 3. Develop the adapter. The adapter developers are in charge of developing and maintaining the test framework and supporting the scripts that are part of the adapter. They must be expert in the automated test execution environment and in the API of the SUT.

Role 4. Analyze test results. This is a traditional task in software testing, which requires a high level of expertise in the application functionality in order to determine whether the failure of a test is caused by a bug in the implementation, an error in the model, or a problem in the adapter.

Based on these roles, the test team can be organized with four kinds of people, which are already well known in software testing automation (see, for example, [FG99]):

Test team leader: The team leader is in charge of defining the test plan and managing the team members. He or she decides which parts of the project will use model-based testing and which parts will use manual development of test cases.

Test developers: The test developers assume roles 1, 2, and 4 of the previous list. They are responsible for developing the test model(s), choosing the test selection criteria, and analyzing test results. They need to be experienced at testing and have a good knowledge of the SUT.

Adapter developers: The adapter developers are responsible for implementing the adapter after its abstraction level and interface to the model have been designed in collaboration with the test developers. They need good programming skills, good knowledge of the system under test API, and familiarity with any test frameworks or test execution environments that are being used by the project. Blackburn and colleagues [BBN04] observe that in their experience, one adapter developer can support several modelers (test developers) because adapters change less frequently than test models and the same adapter can often be reused for several test models.

Automated test execution manager: The test execution manager is responsible for the test framework and the automated test execution environment. He or she may provide some support software that facilitates the development of the adapters within a project.

The main difference with the team organization of other automated testing processes (like the scripting-based testing process or the keyword-based testing process; see Section 2.1) is the requirement that the test developer have modeling skills. This means that the test developer has to be skilled at abstraction (designing interfaces) and have knowledge of the modeling notation and tool. Another difference concerns the required knowledge of basic test selection principles and how to use them with the chosen model-based testing tool.

A sample training course for model-based testing from UML models, that targets test developers, might be structured into two parts, with the first focusing on modeling skills and the second on test generation and concretization skills. Each of these parts could take around two days to cover (including hands-on practical work) and might cover the following topics:

- Modeling for Testing
  - Defining system requirements using UML class diagrams and state machines or activity diagrams
  - Precisely specifying system properties, methods, and transitions using OCL or some other action language
  - Importing a UML model from a UML tool into a model-based testing tool
  - Animating a model for validation purposes

- Test Generation and Concretization
  - Defining test objectives
  - Generating tests by choosing test selection criteria
  - Analyzing test results, model coverage, and requirements coverage
  - Exporting abstract test cases in human-readable formats, such as HTML, text files, and Microsoft Word documents
  - Concretization of abstract test cases for execution
  - Optimizing test generation and coverage

11.4 MODEL-BASED TESTING AND AGILE METHODS

In this section, we discuss how model-based testing fits into agile processes such as Extreme Programming (XP) [Coc01] or SCRUM [SB01]. These are characterized by a number of practices, including strong customer involvement, iterative development, test-driven development, refactoring, frequent or continuous testing, and the like. We discuss three aspects of agile methods that relate to model-based testing: test-driven development, customer acceptance tests, and agile modeling.

11.4.1 Test-Driven Development

One of the most fundamental practices of agile methods is test-driven development (TDD) [Bec03]. This is the practice of writing unit tests for a component before writing the implementation code of the component, then running those tests frequently as the code is developed and refactored (the *test, code, refactor* cycle). This approach claims many benefits, inluding:

- *Code that is documented by tests*: The tests form most of the required documentation for a project (the much-debated "code over documentation" principle).

- *Comprehensive test suites*: New code is written only if an automated test has failed. This means that test suites become quite comprehensive. It is common to have more lines of test code than implementation code.

- *Accurate regression testing*: The resulting test suites serve as regression test suites, giving more confidence in the successive additions of software and the correctness of refactorings.

- *A clean design*: The design will emerge progressively from the tests. TDD plus refactoring is an agile way of converging more effectively toward a simple design.

Recall from Section 5.2 that model-based testing can be used for unit testing. It offers the possibility of generating a suite of unit tests from a small model, which may reduce the cost of developing those unit tests, give deeper understanding of the desired behavior, and allow more rapid response to evolving requirements.

TDD is mostly aimed at getting better code and self-documenting code. At the system level, agile development is driven by acceptance tests, which we discuss next.

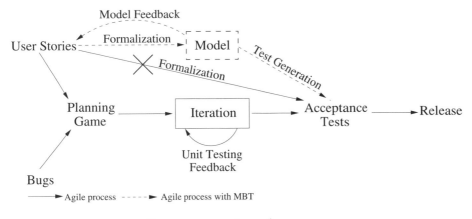

FIGURE 11.2   An agile process.

11.4.2 Acceptance Tests and the Iterative Process

One of the practices of Extreme Programming is that, prior to the start of an iteration, the "customer-on-site" should write acceptance tests that specify what the system is supposed to do. With the help of the testers, these tests are made executable so that they are an executable specification of the desired functionality. This is illustrated in Figure 11.2.

Making the effort of having an executable specification, be it from scripted tests or from a UML model, may look like overkill to many developers. However, in the eyes of the agile practitioners, this has many advantages. First of all, it forces the customer to specify precisely what is required. This usually significantly reduces the number of ambiguous and missing requirements. Second, when the acceptance tests are "green" (the famous success color from the JUnit framework), the customer has much more confidence that real and useful work has been done. Finally, an executable specification gives a clear and measurable objective to the development team!

Model-based testing can be used to good advantage to get more acceptance tests faster. The customer on site can create a model for new user stories or evolve an existing model, focusing only on the relevant requirements that the customer wants to be implemented. Then, with help from the testers, they use model-based testing to get a "reasonable" number of acceptance tests that are given to the developers as input.

This requires a user-friendly modeling notation that can be understood by the customer or perhaps even written by the customer-on-site. For example, the customer might write some detailed use cases to illustrate the desired functionality, and then some model-based testers could convert these into

UML activity diagrams and interact with the customer to ensure that the diagrams capture the requirements.

As well as being used to quickly develop a larger set of acceptance tests, having the acceptance tests centered around a model also facilitates the "embrace change" principle of extreme programming. It is easier to change the model and regenerate the acceptance tests than to modify the tests one by one.

11.4.3 Agile Modeling

Agile modeling is another point where agile methods and model-based testing are in synergy. Agile methods encourage the customer to write acceptance tests in his or her own business language. The adaptation layer is then provided by the development team so that those tests can be executed. This practice is quite close to model-based testing because the business language is actually playing the role of a domain-specific modeling notation. Its semantics is already precise enough to make it executable. The richer the domain-specific language is (for example, supporting selection or iteration constructs), the more tests we can generate from it by using model-based testing principles.

One last thing must be mentioned. There is an "agile modeling" community (*http://www.agilemodeling.com*) that focuses on using models in an "agile" way [Amb02]. The test models that we use for model-based testing match many of the principles advocated by this community:

- Test models have a precise purpose.
- Test models are "light," using only a subset of UML, for instance.
- An iterative approach is encouraged, growing the models incrementally.
- Test models encourage discussion about the exact behavior of the system.
- Test models are not done for documentation's sake; the generated test scripts are what is important.

11.5   MODEL-BASED TESTING AND THE UNIFIED PROCESS

In this section, we discuss how model-based testing fits into the UML Unified Process [AN05].

11.5.1 Introducing the Unified Process

The Unified Process (UP) is a software development technique. The goal of UP is to define who does what, when, and how. It is strongly tied to UML, but they are actually independent. UP is the methodology that explains how to transform requirements into software. UML is the visual language used by the methodology. Both are defined using metamodels, and these metamodels are both instances of the OMG meta-metamodel called MOF. MOF is also the root of several other standards, such as XMI (the XML format used to store UML models) and CWM (Common Warehouse Metamodel).

The UP is not a single prescriptive process but a framework that is intended to be tailored for each project or organization [Kru03]. It is based on research by Ericsson and Rational (now part of IBM) and on other best practice guidelines such as managing requirements, visual modeling of software, component-based architectures, iterative development, verifying software quality, and managing changes of software. The UP is organized into four phases, often with several iterations inside some of these phases.

Inception: The goal of the inception phase is to have an overview of the project. This phase establishes the feasibility of the project, using prototyping and functional behavior modeling. Stakeholders and project managers come to agreement on the scope of the project. Major risks are identified, and a business case is developed to express how the project delivers benefits to the business. The inception phase also evaluates costs and produces a project schedule.

Elaboration: The goal of the elaboration phase is to produce a working skeleton of the architecture of the project. This skeleton should capture the most risky functional behavior expressed in the requirements. By the end of this stage, most of the use cases have been written, the hard engineering decisions have been made, and the final commitment of whether or not to continue with the project can be made.

Construction: The goal of this phase is to build the product. The construction phase is usually a series of development iterations that flesh out the functionality of the skeleton into a deliverable product. Each iteration goes for one to two months, has a fixed deadline, and produces a release that can be tested and evaluated by users.

Transition: The goal of this phase is to deliver the finished product to the users. This includes deployment, beta testing, completion of the user documentation, training of end users, and reacting to user feedback. A project review is done to evaluate the process.

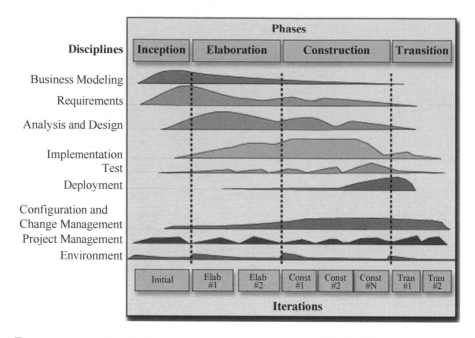

FIGURE 11.3   Combining workflows and phases in the Unified Process.
Source: From *Rational Unified Process: An Introduction*, p. 22, ©2004 Pearson Education, Inc.
Reproduced by permission of Pearson Education, Inc. All rights reserved.

The UP can be visualized as a two-dimensional process, as shown in Figure 11.3. The phases and the iterations within the phases form the horizontal dimension, which corresponds to the passage of time. The *workflows* form the vertical dimension and show the different activities that are going on within each phase of the project. The workflows include the usual software development activities (*requirements, analysis and design, implementation, testing,* and *deployment*), but these are sometimes preceded by *business modeling* to capture the structure, processes, and rules of the business before designing the product. There are also three supporting workflows (*change management, project management,* and *environment*), as shown in Figure 11.3. The environment workflow involves customizing the process and selecting and maintaining tool support for the development team.

11.5.2 Extending the Unified Process with Model-Based Testing

In this section we describe an extension of UP to support a model-based testing process.

We consider a typical construction iteration of UP, as described earlier. Model-based testing introduces, in parallel with the *application design* activi-

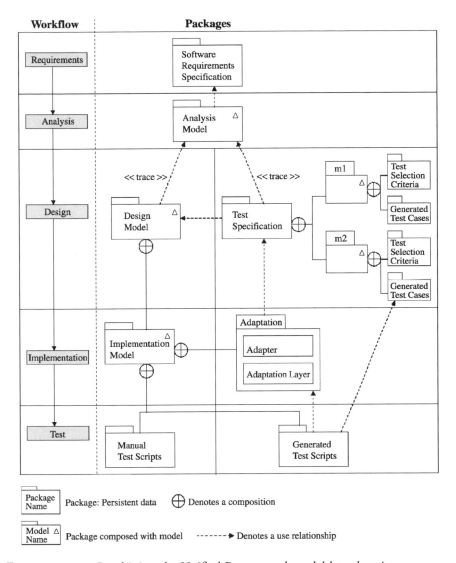

FIGURE 11.4   Combining the Unified Process and model-based testing
workflows.

ties, new *test design* activities. This extension of UP with model-based testing
is summarized in Figure 11.4. It shows the parallelism between the application design workflow and the test design workflow based on automated test
generation from a test model.

From the model-based testing viewpoint, the first activity is the pro-
duction of a test model. This requires the availability of the analysis model.

From this point on, we extend the UP by adding new artifacts in the design, implementation, and test workflows. Two kinds of model are produced; the first is the usual design model of the UP and the second is a test model. Both are derived from the analysis model and the requirements documents.

A *development team* is responsible for the usual design process, and a *test team* follows a model-based testing process (modeling, validating the model, and choosing test selection criteria to generate suites of abstract tests). UP generally recommends assigning a dedicated team to each major process rather than continually moving people between teams. For this model-based testing process, it is good practice to have a dedicated team, first because they must have specific skills, and second because it increases the independence between the test model and the design model, which makes the testing more likely to discover errors (see Section 2.3). To ensure independence, questions raised during the modeling-for-testing process should be answered by the system analyst or a stakeholder rather than by the development team.

The next workflow in the UP is the implementation workflow. The development team produces an implementation of the design model and performs the usual unit testing and integration testing.

Meanwhile the test team performs the concretization and execution stages of model-based testing to produce executable validation test suites and execute them on each iteration of the SUT. Test failures should not be reported immediately, because some analysis is required to determine whether the faults lie in the model, the SUT, or the adapter that connects the test cases to the SUT. If the failure is due to the SUT, then a good diagnostic report can be generated based on the test cases and perhaps using traceability features to relate those test cases to the model and the requirements.

As we introduce model-based testing into the UP, we also have to describe what impacts can be expected on the four phases. The inception phase is not impacted by this approach. Changes mainly concern the elaboration and the construction phase. During those phases the system grows from a skeleton to a final product, and the associated test artifacts evolve with the iterations.

The goal of the elaboration phase for the test team is to produce a skeleton of the model-based testing architecture that will be used during the construction phase. This involves:

- choosing the notation and style of test model, plus a model-based testing tool that supports that notation.
- producing a skeleton test model that covers some basic functionality.
- choosing the automated test execution tools (for online testing, these may be model-based testing tools).

- designing the architecture of the concretization stage and demonstrating that it can connect the abstract tests to the automated test execution tools.

By the end of the phase, the test architecture and tools should be precisely defined, and it should be possible to demonstrate the feasibility of generating some simple tests from a model, concretizing them, and executing them on the SUT skeleton.

The goal of the construction phase for the test team is to construct a series of test models that capture aspects of the functionality of each iteration of the SUT. In parallel with this modeling activity, the concretization layer has to be implemented. Once each test model has been designed and validated, tests can be generated from it and then executed on the SUT. Each iteration made within the construction phase will produce new models and test suites and may also require some evolution of existing test models (and regeneration of the associated test suites). By the end of the construction phase, the test team will have produced a comprehensive set of models and test suites for validation testing during the transition phase.

One benefit of model-based testing is that it identifies faults in the analysis model and in the requirements *earlier* in the design process than is usually the case. This can prevent those faults from flowing into the design model and the SUT implementation. This happens because the modeling and model-validation stages of model-based testing raise questions about the requirements and can expose faults well before any tests are executed.

11.6 EPILOGUE

The idea of model-based testing has been around for a few decades (recall that Moore started the research on FSM-based test generation [Moo56] in 1956!), but in the last few years we have seen a ground-swell of interest in applying it to real applications.

11.6.1 Model-Based Testing

Model-based testing is now used regularly within several dozen product groups at Microsoft (see Section 2.6.2); by most of the four largest smart card companies in the world (Section 2.6.3); by several European automobile manufacturers; by the Software Productivity Consortium,[1] who have successfully applied their Test Automation Framework (TAF) and the T-VEC

---

[1] Now called the Systems and Software Consortium, *http://www.software.org*.

tool (see Appendix C); in a variety of large American defense and avionics companies [BBN03, BBN04]; and by many other companies around the world. They report that model-based testing can reduce the cost of testing, increase software quality, and expose requirements issues earlier in the software life cycle.

Model-based testing tool manufacturers have responded by producing commercial model-based testing tools, and there is now a good selection of tools available for different application domains, styles of testing (online, offline, etc.), and kinds of models. See the tool list in Appendix C and the website associated with this book for an updated list of commercial model-based testing tools.

11.6.2 Future Trends

In the future we expect to see model-based testing expanding from focusing mostly on functional testing into other kinds of testing, such as security testing, performance testing, load testing, robustness testing, real-time testing [LMNS05], and GUI testing. Further research is needed in these areas to find good modeling paradigms and to develop appropriate algorithms and tools.

We also expect to see more good studies that quantitatively measure the benefits and drawbacks of adopting model-based testing. Although empirical evidence is not a necessary prerequisite for widespread adoption, as many earlier technologies have illustrated, it would be nice to have further empirical confirmation of the benefits and limitations of model-based testing.

Three major trends in the software industry seem to be conspiring to make the increased adoption of model-based testing inevitable. One is the increasing level of complexity in modern software: the number of functions in a typical software product is growing rapidly, and there is an increasing demand for that functionality to be online, mobile, or tightly integrated with other tools. This increase in complexity requires an increasingly expensive and sophisticated test phase in order to achieve a reasonable level of error-free functionality and robustness. At the same time, another trend is the increasing demand for software that is less buggy, more secure, and more robust. This requires even more emphasis on testing, as well as other software improvement strategies.

Finally, a third trend is the increasing use of models in software development. We think that it is unlikely that the entire software world will have adopted MDA (model-driven architecture) and be generating all their code from models in the near future, but it does seem to be the case that an increasing number of software developers are becoming comfortable with lightweight models as part of the software design process. This can be viewed as just one more step in the gradual evolution toward higher-level, more expressive languages, from assembler in the 1950s to .NET managed code in this decade.

So the first two trends are driving the cost of testing higher, to the point where traditional testing practices become uneconomic, and the modeling trend is gradually removing the main barrier to the adoption of model-based testing, which is modeling skills (see Section 2.8). For these economic and cultural reasons, we expect to see model-based testing become increasingly widely practiced in the future.

SUMMARY OF B ABSTRACT MACHINE NOTATION

Machine Structure

```
MACHINE
    name
SETS
    set1,set2,...
CONSTANTS
    constant1,constant2,...
PROPERTIES
    properties_of_constants
VARIABLES
    var1,var2,...
INVARIANT
    properties_of_variables
INITIALISATION
    initial_state_assignments
DEFINITIONS
    macros
OPERATIONS
    operations
END
```

Logical Predicates (P, Q)

P & Q	conjunction
P or Q	disjunction
P => Q	implication
P <=> Q	equivalence
not P	negation
!(x).(P=>Q)	universal quantification
#(x).(P&Q)	existential quantification
E = F	equality
E /= F	inequality

Numbers (n, m)

n..m	set of integers from n to m
m>n	greater than
m<n	less than
m>=n	greater than or equal
m<=n	less than or equal
max(S)	maximum of a set of integers
min(S)	minimum of a set of integers
m+n	addition
m-n	difference
m*n	multiplication
m/n	division
m**n	power
m mod n	remainder of division
SIGMA(x).(x:T|E)	sum of E, with x ranging over T

Sets (S, T)

{}	empty set
{E,F}	set enumeration
card(S)	cardinality
S*T	cartesian product
S\/T	set union
S/\T	set intersection
S-T	set difference
E:S	member of
E/:S	not member of
S<:T	subset of

S/<:T	not subset of
S<<:T	strict subset of
S/<<:T	not strict subset of

Relations (r)

S<->T	relation
E|->F	maplet
dom(r)	domain of relation
ran(r)	range of relation
id(S)	identity relation
S<|r	domain restriction
S<<|r	domain subtraction
r|>S	range restriction
r|>>S	range subtraction
r~	inverse of relation
r[S]	relational image
r1<+r2	right overriding

Functions (f)

S+->T	partial function
S-->T	total function
%x.(x:T|E)	lambda function with input x and output E
f(E)	function application

Commands and Substitutions (G, H, I, J)

skip	do nothing
x := E	assignment
f(x) := E	functional override
x::S	nondeterministic choice from a set S
G || H	parallel substitution
ANY x WHERE P(x) THEN G END	nondeterministic choice

```
LET x BE x=E          define a local variable
IN G
END

PRE P                 precondition
THEN G
END

BEGIN                 compound statement
G
END

IF P                  conditional statement
THEN G
ELSE H
END

IF P                  conditional with else = skip
THEN G
END

IF P1 THEN G1         multiconditional statement
ELSIF P2 THEN G2
...
ELSE Gn
END

IF P1 THEN G1         multiconditional with else = skip
ELSIF P2 THEN G2
...
END

CASE E OF             case statement
EITHER m1 THEN G
OR m2 THEN H
OR m3 THEN I
ELSE J
END
```

```
CASE E OF              case statement with else = skip
EITHER m1 THEN G
OR m2 THEN H
OR m3 THEN I
END
```

SUMMARY OF COMMON
OCL CONSTRUCTS

Here are the main OCL constructs:

OCL Construct	Purpose
context *class* **inv:** *predicate*	class invariant
context *class* **def:** *name* : *type* = *expr*	define an attribute
context *class* :: *attribute* **init:** *expr*	define an initial value
context *class* :: *method* **pre:** *predicate*	precondition
context *class* :: *method* **post:** *predicate*	postcondition
context *class* :: *method* **body:** *expr*	define a query method

Since postconditions must talk about a *change* of state, OCL provides a few "postcondition-only" operators to make this more convenient.

- *Attr*@pre returns the *original* value of an attribute or association before the change of state.
- The result keyword indicates the return value from a method.
- The *hasSent* operator (*Object∧Message*) is true when *Message* has been sent to *Object* sometime between the pre and post states. OCL also has a more complex operator (*Object∧∧Message*) that allows one to observe all the messages sent to *Object*, but the details are beyond the scope of this book.

Basic OCL Types

The predefined OCL basic types are Integer, Real, String, and Boolean. Unlike most programming languages, there are no upper or lower bounds on Integer or Real values, and Integer is a subtype of Real. That is, these types follow the ideal mathematical concepts of integers and reals. Here is a list of some of the common OCL Integer and Boolean operators (we do not show Real or String operators because we do not use these types in the OCL examples in this book). We write $b_1, b_2, \ldots$ to stand for Boolean expressions, $i_1, i_2, \ldots$ for Integer expressions, and $e_1, e_2, \ldots$ for expressions of other types such as user-defined classes.

OCL Operator	Result Type	Description
$i_1 + i_2$	Integer	Integer addition
$i_1 - i_2$	Integer	Integer subtraction
$i_1 * i_2$	Integer	Integer multiplication
$i_1.\text{div}(i_2)$	Integer	Integer division
$i_1.\text{mod}(i_2)$	Integer	Integer modulus
$i_1 < i_2$	Boolean	Less than
$i_1 <= i_2$	Boolean	Less than or equal to
$i_1 > i_2$	Boolean	Greater than
$i_1 >= i_2$	Boolean	Greater than or equal to
$e_1 = e_2$	Boolean	Equal to
$e_1 <> e_2$	Boolean	Not equal to
b_1 or b_2	Boolean	Logical disjunction
b_1 and b_2	Boolean	Logical conjunction
$\text{not}(b_1)$	Boolean	Logical negation
b_1 implies b_2	Boolean	Logical implication
if b_1 then e_1 else e_2 endif	Expression	Returns e_1 or e_2

OCL Collections

OCL provides the following four kinds of collection.

Collection	Elements Are Ordered	Duplicates Are Allowed
Set	no	no
OrderedSet	yes	no
Sequence	yes	yes
Bag	no	yes

Note that "ordered" does not mean sorted; it just means that the elements can be accessed via their position in the collection by using an operator like `...->at(N)`.

The most common way to create collections is to follow an association from one class to another. If an association that is going from class A to class B has a multiplicity greater than 1 at the B end, then `self.B` (from within the A class) will return a Set of B objects. However, if the B end of the association is annotated as {ordered}, then self.B will return a Sequence of B objects.

If you traverse several associations consecutively, like self.B.C.D, then the result is flattened into a single collection of D objects. If one of the associations is ordered, then this collection will be a Sequence. Otherwise, it will be a Bag (if several of the associations have a multiplicity greater than one) or a Set.

Here are some examples of collection operators. We assume the following definitions:

set	=	Set{1,3,5}
ordset	=	OrderedSet{5,1,3}
bag	=	Bag{1,1,5}
seq	=	Sequence{5,1,1,3}

Example	**Description**
set->includes(1) = true	Checks if 1 is a member of the set
set->excludes(1) = false	Checks if 1 is *not* a member of the set
set->isEmpty(1) = false	Checks if the collection is empty
bag->size() = 3	Returns the number of elements
bag->count(1) = 2	The number of times 1 occurs
ordset->at(2) = 1	Returns the second element
seq->excluding(1) = Sequence{5,3}	Removes the given element
set->including(2) = Set{1,3,5,2}	Adds an element
set->including(1) = Set{1,3,5}	(because Sets have no duplicates)
set->union(Set{2,3}) = Set{1,2,3,5}	Union of two sets or bags
set->intersection(Set{2,3}) = Set{3}	Intersection of two sets or bags

The most powerful feature of collections is that they provide several *iterator* operations, such as set->collect(x|x*x). This iterates over all the elements in *set* and collects the square of those numbers into a new Set. So this expression returns Set{1,9,25}. The argument to the collect operator, 'x|x*x', is actually a *lambda function*, similar to the lambda functions in B (%x.(x:NAT|x*x)), Groovy (x -> x*x), C# 3.0 (x => x*x), and several other languages.

Here are some of the OCL iterator operations (we use the example from Section 3.2 where drink is a set of eight DrinkShelf objects):

Example	Description
drink->exists(d|d.price<50)	True if there is at least one cheap drink
drink->forAll(d|d.price<50)	True if all drinks are cheap
drink->select(d|d.price<50)	Return the Set of cheap drinks
drink->collect(d|d.price)	Return the Set of prices
drink->sortedBy(d|d.price)	An OrderedSet of DrinkShelf objects, sorted by increasing price

COMMERCIAL TOOLS

This appendix gives a brief overview of commercial (not prototype and research) model-based testing tools. The list is up to date at the time of this writing. A more current list can be found on the website associated with this book. The following parameters are given:

- Product name
- Tool type (as defined in Section 1.2)
- Manufacturer name
- Web link
- Modeling notation
- Very short tool description

Concerning the tool type dimension, the four categories are:

1. Generation of test input data from a domain model
2. Generation of test cases from a model of the environment
3. Generation of test cases with oracles from a behavioral model
4. Generation of test scripts from abstract tests

TABLE C.1 List of Model-Based Tools

Tool Name	Type	Manufacturer	Web Link	Modeling Notation	Brief Description
AETG	1	Telcordia Technologies	*http://aetgweb. argreenhouse.com*	Model of input data domain	The AETG Web Service generates pairwise test cases.
Case Maker	1	Diaz & Hilterscheid Unternehmensberatung GmbH	*www. casemakerinternational. com*	Model of input data domain	CaseMaker uses the pairwise method to compute test cases from input parameter domain specifications and constraints specified by business rules.
Conformiq Test Generator	3	Conformiq	*www.conformiq.com*	UML statecharts	In Conformiq Test Generator, UML statecharts constitute a high-level graphical test script. Conformiq Test Generator is capable of selecting from the statechart models a large amount of test case variants and of executing them against tested systems.
LEIRIOS Test Generator – LTG/B	3	LEIRIOS Technologies	*www.leirios.com*	B notation	LTG/B generates test cases and executable test scripts from a B model. It supports requirements traceability.
LEIRIOS Test Generator – LTG/UML	3	LEIRIOS Technologies	*www.leirios.com*	UML 2.0	LTG/UML generates test cases and executable test scripts from a UML 2.0 model. It supports requirements traceability.
MaTeLo	2	All4Tec	*www.all4tec.net*	Model usage editor using Markov chain	MaTeLo is based on Statistical Usage Testing and generates test cases from a usage model of the system under test.
Qtronic	3	Conformiq	*www.conformiq.com*		Qtronic derives tests from a design model of the SUT. This tool supports multithreaded and concurrent models, timing constraints, and testing of nondeterministic systems.

Tool		Company	URL	Input/Model	Description
Rave	3	T-VEC	www.t-vec.com	Tabular notation	Rave generates test cases from a tabular model. The test cases are then transformed into test drivers.
Reactis	3	Reactive System	www.reactive-systems.com	Mathlab Simulink Stateflow	Reactis generates tests from Simulink and Stateflow models. This tool targets embedded control software.
SmartTest	1	Smartware Technologies	http://www.smartwaretechnologies.com/smarttestprod.htm	Model of input data domain	The SmartTest test case generation engine uses pairwise techniques.
Statemate Automatic Test Generator/Rhapsody ATG	3	I-Logix	www.ilogix.com	Statemate statecharts and UML state machine	ATG is a module of I-Logix Statemate and Rhapsody products. It allows test case generation from a statechart model of the system.
TAU Tester	4	Telelogic	www.telelogic.com/products/tau/tester/index.cfm	TTCN-3	An integrated test development and execution environment for TTCN-3 tests.
Test Cover	1	Testcover.com	www.testcover.com	Model of input data domain	The Testcover.com Web Service generates test cases from a model of domain requirements. It uses pairwise techniques.
T-Vec Tester for Simulink; T-VEC Tester for MATRIXx	3	T-Vec	www.t-vec.com	Simulink and MATRIXx	Generates test vectors and test sequences, verifying them in autogenerated code and in the modeling tool simulator.
ZigmaTEST Tools	3	ATS	http://www.atssoft.com/products/testingtool.htm	Finite state machine (FSM)	ZigmaTEST uses an FSM-based test engine that can generate a test sequence to cover state machine transitions.

GLOSSARY

Animation Bringing to life a formal model by executing certain parts of the model. This is typically an interactive process that allows an engineer to explore particular paths through the model or pose questions such as, "Show me all ways of reaching this state from the initial state." Some models are not directly executable, so an animation tool may place restrictions on the model in order to animate it (e.g., restricting data types to be very small sets, or placing limits on the maximum number of times around a loop).

Application Programming Interface (API) A set of procedures that can be called to control and observe a software system. For example, the Microsoft Windows Win32 API is a large collection of procedures that allows a program to use the facilities of the Windows operating system.

Black-box testing A testing technique whereby the design of tests is based on just the requirements or specification of the system under test, not on knowledge about the implementation of the system.

Complete FSM An FSM in which every state has outgoing transitions that cover all possible input symbols. It is common to make an incomplete (partial) FSM complete by adding an assumption such as "all missing inputs are self-transitions."

Deterministic FSM An FSM that is not **nondeterministic**. That is, all the transitions out of each state are labeled with different inputs.

Environment model For model-based testing, a model that specifies the environment of the SUT (the allowable ranges of inputs, the possible sequences of operations, the expected usage profile of operations, etc.).

Extended finite state machine (EFSM) A finite state machine plus some state variables. The transitions of the finite state machine are labeled with guards and actions to determine when the transition is enabled and how it will update the state variables.

Failure The symptom of a fault. For example, it is the wrong output, the crash, or the infinite loop that may happen when we execute a fault in the SUT.

Fault A defect in the SUT. Also known as a *bug* or an *error*. When a fault is executed, it may cause a **failure**.

Finite state machine (FSM) A model that has a finite number of states and a finite number of transitions between those states.

Initially connected FSM An FSM in which every state is reachable from the initial state. If an FSM is not initially connected, then there must be an error because part of the FSM is unusable and cannot be tested.

Internal transition A transition in a UML state machine that is written within a state. It is similar to a **self-transition**, except that it does not trigger exit and entry actions when it is taken.

Labeled transition systems (LTS) Transition-based modeling notations, similar to finite state machines, but without the restriction that the number of states or transitions has to be finite.

Minimal FSM An FSM that has no redundant states. That is, it does not have two distinct states that generate the same set of input/output sequences. A non-minimal FSM is not a major problem; it just means that there is a simpler equivalent FSM.

Model For model-based testing, a formal description of interactions between the SUT and its environment. There are two main kinds of model: **SUT models** and **environmental models**. Most models for model-based testing are a mixture of SUT and environment models.

Model-based testing In this book, the generation of executable black-box tests from a behavioral model of the SUT. See Section 1.2 for a discussion of alternative definitions.

Nondeterministic FSM An FSM with a state that has several outgoing transitions labeled with the same input symbol.

Offline testing Model-based testing wherein the complete test suite is generated first, then executed later. It decouples the test generation and test execution environments and tools.

Online testing Model-based testing wherein the tests are executed and generated at the same time.

Oracle A mechanism for analyzing SUT output and deciding whether a test has passed or failed.

Oracle problem The question of whether a test case passes or fails when it is executed on the SUT. It can be solved by manual inspection of the test outputs, but this is error-prone and costly. If the test case itself contains code that determines the pass/fail verdict automatically, we call this code the *oracle code* and say that the test case solves the oracle problem.

Self-transition A transition in an FSM, statechart, or UML state machine that loops from a state back to that same state. See also **internal transition**.

Statechart A graphical modeling notation that is similar to a finite state machine, but extended with a hierarchy of nested states, orthogonal states, and broadcast communication. UML state machines are one example of a statechart notation.

Strongly connected FSM An FSM in which every state is reachable from every other state. There are no states or loops to get stuck in—there is always a path out to the rest of the FSM. This is a strong restriction and not always desirable. However, if the SUT has a *reset* method that sets it back to the initial state, then the FSM is automatically strongly connected when it is initially connected.

SUT, or system under test The program, library, interface, or embedded system that is being tested.

SUT model For model-based testing, a model that specifies the input/output behavior of the SUT.

Test case A sequence of SUT interactions. Each SUT interaction includes the SUT inputs and usually includes the expected SUT outputs or some kind of *oracle* for deciding whether the actual SUT outputs are correct.

When testing nondeterministic SUTs, this view of test cases is sometimes generalized so that a test case is a tree or graph of possible SUT interactions. Note that a test case may be executable (though we usually use the term **test script** for an executable test case) or may be non-executable because it is at a higher level of abstraction than the SUT.

Test script An executable version of a **test case**, which is usually written in a programming language, a scripting language, or a tool-specific executable notation.

Test sequence A synonym for **test case**.

Test suite A collection of **test cases**.

Test target A detailed specification of a desired test case (e.g., a node or an arc of a model, a fragment of a path through a model, constraints on the data values of the model). Test targets are usually generated by applying test selection criteria to the model.

Testing The activity of executing a system in order to find failures.

Traceability The ability to trace the connections between the artifacts of the testing life cycle or software life cycle; in particular, the ability to track the relationships between test cases and the model, between the model and the informal requirements, or between the test cases and the informal requirements. Traceability information is often displayed in a traceability matrix.

Traceability matrix A table that shows the relationships between two different artifacts of the testing life cycle. For example, the relationships between informal requirement identifiers and generated test cases.

Unsatisfiable test target A test target that contains some contradictory requirements so that no tests can satisfy it.

Unreachable test target A test target that is internally consistent but is not reachable from the initial state of the model. That is, there is no sequence of operations that starts from the initial state and reaches the test target.

White-box testing A box testing technique wherein the design of tests uses knowledge about the implementation of the system (e.g., tests designed to ensure that all statements of the implementation code are tested).

BIBLIOGRAPHY

[9646-94] ISO/IEC 9646-1. *Information Technology—Open Systems Interconnection—Conformance Testing Methodology and Framework, Part 1: General Concepts.* International Standards Organization, 1994.

[ABM98] P. Ammann, P. E. Black, and W. Majurski. Using model checking to generate tests from specifications. In *International Conference on Forum Engineering Methods*, 46–55. IEEE Computer Society, 1998.

[ABPL02] G. Antoniol, L. C. Briand, M. Di Penta, and Y. Labiche. A case study using the round-trip strategy for state-based class testing. In *13th International Symposium on Software Reliability Engineering*, 269–279. IEEE Computer Society, 2002.

[Abr96] J. R. Abrial. *The B-Book: Assigning Programs to Meanings.* Cambridge University Press, 1996.

[ADLU91] A. Aho, A. Dahbura, D. Lee, and M. U. Uyar. An optimization technique for protocol conformance test generation based on UIO sequences and rural Chinese postman tours. *IEEE Transactions on Communications*, 39(11):1604–1615.

[AFGC03] A. A. Andrews, R. B. France, S. Ghosh, and G. Craig. Test adequacy criteria for UML design models. *Software Testing, Verification & Reliability*, 13(2):95–127.

[Amb02] S. W. Ambler. *Effective Practices for Extreme Programming and the Unified Process.* Wiley & Sons, 2002.

[Ame00] *The American Heritage Dictionary of the English Language.* Houghton Mifflin, 2000.

[AN05] J. Arlow and I. Neustadt. *UML 2 and the Unified Process, Second Edition.* Addison-Wesley Professional, 2005.

[BBN03] M. Blackburn, R. Busser, and A. Nauman. Understanding the generations of test automation. In *STAREAST 2003* (online). Available *http://www.software.org/pub/externalpapers/understanding_generations_of_test_automation.pdf.*

[BBN04] M. Blackburn, R. Busser, and A. Nauman. Why model-based test automation is different and what you should know to get started. In *International Conference on Practical Software Quality and Testing.* Available *http://www.psqtconference.com/2004east/program.php.*

[BCC+05] L. Burdy, Y. Cheon, D. R. Cok, et al. An overview of JML tools and applications. *Software Tools for Technology Transfer*, 7(3):212–232.

[BDM98] P. Behm, P. Desforges, and J. M. Meynadier. METEOR: An industrial success in formal development. In *Proceedings of the 2nd International Conference on the B method*, 29–45. Springer-Verlag, 1998.

[Bec03] K. Beck. *Test-Driven Development by Example*. Addison-Wesley Professional, 2003.

[Bei90] B. Beizer. *Software Testing Techniques, Second Edition*. International Thomson Computer Press, 1990.

[Bei95] B. Beizer. *Black-Box Testing: Techniques for Functional Testing of Software and Systems*. Wiley, 1995.

[BGS84] B. Boehm, T. Gray, and T. Seewaldt. Prototyping versus specifying: A multiproject experiment. *IEEE Transactions on Software Engineering*, SE-10(3):290–303.

[Bin99] R. V. Binder. *Testing Object-Oriented Systems: Models, Patterns, and Tools*. The Addison-Wesley Object Technology Series. Addison-Wesley, 1999.

[BJK+05] M. Broy, B. Jonsson, J.-P. Katoen, et al., editors. *Model-Based Testing of Reactive Systems*. Springer-Verlag, 2005.

[BJL+05] F. Bouquet, E. Jaffuel, B. Legeard, F. Peureux, and M. Utting. Requirement traceability in automated test generation: Application to smart card software validation. In *Proceeding of the ICSE International Workshop on Advances in Model-Based Software Testing*. ACM Press, 2005.

[BL03] F. Bouquet and B. Legeard. Reification of executable test scripts in formal specification-based test generation: The Java card transaction mechanism case study. In *Proceedings of the International Symposium of Formal Methods Europe*, 778–795. Springer-Verlag, 2003.

[BLL05] L. C. Briand, Y. Labiche, and Q. Lin. Improving statechart testing criteria using data flow information. In *13th International Symposium on Software Reliability Engineering*, 95–104. IEEE Computer Society, 2005.

[BLLP04] E. Bernard, B. Legeard, X. Luck, and F. Peureux. Generation of test sequences from formal specifications: GSM 11.11 standard case study. *Software: Practice and Experience*, 34(10):915–948.

[BLPT04] F. Bouquet, B. Legeard, F. Peureux, and E. Torreborre. Mastering test generation from smart card software formal models. In *Proceedings of the International Workshop on Construction and Analysis of Safe, Secure, and Interoperable Smart Devices*, 70–85. Springer-Verlag, 2004.

[BLS04] M. Barnett, K. Rustan, M. Leino, and W. Schulte. The Spec# programming system: An overview. In *Proceedings of the International Workshop on Construction and Analysis of Safe, Secure, and Interoperable Smart Devices*, 49–69. Springer-Verlag, 2004.

[Bow06] J. Bowen. Z website, 2006. *http://vl.zuser.org*.

[BP94] G. V. Bochmann and A. Petrenko. Protocol testing: Review of methods and relevance for software testing. In *Proceedings of the 1994 ACM SIGSOFT International Symposium on Software Testing and Analysis*, 109–124. ACM Press, 1994.

[BS03] M. Barnett and W. Schulte. Runtime verification of .NET contracts. *Elsevier Journal of Systems and Software*, 65(3):199–208. Extended version available as MSR-TR-2002-38, *Contracts, Components, and Their Runtime Verification on the .NET Platform*, available *http://research.microsoft.com/∼schulte*.

[BSC96a] I. Burnstein, C. R. Carlson, and T. Suwannasart. Developing a testing maturity model: Part I. *Crosstalk: The Journal of Defense Software Engineering*, 21–24, August 1996. Available *http://www.stsc.hill.af.mil/crosstalk/1996/articles.html*.

[BSC96b] I. Burnstein, T. Suwannasart, and C. R. Carlson. Developing a testing maturity model: Part II. *Crosstalk: The Journal of Defense Software Engineering*, September 1996. Available *http://www.stsc.hill.af.mil/crosstalk/1996/articles.html*.

[BT01] E. Brinksma and J. Tretmans. Testing transition systems: An annotated bibliography. In *Modeling and Verification of Parallel Processes, 4th Summer School, MOVEP 2000*, Nantes, France, 187–195. Springer-Verlag, 2001.

[Bur02] S. Burton. *Automated Generation of High Integrity Test Suites from Graphical Specifications*. PhD thesis, Department of Computer Science, University of York, March 2002.

[Bur03] I. Burnstein. *Practical Software Testing: A Process-Oriented Approach*. Springer-Verlag, 2003.

[CGN+05] C. Campbell, W. Grieskamp, L. Nachmanson, et al. Model-based testing of object-oriented reactive systems with Spec Explorer. Technical Report MSR-TR-2005-59, Microsoft Research, May 2005. Available *http://research.microsoft.com/SpecExplorer*.

[Cho78] T. S. Chow. Testing software design modeled by finite-state machines. *IEEE Transactions on Software Engineering*, SE-4(3):178–187.

[CJRZ02] D. Clarke, T. Jéron, V. Rusu, and E. Zinovieva. STG: A symbolic test generation tool. In *Proceedings of the 8th International Conference on Tools and Algorithms for the Construction and Analysis of Systems*, 470–475. Springer-Verlag, 2002.

[Cla98] J. Clarke. Automated test generation from behavioral models. In *Proceedings of the 11th Software Quality Week*, 1998.

[CLP04] S. Colin, B. Legeard, and F. Peureux. Preamble computation in automated test case generation using constraint logic programming. *Software Testing, Verification & Reliability*, 14(3):213–235.

[CMM+00] D. A. Carrington, I. MacColl, J. McDonald, L. Murray, and P. A. Strooper. From Object-Z specifications to classbench test suites. *Software Testing, Verification & Reliability*, 10(2):111–137.

[Coc01] A. Cockburn. *Agile Software Development*. Addison-Wesley Professional, 2001.

[Cop04] L. Copeland. *A Practitioner's Guide to Software Test Design*. Artech House Publishers, 2004.

[CS94] D. A. Carrington and P. Stocks. A tale of two paradigms: Formal methods and software testing. In *Proceedings of the 8th Z User Meeting*, 51–68. Springer-Verlag, 1994.

[CSH03] I. Craggs, M. Sardis, and T. Heuillard. AGEDIS case studies: Model-based testing in industry. In *Proceedings of the 1st European Conference on Model-Driven Software Engineering*, 129–132, imbus AG, 2003. Slides from the conference are available from *http://www.agedis.de/conference*.

[CY96] T. Yueh Chen and Y. Tak Yu. A more general sufficient condition for partition testing to be better than random testing. *Information Processing Letters*, 57(3):145–149.

[dBRS+00] L. du Bousquet, S. Ramangalahy, S. Simon, et al. Formal test automation: The conference protocol with TGV/Torx. In H. Ural, R. L. Probert, and G. von Bochmann, editors, *Proceedings of the IFIP 13th International Conference on Testing of Communicating Systems*, 221–228. Kluwer Academic Publishers, 2000.

[DJK+99] S. R. Dalal, A. Jain, N. Karunanithi, et al. Model-based testing in practice. In *Proceedings of the 21st International Conference on Software Engineering*, 285–294. IEEE Computer Society Press, 1999.

[DN84] J. Duran and S. Ntafos. An evaluation of random testing. *IEEE Transactions on Software Engineering*, SE-10(4):438–444.

[DO91] A. DeMillo and J. Offutt. Constraint-based test data generation. *IEEE Transactions on Software Engineering*, SE-17(9):900–910.

[EFW02] I. K. El-Far and J. A. Whittaker. Model-based software testing. In J. J. Marciniak, editor, *Encyclopedia of Software Engineering*, vol. 1, 825–837. Wiley-InterScience, 2002.

[Eur99] European Telecommunications Standards Institute, F-06921 Sophia Antipolis cedex, France. *GSM 11-11 V7.2.0 Technical Specifications*, 1999.

[FG99] M. Fewster and D. Graham. *Software Test Automation*. Addison-Wesley, 1999.

[FGDTS06] R. B. France, S. Ghosh, T. Dinh-Trong, and A. Solberg. Model-driven development using UML 2.0: Promises and pitfalls. *Computer*, 39(2):59–66.

[FHP02] E. Farchi, A. Hartman, and S. S. Pinter. Using a model-based test generator to test for standard conformance. *IBM Systems Journal*, 41(1):89–110.

[FLM+05] J. Fitzgerald, P. G. Larsen, P. Mukherjee, et al. *Validated Designs for Object-Oriented Systems*. Springer, 2005.

[Fow04] Martin Fowler. *UML Distilled: A Brief Guide to the Standard Object Modeling Language, Third Edition*. Addison-Wesley, 2004.

[Fri97] J. E. F. Friedl. *Mastering Regular Expressions*. O'Reilly, 1997.

[FvBK+91] S. Fujiwara, G. von Bochmann, F. Khendek, et al. Test selection based on finite state models. *IEEE Transactions on Software Engineering*, 17(6):591–603.

[GG77] J. B. Goodenough and S. L. Gerhart. Toward a theory of testing: Data selection criteria. *Current Trends in Programming Methodology*, 2:44–79. Prentice-Hall, 1977.

[GPK05] Y. Gurevich, A. K. Petrenko, and A. Kossatchev, editors. *Proceedings of the Workshop on Model Based Testing (MBT 2004)*, volume 111 of *Electronic Notes in Theoretical Computer Science*. Elsevier, January 2005.

[Gro05] H.-G. Gross. *Component-Based Software Testing with UML*. Springer-Verlag, 2005.

[Gua62] M. Guan. Graphic programming using odd and even points. *Chinese Mathematics*, 1:273–277.

[Gut99] W. Gutjahr. Partition testing versus random testing: The influence of uncertainty. *IEEE Transactions on Software Engineering*, 25(5):661–674.

[Ham02] R. Hamlet. Random testing. In J. J. Marciniak, editor, *Encyclopedia of Software Engineering*, vol. 2, 1095–1104. Wiley-InterScience, 2002.

[Har87] D. Harel. Statecharts: A visual approach to complex systems. *Science of Computer Programming*, 8:231–274.

[Har04] A. Hartman. AGEDIS final program report: Deliverable 1.6, February 2004. Available *http://www.agedis.de/downloads.shtml*.

[Hen64] F. C. Hennie. Fault detecting experiments for sequential circuits. In *Proceedings of the 5th Annual Symposium on Switching Circuit Theory and Logical Design*, 95–110, 1964.

[HFT00] L. Heerink, J. Feenstra, and J. Tretmans. Formal test automation: The conference protocol with PHACT. In H. Ural, R. L. Probert, and G. von Bochmann, editors, *Testing of Communicating Systems: Procceedings of TestCom 2000*, 211–220. Kluwer Academic Publishers, 2000.

[HHL+03] H. S. Hong, S. D. Ha, I. Lee, et al. Data flow testing as model checking. In *Proceedings of the Internal Conference on Software Engineering*, 232–242. IEEE Computer Society Press, 2003.

[HHS03] R. M. Hierons, M. Harman, and H. Singh. Automatically generating information from a Z specification to support the classification tree method. In D. Bert, J. P. Bowen, S. King, and M. A. Waldén, editors, *Proceedings of the 3rd International Conference of B and Z Users, June 2003*, 388–407. Springer, 2003.

[Hie97] R. Hierons. Testing from a Z specification. *Software Testing, Verification & Reliability*, 7:19–33.

[Hie03] R. M. Hierons. Generating candidates when testing a deterministic implementation against a non-deterministic finite-state machine. *Computer Journal*, 46(3):307–318.

[Hie04] R. M. Hierons. Testing from a nondeterministic finite state machine using adaptive state counting. *IEEE Transactions on Computers*, 53(10):1330–1342.

[HJ89] I. J. Hayes and C. B. Jones. Specifications are not (necessarily) executable. *IEE/BCS Software Engineering Journal*, 4(6):330–338.

[HN96] D. Harel and A. Naamad. The STATEMATE semantics of Statecharts. *ACM Transactions on Software Engineering and Methodology*, 5(4):293–333.

[HOL05] B. J. Hicks, M. W. Osborne, and N. Ling. Quantitative estimates of fish abundance from boat electrofishing. Proceedings, Australian Society for Fish Biology annual conference, Darwin, NT, 11–15 July 2005.

[Hop71] J. Hopcroft. A $n \log n$ algorithm for minimizing states in a finite automaton. In *Theory of Machines and Computation*, 189–196. Academic Press, 1971.

[HPER05] M. Horstmann, W. Prenninger, and M. El-Ramly. Case studies. In M. Broy, B. Jonsson, J.-P. Katoen, et al., editors, *Model-Based Testing of Reactive Systems*, 439–461. Springer-Verlag, 2005.

[HSS01] R. Hierons, S. Sadeghipour, and H. Singh. Testing a system specified using State-charts and Z. *Information and Software Technology*, 43(2):137–149.

[H+05] B. J. Hicks, N. Ling, M. W. Osborne, D. G. Bell, and C. A. Ring. Boat electrofishing survey of the lower Waikato River and its tributaries. CBER Contract Report No. 39. Client report prepared for Environment Waikato. Centre for Biodiversity and Ecology Research, Department of Biological Sciences, The University of Waikato, Hamilton, 2005.

[ISO02] ISO/IEC 13568. *Information Technology—Z Formal Specification Notation—Syntax, Type System and Semantics, First Edition*. ISO/IEC, 2002.

[JJ05] C. Jard and T. Jéron. TGV: Theory, principles and algorithms. *International Journal on Software Tools for Technology Transfer*, 7(4):297–315.

[Jon90] C. B. Jones. *Systematic Software Development Using VDM, Second Edition*. Prentice-Hall, 1990. Available *http://www.csr.ncl.ac.uk/vdm*.

[Kel76] R. M. Keller. Formal verification of parallel programs. *Communications of the ACM*, 19(7):371–384.

[KLPU04] N. Kosmatov, B. Legeard, F. Peureux, and M. Utting. Boundary coverage criteria for test generation from formal models. In *Proceedings of the 15th International Symposium on Software Reliability Engineering*, 139–150. IEEE Computer Society, November 2004.

[KP99] T. Koomen and M. Pol. *Test Process Improvement: A Practical Step-by-Step Guide to Structured Testing*. Addison-Wesley Professional, 1999.

[KPB+02] V. Kuliamin, A. Petrenko, I. Bourdonov, and A. Kossatchev. UniTesK test suite architecture. In *International Symposium of Formal Methods Europe*, 77–88. Springer-Verlag, 2002.

[KPKB03] V. V. Kuliamin, A. K. Petrenko, A. S. Kossatchev, and I. B. Burdonov. The uniTesK approach to designing test suites. *Programming and Computing Software*, 29(6):310–322.

[Kru03] P. Kruchten. *The Rational Unified Process: An Introduction, Second Edition*. Addison-Wesley Professional, 2003.

[KV05] A. Kervinen and P. Virolainen. Heuristics for faster error detection with automated black box testing. In Gurevich et al. [GPK05], 53–71.

[L+06] G. Leavens et al. The Java Modeling Language (JML) home page. *http://www.jmlspecs.org*, 2006.

[LMNS05] K. G. Larsen, M. Mikucionis, B. Nielsen, and A. Skou. Testing real-time embedded software using UPPAAL-TRON: An industrial case study. In *Proceedings of the 5th ACM International Conference on Embedded Software*, 299–306. ACM Press, 2005.

[LPU02] B. Legeard, F. Peureux, and M. Utting. Automated boundary testing from Z and B. In *Proceedings of the International Conference on Formal Methods Europe*, 21–40. Springer Verlag, 2002.

[LPU04] B. Legeard, F. Peureux, and M. Utting. Controlling test case explosion in test generation from B formal models. *Software Testing, Verification & Reliability*, 14(2):81–103.

[LT87] N. Lynch and M. Tuttle. Hierarchical correctness proofs for distributed algorithms. In *Proceedings of the 6th ACM Symposium on Principles of Distributed Computing*, 137–151. ACM Press, 1987.

[LvBP94] G. Luo, G. von Bochmann, and A. Petrenko. Test selection based on communicating nondeterministic finite-state machines using a generalized WP-method. *IEEE Transactions on Software Engineering*, 20(2), 149–162. IEEE Computer Society, 1994.

[LY96] D. Lee and M. Yannakakis. Principles and methods of testing finite state machines: A survey. *Proceedings of the IEEE*, 84(2):1090–1126.

[MA00] B. Marre and A. Arnould. Test sequences generation from LUSTRE descriptions: GATEL. In *Proceedings of the 15th IEEE Conference on Automated Software Engineering*, 229–237. IEEE Computer Society Press, 2000.

[Mar95] B. Marre. LOFT: A tool for assisting selection of test data sets from algebraic specifications. In *Theory and Practice of Software Development*, 799–800. Springer-Verlag, 1995.

[MC05] R. Mugridge and W. Cunningham. *FIT for Developing Software: Framework for Integrated Tests*. Prentice-Hall, 2005.

[MCLH05] R. E. Miller, D. Chen, D. Lee, and R. Hao. Coping with nondeterminism in network protocol testing. In *Proceedings of the 17th IFIP TD 6/WG 6.1 International Conference, TestCom*, 129–145. Springer-Verlag, 2005.

[Meu97] C. Meudec. *Automatic generation of software test cases from formal specifications*. PhD thesis, Faculty of Sciences, Queen's University of Belfast, 1997.

[Moo56] E. F. Moore. Gedanken-experiments on sequential machines. *Automata Studies*, 129–153. Princeton University Press, 1956.

[Mor90] L. J. Morell. A theory of fault-based testing. *IEEE Transactions on Software Engineering*, SE-16(6):844–857.

[MP02] D. Mosley and B. Posey. *Just Enough Software Test Automation*. Yourdon Press. Prentice-Hall, 2002.

[MP05] J. A. McQuillan and J. F. Power. A survey of UML-based coverage criteria for software testing. Technical Report NUIM-CS-TR-2005-08, Department of Computer Science, NUI Maynooth, Ireland, 2005.

[Mus04] J. Musa. *Software Reliability Engineering, Second Edition*. Authorhouse, 2004.

[Mye79] G. J. Myers. *The Art of Software Testing*. John Wiley & Sons, 1979.

[NML06] D. H. Nam, E. C. Mousset, and D. C. Levy. Automating the testing of object behaviour: A statechart-driven approach. In *Transactions on Engineering, Computing and Technology, Proceedings of Enformatika*, 145–149. World Enformatika Society, 2006. See *http://www.enformatika.org*.

[NT81] S. Naito and M. Tsunoyama. Fault detection for sequential machines by transition-tours. In *Proceedings of the IEEE International Symposium on Fault Tolerant Computer Systems*, 238–243. World Enformatika Society, 1981.

[Nta01] S. C. Ntafos. On comparisons of random, partition, and proportional partition testing. *IEEE Transactions on Software Engineering*, 27(10):949–960.

[OA99] I. Orcutt and A. Abdurazik. Generating test cases from UML specifications. In *Second International Conference on the Unified Modeling Language* (UML99), 416–429. Springer-Verlag, 1999.

[OXL99] A. J. Offut, Y. Xiong, and S. Liu. Criteria for generating specification-based tests. In *Proceedings of the 5th International Conference on Engineering of Complex Computer Systems*, 119–131. IEEE Computer Society Press, 1999.

[Par04] A. M. Paradkar. Towards model-based generation of self-priming and self-checking conformance tests for interactive systems. *Information & Software Technology*, 46(5):315–322.

[Pet01] A. Petrenko. Fault model-driven test derivation from finite state models: Annotated bibliography. In *Modeling and Verification of Parallel Processes*, 196–205. Springer-Verlag, 2001.

[PPW⁺05] A. Pretschner, W. Prenninger, S. Wagner, et al. One evaluation of model-based testing and its automation. In *Proceedings of the 27th International Conference on Software Engineering*, 392–401. ACM Press, 2005.

[Pro03] S. J. Prowell. JUMBL: A tool for model-based statistical testing. In *Proceedings of the 36th Annual Hawaii International Conference on System Sciences*, 331–345. IEEE, 2003.

[Res06a] Microsoft Research. Spec#. Available *http://research.microsoft.com/specsharp*, 2006.

[Res06b] Microsoft Research. Spec Explorer. Available *http://research.microsoft.com/SpecExplorer*, 2006.

[RJB05] J. Rumbaugh, I. Jacobson, and G. Booch. *The Unified Modeling Language Reference Manual, Second Edition*. Addison-Wesley Professional, 2005.

[Rob99] H. Robinson. Graph theory techniques in model-based testing. In *International Conference on Testing Computer Software*, 1999. Available *http://www.geocities.com/harry_robinson_testing/graph_theory.htm*.

[Rob03] H. Robinson. Obstacles and opportunities for model-based testing in an industrial software environment. In *First European Conference on Model-Driven Software Engineering*, 2003. Slides from the conference available from *http://www.agedis.de/conference*.

[Rob05] H. Robinson. Model-based testing. STAREAST 2005 Tutorial, 2005. Available *http://www.geocities.com/harry_robinson_testing/stareast2005.htm*.

[RTC92] RTCA Committee SC-167. *Software considerations in airborne systems and equipment certification, 7th draft to DO-178B/ED-12A*, July 1992.

[SAF04] M. A. Sánchez, J. C. Augusto, and M. Felder. Fault-based testing of e-commerce applications. In *Proceedings of the 2nd International Workshop on Verification and Validation of Enterprise Information Systems*, 66–74. INSTICC Press, 2004.

[Sam02] M. Samek. *Practical Statecharts in C/C++: Quantum Programming for Embedded Systems with CDROM*. CMP Books, 2002.

[SB01] K. Schwaber and M. Beedle. *Agile Software Development with SCRUM*. Prentice-Hall, 2001.

[Sch01] S. Schneider. *The B-Method: An Introduction*. Palgrave, 2001.

[SD88] K. K. Sabnani and A. T. Dahbura. A protocol test generation procedure. *Computer Networks and ISDN Systems*, 15(4):285–297.

[SkL89] D. P. Sidhu and T. K. Leung. Formal methods for protocol testing: A detailed study. *IEEE Transactions on Software Engineering*, 15(4):413–426.

[Som00] I. Sommerville. *Software Engineering, Sixth Edition*. Addison-Wesley, 2000.

[Spi92] J. M. Spivey. *The Z Notation: A Reference Manual, Second Edition*. Prentice-Hall, 1992. Available *http://spivey.oriel.ox.ac.uk/mike/zrm/index.html*.

[Sto93] P. Stocks. *Applying Formal Methods to Software Testing*. PhD thesis, The University of Queensland, 1993. Available *http://www.bond.edu.au/it/staff/publications/PhilS-pubs.htm*.

[Sto05] K. Stobie. Model based testing in practice at Microsoft. In Gurevich et al. [GPK05], 5–12.

[TB03] J. Tretmans and E. Brinksma. TorX: Automated model-based testing. In *First European Conference on Model-Driven Software Engineering*, 31–43, 2003. Slides from the conference available from *http://www.agedis.de/conference*.

[Thi03] H. W. Thimbleby. The directed Chinese postman problem. *Software: Practice and Experience*, 33(11):1081–1096.

[Tre96] J. Tretmans. Test generation with inputs, outputs and repetitive quiescence. *Software: Concepts and Tools*, 17(3):103–120.

[Tre04] J. Tretmans. Model-based testing: Property checking for real. Keynote address at the International Workshop for Construction and Analysis of Safe Secure, and Interoperable Smart Devices, 2004. Available *http://www-sop.inria.fr/everest/events/cassis04*.

[UPL06] M. Utting, A. Pretschner, and B. Legeard. A taxonomy of model-based testing. Technical Report 04/2006, Computer Science Department, The University of Waikato, April 2006. Available *http://www.cs.waikato.ac.nz/pubs/wp*.

[Vas73] M. P. Vasilevskii. Failure diagnosis of automata. *Cybernetics*, 9:653–665. Translated from *Kibernetika* 4, 1973, 98–108.

[VCST05] M. Veanes, C. Campbell, W. Schulte, and N. Tillmann. Online testing with model programs. *SIGSOFT Software Engineering Notes*, 30(5):273–282.

[vL00] A. van Lamsweerde. Formal specification: A roadmap. In *Proceedings of the Conference on the Future of Software Engineering*, 147–159. ACM Press, 2000.

[WC80] L. J. White and E. I. Cohen. A domain strategy for computer program testing. *IEEE Transactions of Software Engineering*, SE-6(3):247–257.

[WDT+05] C. Willcock, T. Deiß, S. Tobies, et al. *An Introduction to TTCN-3*. Wiley, 2005.

[Wea01] T. Weatherill. In the testing maturity model maze. *Journal of Software Testing Professionals*, 2(1):8–13, 2001. Available *http://www.testinginstitute.com/journal* after free registration.

[Whi03] J. A. Whittaker. *How to Break Software: A Practical Guide to Testing*. Addison-Wesley, 2003.

[Wik06] Wikipedia. Global system for mobile communications—Wikipedia, the free encyclopedia, 2006. Accessed 4 April 2006, *http://en.wikipedia.org.wiki/GSM*.

[WK03] J. Warmer and A. Kleppe. *The Object Constraint Language: Getting Your Models Ready for MDA, Second Edition*. Addison-Wesley, 2003.

[WP00] G. Walton and J. Poore. Generating transition probabilities to support model-based software testing. *Software: Practice and Experience*, 30(10):1095–1106.

[WPT95] G. H. Walton, J. H. Poore, and C. J. Trammell. Statistical testing of software based on a usage model. *Software: Practice and Experience*, 25(1):97–108.

[WT94] J. A. Whittaker and M. G. Thomason. A Markov chain model for statistical software testing. *IEEE Transactions on Software Engineering*, 20(10):812–824.

[YU90] B. Yang and H. Ural. Protocol conformance test generation using multiple UIO sequences with overlapping. In *Proceedings of the ACM Symposium on Communications Architectures & Protocols*, 118–125. ACM Press, 1990.

[ZHM97] H. Zhu, P. A. V. Hall, and J. H. R. May. Software unit test coverage and adequacy. *ACM Computing Surveys*, 29(4):366–427.

INDEX